OPERA AND CONCERT SINGERS

GARLAND REFERENCE LIBRARY
OF THE HUMANITIES
(VOL. 466)

OPERA AND CONCERT SINGERS
An Annotated International Bibliography of Books and Pamphlets

Andrew Farkas

with a foreword by
Richard Bonynge

GARLAND PUBLISHING, INC. · NEW YORK & LONDON
1985

Library of Congress Cataloging in Publication Data

Farkas, Andrew.
   Opera and concert singers.

   (Garland reference library of the humanities ; v. 466)
   Includes index.
   1. Singers—Biography—Bibliography.   I. Title.
II. Series.
ML128.S295F37   1985   016.7821′092′2   83-49310
ISBN 0-8240-9001-2

Printed on acid-free, 250-year-life paper
Manufactured in the United States of America

TO
WILLIAM R. MORAN
in gratitude for his untiring help,
guidance and friendship

CONTENTS

FOREWORD

I welcome with enthusiasm this long overdue book and only regret not having had it twenty years ago. So much has been written about the great and lesser singers of the past and present but where to find it at short notice is a major problem.

Mr. Farkas's extensive, thoroughly researched and annotated bibliography will aid enormously in checking the interminable mass of contradictions and misinformation which surround these lives and careers—misinformation often put about by the artists themselves and repeated ad nauseam by numerous writers and sensationalists.

It will always be a task to find the truth but this book will make the task easier, less time consuming and far more pleasurable.

For my own part, whenever I try to put something together for a programme or record sleeve, I spend an inordinate amount of time searching for crumbs of information which this work pinpoints succinctly. I admire the tireless research which has gone into this valuable compilation, and it most assuredly will be treasured by all who have the desire to know more about the art of singing and singers.

Singing is often said to be in a state of decline (the same thing was said a century ago), but it is still a vital part of twentieth-century life and this comprehensive collection will help to make much information concerning its secrets more readily available.

Sydney   Richard Bonynge
August 1984

PREFACE

The present work was born out of selfish motivations: I needed a bio-bibliography of singers for my research and none existed.

In 1975 I became the advisory editor for a 42-volume reprint series entitled Opera Biographies. The books chosen for reprinting were eventually published by Arno Press in 1977. In order to create an appropriate selection tool, I began to compile a bibliography. My naive and optimistic aim was the comprehensive listing of all known and traceable biographical writings about opera and concert singers, which I eventually expected to share in book form with interested readers and researchers. In its present form this bibliography is the result of seven years' casual and two years' intensive research. As my work progressed I came to realize that the quantity of existing material was much greater and more elusive than I ever suspected. This brought the further realization that while an extensive, or nearly exhaustive, listing of biographical works was possible, completeness, even in the loosest sense of this absolute term, will remain unattainable. I also had to accept the fact that the compilation of such a bibliography, in particular an annotated bibliography, was clearly beyond the abilities, resources and energy of one person.

Not more than a couple of decades ago such a project could not have been attempted. However, through the advancement of computer technology, the proliferation of bibliographically reliable printed catalogs and the continuous expansion of on-line databases, information about many collections held by major libraries has become accessible long distance, without the necessity of on-site research. Still, the material is so elusive that for about a fifth of the items listed there is no verifiable institutional ownership.

This bibliography covers only the monographic—as opposed to periodical—literature, i.e., books and pamphlets. A few ex-

ceptions have been made to include some of the best biographical articles published in the most outstanding "little magazine"
of the field, the celebrated *Record Collector*, published in England. A partial consideration guiding the selective inclusion of
this handful of biographies was the fact that the majority of these
are the only available or most authoritative biographical essay
about the artist involved. There was a strong temptation to list
all major biographical articles from the *Record Collector*, and
pending positive reader response they may be incorporated in a
later edition of this work.

The bibliography lists all the known writings *by* and *about*
vocalists who pursued a stage or concert career as a singer, but
not their musical compositions. The validity of this editorial decision can be argued both ways; but the line had to be drawn
somewhere, and it was drawn here.

The bibliography lists, by name, 796 singers. The earliest
entry belongs to Michelangiolo Caccini, born in 1545; the young-
est is Matthew Best, born in 1958. This is a timespan of 413
years, and through these writings one can trace the birth and
evolution of the singer's art, and the seemingly cyclical rise and
fall of old and new vocal styles and musical tastes.

The bibliography contains 1850 individual titles, excluding
variant editions. Not a large number, by any standard. Yet my
research indicates that there is no library in the world, including
the Library of Congress with its vast collection in excess of 20
million books and pamphlets, that could claim ownership of half
of these titles. It would also surprise me if any but the most
specialized private collections would exceed that number. Conversely, in all likelihood there is a large number of titles, not
listed anywhere, of which some collectors may own a few rare
copies.

Several items known to exist (but not handled) were ex-
cluded for want of adequate or reliable data, while some others
were not, on the strength of multiple references found in the
secondary literature. In the instance of works I was unable to
examine first hand yet was convinced deserved inclusion, I
chose to err on the positive side. I hope no glaring errors have

been committed, and if so, I will gladly receive pertinent information from readers.

This obliges me to place an editorial plea early in this introduction.

I ask all music lovers, collectors, laymen and specialists, opera buffs and librarians interested in this project, to give me a helping hand and allow me to capitalize on their collective knowledge. I would greatly appreciate receiving accurate and detailed data about items belonging in this bio-bibliography which are not yet listed. I anticipate that a supplement to the present compilation will be inevitable; a positive response to this open request for worldwide assistance may not only facilitate but also accelerate the process.

I have been repeatedly asked how one goes about locating the bibliographic data of biographical works. My truthful and accurate answer had to be: by the hit-or-miss method. This statement is not made tongue in cheek. Trained as I am in the field of librarianship, my skills as a bibliographer could carry me only up to a certain point. Beyond that I was left to professional intuition, bibliographic sleuthing, following vague leads sprinkled in the secondary literature, examining bibliographies appended to scholarly books, and international correspondence with helpful collectors. Many times I located books of whose existence I was unaware until I was allowed access to private collections. Several of these titles turned out to be unique copies, not listed in any of the conventional bibliographic sources, nor found in other collections.

What were the conventional sources used? First and foremost the printed catalogs of the Library of Congress, the National Union Catalog in its many accumulations, along with other printed catalogs common to the reference collection of research libraries. I also used OCLC, the largest automated bibliographic database in the world. Some less reliable sources were tapped as well: book lists, dealers' sales catalogs, footnotes and special bibliographies. Beyond that I had to fall back on my ingenuity, which more than once failed me completely. Still, I managed to ferret out books that were no more than a passing mention in some text. To this day I take special pride in being able to identify and locate the only biography of Aureliano Pertile without knowing either the author's name or the title of the book, my only lead being an allusion to its existence by Raffaello de Rensis in the preface of his Beniamino Gigli biography.

The books listed were written in 29 languages. Not surprisingly, I was unable to find a qualified and willing collaborator for many of them, hence the absence of some annotations. Others are missing due to a lack of access to the book itself or sufficient time at my disposal.

This prompts me to issue a second plea. I invite readers to contribute annotations for all those works that do not carry one. Brief, concise statements regarding the contents of the books will be enthusiastically welcome.

My primary objective was comprehensiveness. The second objective was the provision of annotations for as many of the books as possible. From the foregoing it can be easily deduced that the annotation of all items has been—and is likely to remain—an impossibility. Because of this, the present bibliography is flawed; and for one often accused of being a perfectionist, I am aggrieved to deliver to the interested public an imperfect work. At the same time I was forced to recognize that were I to own all the items listed, both time and linguistic limitations would render the task of reading and annotating every one of them impossible. With adequate command of only five languages, I had to solicit the help of several distinguished and most cooperative contributors to write annotations. Among them Dr. Peter H. Salus deserves special mention. A true renaissance man and linguist, he has a reading knowledge of over a dozen languages, including Swedish, Norwegian, Dutch, Danish and Icelandic. Placing his rare skills at my serivce deserves special thanks.

Two of the languages posed a special problem. Several books about the same singers have been published both in Russian and Ukrainian, and the spelling of the authors' and biographees' names differ in the two languages. When the nationality of the persons in question could not be ascertained, an arbitrary decision regarding the spelling was made on the grounds of secondary evidence.

Some concession was made to English-speaking readers by appending the majority of annotations of foreign-language books to the English-language edition, unless there was a compelling reason to do otherwise. It will also be noted that sometimes the British, sometimes the American, edition of a book with the same imprint date carries the annotation. If the chronological precedence of an edition could be established or was generally known, that edition was listed first. Although this practice, as many others throughout the book, may present an apparent lack of consistency, decisions of this sort were always based on some sound practical consideration; to explain or defend them all would be time consuming and pointless.

The reader must bear in mind that the annotations are not meant to be either reviews or criticisms. They vary in length according to the information that was deemed appropriate or essential by the contributor. Some books neither required nor deserved more than a few brief sentences. In the case of others, space considerations often compelled the annotator to restrain his or her enthusiasm for the book or its subject. The annotations also assume a certain degree of subject familiarity on the part of the reader, e.g., Caruso is not identified as an Italian tenor, nor Chaliapin as a Russian bass. The objective of each annotation is to tell the prospective reader before he or she has the book in hand, what to expect to find in it. In a few isolated instances critical comments were unavoidable and appropriate. Books containing erroneous or fictitious data had to carry a warning. On occasion, the annotator chose to incorporate some information about the life and career of lesser known artists and it was allowed to stand. Although this bibliography satisfies the criteria of a reference book in every respect—i.e., it is a book one refers to for information rather than reads from cover to cover—the texts, for the most part, aim to go beyond the mere provision of data in order to allow for pleasant and informative reading.

I did use my editorial prerogatives to adjust some of the annotations submitted by my associates, but I made no attempt to rewrite their work in order to force a stylistic conformity upon the texts. By allowing the contributors to retain their individuality, the diversity of styles and formats relieves the monotony to which such a work could fall victim. Even so, some themes or phrases recur out of necessity: these books are about the lives and careers of vocalists, and that can be stated in only so many ways and so many words—a fact that no amount of inventiveness can conceal. For this and similar stylistic inevitabilities I beg the readers' indulgence.

The data supplied in the entries are user oriented. They aim to help the casual reader as well as the specialist to identify the book and ascertain its research value by the features listed: a bibliography, discography, illustrative matter, the presence of an index, etc. This information thus provided largely ignores the needs of a cataloger in a library (secondary subjects and notes are omitted, no book size or unnumbered preliminary leaves are given), or the demands of book dealers (distinguishing marks of typography, binding, the presence of a dust jacket). In short, should a user wish to find out what books and pamphlets exist written by or about a given singer and what research value they have, the data shown here will provide the answers. To identify secondary—non-biographical—subjects, physical characteristics, typographical peculiarities, the user will have to consult the book.

My distinguished confrères in cataloging departments have the infuriating habit of rigidly following the prevailing cataloging rules concerning the collation of a book. They give the last paginated page of the book as the total number of pages, and then show the index or some other concluding portion as having one more page than the book contains. For example, a 182-page book may have an index ending on p. 183. This number is then shown in square brackets to indicate that the actual number is not printed on the page. In light of the irrelevance of this practice for the present bibliography, I made no such distinction in showing pagination. Whenever I was able to establish the actual page number of appendices or the last page of the book, I gave it as such, regardless of whether it carried a number or not.

The singers' names are given in a spelling and format best known to the public. No attempt was made to give a singer's original name when different from the stage name, or to give the married names of the many prima donnas. Although I expected to do so at the inception of the project, I soon found that tracing the correct names as shown on the birth certificates or marriage licenses of our heroes and heroines with any degree of accuracy could be a long-drawn-out project by itself. Giving the information selectively would accomplish little. To list all the husbands of Adelina Patti or the many aliases of Emilio de Gogorza will not assist the user in locating a book. Admittedly, this feature would have enhanced the reference value of the bibliography, but the amount of work involved was disproportionate to the benefit and importance of the result.

The singers' birth and death dates were an inexhaustible source of frustration. Death dates are hardly ever in doubt, as the singer is no longer in a position to falsify it wilfully out of vanity. Dates of birth on the other hand are a different matter. Generally reliable reference works and biographical dictionaries often fail to agree on the birth dates of many singers. Confronted with variant dates I was obliged to make up my mind on the basis of extraneous evidence, conjecture or intuition. The errors that crept into this work—and there are bound to be some—were caused specifically by diligent research: using too many authoritative reference sources I was compelled to choose between dates and I may have made the wrong choice.

Each reader is motivated differently in his or her desire to read biographies. But in the instance of artists of any field the common motivation is likely to be an interest in finding a plausible explanation of what sets these individuals apart from the rest of the world, what distinguishes an artist from an ordinary person. The enduring curiosity to find the secret of what raises the possessor of talent above and beyond the other practitioners of the medium into the rarefied region of stars, seems to ensure willing buyers for the sustained outpouring of biographical works.

Only a handful of biographies ever attain literary greatness;

autobiographies are often barely on the periphery of literature. Few biographers are outstanding stylists or great men of letters; performers seldom are. The gift of literary expression is not often coupled with performing talents. Collaborators, ghost writers or editors can improve upon the narrative of a life story, but they cannot create a work of great literary merit in the absence of the proper ingredients. Insistence upon measuring biographical, especially autobiographical, writings with the yardstick reserved for world literature in the best and most elitist sense of the term would be unfair to the medium, and too high expectations would deprive the reader from enjoying the many qualities that are present in these books. They ought to be taken for what they are: the accurate, semi-accurate or embroidered narrative of artistic lives spent in the public eye, whose aggregate adds up to the history of the lyric stage from the 16th century to our times.

Coverage

The cut-off date of the bibliography is 1983. There are a few items with a 1984 imprint date whose advance publicity or CIP (cataloging in publication) data sheet provided the necessary information for inclusion.

Arrangement

The bibliography is divided into three unequal parts.

Part I, by far the largest, consists of those books that deal with or relate to one singer only or, in a very few instances, to two singers related by blood or marriage. The arrangement of the entries is alphabetical by singer. The books grouped under a singer's name are subdivided into three sections: (a) books written by the singer, including, but not limited to, autobiographical works; (b) books written about the singer by others; (c) cross-references by item number to those books listed in the bibliography that contain chapters or major sections about the singer. The books are alphabetized first by author, then by title. Variant editions of the same work are arranged chronologically.

Part II lists those books which treat multiple subjects, i.e., contain essays, chapters and extensive discussions of several biographees. Encyclopedic works and biographical dictionaries are also included in this part. The arrangement, as in the other sections, is alphabetical by author.

Part III lists those books and translations into English which are known to exist in manuscript. It is hoped that at least some of these will find a publisher, soon.

Numbering

Every item listed has its own distinguishing identification number. There are four types of numbers.

1. Each sequential cardinal number without an alpha suffix denotes an individual item.

2. The alpha-numeric numbers with lower case letter suffixes indicate a variant edition. Different editions of the same work were incorporated only if (a) the book changed publishers between editions, (b) if there was some indication of the expansion, reduction or reworking of the text, or (c) the format and coverage changed substantially. Accordingly, a given title may carry the item number 177; 177-a will be assigned to the same book in a different edition and/or issued by a different publisher. The use of alpha suffixes conveys to the user that the two books are essentially identical. In the very few instances when a separate number without an alpha suffix has been assigned to two editions of the same book, the later edition was known to be sufficiently altered or enlarged to constitute a new work.

3. The T-numbers are sequential numbers with a "T" suffix. The mnemonic "T" communicates to the reader that the book is a translation. In order to retain the strict alphabetical sequence of books within each grouping, translations had to be assigned their own number. Thus it is possible for the original version of a given title and its translations into German, Russian and Hun-

garian to be filed apart from each other, due to the change in title from language to language.

4. In a few instances my sources reported new or newly found items after the identification numbers had been assigned. As it would have been foolish to exclude these important items solely on the grounds of rigidly adhering to the basic numbering system, an addenda number was employed, shown as: / A. There are eleven such numbers in the entire bibliography. Since they, too, are unique numbers, they do not compromise the integrity of the numbering system.

Conversely, in the final preparation of the manuscript some listings had to be deleted for want of sufficient data. In some other instances information about an item for which a number had been reserved did not arrive in time. In these cases the numbers assigned had to be dropped. There are seven of these; they are marked as deleted.

Cross-References

It must be borne in mind that cross-references refer to item numbers, not page numbers.

Alphabetization

Alphabetization of filing elements is letter-by-letter—as opposed to word-by-word—throughout the bibliography. The only exceptions are the names beginning with Mc: they are filed as if spelled Mac.

Elements of Entry

AUTHOR: The authors' names are given as commonly known or established in a major name authority file, e.g., of the Library of Congress. If the established form of a name has changed over the years, the most recent or most simple form is shown. Birth and death dates for all authors are given, if known.

JOINT AUTHOR: The full name of up to three joint authors is given if the names appear on the title page. For four or more authors only the first is shown.

EDITOR: Although the current cataloging rules enter books edited by someone under the title, if the importance of the editorial contribution was deemed significant, the book has been entered (i.e., interfiled) under the editor's name.

TITLE: The title is always given as shown on the title page (or as reported by correspondents). Brief subtitles are always retained, the long ones are cut short (and so indicated by three dots) unless the provision of the entire subtitle is essential to convey the contents of the book.

TRANSLATOR: The translator's name is shown if it appears anywhere in the book.

LANGUAGE: There is no language indicator for books in English. For all others the language is written out in full.

EDITION: No number designator is given for first editions. All others follow the number or descriptive text in the book, in English. Note: The first edition of some titles could not be located.

PLACE: Place of publication is given in the language of the country where the publisher is domiciled, usually as shown on the title page or obtained from some other place in the book. In an international bibliography, aimed at an international readership, it seemed unnecessary to Anglicize the place names.

PUBLISHER: The publisher is identified by name only. The phrase-name of the publisher is retained only when the proper name by itself would not make sense or destroy an intended meaning. Such designators as "Company", "Cie.", "Inc.", "Ltd." have been deleted whenever possible. The inconsistency of publishers' names stems as much from their own inconsistencies in showing it in the imprint as from the great variety of sources from which they were obtained: printed, typed or automated catalog records and private individuals on three continents.

DATE: Date of publication has been taken from the title page, in its absence from elsewhere in the book, or obtained from a reliable bibliographic source. If the date of publication and the copyright date are different, only the publication date is given.

PAGINATION: The inclusive page numbers are given, when known, for the book and its parts, regardless of whether the page carries a printed number or not.

NUMBER OF VOLUMES: For multi-volume sets the number of volumes is given in lieu of pagination.

ILLUSTRATION: If a book has illustrations, it is indicated by the word, "Illustrated." No distinction is made whether the illustrative material is a frontispiece, photographs, drawings, plates, etc.

BIBLIOGRAPHY, REPERTORY, INDEX, DISCOGRAPHY: Inclusive pages are given for all of these elements, if present. If no page numbers were provided by the source, then the word or its appropriate abbreviation is used to indicate their presence.

CHRONOLOGY: Same as above. Note: the term "chronology" relates to the performances given by an artist, not to the major events in his or her life.

BIOGRAPHEES: In the instance of multiple biographies collected in one volume (books listed in Part II) all the biographees' names are given if the total does not exceed twenty. The objective is to help the reader assess the scope and coverage of the book.

SERIES: Publishers' series are shown when known.

NOTES: Unusual features that would not normally constitute an organic part of the annotation are entered here.

Annotations

As has been indicated already, these annotations, written by nine contributors, are neither critiques nor book reviews. They aim to convey to a reader the contents of each book. Critical comments are few, given only when deemed appropriate. Each annotation—except for those written by the editor—is identified by the writer's initials following the text. These are:

(none) Andrew Farkas

TGK   Thomas G. Kaufman (Boonton, New Jersey)
AL   Anna Large (Jacksonville)
AM   Antonio Massísimo (Barcelona)
WRM   William R. Moran (La Cañada, California)
GLN   George L. Nyklicek (San Francisco)
PHS   Peter H. Salus (Mount Kisco, New York)
HCS   Howard C. Sanner, Jr. (Hyattsville, Maryland)
RT   Ruffo Titta, Jr. (Rome)

These friends and associates worked tirelessly and enthusiastically to help improve the quality and usefulness of this reference work. They were motivated by an apparent faith in the project and a desire to help researchers, like themselves, to become better informed in their chosen fields of study or avocation. They considerably lightened my editorial burden and have earned my everlasting gratitude for their excellent contributions.

Acknowledgments

The following individuals also deserve profuse thanks for their generous help in bringing many titles to my attention, their willingness to answer my questions concerning bibliographic details about books, supplying birth and death dates of singers, and for generously opening up their homes and book collections to me. Without their help this work would have been less voluminous and, in consequence, less valuable.

Eduardo Arnosi (Buenos Aires), Richard Bebb (London), Kurt H. Binar (San Francisco), Stanton Golding (San Francisco), Lim M. Lai (San Francisco), Mario Moreau (Lisbon), Tony Murray (London), Frederick M. Manning (Philadelphia), Iván Nádas (Budapest), Harold Rosenthal (London).

Statistics

The reader may be interested in knowing the statistical profile of this bibliography. The data are believed to be accurate. Total number of singers covered or cross-referenced by name: 796.

The books listed were written in 28 languages. These are:

Afrikaans, Basque, Bulgarian, Catalan, Czech, Danish, Dutch, English, Estonian, Finnish, French, German, Hungarian, Icelandic, Italian, Japanese, Latvian, Lithuanian, Norwegian, Polish, Portuguese, Rumanian, Russian, Slovenian, Spanish, Swedish, Ukrainian, Welsh.

Total numbers assigned: 1840. They include:

(a) translations ("T" numbers)	134
(b) manuscripts (monographs)	12
(c) manuscripts (translations)	10
(d) numbers "not used"	7

and exclude:

(a) variant editions	279
(b) addenda ("A" numbers)	11

Total number of books listed: 2123.

It was Corno di Bassetto, a.k.a. Bernard Shaw, who once wrote that "There are people who will read about music and nothing else. To them dead prima donnas are more interesting than saints, and extinct tenors than mighty conquerors." He later paraphrased the same thought in another preface to a collection of his music criticisms, writing "Many people have a curious antiquarian taste (I have it myself) for old chronicles of dead musicians and actors." I offer my work to all those wonderful people with a curious antiquarian taste—they will find it a useful key to locating many an old chronicle.

A companion work to the present bibliography is another Garland publication, *Opera: A Research and Information Guide*, edited and compiled by Guy A. Marco.

February 6, 1984
Jacksonville, Florida

Part I
Single-Subject Monographs

A

ABBOTT, EMMA, 1850-1891

1 Lippincott, Sara Jane (Clarke), 1823-1904. *Emma Abbott, Prima Donna*. By Grace Greenwood (pseud.). New York: Photo Engraving Co., Printers, 1878. 13 pp.

1-a ———. *Emma Abbott, Prima Donna*. By Grace Greenwood (pseud.). New York: n.p., 1879. 10 pp.

2 Martin, Sadie E. *The Life and Professional Career of Emma Abbott*. Minneapolis: L. Kimball Printing Company, 1891. 192 pp. Illustrated.

A very Victorian biography of a very Victorian personage, written by a close friend the year of the singer's death. She studied first with her father, then with Achille Errani in New York. During this period she assisted at concerts featuring Ole Bull and Clara Louise Kellogg. A fund was raised to send her to Europe, where she studied for a short time in Milan, and then in Paris with Marchesi. Patti heard her sing and recommended her to Mapleson; her operatic debut was as Marie in *The Daughter of the Regiment* at Covent Garden February 23, 1877. Later she toured with Mapleson in the United States before founding her own opera company. She took the soprano lead in a re-markable variety of roles, appearing, for example, on successive nights as Anne Boleyn (in Donizetti's opera), Elvira in Balfe's *Rose of Castile*, and Leonora in *Il Trovatore*. She introduced Masse's *Paul and Virginia* to the United States, and was heard as Juliette, Yum-Yum in *The Mikado*, Violetta, the Queen in *Ruy Blas*, Norma, Arline in *The Bohemian Girl*, Lucia, and Marguerite in *Faust*, which score she is said to have improved by the addition of "Nearer My God to Thee." Her programs carried the line "Costumes for this production are by Worth," and the notation that "The Emma Abbott Grand English Opera Company is the Largest, Strongest and Only Successful English Opera Company in America." Certain it is that she introduced a wide variety of operatic fare to many parts of the United States. The appendix (pp. 183-189) traces the musical backgrounds of Miss Abbott's forebears; and there is also a description (pp. 191-192) of the monument Miss Abbott had planned in memory of her husband. WRM

ABENDROTH, IRENE, 1872-1932

3 Abendroth, Irene. *Ein Fragment ihrer Künstlerlaufbahn*. Mit 56 Photographien der Künstlerin. In German. Dresden: E. Pierson, 1904. viii, 95 pp.

4 Thaller, Thomas von. *Irene Abendroth*. In German. Dresden: Pierson, 1904. 43 pp. Illustrated.

ACHTÉ, EMMY, 1850-1924

5 Krohn, Helmi, b. 1871. *Suomalaisen oopperan ensimmäinen tähti;
Emmy Achtén elämä ja työ.* In Finnish. Helsingissä: Otava, 1927.
158 pp. Illustrated.

6 Leppänen, Glory. *Tulesta tuhkaksi; Emmy Achté ja hänen maailmansa.*
In Finnish. Helsingissä: Otava, 1962. 339 pp. Illustrated.

ACKTÉ, AINO, 1876-1944

7 Ackté, Aino. *General Bruno Jalanders minnen; kaukasiska år och
politiske kristider,* upptecknade av Aino Ackté-Jalander. In Swedish.
Helsingfors: Söderström & Co. förlagsaktiebolag, 1932. 209 pp.
Illustrated.

These memoirs were written by Aino Ackté-Jalander about her second
husband, General Bruno Jalander. She is not mentioned in the book;
nor does she obtrude as narrator. PHS

8 ———. *Minnen och fantasier.* Translated by Bertel Gripenberg.
In Swedish. Stockholm: A. Bonnier, 1916. 128 pp.

A well-written series of "memories" of various sorts by Ackté.
Most of them do not concern opera or music, but one: a "Hymn til
grammofonen" is a brief tribute to John Forsell's recording of
Escamillo's aria from *Carmen.* PHS

9 ———. *Minnen och upplevelser.* In Swedish. Helsingfors:
Söderström & Co., 1925.

10 ———. *Muistoja ja kuvitelmia.* In Finnish. Helsingissä:
Kustannusosakeyhtiö Otava, 1916. 127 pp.

11 ———. *Muistojeni kirja.* I. In Finnish. Helsingissä: Otava,
1925. 330 pp. Illustrated. Note on National Union Catalog card,
"No more published."

The number following the title, which translates as "My book of
memories," suggests that Ackté planned to continue her memoirs. This
volume brings the account of her life up to 1905. The book begins
with a brief narrative of her childhood and operatic training in
France, then becomes a rather self-righteous recitation of the
machinations within the operatic world. References to other artists
are rarely complimentary, but there are many accounts of the admiration
that surrounded Ackté herself. The book contains a generous selection
of reviews of Ackté's performances from 1893 to 1902 (pp. 303-330)
published in Finnish, Swedish and French publications, presumably
translated into Finnish by Ackté. There is no index or bibliography.
AL

12 ———. *Taiteeni taipaleelta.* In Finnish. Helsingissä: Kustannusosakeyhtiö Otava, 1935. 212 pp. Illustrated.

This continues the narration begun in the author's *Muistojeni kirja,*
and covers the years 1905-1920. The book is primarily a description

of her performances throughout Europe, with a great deal of emphasis on her interpretation of Richard Strauss's *Salome*. She also describes how she and Edvard Fazer, a Finnish pianist, founded the Finnish opera in 1911. The book ends with her leaving the opera stage in 1920. Appended to the book are twelve pages of quotations from international reviews, most of them quite complimentary, but some downright vitriolic. AL

13 Leppänen, Glory, b. 1901. *Arkkipiispan perhe ja Aino Ackté*. In Finnish. Helsinki: Otava, 1966. 209 pp. Illustrated.

The author was Aino Ackté's daughter; her father, Heikki Renvall, was the son of the Archbishop of Finland. The book is concerned with family history, much of it written from family letters. WRM

14 Savolainen, Pentti. *Savonlinnan Ooperajuhlat Aino Acktésta Martti Talvelaan*. In Finnish. Savonlinna: Savonlinnan Kirjapaino Osakeyhtiö, 1980. 211 pp. Illustrated.

The opera festival at Savonlinna, Finland, was under the directorship of soprano Aino Ackté from its conception in 1911 through the 1916 season, then again in 1930. The festival was reestablished in 1967 in this popular seaside resort of southeast Finland; Martti Talvela was appointed Chairman of the Artistic Committee in 1972. This book tells the story of the festival which is now staged annually in the courtyard of St. Olaf's Castle, built in 1475. The original festival booklet of 1912 is reproduced on pp. 30-48. Reviews are given for each season, with programs for concerts and casts for the operas. WRM

15 Wennevirta, Ludvig, b. 1882. *Aino Ackté--Albert Edelfelt, eräs taiteemme episodi*. In Finnish. Porvoo: W. Söderström, 1944. Illustrated.

ADAM, THEO, b. 1926

16 Adam, Theo. *"Seht, hier ist Tinte, Feder, Papier ..."*: aus der *Werkstatt eines Sängers*. Edited by Hans-Peter Müller. In German. Berlin: Henschelverlag, 1980. 240 pp. Illustrated. Index, pp. 224-225. Discography, pp. 221-223. Chronology of Performances, pp. 218-220.

An autobiography of Theo Adam from his birth up to the publication date. He discusses his early life and career and talks about many of his engagements in chronological order, his approach to the roles, what was going on around him and in his life when he learned and sang them. He does this in especially deep detail in the *Probetagebuch* section. The book concludes with an interview between Adam and Hans-Peter Müller. It is especially valuable for its profuse illustrations; it contains formal and informal portraits on and off stage, in productions, costumes, and with family and friends. The discography, unfortunately, lists only the titles of works and company names; there are no record numbers included and only a list of the conductors involved at the end. HCS

17 Olivier, Philippe. *Theo Adam*. In French. Les Trésors de l'Opéra, no. 2. Paris: Opéra International, 1979. 64 pp. Illustrated. Discography, pp. 57-61.

A rather sketchy biography, written in a "with it" style of clipped sentences, some of them grammatically incomplete for emphasis or effect. The inadequate discography gives neither record numbers nor the names of other artists in the cast. Did Adam sing the complete *Ring* by himself?

ADAMI CORRADETTI, IRIS, b. 1909

18 Padoan, Paolo, b. 1938. *Iris Adami Corradetti fra storia e critica*. In Italian. Bologna: Bongiovanni, 1979. 103 pp. Illustrated. Repertory, pp. 95-96. Index, pp. 97-101. Discography, p. 94. Chronology of Performances, pp. 75-93.

A quilt of documents and reviews relating only to the professional life of the soprano. Her career began in 1926 and ended in 1957; she appeared almost exclusively in Italy. RT

AKIMOVA, SOF'IA VLADIMIROVNA, 1887-1972

19 Akimova, Sof'ia Vladimirovna. *Vospominaniia pevtsy*. Predisl. G. Tigranova. In Russian. Leningrad: Muzyka, 1978. 96 pp. Illustrated.

ALBANI, EMMA, 1847-1930

20 Albani, Emma. *Forty Years of Song*. London: Mills & Boon, 1911. 285 pp. Illustrated. Discography, pp. i-v.

20-a ———. *Forty Years of Song*. With a discography by W.R. Moran. Opera Biographies. New York: Arno Press, 1977. 285, v pp. Illustrated.

Reprint of the 1911 edition published by Mills & Boon (q.v.), augmented by the discography prepared for this reprint edition.

21 Charbonneau, Hélène. *L'Albani, sa carrière artistique et triomphale*. Préface de Victor Morin. In French. Montréal: Imprimerie Jacques-Cartier, 1938. 171 pp. Illustrated. Index, pp. 167-171.

A well-researched biography marred only by the style and tone of excessive adulation. The author was also a singer, which explains not only her affinity toward her subject but her ego as well that induced her to have her own photograph as frontispiece in a biography about a legendary opera singer. This book well complements Albani's own *Forty Years of Song* (q.v.).

See also items 1567, 1597, 1658

ALBONI, MARIETTA, 1823-1894

22 Pougin, Arthur, 1834-1921. *Marietta Alboni*. In French. Paris: Plon-Nourrit, 1912. x, 269 pp. Illustrated. Repertory, pp. 245-247.

A skilled writer and an expert musicologist, Pougin presents a well-written and informed biography of the famous contralto. There are frequent quotations from the autobiographical notes left by Alboni. RT

See also items 1612, 1658, 1694

ALCAÏDE, TOMÁZ, 1901-1967

23 Alcaïde, Tomáz. *Um cantor no palco e na vida; memórias*. In Portuguese. Lisboa: Publicações Europa-America, 1961. 293 pp. Illustrated. Chronology of Performances.

24 *Tomas Alcaïde*. In Portuguese. Lisboa: Teatro da Trinidade, 1968. 77 pp. Illustrated. Chronology, pp. 35-49.

The catalog of an exhibit commemorating the Portuguese tenor, Tomáz Alcaïde. Among the many brief tributes there is one by the baritone Gino Bechi.

ALCHEVSKII, IVAN

25 Alchevskii, Ivan. *Spogadi. Materiali. Listuvanniia*. In Ukrainian. Kiev: Muzichna Ukraina, 1980. 294 pp. Illustrated.

ALDA, FRANCES, 1883-1952

26 Alda, Frances. *Men, Women and Tenors*. Boston: Houghton Mifflin Company, 1937. 307 pp. Illustrated.

That Frances Alda's tenure at the Metropolitan Opera House (1908-1929) was not entirely due to her being the wife of the General Manager, Giulio Gatti-Casazza, from 1910 to 1928, is attested to by the many fine recordings which she left, many of them in ensembles with such worthy partners as Caruso. Alda's book reminds us that she could be witty, sarcastic, seldom subtle and brutally frank. She is all these things, whether speaking of her marriage or her fellow artists. Few of the latter go unmentioned, and the reader at least knows how Mme. Alda felt about them. In her book, she says that her world is active and amusing, sometimes exciting, never dull. The same can be said for her book. You do not have to be an Alda fan to enjoy it; it is a book which can be read again and again, and in some ways is a model which more singers should follow. Its reference use is somewhat marred by the fact that there is no index. WRM

26-a ————. *Men, Women and Tenors*. Freeport, N.Y.: Books for Libraries Press, 1970. 307 pp. Illustrated.

Reprint of the 1937 edition published by Houghton Mifflin, Boston (q.v.).

26-b ———. *Men, Women and Tenors.* New York: AMS Press, 1971. 307 pp.

Reprint of the 1937 edition published by Houghton Mifflin, Boston (q.v.).

See also item 1581

ALTUBE, CRISTOBAL, 1898-1951

27 Altube-Vergara, Cristobal. *Articulación de la voz humana.* In Spanish. Madrid: Publicaciones Españolas, 1951? 57 pp. Illustrated.

Altube was à good Basque tenor with a meritorious international career, even though he was overshadowed by his contemporaries, among them the three great Spanish tenors: Cortis, Fleta and Lázaro. He ended his short life as a voice teacher and lecturer at the Madrid Conservatory. The section written by Altube (pp. 25-55) contains singing exercises, advice and warnings to singers and comments on his own experiences. Director of the Conservatory, Nemesio Otaño, offers an interesting biographical sketch of Altube (pp. 15-20). AM

AMATO, PASQUALE, 1878-1942

See items 1541, 1581

AMELING, ELLY, b. 1934

28 Jong, Janny de. *Elly Ameling; vocaal avontuur.* In Dutch. Soest: Gooise Uitgiverij, 1978. 104 pp. Illustrated. Discography, pp. 102-104.

Published with a 12" 33 rpm disc.

AMSTAD, MARIETTA, 1882-1972

29 Amstad, Marietta. *Erinnerungen einer Nidwaldner Sängerin.* Edited by Jakob Wyrsch. In German. Beckenried: Martha Amstad, 1973. 116 pp. Illustrated.

ANCONA, MARIO, 1860-1931

30 Moran, William R. "Mario Ancona." *The Record Collector* XVI, nos. 5 & 6 (April 1965), 100-139. Discography, pp. 131-139.

Mario Ancona was one of the principal baritones of the operatic capitals in Europe and America in the latter part of the 19th and beginning of the 20th centuries. His name is frequently found with those of Caruso (with whom he recorded), Melba, the de Reszkes, Plançon, Eames, Nordica and other stars of the period. This biographical article was written with the assistance of the singer's son, and with reference to family files and letters. It also includes

previously unpublished letters from Leoncavallo and Giordano, and a
discography by the author.

ANDERS, PETER, 1908-1954

31 Pauli, Friedrich Wilhelm. *Peter Anders.* In German. Rembrandt-
Reihe, Bd. 47. Berlin: Rembrandt Verlag, 1963. 61 pp. Illustrated.

ANDERSON, MARIAN, b. 1902

32-T Anderson, Marian. *Marian Anderson vertelt haar leven.* In
Dutch. Antwerpen: H. Nelissen, Bilthoven 't Groeit, 1957. 299 pp.
Illustrated.

Dutch translation of *My Lord, What a Morning* (q.v.).

33 ————. *My Lord, What a Morning; an Autobiography.* New York:
Viking Press, 1956. 312 pp. Illustrated.

This autobiography was written and published a year after Anderson's
Met debut, the occasion that marked the end of racial discrimination
at the Metropolitan Opera House. Even though the singer acknowledges
being "indebted to Mr. Howard Taubman for editorial and critical
assistance in the preparation of this book," there can be no doubt
that the words and the narrative are hers. It is a detailed, enjoyable
book that touches on all the highlights of her career as well as her
childhood and adult life. She mentions acts of discrimination
without bitterness and with so much dignity that it humiliates the
perpetrators of the incidents.

33-a ————. *My Lord, What a Morning; an Autobiography.* London:
Cresset Press, 1957. 240 pp. Illustrated.

34 Albus, Harry James, b. 1920. *The "Deep River" Girl; the Life of
Marian Anderson in Story Form.* Grand Rapids: W.B. Eerdmans Publishing Co., 1949. 85 pp. Illustrated.

Marian Anderson's life story written in fictional style, at the
juvenile literature level.

35 Newman, Shirlee Petkin. *Marian Anderson: Lady from Philadelphia.*
Philadelphia: Westminster Press, 1965. 175 pp. Illustrated. Bibliography, pp. 163-165.

36 Piquion, René, with a poem by Jean Fernand Brierre. *Marian
Anderson.* In French. Collection du bi-centenaire de Port-au-Prince.
Port-au-Prince: Henri Deschamps, 1950. 13 pp. Illustrated.

A brief summary of the Anderson career, written with simplicity,
dignity and racial pride. It is preceded by a laudatory poem by
Jean F. Brierre.

37 Richardson, Ben Albert. *Great American Negroes.* New York:
Thomas Y. Crowell, 1947. viii, 223 pp.

This book contains brief biographies of outstanding Blacks. It includes politicians, educators, entertainers, etc., among them a singer and a singing actor: Marian Anderson and Paul Robeson. The biographies are superficial and cover only half of the careers of these artists.

38 Sims, Janet L. *Marian Anderson; an Annotated Bibliography and Discography*. Westport, Conn.: Greenwood Press, 1980. viii, 243 pp. Index, pp. 239-243. Discography, pp. 235-237.

A researcher's dream, this is an exhaustive bibliography of Marian Anderson. The material is divided into three main sections: (1) personal data, (2) career activities, (3) awards and honors. Each section is further subdivided into major subject categories. The entries include books (monographs, encyclopedias, other reference works), articles (magazine and newspaper), and all other material (portraits, busts, murals, honorary degrees, etc.) relating to Anderson's life and career. The annotations are brief and informative. The appendix contains a listing of manuscript holdings and an elementary, barely useful discography.

39 Spivey, Lenore. *Singing Heart; a Story Based on the Life of Marian Anderson*. Illus. by Howard and Thelma Hogan. Largo, Fla.: Community Service Foundation, 1963. 66 pp. Illustrated. Bibliography, p. 66.

40 Stevenson, Janet. *Marian Anderson; Singing to the World*. Britannica Bookshelf. Great Lives. Chicago: Encyclopedia Britannica Press, 1963. 189 pp. Illustrated.

This book concentrates on the one major--notorious--event of the singer's life up till 1963, the D.A.R.'s ban on her appearance in Constitution Hall in Washington, D.C. The outline of her whole life story is sandwiched between the segmented retelling of the events that led up to the Lincoln Memorial Concert on Easter Sunday, 1939. The largely fictitious dialogue and the labored structure of the biography get in the way of the otherwise interesting life story.

41 Stokes, Anson Phelps, b. 1874. *Art and the Color Line; an Appeal made May 31, 1939, to the President General and other Officers of the Daughters of the American Revolution to Modify their Rules so as to Permit Distinguished Negro Artists such as Miss Marian Anderson to be Heard in Constitution Hall*. Printed for consideration of the Executive Committee of the D.A.R. at Their Meeting, October 23, and for the Marian Anderson Committee. Washington, D.C., 1939. 26 pp.

42 Tobias, Tobi. *Marian Anderson*. Illustrated by Symeon Shimin. Crowell Biographies. New York: Thomas Y. Crowell, 1972. 40 pp. Illustrated.

The merest outline of the Anderson career, retold for children. Shimin's illustrations are stylish and appropriate. Of the few dates given, Anderson's date of birth is shown incorrectly as 1903 instead of 1902.

43 Vehanen, Kosti, b. 1887, and George J. Barnett. *Marian Anderson, a Portrait*. New York: McGraw-Hill, 1941. 270 pp. Illustrated.

Written by Anderson's Finnish accompanist, this is not a biography
in the conventional sense, but rather the retelling of the highlights
of ten years' collaboration. The book is little more than a succession of anecdotes, yet it illuminates many details about Anderson's
early career. It is particularly noteworthy that the singer had many
offers to sing opera in Europe, including one made by Stanislavskii
during her Russian tour, yet she turned them down. The great director
offered to stage *Carmen* for her but Anderson declined. The book concludes with the celebrated 1939 Easter Sunday concert in front of the
Lincoln Memorial, the last major collaboration between Anderson and
Vehanen before the latter's return to Finland. This biography was
"written with the collaboration of George J. Barnett" and published
simultaneously in New York and London (Whittlesey House). No bibliographic entry has been located for the London edition.

43-a ————. *Marian Anderson, a Portrait.* Westport, Conn.: Greenwood Press, 1970. 270 pp. Illustrated.

Reprint of the 1941 edition of McGraw-Hill, New York (q.v.).

44 Westlake, Neda M., and Otto E. Albrecht. *Marian Anderson: A
Catalog of the Collection at the University of Pennsylvania Library.*
Philadelphia: University of Pennsylvania Press, 1981. vii, 89 pp.
Illustrated.

A quarto-size volume that is neither more nor less than the inven-
tory list of the 248 boxes of music, correspondence, records and
memorabilia the singer donated to the University of Pennsylvania in
April 1977. The compilers did an excellent job; the book contains
the key to research material for more than one doctoral dissertation.

See also items 1607, 1608, 1792

ANDRADE, FRANCISCO DE, 1859-1921

45 *Andenken an die erste Gastspielreise d'Andrade in Deutschland
und Holland.* In German, Dutch, French. Elberfeld: S. Lucas, 1889?
146 pp. Illustrated.

A volume of press notices from German and Dutch papers, with French
translations.

46 Imiela, Hans-Jürgen. "Max Slevogt; das Bildnis des Sängers
Francisco D'Andrade als Don Giovanni, 1902." *Wallraf-Richartz-
Jahrbuch* (Köln) 23 (1961), 251-274. In German. Illustrated.

ANGELES, VICTORIA DE LOS, b. 1923

47 Burian, Karel Vladimir. *Victoria de los Angeles.* In Czech.
Praha: Supraphone, 1970. 48 pp. Illustrated.

A brief appreciation of de los Angeles, with 17 pages of plates
and a 7" 45 rpm record.

48 Fernández-Cid, Antonio, b. 1916. *Victoria de los Angeles.* In
Spanish. Madrid: Aldus, 1970. 269 pp. Illustrated. Repertory, pp.

161-172. Index, pp. 251-260. Discography, pp. 173-191.

49 Gavoty, Bernard. *Victoria de los Angeles*. Portraits de Roger Hauert. In French. Les grands interprètes. Genève: René Kister, 1956. 32 pp. Illustrated. Discography, p. 32.

A simple, short article about de los Angeles, complemented by many excellent photographs. The discography, marked "for the reader's guidance only," is certainly no more than that.

49-T-a ————. *Victoria de los Angeles*. Fotografías de Roger Hauert. Translated by J. Peral. In Spanish. Los Grandes Intérpretes. Ginebra: René Kister, 1956. 32 pp. Illustrated.

The Spanish translation of the 1956 French edition by the same publisher (q.v.).

49-T-b ————. *Victoria de los Angeles*. With portraits by Roger Hauert. Translated by F.E. Richardson. Great Concert Artists. Geneva: René Kister, 1956. 30 pp. Illustrated. Discography, p. 30.

The English translation of the 1956 French edition by the same publisher (q.v.).

50 Llopis, Artur. *Victòria dels Àngels*. In Catalan. Collecció biografies populars, serie 2, no. 5. Barcelona: Editorial Alcides, 1963. 75 pp. Illustrated.

51 Roberts, Peter. *Victoria de los Angeles*. London: Weidenfeld & Nicolson, 1982. vii, 184 pp. Illustrated. Index, pp. 179-184. Discography, pp. 169-177.

This "authorized" biography, written with the full cooperation of the singer herself, is the first full-length English-language biography of de los Angeles. It covers the private and public side of her life, with many incidents told in her own words. The discography includes her 78 rpm records; the LP listings only give the names of the principal performers of complete works.

See also item 1702

ANITÚA, FANNY, 1887-1968

See item 1631

ANSELMI, GIUSEPPE, 1876-1929

See item 1731

ARDER, ALEKSANDR, 1894-1966

52 Kits, Malev, and Arne Mikk. *Aleksandr Arder*. In Estonian. Tallinn: Kirjastus "Eesti Raamat," 1969. 119 pp. Illustrated. Repertory, pp. 117-118.

Biography of the Estonian bass-baritone. His repertory of 38 roles ranged from Silvio (debut, 1919) through Scarpia, Boris and Onegin to the Verdi baritone repertory. It speaks for the range of his voice that toward the end of his career he took on Prince Gremin, his last new role.

ARKHIPOVA, IRINA KONSTANTINOVNA, b. 1925

See item 1732

ARNDT-OBER, MARGARETE, 1885-1971

See item 1743

ARNOULD, SOPHIE, 1740-1802

53 Billy, André, b. 1882. *La vie amoureuse de Sophie Arnould (avec des documents inédits).* In French. "Leurs amours." Paris: E. Flammarion, 1929. 191 pp.

54 Deville, Albéric, 1773-1832. *Arnoldiana, ou Sophie Arnould et ses contemporaines; recueil choisi d'anecdotes piquantes, de reparties et de bons mots de Mlle Arnould; précédé d'une notice sur sa vie et sur l'Académie impériale de musique.* In French. Paris: Gérard, 1813. 380 pp. Illustrated.

55 Douglas, Robert Bruce, b. 1848. *Sophie Arnould, Actress and Wit.* With seven copper-plate engravings by Adolphe Lalauze. Paris: C. Carrington, 1898. x, 272 pp. Edition limited to 500 copies.

56-T ————. *Sophie Arnould.* Compositions par Adolphe Lalauze. Translated by Charles Grolleau. In French. Paris: C. Carrington, 1898. ix, 264 pp. Illustrated. Edition limited to 425 numbered copies.

French translation of the English edition published by the same firm in the same year, 1898 (q.v.).

57 Dusanne, Beatrix, b. 1886. *Sophie Arnould, la plus spirituelle des bacchantes.* In French. Les grandes pécheresses. Paris: A. Michel, 1938. 254 pp.

58 Fayolle, François Joseph Marie, 1774-1852. *Esprit de Sophie Arnould.* In French. Paris: F. Louis, 1813. 106 pp.

59 Goncourt, Edmond de, 1822-1896, and Jules de Goncourt. *Sophie Arnould d'après sa correspondance et ses mémoires inédits.* In French. Paris: Poulet-Malassis et de Broise, 1857. iv, 197 pp.

59-a ————. *Sophie Arnould d'après sa correspondance et ses mémoires inédits.* In French. Paris: E. Dentu, 1877. vii, 223 pp. Illustrated.

59-b ———. *Sophie Arnould d'après sa correspondance inédits.*
In French. Paris: G. Charpentier, 1885. xv, 327 pp.

59-c ———. *Sophie Arnould d'après sa correspondance et ses
mémoires inédits.* In French. (On cover:) Les actrices du XVIIIme
siècle. Paris: E. Fasquelle, 1902. xv, 327 pp.

59-d ———. *Sophie Arnould d'après sa correspondance et ses
mémoires inédits.* Postface de Émile Bergerat. In French. Les
actrices du XVIIIme siècle. Paris: E. Flammarion, 1922. 228 pp.
Illustrated. On title page: Edition définitive publiée sous la
direction de l'Académie Goncourt.

60 Lamothe-Langon, Étienne Léon, baron de, 1786-1864. *Mémoires de
Mademoiselle Sophie Arnoult*; recueillis et publiés par le baron de
Lamothe-Langon. In French. Paris: Allardin, 1837. 2 vols.

61 Stern, Jean. *À l'ombre de Sophie Arnould. François-Joseph
Bellanger, architecte des Menus Plaisirs, premier architecte du comte
d'Artois....* In French. Paris: Plon, 1930. 2 vols. Illustrated.

62 Wahl, Roger, b. 1898. *La folie Saint-James, notamment d'après
les "secrets" de Bachaumont, Bellanger et Mlle Sophie Arnould.* In
French. Neuilly-sur-Seine: Chez l'auteur, 1955. 149 pp. Illustrated.

The story of the walled country house at Neuilly, called La Folie
Saint-James, its builder François-Joseph Bellanger, along with a disorganized chapter of obscure relevance about Sophie Arnould.

63 Williams, Noel H. *Later Queens of the French Stage.* New York,
1906. 360 pp. Illustrated. Unverified; information taken from
dealer's catalog.

Contains a chapter on Sophie Arnould.

See also items 1596, 1597, 1612

ARRAL, BLANCHE, 1865-1945

See item 1819

ARROYO, MARTINA, b. 1935

See item 1654

ASZTALOS, ELISE VON

64 Asztalos, Elise (Berndes) von. *Aus meinem Künstlerleben als
Primadonna in Deutschland, Österreich und Italien.* In German.
Hamburg: Verlagsanstalt Aktien-Gesellschaft, 1901. 272 pp. Illus-
trated.

ATHANSASIU, JEAN, 1885-1938

65 Istratty, Ella. *Jean Athanasiu.* In Rumanian. Bucureşti:
Editura Muzicală, 1966. 149 pp. Illustrated. Repertory, pp. 147-148.

A fairly detailed biography that made use of Rumanian archives and
magazines in establishing the exact chronology of the singer's life.
The events of his childhood are covered quickly, with greater detail
on his student years and career. The list of his repertory gives the
place and year of his first performance in each role. HCS

ATLANTOV, VLADIMIR, b. 1939

See item 1732

AVERKAMP, ANTOON, 1861-1934

66 Averkamp, Antoon. *Uit mijn practijk. Wenken en raddgevingen bij
het onderwijs en de studie van den solozang.* In Dutch. Groningen,
Den Haag: J.B. Wolters, 1916. 140 pp. Illustrated.

AYRES, PATTI, 1876-1921

67 Ayres, Patti. *A Few Hints to Singers.* Seattle?, 1929? 9 pp.

The "hints" run little more than a page and are concerned almost
exclusively with proper formation of vowels and nearly obsessive
admonitions to eschew obesity, citing many famous singers who were
slender. The remainder is a compilation of reviews and promotional
literature about Patti Ayres; there is a facsimile of one of her
recital programs with a portrait in the upper right-hand corner and
other portraits of her in the book. A brief biography, taken from
the *National Cyclopedia of American Biography* is on p. [8], giving
an outline of her life and career. HCS

B

BABINI, MATTEO, 1754-1816

68 Brighenti, Pietro. *Elogio di Matteo Babini detto al Liceo
filarmonico di Bologna nella solenne distribuzione dei premi musicali
il 9 luglio 1819.* In Italian. Bologna: Nobili, 1821. 28 pp.

BĂDESCU, DINU, b. 1904

69 Bădescu, Dinu. *Pe cărările unei vieți de boem. Evocări.*
In Rumanian. Bucureşti: Editura muzicală, 1973. 188 pp. Illustrated.

BADÍA, CONCHITA, 1897-1975

70 Alavedra, Juan. *Conxita Badia: una vida d'artista.* In Catalan.
Collecció Memòries, no. 18. Barcelona: Pòrtic, 1975. 255 pp.
Illustrated. Index, pp. 245-254. Discography, pp. 239-243.

BAHR-MILDENBURG, ANNA, 1872-1947

71 Bahr-Mildenburg, Anna, and Hermann Bahr. *Bayreuth.* In German.
Leipzig: E. Rowohlt, 1912. 114 pp.

The titles of the first three chapters are "Cosima Wagner," "Rehearsal time in Bayreuth" and "Conductor Müller." Only these are by
Anna Bahr-Mildenburg; the rest are by Hermann Bahr.

72-T ————. *Bayreuth and the Wagner Theatre.* Translated by T.W.
Makepeace. London: T.F. Unwin, 1912. 95 pp.

This is the English translation of the German original published
in 1912 under the title *Bayreuth* in Leipzig by E. Rowohlt (q.v.).
Only the first three chapters are written by Anna-Bahr Mildenburg;
the rest are by Hermann Bahr.

73 Bahr-Mildenburg, Anna. *Darstellung der Werke Richard Wagners aus
dem Geiste der Dichtung und Musik. Tristan und Isolde;* vollständige
Regiebearbeitung sämtlicher Partien mit Notenbeispielen. In German.
Leipzig: Musikwissenschaftlicher Verlag, 1936. 115 pp. Illustrated.

74 ————. *Erinnerungen.* In German. Wien: Wiener literarische
Anstalt Gesellschaft, 1921. 230 pp. Illustrated.

75 Bahr, Hermann, 1863-1934. *Salzburger Landschaft. Aus Briefen an
seine Frau Anna Bahr-Mildenburg und aus seinen Tagebüchern.* With
drawings by Anton Steinhart. In German. Innsbruck: F. Rauch, 1937.
54 pp. Illustrated.

76 Stefan-Gruenfeldt, Paul, 1879-1943. *Anna Bahr-Mildenburg.* In
German. Wien: "Wila," 1922. 37, 5 pp. A copy of this book is in
the collection of the Széchenyi Library, Budapest.

BAJENARU, IOAN, 1863-1921

77 Massoff, Ioan. *Tenorul Ioan Băjenaru şi vremea lui.* In Rumanian.
Bucureşti: Editura muzicală, 1970. 232 pp. Illustrated. Bibliography, pp. 227-229.

BAKER, JANET, b. 1933

78 Baker, Janet. *Full Circle; an Autobiographical Journal.* With
photographs by Zoë Dominic. London: Julia MacRae, 1982. 270 pp.
Illustrated. Repertory, pp. 267-270.

   As the subtitle suggests, this is the diary of the singer, written
during the 1981-82 season, which marked the conclusion of her operatic--
as opposed to concert--career. It is an interesting record of her
professional and off-stage activities during that busy year. Although
it contains a good deal of commentary on a variety of topics, it lacks,
intentionally, the elements of a conventional autobiography. To find
out more about the life and career of Dame Janet Baker, those details
that made her retirement a musical event of international significance,

the reader must turn to other publications. Just as the singer intended, Zoë Dominic's superb photographs bring unity to this beautifully produced book.

78-a ———. *Full Circle; an Autobiographical Journal*. With photographs by Zoë Dominic. New York: Franklin Watts, 1982. 270 pp. Illustrated. Repertory, pp. 267-270.

79 Blyth, Alan. *Janet Baker*. New York: Drake, 1973. 64 pp. Discography, pp. 61-64.

A simple, straightforward biography, with many extensive quotations from the artist herself. The well-chosen photographs show her mostly in her professional activities.

See also item 1654

BAKLANOV, GEORGE, 1882-1938

See item 1811

BARONI, ADRIANNA BASILE, ca. 1580-ca. 1640

80 Ademollo, Alessandro, 1826-1891. *I Basile alla corte di Mantova, secondo documenti inediti o rari (1603-1628)*. In Italian. Genova: Tipografia del R. Istituto Sordo-muti, 1885. 29 pp.

81 ———. *La bell'Adriana a Milano (1611)*. In Italian. Milano: R. stabilimento musicale Ricordi, 1885. 14 pp. Illustrated.

82 ———. *La bell'Adriana ed altre virtuose del suo tempo alla corte di Mantova; contributo di documenti per la storia della musica in Italia nel primo quarto del seicento*. In Italian. Città di Castello: S. Lapi, 1888. ix, 359 pp. Illustrated.

BARRIENTOS, MARIA, 1883-1946

See items 1543, 1565

BARSOVA, VALERIIA VLADIMIROVNA, 1892-1967

83 Moscow. Gosudarstvennyi akademicheskii Bol'shoi teatr. *Valeriia Vladimirovna Barsova*. Edited by Anisimov. In Russian. Moskva: Iskusstvo, 1954. Unpaged. Illustrated.

A small booklet with a brief introduction, consisting mostly of illustrations. Interesting photos, poor printing. Barsova's roles include: Lakmé, Cio-Cio-San, Marfa (in *Tsar Saltan*), Violetta, Leonora (*Il Trovatore*), Marguerite de Valois, Ludmila, Juliette, Antonida (*Life for the Tsar*).

84 Polianovskii, Georgii Alekseevich. *V.V. Barsova*. In Russian. Moskva: Muzyka, 1975. 158 pp. Illustrated.

BASILIDES, MÁRIA, 1886-1946

85 Horváth, Árpád, editor. *Szerep nélkül. Basilides Mária, Kiss Manyi, stb. irásai.* In Hungarian. Budapest: Uj Hang, 1943. 158 pp.

86 Molnár, Jenö Antal. *Basilides Mária.* In Hungarian. Nagy magyar elöadómüvészek, 1. Budapest: Zenemükiadó, 1967. 70 pp. Illustrated. Repertory, pp. 66-69.

Basilides, one of the great contralto voices Hungary produced, had a large operatic repertory but was best known for her oratorio work and as the foremost interpreter of the music of Bartók and Kodály. Molnár gives an excellent overview of her career. The two records in a pocket (7", 33 rpm) include Bartók and Kodály folk songs with the piano accompaniment of Bartók himself.

BATHORI, JANE, 1876-1970

87 Bathori, Jane. *Sur l'interprétation des mélodies de Claude Debussy.* (Lettre-préface de Darius Milhaud.) In French. Paris: Editions ouvrières, 1953. 40 pp.

BÁTHY, ANNA, 1901-1962

88 Somogyi, Vilmos, and Imre Molnár. *Báthy Anna.* In Hungarian. Nagy magyar elöadómüvészek, 8. Budapest: Zenemükiadó, 1969. 58 pp. Illustrated. Repertory, pp. 57-58.

A fair account of the distinguished career of this excellent soprano. Apart from a few foreign engagements she spent her career at the Hungarian Opera House in Budapest. The two 7" 33 rpm records in the pocket of the back cover contain six selections of opera and song.

BATTISTINI, MATTIA, 1856-1928

89 Fracassini, Gino. *Mattia Battistini*, profilo artistico illustrato di Gino Fracassini. In Italian. Milano: C. Barbini, 1914. 160 pp.

90 Palmegiani, Francesco. *Mattia Battistini, il re dei baritoni.* In Italian. Milano: Stampa d'oggi, 1949. 199 pp. Illustrated. Bibliography, p. 197.

A well-written biography whose overall value is diminished by the large number of factual errors, some of them of great significance. For instance, Battistini traveled twice to South America, not once; he first sang in Russia in 1893, not 1888; the list goes on. This being one of only two full-length biographies ever written about Battistini, the limited choice lends undue importance to this book. TGK

90-a ———. *Mattia Battistini: il re dei baritoni.* With a discography by W.R. Moran. In Italian. New York: Arno Press, 1977. 199 pp. Illustrated. Bibliography, p. 197. Discography, pp. 198- (unpaged).

Reprint of the 1949 edition published by Stampa d'oggi, Milano (q.v.). The discography by William R. Moran was prepared for this edition.

91 Deleted

92 Sillanpa, Tom. *An Artistic Profile of Mattia Battistini: A Biography of the World's Premier Baritone.* "Lest We Forget" series; no. 2. N.p.: T. Sillanpa, 1983. 46 pp. Illustrated. Repertory, pp. 41-42. Discography, pp. 39-44. Songs Recorded, p. 43.

A superficial, poorly written, sometimes inaccurate biography, it is chiefly valuable for the photographs of Battistini in and out of costume. The discography—a misleading title—lists and discusses a few recordings; it is by no means exhaustive. HCS

See also items 1617, 1680, 1831

BATURIN, ALEKSANDR IOSIFOVICH, b. 1904

93 Moscow. Gosudarstvennyi akademicheskii Bol'shoi teatr. *Aleksandr Iosifovich Baturin.* Edited by A. Anisimov. In Russian. Moskva: Iskusstvo, 1953. 16 pp. Illustrated.

A brief appreciation of the artist followed by a large selection of photographs. The reproductions are poor.

See also item 1708

BAUR, CAROLINE

94 Baur, Caroline. *Memoirs.* Boston: Roberts Brothers, 1885. 544 pp.

BEDFORD, PAUL JOHN, 1792-1871

95 Bedford, Paul John. *Recollections and Wanderings of Paul Bedford. Facts, Not Fancies.* London: Routledge, Warne, and Routledge, 1864. 160 pp. Illustrated.

The recollections of actor-singer Paul Bedford, consisting of only a little biographical material and even less music. There is a long succession of loosely connected inane anecdotes, one of them involving Malibran. Bedford appeared in many plays, including *Richard the Third* with Edmund Kean; he also sang the bass repertory, including Dulcamara, Don Pasquale, Caspar and Beppo (*Fra Diavolo*).

95-a ———. *Recollections and Wanderings of Paul Bedford. Facts, Not Fancies.* London: Strand Printing and Pub. Co., 1867. 132 pp.

BELLINCIONI, GEMMA, 1864-1950

96 Bellincioni, Gemma. *Io e il palcoscenico (trenta e un anno di vita artistica)*. In Italian. Milano: R. Quintieri, 1920. 137 pp.

A sketchy and only moderately informative memoir by the creator of Santuzza in *Cavalleria rusticana*. She was the most famous Italian Salome, the first primadonna to sing the role *and* dance the Dance of the Seven Veils. While the book contains valuable details, Bellincioni omits even more that only she could have told.

97 Baccioni, G.B. *Gemma Bellincioni*. In Italian. Palermo, 1902. Listed as a footnote to the Bellincioni entry in the *Enciclopedia dello Spettacolo*. Not located in any other source.

See also items 1375, 1376, 1620, 1680, 1733

BELLOC, TERESA, 1784-1885

98 Della Croce, Vittorio, b. 1924. *Una giacobina piemontese alla Scala: la primadonna Teresa Belloc*. Prefazione di Giorgio Gualerzi. In Italian. Realtà musicali. Torino: Eda, 1978. 222 pp. Illustrated. Bibliography, pp. 201-204. Repertory, pp. 163-165. Index, pp. 213-220. Discography, pp. 193-199. Chronology, pp. 167-191.

A well-researched biography of Maria Teresa Belloc (née Trombetta), the celebrated mezzo-soprano of the first quarter of the 19th century. The author sets her career in the proper perspective by an extensive discussion of her predecessors and contemporaries. The supporting documentation is excellent, the chronology of her performances includes all the essential data *and* the publication, by date, which carried a review of her performance!

BELOCCA, ANNA DE, b. 1854

99 Berlioze, Victor. *Esquisses biographiques. Anna de Belocca*. In French. Paris: Librairie nouvelle, 1874. 28 pp. Illustrated.

BENTON, JOSEPH, 1898-1971

100 Benton, Joseph. *Oklahoma Tenor: Musical Memories of Giuseppe Bentonelli*. Foreword by Eva Turner. Introduction by B.A. Nugent. Norman: University of Oklahoma Press, 1973. xiii, 150 pp. Illustrated.

BERGANZA, TERESA, b. 1935

101 Segalini, Sergio, b. 1944. *Teresa Berganza*. In French. Paris: Fayard. 108 pp. Discography, pp. 106-108. Chronology, pp. 96-105.

This beautifully designed and printed book consists of a twelve-page biographical introduction and an annotated collection of superb photographs. Although the biography successfully captures the essence of the singer, it is too sketchy and superficial to do justice to this artist. The very extensive notes that accompany the photographs are informative and well complement the introduction.

BERGER, ERNA, b. 1900

102 Höcker, Karla, b. 1901. *Erna Berger, die singende Botschafterin.* In German. Rembrandt-Reihe, 29. Berlin: Rembrandt, 1961. 62 pp. Illustrated.

A short summary of the career of the famous German coloratura soprano. Half of the book is taken up by photographs. The list of her recordings on the last page is not a discography in the conventional sense, but rather an advertisement for Electrola.

BERNAC, PIERRE, 1899-1979

103 Bernac, Pierre. *Francis Poulenc et ses mélodies.* Préface d'Henri Sauget; quelques mots par Bernard Gavoty. In French. Paris: Buchet-Chastel, 1978. 220 pp. Index.

This is the French original of Bernac's book published a year earlier in New York and London under the title *Francis Poulenc, the Man and His Songs* (q.v.). In spite of the reversal of the usual chronological sequence, considering Bernac's nationality and the absence of indication of a translator, this book is assumed to contain the original text as written by Bernac.

104-T ——. *Francis Poulenc, the Man and His Songs.* With a foreword by Sir Lennox Berkeley. Translated by Winifred Radford. New York: B. Norton, 1977. 233 pp. Bibliography, p. 225. Index of Titles, pp. 227-229. Index of First Lines, pp. 230-233.

The English translation of *Francis Poulenc et ses mélodies* (q.v.). One of the foremost interpreters of Poulenc's music and a friend of the composer, French singer and voice teacher Bernac brings to the subject a wealth of privileged information. An excellent book on the interpretation of these songs.

104-T-a ——. *Francis Poulenc, the Man and His Songs.* With a foreword by Sir Lennox Berkeley. Translated by Winifred Radford. London: V. Gollancz, 1977. 233 pp. Illustrated. Bibliography, p. 224. Index of Titles and Index of First Lines as in 1977 Norton ed. (q.v.).

105 ——. *The Interpretation of French Song.* Translation of song texts by Winifred Radford. New York: Praeger, 1970. xiv, 326 pp. Index of Titles, First Lines, and Composers as in 1970 Cassell edition (q.v.).

An outstanding study on the topic as indicated by the title: the interpretation of the French song. Bernac, an accomplished singer specializing in the music this book discusses, and a recognized authority on interpretation as well as a voice teacher, communicates his ideas with clarity and insight.

105-a ——. *The Interpretation of French Song*; translation of song texts by Winifred Radford. London: Cassell, 1970. xiv, 327 pp.

Index of Titles, pp. 319-322. Index of First Lines, pp. 323-326.
Index of Composers, p. 327.

See also item 1623

BERRY, WALTER, b. 1929

See item 879

BEST, MATTHEW, b. 1958

See item 1024

BETETTO, JULIJ, b. 1885

106 Ukmar, Vilko. Srecanja z Julijem Betettom. In Slovenian.
Ljubljana: Drzavna zalozba Slovenije, 1961. 126 pp. Illustrated.

BILINNIK, PETRO SERGIIOVICH

107 Stebun, Illia Isakovych, b. 1911. Petro Sergiiovich Bilinnik.
In Ukrainian. Kiev: Derzh. izd-vo obrazotvorchogo mistetsva i
muzichnoi lit-ri URSR, 1958. 14 pp. Illustrated.

108 Stefanovych, Mykhailo Pavlovych. Petr Sergeevich Belinnik.
In Russian. Kiev: Derzh. vid-vo obrazotvorchogo mistetsva i muzichnoi
lit-ri URSR, 1960. 28 pp. Illustrated.

BILLINGTON, ELIZABETH (WELCHSEL), afterwards Mme. Felissent, 1765-1818

109 An Answer to the Memoirs of Mrs. Billington. With the Life and
Adventures of Richard Daly, Esq. and an Account of the Present State
of the Irish Theatre. Written by a Gentleman, Well Acquainted with
Several Curious Anecdotes of All Parties. London: For the author,
1792. 71 pp.

Her date of birth is given as 1768 by the Library of Congress.
Rosenthal gives her birth date as 1765; the new Grove's as ?1765-8.

110 Memoirs of Mrs. Billington, from Her Birth: Containing a Variety
of Matter, Ludicrous, Theatrical, Musical, and --; with Copies of
Several Original Letters.... London: J. Ridgway, 1792. xv, 78 pp.

See also items 1562, 1612

BISHOP, ANNA

See item 1694

BISPHAM, DAVID SCULL, 1857-1921

111 Bispham, David Scull. *A Quaker Singer's Recollections.* New York: Macmillan Company, 1920. 401 pp. Illustrated. Index, pp. 375-401.

David Bispham began and ended his life in Philadelphia: it was in that city that he first studied voice, later perfecting his technique with Lamperti in Milan and Shakespeare in London. His Covent Garden debut was in 1892, his debut at the Metropolitan 1896; in each company he performed major roles, especially in the Wagner operas, with the great artists of his time. Later he was famous as an oratorio and concert singer, one of the most prestigious of his time. As an American singer, he took pride in his heritage, and encouraged American artists. His many stories about his fellow artists, Plançon, the de Reszkes, Nordica, Melba, Eames, as well as many of the lesser lights of his times are told in a kindly and gentlemanly fashion. A well-travelled, educated man, Bispham writes with enviable ease, charm, and sensible combination of modesty and awareness of his artistic worth. The breadth of coverage is indicated by the 25-page index. WRM

111-a ————. *A Quaker Singer's Recollections.* New York: Arno Press, 1977. ix, 401 pp. Illustrated. Index, pp. 375-401.

Reprint of the 1921 edition published by Macmillan, New York (q.v.). This edition, as well as the 1922 "new edition," contains a new preface.

See also items 1565, 1581

BJÖRLING, JUSSI, 1911-1960

112 Björling, Jussi. *Med bagaget i strupen.* In Swedish. Stockholm: Wahlström and Widstrand, 1945. 175 pp. Illustrated. Repertory, pp. 174-175. Discography, pp. 118-122.

A well-illustrated, detailed, egocentric autobiography by the 34-year-old Björling. He begins his story with the tours of the "Björling Male Quartet" (father David and his three sons) and carries the narrative through his Viennese, Chicago, New York and San Francisco engagements. The volume is full of anecdotes and comments about operatic notables like Tibbett, Marian Anderson (shown in a snapshot at a New Year's Eve party with the Björlings in Sweden), Thorborg, Kiepura and many others. The list of his roles is arranged chronologically as he added each to his repertory and is thus complete only until 1938. In addition to the anecdotes, this volume is valuable for the insight it gives of the tenor's view of himself. A brief list of his 78s is incorporated in the text on pp. 118-122. PHS

113 Björling, Gösta, b. 1912. *Jussi, boken om storebror.* In Swedish. Stockholm: Steinsvik, 1945. 223 pp. Illustrated.

Published in 1945, the same year the 34-year-old Jussi's own autobiography appeared, this book also excludes the last fifteen years of the tenor's life and career. It is an excellently written, personal view by the singer's younger brother. There is a wealth of personal

material along with remarkable illustrations that range from a reproduction of a concert program shared by father David, John Forsell and
two ladies, to a large number of professional and family photographs
including movie stills from Jussi's film *Fran för framgång*. Documentary
material includes a list of the Swedish appearances of the "Björling
Quartet" consisting of the three boys in their pre-teen years and
their father, a list of the 26 U.S. cities where Jussi concertized in
1937-1941, and a list of roles with the dates of his first assumption
of each role at the Swedish Royal Opera House: fifty minor and major
roles between 1930 and 1938! The simple discography is an elementary
effort, and has been rendered obsolete by subsequent compilations.
PHS

114 Hagman, Bertil, editor. *Jussi Björling, en minnesbok.* In
Swedish. Stockholm: Albert Bonniers förlag, 1960. 212 pp. Illustrated. Repertory, pp. 182-186. Discography, pp. 189-208.

A collection of reminiscences by friends, associates, colleagues,
written and published in the year Björling died. The authors of the
thirty-nine chapters include such internationally famous names as Set
Svanholm, Hjördis Schymberg, Birgit Nilsson, Elisabeth Söderström,
Joseph Hislop, Kurt Herbert Adler, Harold Rosenthal and others. The
list of his roles, with dates, includes only Swedish performances; the
discography of his commercial recordings (no dates or matrix numbers
for the 78 rpm records) appears complete up to 1960. The profuse
illustrations are from all stages of Björling's life. This is certainly a book that deserves to be translated for wider accessibility.

BLACHUT, BENO, b. 1913

115 Brožovská, Jarmila. *Beno Blachut.* In Czech. Umělci Národního
divadla, sv. 3. Praha: Panton, 1964. 63 pp. Illustrated.

BLAHO, JANKO, b. 1901

116 Blaho, Janko. *Zo skalického rínku.* In Czech. Memoáre, zv. 6.
Bratislava: Tatran, 1974. 202 pp. Illustrated.

The memoirs of Dr. Janko Blaho, one of the important Czech tenors
of the interwar years. He made his debut on March 23, 1924, and took
on his last new role (Pong) on January 6, 1966. He sang the title
role of *Faust* opposite Chaliapin at the Narodne Divadlo in 1934. His
repertory included over 150 roles, among them Jenik, Alfredo, Rodolfo,
Cavaradossi, Des Grieux, Pinkerton, Almaviva, Hoffmann, Riccardo,
Lyonel and others.

BOCKELMANN, RUDOLF, 1892-1958

See item 1811

BÖHME, KURT, b. 1908

117 Richter, Karl. *Kurt Böhme: selbstverständlich empfängt mich Ihro Gnaden!* In German. Augsburg: Schroff, 1977. 238 pp. Illustrated. Discography, pp. 230-233. Chronology, pp. 207-229.

BOHNEN, MICHAEL, 1887-1965

See items 1742, 1811

BOLLMANN, HANS HEINZ, 1889-1974

See item 1811

BONCI, ALESSANDRO, 1870-1940

118 Bennati, Nando. *Alessandro Bonci, impressioni.* In Italian. Ferrara, 1901. Located only as a footnote to the Bonci article in the *Enciclopedia dello Spettacolo.*

See also item 1620

BONINSEGNA, CELESTINA, 1877-1947

119 Moran, William R. "Celestina Boninsegna in the United States: Contemporary Critics Speak." *The Record Collector* XII, no. 12 (February 1960), 267-283.

Excerpts from contemporary reviews of Boninsegna's debut at the Metropolitan (as Aida, with Caruso, Stracciari, Kirkby-Lunn and Plançon on December 21, 1906) through a Tosca at the Boston Opera House on March 7, 1910; some 30 performances in the United States are traced. In these performances, the singer seldom received unqualified praise. The most used adjective is "conventional," with "uneven" a close second. The author concludes that Boninsegna's place in operatic history must rely mainly on her recordings where her fame is and will continue to be appreciated because of her many truly sensational performances.

120 Williams, Clifford, and John B. Richards. "Celestina Boninsegna." *The Record Collector* XII, nos. 1 and 2 (January-February 1958), 4-33.

Celestina Boninsegna has always been the darling of record collectors: her vibrant, full dramatic soprano voice was treated kindly by the acoustical recording process in use from 1904 to 1920 when her name could be found in many record company catalogs. Detailing the events of her career, however, proved a real challenge, which the authors discharged in an excellent fashion. This seems to be the only biographical account of her operatic career which encompassed opera houses in Italy, South America, and for shorter periods, London, New York, Boston, Chicago and other cities in the United States.

BOOTH, WEBSTER, b. 1905

See item 1536

BORDONI-HASSE, FAUSTINA

See Hasse, Faustina (Bordoni)

BORGATTI, GIUSEPPE, 1871-1950

121 Borgatti, Giuseppe. *La mia vita d'artista, ricordi e aneddoti.*
Prefazione di Giuseppe Lipparini. In Italian. Confessioni di attori
collana di memorie teatrali. Bologna: L. Cappelli, 1927. 181 pp.
Illustrated.

The autobiography of the greatest Wagnerian tenor Italy has produced. Borgatti introduced most of the Wagner operas to Italy and
sang many performances under the baton of Toscanini. Because of
acute glaucoma, first one, later the other eyeball had to be removed,
bringing to a premature end a gloriously successful career. The
passage where he describes wishing to fix the image of his children
on his memory one last time before the second operation is profoundly
moving in its tragic simplicity. The chronological continuity of the
narrative should have been better organized by a capable editor.
Under the circumstances, with the author unable to read his own manuscript, one must be grateful for his reminiscences as they are.

See also items 1620, 1832

BORI, LUCREZIA, 1887-1960

122 Marion, John Francis. *Lucrezia Bori of the Metropolitan Opera.*
American Background Books, 22. New York: P.J. Kennedy, 1962. 189
pp. Illustrated. Index, pp. 183-189.

Bori's life story in outline, told at the reading level of a 12-
year-old, complete with fictional dialogues. It is to be regretted
that this is the only book to date devoted to this important singer.

See also items 1541, 1695

BOSIO, ANGIOLINA, 1830-1859

See item 1597

BOUÉ, GÉORI, b. 1918

123 Mancini, Roland, and Jean-Louis Caussou. *Géori-Boué.* In
French. Montres sacrés--Les cahiers d'opéra, no. 6. Paris: SODAL,
1967. 32 pp. Illustrated.

BOVY, VINA, 1900-1983

124 Deleersnyder, Jacques. *Vina Bovy*. In French. Ghent: The Author, 1965. 112, xvi pp. Illustrated.

BRAHAM, JOHN, 1774?-1856

125 Gilliland, Thomas, fl. 1804-1816. *Jack in Office; Containing Remarks on Mr.· Braham's Address to the Public, with a Full and Impartial Consideration of Mr. Kemble's Conduct with Respect to the Above Gentlemen*. London: C. Chapple, 1805. 40 pp.

126 Levien, John Joseph Mowburn, b. 1863. *The Singing of John Braham*. London: Novello and Company, 1944. 40 pp. Illustrated.

See also items 1562, 1682

BRANDT, MARIANNE, 1842-1921

See items 1615, 1658

BRASLAU, SOPHIE, 1892-1935

See items 1565, 1695

BREMA, MARIE, 1856-1925

See item 1567

BROSCHI, CARLO

See Farinelli

BROUWENSTIJN, GRÉ, b. 1915

127 Brouwenstijn, Gré, and J.P.M. van Elswijk. *Gré Brouwenstijn met en zonder make-up*. In Dutch. Bussum: Teleboek, 1971. 224 pp. Illustrated. Discography, p. 224. Chronology of Career, pp. 201-222.

A charming, profusely illustrated narrative of the life and career of Gré Brouwenstijn, related by the soprano and her husband, A.C. van Swol. Born in 1915 as Gerarda Demphina Brouwenstijn, Gré made her first mark in the post-war period singing Santuzza in Limburg, the title role of *Fidelio* in Amsterdam, and Tatiana's letter aria in a Henry Wood concert in 1949. Her distinguished career came to a close with a farewell concert in Amsterdam, on June 25, 1971. There are a few interesting anecdotes of singers, conductors and tours, but the thrust of the book is non-chronological and comparatively disorganized. Nonetheless, it is interesting and well written. The profuse photos are fascinating. PHS

See also item 1744

BRUCKMANN, HANNA VON, b. 1869

128 Bruckmann, Hanna von. *Dreissig Jahre aus meinem Leben.* In German. München: K. Thiemig, 1958? 273 pp.

Daughter of a lyric tenor and a coloratura soprano, von Bruckmann wrote this charming, literate autobiography in her eightieth year. Born in 1869, she retired after a successful career of only twelve years that included several Bayreuth engagements. Because of her imminent marriage, she sang her last performance on the stage of the Royal Court and National Theater in Munich on November 25, 1900.

BUCKMAN, ROSINA, 1880?-1948

See items 1594, 1629

BURIAN, KAREL, 1870-1924

129 Bartoš, Josef, b. 1887. *Karel Burian.* In Czech. Praha, 1934. Unverified; information taken from the Burian article of *Enciclopedia dello Spettacolo.*

130 Burian, Emil František. *Karel Burian.* In Czech. Kdo je, 96. Praha: Orbis, 1948. 26 pp.

131 ———. *Památnik bratři Burianů.* In Czech. Praha, 1929. Unverified; information taken from the Burian article in the *Enciclopedia dello Spettacolo.*

132 Pujman, Ferdinand, b. 1889. *Burianům k poctě.* In Czech. Praha, 1933. Unverified; information taken from the Burian article in the *Enciclopedia dello Spettacolo.*

BURKE, THOMAS, 1890-1968

133 Vose, John D. *The Lancashire Caruso; the Life of Tom Burke.* Blackpool: By the author, 1982. 201 pp. Illustrated.

BUTT, CLARA, 1873-1936

134 Ponder, Winifred. *Clara Butt: Her Life-Story.* With a foreword by Dame Clara Butt. London: George G. Harrap, 1928. 261 pp. Illustrated.

What seemed to be destined to be a rather pedestrian "singer's authorized biography" (which it is in nearly every respect) turned out to be a time bomb when the first printing reached Australia. Let the London published *Musical Times* for September 1928 tell the story:

The "Sing 'em muck" controversy has livened a few weeks of the "off" season. Dame Nellie Melba cabled wrathfully protesting against a statement in Dame Clara Butt's biography that the former had said to the latter, who was about to tour Australia, "Sing 'em muck; it's all they can understand." Whereupon Dame Clara cabled to Dame Nellie assuring her that she was innocent, having neither ascribed the remark to Dame Nellie, nor seen the proofs of the book in which it appeared. Exhibit No. 3 (as they say in the Courts) was a cable from Miss Ponder, the writer of the book. Writing from India, Miss Ponder affirms that the proofs were duly passed by Dame Clara.
The result of this long-distance argument is that we have three irreconcilable statements, and, one man's word being as good as another's (especially when they are women), the case must be dismissed, the parties paying their own costs. The only thing that is certain is that both these eminent singers, however emphatically they may decry the "Sing 'em muck!" principle, have consistently acted on it in arranging their programmes. The fact of their having sung a good deal of fine music as well can never alter that.

The offending remark can be found on page 138 of the first issue of the book. As a result of the international fuss, the publisher quickly recalled all unsold copies and replaced pages 138 and 139. In the new version, page 138 ends with the line "What are you going to sing?" and page 139 begins with "Australian audiences, it is interesting to note, proved as appreciative of the classical items which both Clara Butt and (her husband) Kennerley Rumford invariably included in their programmes as of the more popular type of songs and ballads...." The final word, however, came from Percy Colson, who declared: "I do not for a moment believe that (Melba) ever told Clara Butt to sing 'muck' to the Australians. Such advice to Clara Butt would be so entirely unnecessary." WRM

134-a ———. *Clara Butt, Her Life-Story*; with a foreword by Dame Clara Butt. Da Capo Press Music Reprint Series. New York: Da Capo Press, 1978. Illustrated. 261 pp.

Reprint of the 1928 edition published by G.G. Harrap, London (q.v.).

See also items 1581, 1635, 1648

C

CABALLÉ, MONTSERRAT, b. 1933

135 Farret, Georges. *Montserrat Caballé*. In French. Les trésors de l'opéra, no. 6. Paris: Opéra International, 1980. 62 pp. Illustrated. Discography, pp. 51-61.

A generously illustrated, beautifully executed booklet. Farret gives a chronological overview of Caballé's career, according the proper weight to the pivotal *Lucrezia Borgia* concert performance at Carnegie Hall (April 20, 1965) that catapulted the singer overnight to world fame. Until the appearance of a full-length biography this

is a satisfactory, informative work. The discography contains all the
commercial and several private recordings. The recordings are identified by the company but without record numbers. There is one embarrassing error: the listing of Verdi's *Ballo in maschera* under
Donizetti.

See also item 1788

CACCINI, GIULIO DI MICHELANGIOLO, called GIULIO ROMANO, 1545-1618

136 Ehrichs, Alfred (Karl Alfred), b. 1880. *Giulio Caccini.* In
German. Leipzig: Hesse & Becker, 1908. 111 pp. Inaug. Dissertation.

CAFFARELLI, GAETANO MAJORANO, called, 1710-1783

See item 432

CALLAS, MARIA, 1923-1977

137 Ardoin, John. *The Callas Legacy.* New York: Scribner, 1977.
xi, 224 pp. Illustrated. Bibliography, pp. 212-213. Index, pp.
218-224. Recorded Interviews, pp. 206-211. Recorded Performances,
pp. 214-217.

In his preface Ardoin writes "To create as complete a picture as
possible, I have dealt with every scrap of recorded sound by Callas
that I have been able to unearth, including recorded interviews."
This statement sums up the contents of this book, written with
understanding, insight and a commendable degree of objectivity for
one so devoted to his subject. "Every scrap of recorded sound" is
critically evaluated, thus providing a unique guide to Callas's
recorded legacy. The arrangement of the main body--the musical re-
cordings--is chronological. A separate chronology contains the recorded interviews, followed by an extensive bibliography. There is
also an index of recorded performances followed by an index of names.

137-a ———. *The Callas Legacy.* London: Duckworth, 1977. xi,
224 pp. Illustrated. Bibliography, pp. 212-213. Index, pp. 218-224.
Recorded Interviews, pp. 206-211. Recorded Performances, pp. 214-217.

138 ———. *The Callas Legacy; a Biography of a Career.* Revised
Edition. New York: Charles Scribner's Sons, 1982. 240 pp. Illustrated. Bibliography, pp. 223-226. Index, pp. 233-240. Interviews,
pp. 215-220. Filmed Performances, pp. 221-222.

The revised edition of this annotated discography of the Callas
voice, singing and speaking, as preserved in various forms, retains
the format and contents of the original, 1977, edition (q.v.). The
revision consists of the correction of some minor mistakes and the
addition of "new" Callas recordings that have surfaced in the meantime.
The valuable commentary and fair appraisal of each recording makes
this a model work of its kind and a definitive guide to Callas's
recorded voice.

139 Bragaglia, Leonardo, b. 1932. *L'arte dello stupore: omaggio a Maria Callas; un saggio con bibliografia, discografia, cronologia della vita e dell'arte, antologia critica*; presentazione di Giacomo Lauri-Volpi con due lettere inedite di Maria Callas a Lauri-Volpi. In Italian. Roma: Bulzoni, 1977. 81 pp. Illustrated. Bibliography, p. 67. Repertory, pp. 79-80. Discography, pp. 71-78.

Callas died on September 16, 1977. Author Bragaglia and the publisher must have worked overtime to bring out this book in 1977. The main essay was written, according to its subtitle, on the thirtieth day of her death. Both essays and the supporting material reflect the haste of production. The book contains two of her letters written to Lauri-Volpi; out of context they are of minimal interest. The photographs are adequate, the chronology and discography are incomplete. An inconsequential book.

140-T *Callas: el arte y la vida, por John Ardoin. Los grandes años, por Gerald Fitzgerald.* Diagramado por Howard Sperber. Translated by María Canyelles, Juan Faci. In Spanish. Barcelona: Editorial Pomayre, 1979. vi, 282 pp. . Illustrated. Repertory, p. 275. Index, pp. 276-281. Discography, pp. 265-275.

The Spanish translation of *Callas: The Art and the Life* (q.v.).

141 Callas, Evangelia, in collaboration with Lawrence G. Blochman. *My Daughter Maria Callas.* New York: Fleet Publishing Co., 1960. 186 pp. Illustrated.

Callas chose to sever all relations with her mother at the brink of her international stardom. Evangelia's book, written with unconcealed hurt, gives the "mother's side" of the family story. It casts some light on the early family life of Callas; otherwise it is an ill-advised book that contributes little to the Callas lore.

141-a ———, as told to Lawrence G. Blochman. *My Daughter Maria Callas.* London: Frewin, 1967. 175 pp. Illustrated.

141-b ———, in collaboration with Lawrence G. Blochman. *My Daughter Maria Callas.* New York: Arno Press, 1977. 186 pp. Illustrated.

Reprint of the 1960 edition published by Fleet Publishing Corporation, New York (q.v.). This edition contains some additional photographs.

142 *Callas: The Art and the Life*, by John Ardoin. *The Great Years*, by Gerald Fitzgerald. New York: Holt, Rinehart and Winston, 1974. 282 pp. Illustrated. Index, pp. 276-282. Chronology of Performances, pp. 265-275.

Two major essays by the authors, each writing separately on different aspects of the Callas career. Ardoin tries to place her art in the proper historical perspective; Fitzgerald analyzes the performances she gave in her prime. Both authors make generous use of statements made by the soprano's former associates. The bulk of the book is taken up by a large number of photographs, many of them previously unpublished. The chronology is comprehensive but less detailed than the one by Arthur Germond in Henry Wisneski's *Maria Callas* (q.v.). A beautifully produced book.

143 Deleted

144 Cederna, Camilla. *Callas*. I dischi della Callas, di Mario Pasi. In Italian. Milano: Longanesi, 1968. 149 pp. Discography, pp. 147-149.

145 Celletti, Rodolfo, b. 1917. *Tu che la vanità*. In Italian. Milano: Rizzoli, 1981. 249 pp. Fiction.

A writer and an acknowledged expert of voices and the art of singing, Celletti turns to a narrative of fantasy with this novel. It is permeated with the theater according to the title, the opening line of the soprano aria from *Don Carlo*. It is a long, unusual and complex story with three protagonists: the author himself as narrator, and two *prime donne* Giulia Pascucci and Sdenka Di Carlo, thin and easily dispersible guises for Tebaldi and Callas. RT

146 Galatopoulos, Stelios. *Callas, la Divina; Art that Conceals Art*. London: Cunningham Bass, 1963. 191 pp. Illustrated. Discography, pp. 177-186.

146-a ————. *Callas: la Divina; Art that Conceals Art*. Revised and Enlarged Edition. London: Dent, 1966. xii, 218 pp. Illustrated.

146-b ————. *Callas: la Divina; Art that Conceals Art*. Elmsford, N.Y.: London House and Maxwell, 1970. xii, 218 pp. Illustrated.

147 ————. *Callas: Prima Donna Assoluta*. London: Allen, 1976. xviii, 353 pp. Illustrated. Index, pp. 343-353. Chronology of Performances, pp. 325-341.

Callas's life, broken down into six chronological periods, concludes in 1976, just one year before her death. A long chapter entitled "The art of the singer" is followed by an analysis of "Maria Callas' most famous roles." An undistinguished entry in the large Callas literature, inspired more by a devotion to the artist than any particular insight.

148 Gara, Eugenio, b. 1888. *Maria Callas*. Fotografie di Roger Hauert, testo di Eugenio Gara, edizione italiana a cura di Guido M. Gatti. In Italian. I grandi interpreti. Milano: G. Ricordi, 1957. 32 pp. Illustrated. Discography, p. 32.

A brief article of little originality, enhanced by excellent photographs of Callas at the peak of her career. Gara goes to great lengths to justify Callas's vocal shortcomings on the grounds that both Pasta and Malibran had imperfect voices yet they achieved greatness and lasting fame. Callas is allowed to speak for herself on matters of interpretation. The discography "for the reader's guidance only" is barely that.

149-T ————. *Maria Callas*. Portraits de Roger Hauert. Translated by J. Horneffer. In French. Les grands interprètes. Genève: R. Kister, 1957. 32 pp. Illustrated. Discography, p. 32.

French translation of the 1957 edition published in Italian by
G. Ricordi, Milan (q.v.).

149-T-a ————. *Maria Callas*. Portraits by Roger Hauert. Translated by Barbara Wall. Great Concert Artists. Geneva: R. Kister,
1958. 32 pp. Illustrated. Discography, p. 32.

English translation of the 1957 edition published in Italian by
G. Ricordi, Milan (q.v.).

150 Gastel Chiarelli, Cristina. *Maria Callas. Vita, immagini,
parole, musica*. In Italian. Saggi, n. 89. Venezia: Marsilio, 1981.
213 pp. Illustrated. Chronology of Performances, pp. 149-212.

An enthusiastic yet objective biography, without gossip, generously
illustrated. Especially noteworthy is the detailed chronology that
covers all the artistic activities of Callas: opera, concert, recordings, film and directing. Finally, there is a list of concert
programs. RT

151 Goise, Denis. *Maria Callas, la diva scandale: sa vie, ses
amours, ses folies, sa mort*. In French. Rayon souvenirs et mémoires.
Paris: Guy Authier, 1978. 196 pp. Illustrated.

Goise's objective was not to write yet another Callas biography.
In fact, he touches on the various aspects of her career only when
it is necessary to provide a setting or an explanation to the many
stories and anecdotes about the successes, passions, love affairs
and complexes of this *prima donna assoluta*. How many of these stories
are true are left to the reader to decide. AM

152 Herzfeld, Friedrich, b. 1897. *Maria Meneghini-Callas; oder, Die
grosse Primadonna*. In German. Rembrandt-Reihe, Bd. 18. Berlin:
Rembrandt-Verlag, 1959. 60 pp. The second edition, published in
1962, dropped "Meneghini" from the title.

153 Jellinek, George, b. 1919. *Callas; Portrait of a Prima Donna*.
New York: Ziff-Davis Publishing Co., 1960. 354 pp. Illustrated.
Repertory, pp. 338-340. Index, pp. 348-354. Discography, pp. 341-
346.

For a decade or more Jellinek's book was the only major English-
language biography of Callas. The book keeps in balance the private
and public lives, avoiding partisanship, exaggeration or superlatives.
The Callas story is brought up to 1960; however, by then her career
was nearly over. There are 24 pages of well-chosen photographs and
a now obsolete discography.

153-a ————. *Callas, Portrait of a Prima Donna*. London: Gibbs &
Phillips, 1961. 346 pp. Illustrated. Index.

Same as the Ziff-Davis edition, New York, 1960 (q.v.).

154 Krynauw, Jan. *Maria Callas*. In Afrikaans. Pretoria, S.A.:
Daan Retief Uitgewers, 1980. 85 pp. Illustrated.

154/A Linakis, Steven, b. 1923. *Diva; the Life and Death of Maria Callas*. Englewood Cliffs, N.J.: Prentice-Hall, 1980. 169 pp. Illustrated. Index, pp. 167-169.

The foundation and "birthright" of this book rests on the author's relationship with his subject: they were cousins. Callas spent her New York years in the proximity of Linakis: he was a frequent visitor in the Kalogeropoulos home and was for awhile--or so he wants the reader to believe--Maria's friend and confidant. His narrative capitalizes on the unpleasant side of Callas's personality, sharing for the first time family incidents and fights, physical and emotional, with the reading public. Since Linakis fails to probe deeply, the incidents and his observations are inconsequential. Comments of a musical nature are fortunately few. A minor brush stroke in Callas's literary portrait.

155 Lorcey, Jacques. *Maria Callas*. In French. Collection Têtes d'affiche. Paris: PAC, 1977. 428 pp. Illustrated. Bibliography, pp. 420-425.

156 ————. *Maria Callas: d'art et d'amour*. In French. Collection Têtes d'affiche. Paris: PAC, 1983. 615 pp. Illustrated. Index, pp. 595-607. Discography, pp. 537-585; 609-612. Filmography, p. 586. Dedicated to the memory of Bernard Gavoty.

A greatly expanded reworking of the original book published by PAC in 1977 (q.v.).

157 Mancini, Roland, and Jean-Louis Caussou. *Maria Callas*. In French. Monstres sacrés--Les cahiers d'opéra, no. 1. Paris: SODAL, 1964. 32 pp. Illustrated.

158 *Maria Callas*. In French. L'Avant-scène opéra, no. 44. Paris: L'Avant-scène, 1982. 191 pp. Illustrated. Bibliography, p. 166. Discography, pp. 170-176. Chronology of Performances. "Vidéographie."

159 *Mariia Kallas; biografiia, stat'i, interv'iu*. In Russian. Moskva: Progress, 1978. 216 pp. Illustrated.

160 Meneghini, Giovanni Battista, 1895-1981, and Renzo Allegri. *Maria Callas, mia moglie*. In Italian. Milano: Rusconi Libri, 1981. 322 pp. Illustrated. Index, pp. 317-322.

161-T ————. *My Wife Maria Callas*. Translated by Henry Wisneski. New York: Farrar, Straus, & Giroux, 1982. xiv, 331 pp. Illustrated. Index, pp. 323-331.

Meneghini entered operatic history as the manager-husband of Maria Callas and the man largely responsible for her rapid rise to the top of her profession. Callas was the great love of his life and he never recovered from the blow of losing her to Onassis. He wrote his memoirs shortly before his death, mainly to refute the persistent claim that Callas never loved him. In this he succeeds, but at the cost of making public many intimate details about their life together. Meneghini also contributes his side of the Callas story, which makes this book an essential source work in the ever-growing Callas literature.

162 Owen, Peter. *Callas: Diva*. London, 1980. Unpaginated. Illustrated.

163 Picchetti, Maria Teresa, and Marta Teglia. *El arte de Maria Callas como metalenguaje*. In Spanish. Buenos Aires: Editorial Bocarte, 1969. 97 pp.

164 Rémy, Pierre Jean (Jean-Pierre Angrémy). *Callas: une vie*. In French. Paris: Editions Ramsay, 1978. 281 pp. Illustrated. Repertory.

A factually near-complete recapitulation of the Callas story, written in the characteristically French journalistic style that gives the reader the sensation of reading a book-length magazine article.

165-T ————. *Maria Callas*. Translated by Vera Somló. In Hungarian. Budapest: Zenemükiadó, 1982. 335 pp. Illustrated. Repertory, pp. 319-334.

Hungarian translation of the French original published under the same title in 1978 (q.v.).

165-T-a ————. *Maria Callas, a Tribute*. Translated by Catherine Atthill. London: Macdonald and Jane's, 1978. 192 pp. Illustrated. Repertory, pp. 185-189. Discography, pp. 189-192.

English translation of the French edition published in 1978 by Editions Ramsay, Paris (q.v.).

166 Riemens, Leo. *Maria Callas*. In Dutch. Zwarte beertjes, 266. Utrecht: A.W. Bruns, 1960. 156 pp. Illustrated.

167 Rizzi, Luigi. *La Callas y Onassis*. In Spanish. Enciclopedia popular ilustrada, serie M, no. 27. Barcelona: G.P. (Distributed by Plaza y Jane's), 1963. 76 pp. Illustrated.

168 Segalini, Sergio, b. 1944. *Callas; les images d'une voix*. In French. Paris: F. Van De Velde, 1979. 171 pp. Illustrated. Discography, pp. 170-171.

169-T ————. *Callas: imágenes de una voz*. Translated by Carles Alier-Aixelá. In Spanish. Barcelona: Daimon, 1980. 173 pp. Illustrated. Discography, pp. 170-171. Chronology of Performances, pp. 159-169.

Spanish translation of *Callas; les images d'une voix* (q.v.).

169-T-a ————. *Callas: Portrait of a Diva*. Translated by Sonia Sabel. London: Hutchinson, 1980. 171 pp. Illustrated. Discography, pp. 170-171.

The English translation of *Callas; les images d'une voix* (q.v.).

170 Soprano, Franco. *Per Maria Callas*. In Italian. Bologna: Recitar Cantande, 1981. 366 pp. Illustrated.

171-T Stassinopoulos, Arianna, b. 1950. *Maria Callas al di là della leggenda*. Translated by Riccardo Mainardi. In Italian. Milano: A. Vallardi, 1982. 431 pp. Illustrated. Index, pp. 419-430.

Italian translation of *Maria Callas, the Woman Behind the Legend* (q.v.).

171-T-a ————. *María Callas: la mujer detrás de la leyenda*. Translated by L. Tejada Conde-Pelayo. In Spanish. México, D.F.: Lasser Press, 1981. 371 pp. Illustrated.

Spanish translation of *Maria Callas, the Woman Behind the Legend* (q.v.).

171-T-b ————. *Maria Callas par de là sa légende*. Translated by Philippe Delamare, Éric Diacon and Claude Gilbert. In French. Paris: Fayard, 1981. 443 pp. Illustrated. Discography, pp. 415-426.

French translation of *Maria Callas, the Woman Behind the Legend* (q.v.), with an annotated discography by Sergio Segalini added to the French edition only.

172 ————. *Callas; the Woman Behind the Legend*. New York: Ballantine Books, 1982. xiv, 366 pp. Illustrated. Bibliography, p. 343. Index, pp. 353-366.

The paperback edition of *Maria Callas, the Woman Behind the Legend* (q.v.).

172-a ————. *Maria Callas, the Woman Behind the Legend*. New York: Simon & Schuster, 1981. 320 pp. Illustrated. Index, pp. 368-383.

As the subtitle indicates, this book concentrates on the woman rather than the artist. The author presents a good deal of previously unavailable information. She does not discuss Callas's art, but rather tries to put her career in the context of her life by analyzing the behavior and actions of this gifted, sensitive, vulnerable and pathetically insecure woman. Her romance with Onassis, freed from journalistic distortions, affords the reader a glimpse of what the relationship meant to Callas. This is an indispensable book for anyone wishing to probe beyond the glitter that surrounds a celebrity and trying to understand her artistic achievement in human terms, through the life of Callas, the private person. The illustrations are chosen mostly for their significance to Callas's life off stage.

173 Tortora, Giovanna, and Paolo Barbieri. *Per Maria Callas*. In Italian. Bologna: Edizioni Recitar Cantando, 1979. 367 pp. Illustrated.

174 Verga, Carla. *Maria Callas: mito e malinconia*. In Italian. Roma: Bietti, 1980. 175 pp. Chronology, pp. 118-171.

A rich iconography placed within the framework of a slender text, gentle and friendly, written by someone who was close to Callas in her private life also. The preface is by Giampiero Tintori. RT

175 Wisneski, Henry. *Maria Callas: The Art Behind the Legend*; with Performance Annals, 1947-1974, by Arthur Germond. New York: Doubleday,

1975. x, 422 pp. Illustrated. Bibliography, pp. 397-399. Index, pp. 401-422. Discography, pp. 385-396. Chronology of Performances, pp. 251-384. Index to Performance Annals, pp. 407-422.

Wisneski's book, one of the major works in the ever-expanding Callas literature, presents a wealth of information about Callas's stage career. Following a brief biography, each chapter is devoted to the discussion of one role in Callas's repertory. The book covers all the roles she sang after leaving Athens in 1945, her only motion picture (*Medea*), and her master classes at Juilliard in 1971 and 1972. Wisneski has a polished style and a fine sense of proportion. He documents critical opinions with excerpts from reviews; his own observations are appropriate and, in light of his obvious affinity toward the subject, commendably objective. Arthur Germond's exhaustive Performance Annals is sufficiently detailed, with its own index. The book is beautifully produced; to say that it is profusely illustrated is a gross understatement. The discography of private recordings by Wisneski was complete at the time of publication.

See also items 1813, 1820

CALVÉ, EMMA, 1858-1942

176 Calvé, Emma. *My Life*. Translated by Rosamond Gilder. New York: D. Appleton, 1922. xiii, 279 pp. Illustrated. The French edition, if there was one, cannot be traced.

176-a ─────. *My Life*. With a discography by W.R. Moran. Translated by Rosamond Gilder. Opera Biographies. New York: Arno Press, 1977. xiii, viii, 279 pp. Illustrated. Discography, pp. i-viii.

Reprint of the 1922 edition published by D. Appleton, New York (q.v.). The discography by William R. Moran was prepared for this edition.

177 ─────. *Sous tous les ciels j'ai chanté. Souvenirs*. In French. Paris: Plon, 1940. 295 pp. Illustrated.

A series of vignettes, ranging in length from two lines to several pages, that barely adds up to the life story of the singer. The subject matter ranges from events to places, from music to people. The diary-like arrangement and chronological information are discredited by the large number of errors. Placing a performance of Mascagni's *Cavalleria rusticana* in 1886, four years before its world premiere, suggests faulty memory rather than intentional misstatement; after all, the book was written at the end of the singer's life. In spite of its defects, it is an interesting, enjoyable document from the pen of one of the great singing actresses and the most colorful operatic stage personality of the turn of the century.

178 Girard, Georges. *Emma Calvé: la cantatrice sous tous les ciels*. In French. Millau: Editions Grandes Causes, 1983. 295 pp. Illustrated. Bibliography, pp. 292-295. Discography, pp. 287-291.

179 Wisner, Arthur, b. 1847. *Emma Calvé; her Artistic Life*. By A. Gallus (pseud.) ... with numerous autograph pages especially

written by Mlle. Calvé. New York: R.H. Russell, 1902. 40 leaves.
Illustrated.

See also items 1567, 1615, 1635, 1658, 1662, 1663, 1695, 1792, 1803,
1804, 1805

CAMPANARI, GIUSEPPE, 1855-1927

See item 1581

CAMPANINI, ITALO, 1845-1896

See item 1615

CAPOUL, VICTOR (JOSEPH AMÉDÉE VICTOR), 1839-1924

180 Grand, Georges, b. 1831. *Victor Capoul. Étude ornée d'un beau
portrait par Nadar.* In French. Paris: Imprimerie de E. Donnaud,
1877. 15 pp.

CAPUZZO, AGOSTINO

See item 338

CARAZA, MERCEDES, b. 1908

See item 1631

CARBONE, AGOSTINO

181 *Memoriale artistico del baritono buffo Agostino Carbone.* In
Italian. Genova: Tipografia dei Tribunale, 1899. 11 pp.

CARELLI, EMMA, 1877-1928

182 Carelli, Augusto, b. 1873. *Emma Carelli; trent'anni di vita del
teatro lirico.* In Italian. Roma: P. Maglione, 1932. 323 pp.
Illustrated.

An excellent biography written with intelligence and verve by
Carelli's brother, himself a singer, stage designer and art critic.
The work covers Emma Carelli's singing career and her activities as
impresaria of the Teatro Costanzi of Rome. RT

CARELLI, GÁBOR, b. 1915

183 Carelli, Gábor. *Utam a Metropolitanbe.* In Hungarian. Budapest:
Zeneműkiadó, 1979. 207 pp. Illustrated.

Before his 1938 debut in Florence as Rodolfo in *La Bohème* Gábor Krausz of Budapest became Gábor Carelli at the suggestion of his teacher and mentor, Beniamino Gigli. During his years of study in Rome he was treated as a member of the Gigli family, and the chapters devoted to his association with the great tenor show him from a side wholly unknown to the public. Carelli's well-known association with Gigli became a nearly insurmountable liability during the war years in the United States because of Gigli's widely publicized Fascist alignment. In addition to the lengthy passages about Gigli, the book is of interest to readers who remember Carelli's pleasant lyric tenor from his many seasons at the Met.

CARON, ROSE, 1857-1930

184 Solenière, Eugène de, 1872-1904. *Rose Caron; monographie critique*. In French. Paris: Bibliothèque d'art de la critique, 1896. 47 pp. Illustrated.

See also item 1588

CARPI, VITTORIO, 1846-1917

185 Carpi, Vittorio. *Al di qua e al di là dell'Atlantico; impressioni di un artiste di canto*. In Italian. With a preface by Prof. Arnaldo Bonaventura. Firenze: F. Lumachi, 1909. x, 298 pp.

A collection of reminiscences with which the author wished to seal his active career as a distinguished baritone and esteemed singing teacher. "Vittorio" was his stage name; his real name was Michelangelo. RT

CARREÑO, TERESA, 1853-1917

186 Marciano, Rosario. *Teresa Carreño, o un ensayo sobre su personalidad a los 50 años de su muerte*. In Spanish. Colección musica, 2. Caracas: Instituto Nacional de Cultura y Bellas Artes, 1966. 28 pp. Illustrated.

187 Milinowski, Marta, b. 1885. *Teresa Carreño, "by the Grace of God."* New Haven: Yale University Press, 1940. xvi, 410 pp. Illustrated. Bibliography, pp. 399-403.

A detailed biography of the celebrated pianist and singer. In spite of her great success as a singer she spent the major part of her musical life on the concert stage as a distinguished, sought-after pianist. This work gives an excellent overview of her dual career.

188-T ————. *Teresa Carreño*. Translated by Luisa Elena Monteverde Basalo. In Spanish. Caracas: Ediciones EDIME, 1953. xxiii, 427 pp. Illustrated. Bibliography.

Spanish translation of the 1940 edition published by Yale University Press, New Haven (q.v.).

189 Peña, Israel. *Teresa Carreño (1853-1917)*. In Spanish.
Colección de biografías, no. 11. Caracas: Fundación Eugenio Mendoza,
1953. 64 pp.

190 Plaza, Juan Bautista, 1898-1965. *Teresa Carreño*. In Spanish.
Caracas: Tipografía americana, 1938. 33 pp.

CARUSO, ENRICO, 1873-1921

191 Caruso, Enrico. *L'altro Caruso*. In Italian. Milano: Eiot-
Nuova Editrice Internazionale, 1961. 159 pp. Illustrated.

192 ———. *Caricatures by Enrico Caruso. In Four Parts....*
Caricature di Enrico Caruso. New York: "La Follia di New York,"
1908. 182 pp. Illustrated. Advertising Matter, pp. 176-182.

193 ———. *Caruso's Book; Being a Collection of Caricatures and
Character Studies from Original Drawings of the Metropolitan Opera
Company*. New York: R.G. Cooke, 1906. 47 pp. Illustrated.

This is the first printed collection of Caruso's celebrated caricatures. Exceedingly rare; the Library of Congress owns an autographed
copy.

194 ———. *Caruso's Caricatures*. New York: Dover Publications,
1977. 214 pp. Illustrated. Index.

Contains a new selection of pictures from three editions (1922,
1939, 1965) of *Caricatures* by Enrico Caruso, published by La Follia
di New York.

195 ———. *How to Sing: Some Practical Hints*. London: The John
Church Company, 1913. 61 pp. Illustrated.

Published under Caruso's name. The tenor disclaimed authorship in
court.

195-a ———. *How to Sing*. Brooklyn: Opera Box, 1973. 61 pp.

"This is an unabridged republication of the first edition published
by The John Church Company, London." (q.v.)

196 ———. *The New Book of Caricatures*. New York: La Follia di
New York, 1965. Unpaged. Illustrated. Previous editions published
under the title *Caricatures*.

A re-edition of Caruso's caricatures originally published in La
Follia di New York. This volume includes letters from Caruso to the
publisher, his friend Marziale Sisca, with English translations.

197-T ———. *Wie man singen soll*. *Praktische Winke*. Translated
by August Spanuth. In German. Mainz: B. Schott's Söhne, 1914.
61 pp. Illustrated.

The German translation of the booklet *How to Sing* (q.v.), whose
authorship has been attributed to Caruso, for commercial reasons,
even though the tenor publicly disclaimed any connection with it.

198 Armin, George. *Enrico Caruso. Eine Untersuchung der Stimme
Carusos und ihr Verhältnis zum Stauprinzip im Spiegel eines eigenen*

Erlebnisses. In German. Berlin-Wilmersdorf: Verlag der "Gesellschaft für Stimmkultur," 1929. 111 pp. Illustrated.

199 Barát, Endre, and Endre Lévay. *Caruso csodálatos élete; regényes életrajz.* In Hungarian. Budapest: Bibliotheca, 1957.

A fictionalized, superficial account of Caruso's life. This is the Hungarian translation of the biography originally published in French under the joint author's name, Endre Lévay (q.v.).

200 Barthelemy, Richard. *Memories of Caruso.* Introduction by James Camner. Translated by Constance S. Camner. Plainsboro, N.J.: La Scala Autographs, 1979. 15 pp. Illustrated. Edition limited to 500 copies.

Translated for the first time from the author's manuscript, these are the brief and not particularly well-written recollections of the man who first met Caruso in 1901 and later became his coach and accompanist for fourteen years. It is the sole source of the spurious story of Caruso's having sung the "Prologo" of *Pagliacci* at the Colón for an ailing Titta Ruffo who was replaced in the rest of the performance by Giuseppe Danise. Since Danise sang 2 of the 5 complete performances of *Pagliacci* with Caruso (Ruffo sang the entire first act with Caruso in a gala at the Colón on August 4, 1915, and a complete performance in Buenos Aires on August 16, 1915), the story lacks all credibility. Dr. Ruffo Titta, Jr., believes it is pure fabrication. It is distressing that of the memories of fourteen years' association and daily contact with Caruso all Barthelemy found worth retelling could fit into 15 poorly organized pages.

201 Bello, John. *Enrico Caruso; a Centennial Tribute.* Providence: Universal Associates, 1973. Unpaged. Illustrated.

This is, as the subtitle indicates, a centennial tribute to the singer, a part of the Caruso Centennial Exhibit organized and directed by the author, John Bello. The booklet's main value is the brief interviews with individuals who knew the singer, former colleagues, friends and his grandson. Other sections of interest are a list of performances Caruso sang with the Met on tour and a list of items on display at the Centennial Exhibit. There are many unusual photographs; however, the quality of reproduction is barely adequate.

202 Blanco, Eumenio. *El inmortal Enrico Caruso.* In Spanish. Hollywood: Orbe Publications, 1964. 60 pp. Illustrated.

This rather emotional little volume purports to draw on personal association of the author and the great tenor (a fact alluded to by the inclusion of a caricature of the author drawn by the tenor in 1919), plus information gathered from many of the singer's fellow artists and William J. Guard of the Metropolitan. For an account of this length, a great deal of emphasis is placed on the singer's romance with Ada Giachetti, who receives a full-page illustration, and is the subject of one full chapter entitled "The Terrible Tragedy: The Most Anguished Days of His Life!" In this chapter, the author describes Caruso's arrival in London in May, 1908, and his receipt of a letter from Giachetti informing him that he was abandoned for another love; "Giachetti, whom Caruso had known since 1897 and who

was the great love of his life, with whom he had lived for eleven
idyllic years...." The same events are described with less emotion
in *Enrico Caruso* by Key and Zirato (q.v.). Not all of Blanco's "facts"
can bear close examination. WRM

203 Bolig, John Richard. *The Recordings of Enrico Caruso; a Discography.* Dover, Del.: Eldridge Reeves Johnson Memorial, Delaware
State Museum, 1973. v, 88 pp.

Of the several Caruso discographies now in existence, this is by
far the most complete. The recording information of all the Caruso
records, every take, published and unpublished, is arranged chronologically by recording session. The data given are as complete as
humanly possible, representing "about twenty-five years of data
gathering from many sources." The compiler re-calculated the playing
speed of each record, comparing the results (which he found "virtually
identical") with the playing speeds given by Favia-Artsay in her
discography (q.v.). The layout is spacious, clear, easy to use.
The discography is generously cross-indexed. There is no information
about Lp transfers. For the benefit of those wishing to acquire
this hard-to-locate discography, it can be purchased from the Margaret
O'Neill Visitor Center, Court and Federal Street, Dover, Delaware
19901.

204 Bruns, Paul, b. 1867. *Carusos Technik in deutscher Erklärung.*
In German. Charlottenburg: Otto Sorge, 1922. 42 pp.

205 Burian, Karel Vladimir. *Enrico Caruso.* "Kdo je?" Praha:
Orbis.

206 Caruso, Dorothy Park (Benjamin), 1893-1955. *Dorothy Caruso, a
Personal History.* New York: Hermitage House, 1952. 191 pp. Illustrated.

The circumstance that lends operatic interest to this autobiography
is its being the self-portrait of the woman whom Enrico Caruso, in
mature manhood, married. The book devotes only two chapters to
husband Enrico, who, after three short years of marriage, left
his widow with the memory of happiness she claims to have tried
in vain to recapture for the rest of her life. Mrs. Caruso's in-
dividualistic style is not to everyone's liking and was probably a
hindrance to the success of the book. Had she any accomplishments
of her own, the critical esteem of her writing probably would have
been greater.

207 ———. *Enrico Caruso, His Life and Death.* New York: Simon
and Schuster, 1945. viii, 303 pp. Illustrated. Repertory, p. 288.
Discography, pp. 289-301.

This is the second biography of Enrico Caruso written by his widow.
Well organized and well written, it dwells only briefly on Caruso's
early life and only to the extent of retelling the information and
stories Mrs. Caruso must have heard from her husband. Details about
Caruso, the person, become more abundant concerning the last three
years of his life, i.e., the period of their marriage. The greatest
value of the book lies on the numerous letters Caruso wrote to his
"Doro darling" that Mrs. Caruso so generously shares with the reading

public. Each charmingly misspelled letter in faulty English is an
inimitable portrait of the man. Rather than clarify, it renders more
elusive the explanation of how a simple, more or less uneducated man
could attain such depth of feeling in his interpretations and acquire
the ability to communicate it to his hearers. With a good, but now
obsolete, discography by Jack L. Caidin.

207-a ─────. *Enrico Caruso, His Life and Death.* London: T.W.
Laurie, 1946. viii, 312 pp. Illustrated. Discography, pp. 289-310.

207-b ─────. *Enrico Caruso, His Life and Death.* "An Essandess
Paperback." New York: Simon and Schuster, 1963. 305 pp. Illustrated.
Discography, pp. 289-301.

The first paperback edition of this well-known biography. "Essandess" presumably stands for Simon and Schuster's initials: S and S.

208-T ─────, and Torrance Goddard. *Das Leben Enrico Carusos.*
Erinnerungen. Translated by Else Werkmann. Dresden: P. Aretz, 1929.
205 pp. Illustrated.

German translation of *Wings of Song* (q.v.).

209 ─────. *Wings of Song; the Story of Caruso.* New York: Minton,
Balch and Company, 1928. 218 pp. Illustrated.

209-a ─────. *Wings of Song; an Authentic Life Story of Enrico
Caruso,* by Dorothy Caruso and her sister Mrs. Torrance Goddard.
London: Hutchinson, 1928? 256 pp. Illustrated.

210 *Collezione del fu Comm. Enrico Caruso, monete e medaglie in oro,
greche, romane, bizantine, medioevali e moderne, italiane e estere,
medaglie papali, italiane e estere; la vendita avrà luogo ... dal 28
giugno e giorni seguenti.* In Italian. Paris: C. & E. Canessa, 1923.
104 pp. Illustrated. Publication date misprinted as 1823. The
British Museum General Catalog lists a copy of the catalog, with the
same misprinted date, but as printed in Naples.

A sales catalog of Caruso's coin collection.

210-a *Collezione Enrico Caruso monete e madaglie d'oro.* In Italian.
Bologna: Forni, 1970. viii, 104. Illustrated.

The reprint of the Paris, Naples, New York 1923 editions of this
sales catalog of Caruso's coin collection. The cover title reads:
"Catalogo dell'asta Canessa tenutasi in Napoli nel giugno 1923. Con
prefazione e prezzi aggiornati al giugno 1969 di C. Camberini di
Scarfèa." Original title page reads: "Collezione del fu Comm. Enrico
Caruso monete e medaglie in oro."

211 Corda, Alfredo. *Caruso in der Westentasche; Schmunzeleien eines
Tenors: Kurzgeschichten und Anekdoten.* In German. Darmstadt:
Bläschke, 1977. 285 pp. Illustrated.

212 Daspuro, Nicola, 1853-1941. *Enrico Caruso.* In Italian. Milano:
Casa Editrice Sonzogno, 1938. 79 pp. Illustrated.

A biography based on the unpublished memoirs of the author, a journalist and librettist better known by his pseudonym P. Suardon. Amusing and at times moving incidents are provided, but the book is sprinkled with inaccuracies and errors. RT

213-T ————. *Enrico Caruso*. Translated by Arrigo Coen Anitúa. In Spanish. Mexico: Ediciones Coli, 1943. xvii, 124 pp. Illustrated.

214 Favia-Artsay, Aida. *Caruso on Records*. *Pitch, Speed and Comments for All the Published Recordings of Enrico Caruso*. Valhalla, N.Y.: Historic Record, 1965. 218 pp.

A complete analytical discography of all of Caruso's published recordings, critically evaluating every record. Although the reader may not always agree with the author, her statements are lucid and her conclusions well reasoned. In addition to the necessary particulars (minus take numbers) pertaining to the individual recordings, the book provides the recommended playing speed for each. To facilitate the correct "pitching" for owners of the original 78s, two special Caruso stroboscopes are provided, one for 50 and one for 60 cps (cycles per second) electric current. To further facilitate establishing the correct pitch, the score of the opening bars of music is given for every selection. The arrangement is chronological, by recording session. There is no information regarding the transfer of 78s to LP.

215 Feldinger, Heinrich. *Der Schatten des Enrico Caruso*. Herausgegeben von Otto Eicke. In German. Der neue Excentric-Club, 44. Heft. Dresden: Mignon-Verlag, 1924? 32 pp.

216 Finck, Henry Theophilus, 1854-1926. *The Secret of Caruso's Glorious Voice*. The Etude Musical Booklet Library. Philadelphia: Theodore Presser Co., 1929. 19 pp. Illustrated.

An article by the famed music critic Henry T. Finck is followed by "A Short Biography of Caruso" and "Italy, the Home of Grand Opera" from an interview with Signor Caruso shortly before his death, by James Francis Cooke. WRM

217 Fitzgerald, Gerald, editor. *Caruso; 1981*. *The Opera Engagement Calendar*. New York: Metropolitan Opera Guild, 1980. Unpaged. Illustrated.

A good collection of photographs of Caruso and persons--professional and private--of importance in his life and career. The quality of all reproductions is uniformly excellent, the editorial notes on the pictures informative and accurate.

218 Flint, Mary H. *Impressions of Caruso and His Art as Portrayed at the Metropolitan Opera House*. New York: Privately printed by J.P. Paret and Co., 1917. 23 pp. Illustrated.

A brief biographical sketch is followed by individual chapters (each accompanied by a photograph either by Mishkin or White Studios) entitled: Des Grieux in *Manon* and *Manon Lescaut*, the Duke in *Rigoletto*, Nadir in *The Pearl Fishers*, Lionel in *Martha*, Nemorino in *L'Elisir d'amore*, Rodolfo in *La Bohème*, Don José in *Carmen*, Radames in *Aida*, Samson in *Samson and Dalila*, and Canio in *Pagliacci*. The frontispiece is a Mishkin portrait of Caruso, inscribed to the author and dated "N.Y., 1917." WRM

219 Freestone, John, and H.J. Drummond. *Enrico Caruso; His Recorded Legacy.* With a foreword by Compton Mackenzie. London: Sidgwick and Jackson, 1960. x, 130 pp. Illustrated.

A chronological listing by recording session of all published Caruso records, giving the history of the various pressings along with critical comments. Take numbers and playing speeds are not given; nor is information about LP transfers. Although the commentary contains worthwhile observations, as a discography this work has been superseded by the one compiled by John Bolig (q.v.).

219-a ————. *Enrico Caruso: His Recorded Legacy.* With a foreword by Compton Mackenzie. Minneapolis: T.S. Denison and Company, 1961. x, 130 pp.

220 Fucito, Salvatore, and Barnet J. Beyer. *Caruso and the Art of Singing, Including Caruso's Vocal Exercises and His Practical Advice to Students and Teachers of Singing.* New York: Frederick A. Stokes Company, 1922. vii, 219 pp. Illustrated.

221-T ————. *Caruso: Gesangkunst und Methode.* Translated by Curt Thesing. In German. 3rd ed. Berlin: E. Bote & G. Bock, 1924. 60 pp. Illustrated. Probably third printing; first edition likely to have same imprint date. A "new edition" was issued by the same publisher in 1928.

The German translation of *Caruso and the Art of Singing* (q.v.).

222-T Gara, Eugenio, b. 1888. *Caruso.* Translated by Concepción Valero. In Spanish. Collección Quien fua. Barcelona: Ediciones G.P., 1959. 128 pp.

Spanish translation of the author's work of the same title (q.v.).

223 ————. *Caruso, storia di un emigrante.* In Italian. Milano: Rizzoli, 1947. 282 pp. Illustrated. Bibliography, pp. 268-272. Index, pp. 275-282. Discography, pp. 263-265.

223-a ————. *Caruso. Storia di un emigrante.* In Italian. Milano: Cisalpino-Goliardica, 1973. 282 pp. Bibliography, pp. 268-272. Repertory, p. 262. Index, pp. 275-282.

Republication of the 1947 edition of Rizzoli, Milano (q.v.).

224 Greenfeld, Howard. *Caruso.* New York: G.P. Putnam's Sons, 1983. 275 pp. Illustrated. Bibliography, pp. 258-263. Repertory, pp. 255-257. Index, pp. 264-275.

The most complete retelling to date of Caruso's life, synthesizing the information contained in previous biographies. The book contains a great deal of material drawn from heretofore untapped sources, using long quotations from books and articles. Several brief statements obtained from the singer's son, Enrico Caruso, Jr., are incorporated in the narrative. The easy style is flowing and unobtrusive; the documentations, photographs, bibliography and index are excellent.

225 Grignaffini, Arnaldo. *Caruso. Note biografiche ed aneddotiche.* In Italian. Parma: Officina Grafica Freschig, 1923. 38 pp. Illustrated.

226 Hacker, Werner, b. 1897. *Enrico Caruso. Ein Lebensroman.* In German. Berlin: P. Neff, 1944. 182 pp.

227 Huefner-Berndt, Bernhard. *Die praktischen Winke Carusos an Hand von Schallplatten.* In German. Leipzig: Selbstverlag, 1927. 52 pp.

227-a ———. *Die praktischen Winke Carusos an Hand von Schallplatten.* In German. 2nd ed. Leipzig: Hug & Co. in Komm, 1928. iv, iv, 86 pp.

228 *Illustrated Catalogue of the Rare and Beautiful Antique Art Treasures, American and Foreign Gold Coins and Many Operatic Costumes, the Property of the Late Enrico Caruso, to Be Sold at Unrestricted Public Sale at the American Art Galleries.* New York: Canessa?, 1921. 172 pp. Illustrated.

229 Jackson, Stanley, b. 1910. *Caruso.* New York: Stein and Day, 1972. xiii, 302 pp. Illustrated. Bibliography, pp. 294-296. Index, pp. 297-302.

A bold rehash of the Caruso literature with enough inaccuracies and pure inventions to discredit the whole book. Jackson places Chaliapin in New York in 1918-19 as a regular dinner guest of the Carusos; however, Chaliapin was firmly held in his native Russia by the Bolshevik government until 1921. He didn't set foot in New York between 1908 and 1921! Jackson also claims that Caruso had an "Oedipus complex as wide as a barn" (p. 248) and "He then turned for sympathy to various matrons: 'Mammina' Farrar, stately Belle Goelet and Chaliapin's aged mother whom he used to slobber over like a spaniel." The fact is that Chaliapin's mother never "aged"; the good lady died in Kazan (Russia) before the turn of the century, before Chaliapin and Caruso ever met in Milan in 1901. If Jackson meant Chaliapin's mother-in-law, the tenor could not have slobbered over her either, were he inclined to do so in the first place, since the Chaliapins emigrated to Paris the year after Caruso died. Ada Giachetti was 22 months younger, not ten years older, than Enrico. The list of factual errors goes on.... What is original in this book cannot be accepted at face value; all else is available from sources of proven reliability.

229-a ———. *Caruso.* London: W.H. Allen, 1972. x, 302 pp. Illustrated. Bibliography, pp. 294-296.

230-T ———. *Caruso.* Appendix: Iván Kertész, *Caruso bukása Budapesten a korabeli sajtó tükrében.* Translated by Mária Borbás. In Hungarian. Budapest: Gondolat, 1976. 447 pp. Illustrated.

The Hungarian translation of Jackson's book published in English (q.v.) with one important difference: appended to it is Kertész's excellent essay entitled "Caruso's Failure in Budapest as Reflected in the Contemporary Press." It gives the reader a generous selection of press releases and reviews, along with editorial commentary, of the celebrated fiasco Caruso suffered in the Hungarian capital in 1907.

231-T Key, Pierre Van Rensselaer, b. 1872, and Bruno Zirato. *Caruso.*
[Published with:] Salvatore Fucito and Barnet J. Beyer. *Carusos
Gesangmethode.* Translated by Curt Thesing. In German. München:
Buchenau & Reichert, 1924. 395 pp. Illustrated.

The German translation of P.V.R. Key's *Enrico Caruso* (q.v.) and
Salvatore Fucito's *Caruso and the Art of Singing* (q.v.).

232 ———. *Enrico Caruso; a Biography.* Boston: Little, Brown and
Company, 1922. xv, 455 pp. Illustrated. Repertory, pp. 396-397.
Index, pp. 443-455. Chronology of Performances, 398-442.

232-a ———. *Enrico Caruso; a Biography.* New York: Vienna House,
1972. xv, 455 pp. Illustrated. Repertory, pp. 396-397. Index, pp.
443-455. Chronology, pp. 398-442.

Reprint of the 1922 edition published by Little, Brown and Company,
Boston (q.v.).

233-T Kronberg, Max. *Pucini un Karuzo dzives romans. Melodijas
uzvara.* Translated by Tulkojis E. Feldmanis. In Latvian. Riga:
Gramatu draugs, 1936. 232 pp.

Translation of *Der Sieg der Melodie* (q.v.).

234 ———. *Der Sieg der Melodie; ein Puccini-Caruso-Roman.* In
German. Leipzig: Koehler und Amelang, 1935. 267 pp. Illustrated.

235 Ledner, Emil. *Erinnerungen an Caruso.* With a foreword by Leo
Blech. In German. Hannover: P. Steegemann, 1922. 91 pp. Illustrated.

The contents of this book first appeared in the *Berliner Tageblatt* in
1922 (February 16, 18, 25; March 14, 18, 23), within six months
following the death of the singer. A translation appeared in the
April 14 and May 13, 1922, issues of *Living Age*, the only English
translation to date. Ledner was Caruso's European manager; his
poorly written, gossipy articles add up to a poorly written, gossipy
little book which contributes little to the Caruso story. It contains Ledner's eyewitness account of the enigmatic Budapest fiasco
(October 2, 1907), the only known occasion when a major artist received
absolutely no applause for "Celeste Aida." Considering the extensive
association between the artist and his manager, a disappointing contribution to the Caruso literature.

236 Lehrmann, Johannes. *Caruso singt! Ernstes und Lustiges um
Caruso und die Gastspielzeit vor 30 Jahren in Wort und Bild.* In
German. Berlin: Lehrmann, 1940. 80 pp. Illustrated.

237 Lévai, Endre, and Endre Barât. *La vie fantastique de Caruso.
Roman.* Traduit de l'américain. Translated by Jacques Ancelot. In
French. Paris: Les Editions Artistique et Documentaires, 1946. 227 pp.
Illustrated.

A fictionalized, superficial account of Caruso's life. The provenance
of this book is rather mysterious. All efforts to locate the
"américain" edition from which it has been allegedly translated have
failed. This French edition is listed in the 1947 volume of the French

trade bibliography *Biblio* and a copy is held in the Hungarian National
Library, the Széchenyi Library. A final and relatively insignificant
curiosity is the switch of the joint author's name when the book was
finally published in Hungarian (see Endre Barát, *Caruso csodálatos
élete*).

238 Marafioti, Pasqual Mario. *Caruso's Method of Voice Production;
the Scientific Culture of the Voice*. Preface by Victor Maurel.
New York: D. Appleton, 1922. xix, 308 pp. Illustrated. Vocal
Exercises, pp. 285-302.

Although the manuscript was completed in the singer's lifetime,
this is a book about voice production in general and only coincidental-
ly of Caruso's method. The author was for many years Caruso's personal friend and throat specialist; many other Met artists were his
regular patients. Dr. Marafioti writes in the foreword: "By closely
observing his (Caruso's) method of singing, I saw the correct ap-
plication by the master himself of the natural laws governing the
mechanism of voice production, and I had the opportunity, by testing
his ideas and principles, of ascertaining that they conformed with
those I have developed in the scientific part of this book." A
bold claim, allegedly untrue.

238-a ———. *Caruso's Method of Voice Production; the Scientific
Culture of the Voice*. Preface by Victor Maurel. Austin, Texas:
Cadica Enterprises, 1950. xix, 308 pp. Illustrated.

239 Maria y Campos, Armando de, b. 1897. *El canto del cisne; una
temporada de Caruso en 1919, recuerdos de un cronista*. In Spanish.
Mexico: Editorial Arriba el Telón, 1952. 159 pp.

240 Marone, Silvio. *Caruso: aspectos de sua personalidade psico-
dinâmica, suas atividades em São Paulo*. In Portuguese. São Paulo:
Grafica Gentleman, 1973. 25 pp. Illustrated.

241 Milan. Museo teatrale alla Scala. *Enrico Caruso*. In English
and Italian. Milano: Arti Grafiche E. Milli, n.d. Unpaged. Illustrated. Chronology of Life.

Contains a chronology of his life in English and Italian, and 25
pages of photographs, caricatures and letters.

242 Metropolitan Opera Association, Inc., New York. *Special Gala
Performance Celebrating the Twenty-Fifth Year in the Career of Enrico
Caruso, Metropolitan Opera House ... March the 22nd, 1919*. New York:
The Theatre Magazine Co., 1919. 32 leaves. Illustrated.

243 Mouchon, Jean-Pierre, b. 1937. *Enrico Caruso, 1873-1921, sa vie
et sa voie. Étude psycho-physiologique, physique, phonétique et
esthétique*. In French. Langres: Imprimerie du Petit Cloître, 1966.
106 pp. Illustrated. Bibliography, pp. 95-102. Discography, pp.
103-104.

A creditable effort by a devoted admirer of Caruso's artistry who
heard his first Caruso record in 1957. "Enraptured by the sound of
his strong, manly voice and, fascinated by the legend in which the
singer was enswathed," the author set out not only to find all other

recordings made by the tenor but to prove, by scientific methods and written documents, his superiority to all other tenors. A brief biographical sketch is followed by discussions of the physiology of voice production and analyses of Caruso's singing documented by the reproduction of sonagrams of various notes. The editor does not feel himself qualified to pass judgment on the scientific validity of Dr. Mouchon's findings. The discography is incomplete.

244-T ————. *Enrico Caruso: His Life and Voice.* Translated by the Author. Gap, France: Editions Ophrys, 1974. 74 pp. Illustrated.

The English translation of the French edition (q.v.) with some changes. Some of the many footnotes postdate the original French edition. The appendix of the original edition (pp. 81-106) is omitted. RT

245 Narciso, Adolfo. *Enrico Caruso e i vermicelli a vongole....* In Italian. Napoli, 1935. 31 pp.

246 Niemand, Szymon. *Enrico Caruso 1873-1921 (W. 40 rocznice smierci).* In Polish. Katowice (mimeographed), 1961. 29 pp. Published on the fortieth anniversary of Caruso's death.

247 Petriccione, Diego, b. 1867. *Caruso nell'arte e nella vita.* In Italian. Napoli: Edizione Santojanni, 1939. 61 pp. Illustrated.

248 Reis, Kurt. *Caruso, Triumph einer Stimme; Roman nach zeit-genössischen Quellenwerken und Memoiren frei bearbeitet.* In German. Männer-Serie II. Berlin: Deutsche-Buchvertriebs- und Verlags-Gesellschaft, 1955. 350 pp.

249 Rietsch, Gertrud. *Kann man die ideale Tongebung Carusos lehren? "Stimmturnen", der kürzeste und scherste Weg zum Ziel.* In German. München: Buchenau & Reichert, 1924. 29 pp.

250 Robinson, Francis Arthur, 1910-1980. *Caruso: His Life in Pictures.* With Caruso discography by John Secrist. New York: Studio Publications, 1957. 160 pp. Illustrated. Discography, pp. 149-160.

This is Francis Robinson's contribution to the Caruso literature. Robinson, the Metropolitan Opera's assistant manager for public relations, had an obsessive interest in Caruso, a singer he never heard on stage. His determination to collect everything relating to him resulted in this annotated iconography, perhaps the best ever assembled about the tenor. Each illustration is accompanied by enlightening commentary, and four biographical chapters tell the Caruso story. John Secrist's excellent discography (originally published in the November-December issue of *The Record Collector*) completes the volume. It has since been superseded by the one by John R. Bolig (q.v.).

250-a ————. *Caruso: His Life in Pictures.* With Caruso discography by John Secrist. New York: Bramhall House, 1957. 160 pp. Illustrated. Discography, pp. 149-160.

The verso of the title page reads: "This edition published by Bramhall House, a division of Clarkson N. Potter, Inc., by arrangement with The Viking Press." The reason for publishing the same book, identical in every respect, simultaneously but with different imprints remains one of the inconsequential mysteries of the publishing world.

251 Steen, Hans, b. 1905. *Caruso; eine Stimme erobert die Welt.* In German. Essen-Steele: W. Webels, 1946. 105 pp. Illustrated.

252 Thiess, Frank, b. 1890. *Caruso, Roman einer Stimme.* In German. Wien: K.H. Bischoff, 1942. Fictionalized biography.

252-a ———. *Caruso; Roman einer Stimme.* In German. Hamburg: P. Zsolnay, 1952. 719 pp. Fictionalized biography.

253 ———. *Caruso, Vortrag gehalten am 26. Februar 1943 in der Deutsch Italienischen Gesellschaft in Frankfurt am Main.* In German. Berlin: K.H. Bischoff, 1943. 55 pp.

254 ———. *Der Tenor von Trapani.* In German. Reclams universal Bibliothek, 7506. Leipzig: P. Reclam jun., 1942. 74 pp. Fictionalized biography.

255-T ———. *Il tenore di Trapani.* Translated by Anita Rho. In Italian. Collana di opere brevi, 2. Torino: Frassinelli, 1942. x, 195 pp.

256 Tortorelli, Vittorio. *Enrico Caruso nel centenario della nascita.* Preface by Ivan Martynov. In Italian. Rimini: Artisti asociati, 1973. 188 pp. Illustrated. Bibliography, pp. 186-187. Repertory, pp. 183-185.

257-T ———. *Enriko Karuzo.* In Russian. Moskva: Muzika, 1965. 176 pp. Illustrated.

Russian translation of the author's *Enrico Caruso* (q.v.).

258 Wagenmann, Josef Hermann, b. 1876. *Enrico Caruso und das Problem der Stimmbildung.* In German. Altenburg: S.-J. Räde, 1911. 73 pp. Illustrated.

258-a ———. *Enrico Caruso und das Problem der Stimmbildung.* In German. 3rd ed. Leipzig: A. Felix, 1924. 107 pp.

259 ———. *Umsturz in der Stimmbildung (Lösung des Stimmbildungs- und Carusoproblems). Schrift für Sänger, Schauspieler, Redner und jedermann.* 2nd ed. Leipzig: A. Felix, 1922? 37 pp.

260 Ybarra, Thomas Russell, b. 1880. *Caruso; the Man of Naples and the Voice of Gold.* New York: Harcourt, Brace, 1953. 315 pp. Illustrated. Bibliography, pp. 313-315. Chronology of Performances, pp. 311-312.

One of the major Caruso biographies, bringing together the published information available up to the time of writing. While Ybarra's affinity to his subject is obvious, he presents the pleasant as well as the unattractive sides of the singer's personality with commendable objectivity. The book reads well; the style is that of a skilled journalist. The fictional dialogues, although used sparingly as a writer's device, are hard to accept when they deal with conversations never recorded and whose participants or eyewitnesses were long dead at the time of writing. The chronology pertains only to his Metropolitan appearances.

260-a ————. *Caruso, the Man of Naples and the Voice of Gold.* London: Cresset Press, 1954. 230 pp. Illustrated. Bibliography, pp. 225-226. Index, pp. 227-230.

261 Young, Patricia, b. 1922. *Great Performers.* The Young Reader's Guides to Music, 10. London: Oxford University Press, 1964. 58 pp. Illustrated.

Simple, straightforward biographical summaries of the lives of Paganini, Liszt, Caruso, Pavlova and Toscanini. Though nicely done for young adults, a book of little consequence for anyone with more than a passing interest in these artists.

261-a ————. *Great Performers.* The Young Reader's Guides to Music. New York: H.Z. Walck, 1967. 71 pp. Illustrated.

See also items 1429, 1430, 1431, 1541, 1565, 1581, 1620, 1635, 1647, 1663, 1680, 1744, 1821

CARVALHO, CAROLINE MARIE, 1827-1895

262 Spoll, Edouard Accoyer, b. 1833. *Mme. Carvalho; notes et souvenirs*, avec un portrait à l'eau-forte par Lalauze. In French. Paris: Librairie des bibliophiles, 1885. 104 pp. Illustrated.

See also item 1588

CASA, ANNA, b. 1889

See items 1565, 1695

CASTRO-ESCOBAR, CONSUELO, b. 1917

See item 1631

CASTRO-PADILLA, CARLOS, 1889-1938

See item 1631

CATALANI, ANGELICA, 1780-1849

263 Gatti, Carlo. *Catalani.* In Italian. Milano: Garzanti, 1953. 250 pp. Information taken from dealer's catalog.

263/A Satter, Heinrich. *Angelica Catalani; Primadonna der Kaiser und Könige.* In German. Frankfurt am Main: Frankfurter Bücher, 1958. 512 pp. Fiction.

264 Simpson, Arthur. *Secret Memoirs of Madame Catalani.* Bath: Printed for the author by M. Gye, 1811. 46 pp.

See also items 943, 1562, 1612, 1615, 1745

CATLEY, ANNE, 1745-1789

265 *The Life of Miss Anne Catley, Celebrated Singing Performer of the Last Century, Including an Account of Her Introduction to Public Life, Her Professional Engagements in London and Dublin, and Her Various Adventures and Intrigues....* Carefully compiled and edited from the best and most authentic records extant. London, 1888. 78 pp. Illustrated.

CAVALIERI, LINA, 1874-1944

266 Cavalieri, Lina. *Le mie verità.* Edited by Paolo D'Arvanni. In Italian. Roma: S.A. Poligrafica Italiana, 1936. 201 pp. Illustrated.

This is the autobiography of Lina Cavalieri, who promoted herself as "the most beautiful woman of the world." From an impoverished childhood in a Roman slum she rose in the world of variety shows to the *Folies Bergère* in Paris and the *Empire* in London. Barely out of her teens, during her Russian tour she became the Princess Bariatinsky. The newly acquired riches enabled her to cultivate her voice; she divorced her husband and launched her operatic career in 1900. The narrative lacks continuity; the incidents from her career are few and inconsequential. The image that emerges is that of a woman spoiled by the incessant attention paid to her by men; her whims included a one-week marriage to an American millionaire on a bet. Her third marriage to tenor Lucien Muratore also ended in divorce. She spent her retirement years managing her cosmetic salons in Paris. The chronology of events in the book is erratic and difficult to reconcile. Even at the age of 62, men, marriage, jewels and beauty seem to have preoccupied her more than her "one true love": singing. Most unfortunately, the large number of excellent illustrations are poorly reproduced.

267 ———. *My Secrets of Beauty ... Including More Than 1,000 Valuable Recipes for Preparations Used and Recommended by Mme. Cavalieri Herself;* illustrated with new photographs of Mme. Cavalieri and other famous beauties. New York: The Circulation Syndicate, 1914. 317 pp. Illustrated.

268 Dusan, Paula. *Lina Cavalieri.* In Italian. Roma: Edizioni "La Chiglia," 1944? 36 pp. Illustrated.

This booklet was part of the extremely modest and inexpensive series entitled "Famous Women." The biography is written in the tone and spirit of the series. RT

See also item 1680

CEBOTARI, MARIA, 1910-1949

269 *Kammersängerin Maria Cebotari von der Staatsoper Berlin und Dresden, Salzburger Festspiele.* In German. Bremen: Harlip, 1934? 11 unnumbered leaves.

270 Mingotti, Anton. *Maria Cebotari, das Leben einer Sängerin.* In German. Salzburg: Hellbrunn-Verlag, 1950. 145 pp. Illustrated.

Capitalizing on the sympathy of the public over the loss of one of their favorites, this short biography of Cebotari was written and rushed to print within a year after she died of cancer at the age of thirty-nine. The biography, a "rush job" by a skilled writer, concentrates on the public side of her life and the hardships and deprivations of the war. Confined by political circumstances to the Axis countries, her stage and film career were easily researched. The basic facts of her activities are well covered. The list of her repertory includes eight motion pictures, in two of which she was partnered by Beniamino Gigli.

270-a ─────. *Maria Cebotari; das Leben einer Sängerin.* In German. Opera Biographies. New York: Arno Press, 1977. 145 pp. Illustrated.

Reprint of the 1950 Hellbrunn-Verlag edition (q.v.).

CEPEDA, CAROLINA CASANOVA DE, 1851-1910

See item 1756

CHALIAPIN, FEDOR IVANOVICH, 1873-1938

271-T Chaliapin, Fedor Ivanovich. *Aus meinem Leben: Bilder aus meinem Leben--Maske und Seele.* Translated by Lothar Fahlbusch. In German. Leipzig: Philipp Reclam jun., 1972. 595 pp. Repertory, pp. 559-568. Index, pp. 569-593. Chronology of Performances, pp. 559-568.

This translation is based on the "official" two-volume Russian edition of 1958-60 (q.v.), which omits some of the politically controversial passages. The two works incorporated here are the auto-biography told to Maksim Gorky, *Fedor Ivanovich Chaliapin* (q.v.) in Russian, *Chaliapin* (q.v.) in English; and *Maska i dusha* (q.v.), completed and dated by the singer on March 8, 1932. A useful collection of 173 explanatory notes follow on pp. 531-557. AM

272-T ─────. *Ifjúságom. Az elö- és utószót irta István Albert.* Translated by Pongrác Galsai, Mária G. Bolgár. In Hungarian. Budapest: Zenemükiadó Vállalat, 1960. 222 pp. Illustrated.

This is the incomplete Hungarian translation of *Stranitsy iz moei zhizny* (q.v.). For some inexplicable reason the text concludes with

chapter 6 of the 1927 Katharine Wright translation, or chapter 8 of
the Froud and Hanley translation. There is no reference to the missing
chapters and more importantly, there is no mention of Maksim Gorky's
co-authorship.

273-T ———. *Lied meiner Jugend*. Mit einem Nachwort von Grigori
Schneerson. Translated by Ruth Elisabeth Riedt. In German. Berlin:
Henschelverlag, 1958. 234 pp. Illustrated.

German translation of *Stranitsy iz moei zhizni* (q.v.).

274 ———. *Literaturnoe nasledstvo*. In Russian. Moskva: Iskusstvo,
1960. 2 vols. Illustrated.

275-T ———. *Ma vie*. Translated by André Pierre. In French.
Paris: A. Michel, 1932. 385 pp.

French translation of *Maska i dusha* (q.v.).

276 ———. *Chaliapin; an Autobiography as Told to Maxim Gorky*.
Translated by Nina Froud and James Hanley. New York: Stein and Day,
1967. 320 pp. Bibliography, pp. 307-308. Repertory, pp. 303-306.
Index, pp. 313-320. Notes on Persons Mentioned, pp. 309-312.

The complete translation of Chaliapin's first autobiography as told
to Gorky in the course of the former's extended visit to the exiled
writer then living on the island of Capri. Not surprisingly, the
biography is literate and quite dramatic, and reads like a Gorky
novel written in his characteristic stark and powerful prose, full
of evocative imagery and revealing details. The collaboration represents the fusion of twin souls whose lifelong friendship in the end
fell victim to divergent political views. Chaliapin's life story is
brought up to the outbreak of World War I, his forty-first year.
Over two decades of enormously successful and lucrative international
appearances were still to come.
Appended to the book are several important and revealing letters
of Chaliapin, his family and friends. There is a special group
of letters from Gorky, ending with a scathing missive upon the publication of the anti-Soviet second autobiography (*Maska i dusha*, q.v.).
There are also reminiscences of varying length by Rachmaninov,
Angelo Masini, Nemirovich-Danchenko, Stassov, Stanislavsky and Nikulin.
Gorky's contribution makes this one of the jewels of operatic biographical literature.

277 ———. *Man and Mask; Forty Years in the Life of a Singer*.
Translated by Phyllis Mégroz. London: V. Gollancz, 1932. 413 pp.
Illustrated.

This is the British edition of the book, published the same year,
by A.A. Knopf (q.v.). It was reprinted ("republished," according to
the publisher) in 1973, by Scholarly Press.

277-a ———. *Man and Mask; Forty Years in the Life of a Singer*.
Translated by Phyllis Mégroz. New York: A.A. Knopf, 1932. xxvi,
358 pp. Illustrated. "First American edition."

This is the English translation of Chaliapin's second autobiography
originally published under the title *Maska i dusha* (q.v.). Several

chapters deal with politics and the Soviet state whose tone caused the final rift between the singer and his lifelong friend, Maksim Gorky. He retraces his youth, but only briefly in order not to duplicate the previous biography. The most valuable portions are Chaliapin's statements about his own artistic development, his operatic stagework and his views about art in general and performing arts in particular. Pro-Soviet sources attribute his critical statements of the Revolution to a ghost writer, supposedly a former officer of the white guard. Be that as it may, his narrative dovetails with historical facts, contrary to Gorky's objections. Chaliapin's identification with the Russian people and their striving for freedom from tsarist oppression permeates his story, and he makes the reader understand that it was the excesses of the Revolution that had alienated him from the cause. The irony of his becoming a victim of a political movement becomes apparent from his statement "I knew very little about politics, and the little I knew failed to interest me." The book, as a whole, reveals much about the greatest singing-actor to emerge in the last hundred years and whose musical stagecraft revolutionized theatrical life in Russia.

277-b ————. *Man and Mask; Forty Years in the Life of a Singer.* Translated by Phyllis Mégroz. New York: Garden City Publishing Co., 1932. 358 pp. Illustrated.

This edition seems to have been printed from the same plates as that published by A.A. Knopf the same year. The inconsequential differences are a slightly smaller page size, the same illustrations reproduced on different paper and located elsewhere in this edition, and the *absence* of the statement: "First American edition." Since Knopf is still shown as the copyright holder, it is hard to explain why another edition with the Garden City Publishing Co. imprint was deemed necessary.

277-c ————. *Man and Mask; Forty Years in the Life of a Singer.* Translated by Phyllis Mégroz. Westport, Conn.: Greenwood Press, 1970. xxvi, 358 pp. Illustrated.

English translation of *Maska i dusha* (q.v.); reprint of the 1932 edition by A.A. Knopf, New York (q.v.).

277-d ————. *Man and Mask; Forty Years in the Life of a Singer.* Translated by Phyllis Mégroz. St. Clair Shores, Mich.: Scholarly Press, 1973. 413 pp. Illustrated.

English translation of *Maska i dusha* (q.v.); reprint of the 1932 edition by V. Gollancz, London (q.v.).

278 ————. *Maska i dusha; moi sorok' let' na teatrakh.* Paris: Sovremennyie zapiski, 1932. 356 pp. Illustrated.

This is the original Russian edition of Chaliapin's second autobiography. It was published concurrently in London by V. Gollancz and in New York by A.A. Knopf under the title: *Man and Mask; Forty Years in the Life of a Singer* (q.v.). The exact translation from the Russian would be "my forty years in the theater." For a full annotation see the 1932 Knopf edition of this book.

279-T ──────. *Mein Freund Fjodor; das Leben Schaljapins, von Maxim Gorkij*. Übertragung aus dem Russischen, Anmerkungen und Nachwort von Erich Müller-Kamp. Translated by Erich Müller-Kamp. In German. Tübingen: Rainer Wunderlich, 1970? 323 pp. Illustrated.

This is the German translation of Chaliapin's autobiography told to Maksim Gorky (q.v.). The preface, on pp. 9-11, is a letter from Gorky to a certain W.A. Posse dated October 27, 1901, and titled "Einer von uns" (one of us). Pages 269-301 contain an exchange of 17 letters between the two friends. There is also an article by Chaliapin (pp. 303-307) about Gorky. The translator's explanatory notes close the volume. AM

280-T ──────. *Mein Werden*. Translated by Arthur Knüpffer. In German. Berlin: Adlerverlag, 1928. 276 pp. Illustrated.

German translation of *Stranitsy iz moei zhizni* (q.v.).

281-T ──────. *Meine Jugend; Erinnerungen*. Mit einem Nachwort von Edzard Schaper. Translated by Arthur Knüpffer. In German. Zürich: Werner Classen, 1949. 228 pp.

German translation of *Stranitsy iz moei zhizni* (q.v.).

282-T ──────. *Minha vida*. Translated by Costa Neves. In Portuguese. Rio de Janeiro: Casa editora Vecchi, 1942. 273 pp. Illustrated.

Portuguese translation of *Maska i dusha* (q.v.), excluding the first four chapters.

283-T ──────. *Mi vida*. Translated by Hugo Lamel. In Spanish. Biblioteca Tota, no. 26 (Memorias y autobiografías VII). Buenos Aires: Centro Editor de América Latina, 1977. 134 pp.

Without comments or explanations, this translation of the auto-biography told to Maksim Gorky (q.v.) contains only the first 19 chapters of the 36 that make up the Russian-language original. AM

284-T ──────. *Ohne Maske; Erinnerungen. 40 Jahre Sänger*. In German. Berlin: Drei Masken Verlag, 1933. 292 pp. Illustrated.

German translation of *Maska i dusha* (q.v.).

285-T ──────. *Pages de ma vie*. Translated by H. Pernot. In French. Paris: Librairie Plon, 1927. 256 pp. Illustrated.

French translation of *Stranitsy iz moei zhizni* (q.v.).

286-T ──────. *Pages from My Life; an Autobiography*. Revised, en-larged and edited by Katharine Wright. Translated by H.M. Buck. New York: Harper & Brothers, 1927. 345 pp. Illustrated.

This, the first Chaliapin autobiography to appear in English, is a curious hybrid, textually speaking. It was entitled *Stranitsy iz moei zhizni* (q.v.) when it appeared in Leningrad, in 1926. The first ten chapters, in spite of numerous minor omissions, mostly agree with the version co-authored by Maksim Gorky (published in its entirety in English in 1967, under the title *Chaliapin, an Autobiography, as Told to Maksim Gorky*, q.v.). Chapters 11 and 12, however, were specifically

written for this edition with Western audiences in mind. As is explained in the work, it was necessary to make this edition different
from the one published in Leningrad in 1926 to avoid preempting the
claim of first publication, unless the text was altered, augmented,
etc. The new chapters make only few references to the Russian Revolution. While they aren't flattering, they are simply too brief to
have allowed Chaliapin's political detractors to capitalize on them.
At this stage of his life Chaliapin, apparently, wasn't quite ready
to break away from his homeland permanently. He also condenses in a
single sentence his elaborate scheme of leaving Russia for good in
1922: "In June I again left Russia, this time taking with me members
of my family." The last chapter summarizes his American experiences
up to December, 1926, including the story of a private screening given
him by Charlie Chaplin in his own studio, and the story of his concert
at Sing Sing prison.

In spite of the clumsy translation the book has a stylistic unity
that gives the impression of Chaliapin narrating the story of his
life. The illustrations, that reappeared with some regularity in
subsequent publications, are of good quality.

287-T ———. *Pei sentieri della vita*. Translated by Ermet Libe-
rati. In Italian. Collezione "Memorie e documenti ..." 8. Milano:
Treves-Treccani-Tumminelli, 1932. xi, 334 pp. Illustrated.

Italian translation of *Maska i dusha* (q.v.).

288 ———. *Povesti o zhizni. Stranitsy iz moei zhizni. Maska i
dusha*. (Komment. E.A. Groshevoi i I.F. Shaliapinoi). In Russian.
Perm': Kn. izd., 1969. 372 pp. Illustrated.

The combined edition of Chaliapin's two autobiographies, edited by
Grosheva and the singer's daughter, Irina.

289 ———. *Stranitsy iz moei zhizni; avtobiografiia*. In Russian.
Biblioteka dlia vsekh, no. 51-57. Leningrad: Rabochee izdatel'stvo
"Priboi," 1926. 220 pp.

289-a ———. *Stranitsy iz moei zhizni*. In Russian. Kiev: Gos.
izd-vo izobrazitel'nogo iskusstva i muzykal'noi lit-ri, 1956. 215 pp.
Illustrated.

This edition was republished in 1958 by the Derzh. vyd-vo obrazot-
vorchoho mystetsva i muzychnoi lit-ry URSR, Kiev.

289-b ———. *Stranitsy iz moei zhizni*. In Russian. Perm':
Permskoe knizhnoe izd-vo, 1961. 238 pp. Illustrated.

290-T ———. *Wspomnienia z mojego zycia*. Translated by Ludwicka
Rakowska. In Polish. Kraków: Polskie Wydawn. Muzyczne, 1961. 399 pp.
Illustrated. Bibliography, p. 398.

Polish translation of *Stranitsy iz moei zhizni* (q.v.).

291 Almedingev, B.A. *Golovin i Shaliapin*. In Russian. Moskva,
1975. 31 pp. Illustrated. Information taken from dealer's catalog.

292 Dmitrievskii, Vitalii Nikolaevich, and E.R. Katerinina. *Shaliapin v Peterburge-Petrograde*. In Russian. Seriia Vydaiushchiesia deiateli literatury, iskusstva, nauki v Peterburge-Petrograde-Leningrade. Leningrad: Lenizdat, 1976. 263 pp. Illustrated. Bibliography, pp. 258-262. List of Chaliapin's Peterburg Addresses, pp. 250-257.

293 Dmitrievskii, Vitalii Nikolaevich. *Velikii artist. Dokum. povest' o zhizni i tvorchestve F.I. Shaliapina. K 100-letiiu so dnia pozhdeniia, 1873-1973*. In Russian. Leningrad: "Muzyka," 1973. 216 pp. Illustrated.

294 Drankov, Vladimir L'vovich. *Priroda talanta Shaliapina*. In Russian. Leningrad: "Muzyka," 1973. 215 pp. Illustrated.

295 Feschotte, Jacques. *Ce géant: Féodor Chaliapine*. Préface de Bernard Gavoty. In French. Paris: La Table Ronde, 1968. 228 pp. Illustrated. Discography, pp. 223-226.

In his preface Bernard Gavoty writes: "The book these lines preface is something else and better than a biography: it is an act of love." Unintentionally, Gavoty thus summed up the interest and value of this book. The author's worshipful admiration is the source, inspiration and essence of this book. It is well worth reading but will tell the reader little that cannot be found, better presented, elsewhere. The discography is an insignificant, amateur effort.

296 Fokine, Michel, 1880-1942. *Feodor Chaliapin, the Ingenious Artist; His Stage Career*. New York: N.p., 1952. 23 pp. Illustrated.

297 Georgievich, N. *Zhizn' F.I. Shaliapina i ego artisticheskaia deiatel'nost'*. In Russian. Odessa: M.S. Kozmana, 1903. 24 pp.

298 Goury, Jean. *Fedor Chaliapin*. In French. Monstres sacrés. Paris: SODAL, 196?. 81 pp. Illustrated. Bibliography, p. 75. Discography, pp. 65-74.

The biography relies too heavily on Chaliapin's own reminiscences to have any claim of originality. Of minor value are the taped or published testimonials of some singers who appeared with Chaliapin. The chronology of his life emphasizes the events of special relevance to Paris. The illustrations are good, the discography and the bibliography incomplete and inadequate.

299 Gozenpud, Abraham Akimovich. *Russkii opernyi teatr na rubezhe XIX-XX vekov i F.I. Shaliapin: 1890-1904*. In Russian. Leningrad: Muzyka, 1974. 262 pp. Illustrated.

300 Grevina, Anna. *Salapins*. In Latvian. Riga: A. Gulbis, 1935. 219 pp. Illustrated.

301 Grosheva, Elena Andreevna, editor. *Fedor Ivanovich Shaliapin*. In Russian. 2nd ed.? Moskva: Iskusstvo, 1959-60. 2 vols. Illustrated. Repertory. Discography.

302 ———. *Fedor Ivanovich Shaliapin*. In Russian. 3rd ed. Moskva: Iskusstvo, 1976-1979. 3 vols. Illustrated. Repertory, Vol. 3, pp. 331-342. Index, Vol. 3, pp. 362-392. Chronology of Performances,

Vol. 3, pp. 248-330.

Without a doubt this is the most substantial item in the vast
Chaliapin literature. Time obviously heals many things, including the
wounded pride of the Soviet government that lost Chaliapin to the West.
He is, by now, a national hero whose memory is worshipped and whose
legend is duly exploited in his homeland. As far as it can be established, this is the much-expanded reworking of the two-volume anthology
that first appeared in 1957-60 by the same editor. This three-volume
set contains an editorial introduction; the two autobiographies; correspondence; a 90-page reminiscence by daughter Irina and three pages
by daughter Lydia; about 720 pages of reminiscences, appreciation,
essays, etc., by some 75 other individuals; an exhaustive (but by no
means complete) chronology of his appearances; his operatic and concert repertory; an elementary discography; and exhaustive notes and
indices. There are about 200 interesting photographs. Unfortunately,
with a few exceptions, the quality of reproduction is annoyingly poor
and that is due to the printing process, not the quality of the
originals. A remarkable work that deserves to be translated.

303 IAnkovskii, Moisei Osipovich, b. 1898. *F.I. Shaliapin.* In
Russian. Mastera Bol'shogo teatra. Moskva: Gos. muzykal'noe izd-vo,
1951. 127 pp. Illustrated. Bibliography, p. 127.

304-T ———. *Saljapin.* Appendix: Pál Komár, "Saljapin és
Magyarország." Translated by Ferenc Aczél. In Hungarian. Budapest:
Gondolat, 1976. 469 pp. Illustrated. Index, pp. 452-467.

This is the Hungarian translation of the 1972 Russian edition of
IAnkovskii's book (q.v.). The appendix by Pál Komár, entitled "Chaliapin
and Hungary," discusses the singer's eight visits to Budapest. Illustrations include two theater posters of Chaliapin's Budapest engagements in *Faust* and in *Don Quichotte*.

305 ———. *Shaliapin.* In Russian. Zhizn v iskusstve. Leningrad:
Iskusstvo, 1972. 374 pp. Illustrated.

A detailed biographical account of Chaliapin's life. Up to the
years of emigration it is heavily dependent on the two volumes of
autobiography. IAnkovskii claims that the second autobiography (*Maska
i dusha*) was dictated to S.L. Poliakov-Litovtsev, a former member of
the white guard, the person solely responsible for the anti-Soviet
chapters of the book.

For information about the last ten years of the singer's life
IAnkovskii relies on various Russian sources, emigrant eyewitness
accounts, and the memoirs of prominent Soviet nationals allowed to
travel abroad, all of them properly identified.

306 ———. *Shaliapin.* In Russian. Massovaia musykal'noe biblioteka. Moskva: Gos. musykal'noe izd-vo, 1955. 71 pp.

307 ———. *Shaliapin i russkaia opernaia kul'tura*; pod red. Evg.
Kuznetsova. In Russian. Leningrad: Iskusstvo, 1947. 222 pp.
Illustrated.

308 Karatygin, Viacheslav Gavrilovich, 1875-1925. *I. Musorgskii.*
II. Shaliapin. In Russian. Peterburg: Izdanie Biblioteki Gosud.

akad. teatra, operny i baleta, 1922. 82 pp. Illustrated.

309 Kopylov, Aleksandr Aleksandrovich, 1854-1911? *F.I. Shaliapin.*
In Czech. Praha, 1947. Information taken from the Chaliapin article
in the *Enciclopedia dello Spettacolo.*

310 Korovin, Konstantin Alekseevich, 1861-1939. *Shaliapin; vstrechi
i sovmestnaia zhizn'.* In Russian. Paris: "Vozrozhdenie," 1939.
213 pp. Illustrated.

311 Less, Aleksandr Lazarevich. *Rasskazy o Shaliapine.* Predicl.
I. Bielzy. In Russian. Moskva: "Sov. Rossiia," 1973. 174 pp.
Illustrated.

312 Makovskii, Sergei Konstantinovich, b. 1877. *Portrety sovremennikov.*
In Russian. N'iu Iork: Izd-vo im. Chekhova, 1955. 413 pp.

Contains a long chapter devoted to Chaliapin (pp. 169-190).

313 Nikulin, Lev Veniaminovich, 1891-1967. *Fedor Shaliapin; ocherk
zhizni i tvorchestva.* In Russian. Moskva: Iskusstvo, 1954. 191 pp.
Illustrated.

314 ———. *Liudi russkogo iskusstva.* In Russian. Moskva:
Sovetskii pisatel', 1947. 208 pp.

314-a ———. *Liudi russkogo iskusstva.* In Russian. 2nd revised,
enlarged ed. Moskva: Iskusstva, 1952. 332 pp.

315 Rozenfel'd, Semen Efimovich. *Povest' o Shaliapine.* In Russian.
Leningrad: Lenizdat, 1966. 277 pp.

316-T ———. *Saljapin. Emlékeim a müvészröl és az emberröl.*
Translated by Ágnes Békési, Irén Szantó. In Hungarian. Bucharest:
Orosz Könyv, Áll. Irodalmi es Müvészeti Kiadó, 1969. 237 pp.

Hungarian translation of *Povest' o Shaliapine* (q.v.).

317 Stark, Eduard Aleksandrovich. *Shaliapin.* Eduard Stark (Zigfrid).
In Russian. Petrograd: R. Golike i A. Vil'borg, 1915. iv, 210 pp.
Illustrated.

318 Stasov, Vladimir Vasil'evich, 1824-1906. *Stat'i o Shaliapine.*
In Russian. Russkaia klassicheskaia muzykal'naia kritika. Moskva:
Gos. muzykal'noe izd-vo, 1952. 22 pp.

319 Teliakovskii, Vladimir Arkad'evich, 1861-1924. *Moi sosluzhivets
Shaliapin.* In Russian. Teatral'nye memuary ... seriia knig, 1.
Leningrad: Akademiia, 1927. 167 pp.

320 Thury, Zoltán. *Ej uhnyem. Saljapin csodálatos élete.* In
Hungarian. Budapest: Aesopus, n.d. 224 pp. Illustrated.

A Chaliapin biography in Hungarian, based very closely on *Maska i
dusha* (q.v.) which the author read in the German translation (*Ohne*

Maske, q.v.). Because of its anti-Soviet statements this book was on restricted circulation in Hungarian libraries after World War II.

See also items 665, 1471, 1472, 1617, 1680, 1702, 1716, 1795, 1796, 1811

CHAVDAR, ELIZAVETA IVANIVNA, b. 1925

321 Kaufman, Leonid Serhilovych. *Elizaveta Ivanovna Chavdar, narodnaia artistka SSSR.* In Ukrainian. Kiev: Derzh. vid-vo obrazot-vorchogo mistetsva i muzichnoi lit-ri URSR, 1960. 22 pp. Illustrated.

322 Kyrychenko, T. *IElizaveta Ivanivna Chavdar.* In Russian. Kiev: Derzh. vid-vo obrazotvorchogo mistetstva i muzichnoi lit-ri URSR, 1958. 14 pp.

CHOLLET, JEAN-BAPTISTE-MARIE, 1798-1892

323 Laget, Auguste, 1821-1902. *Chollet, premier sujet du théatre de l'Opéra-Comique.* In French. Toulouse, 1880.

CHRISTOFF, BORIS, b. 1914

324 Goury, Jean. *Boris Christoff.* In French. Collection "Spécial OPÉRA." Paris: SODAL, 1970. 32 pp. Illustrated. "Supplément semestriel au no. 90 d'Opéra."

A good illustrated summary of Christoff's life and career up to the time of publication. Considering his importance as a singer in post-war operatic life, it is surprising that there has been no other biography about him or by him (unless one of the Slavic countries produced one the editor was unable to trace). A pupil of Riccardo Stracciari, Christoff was still active in 1982, 36 years after his debut. From his repertory of over 100 roles he retained only a few that he refined to perfection over the years. These roles brought him lasting fame and a secure place in operatic history.

See also item 1545

CINTI-DAMOREAU, LAURE, 1801-1863

See item 1601

CLAUSSEN, JULIA, 1879-1941

See item 1581

COATES, EDITH, 1906-1983

See item 1545

COATES, JOHN, 1865-1941

See items 1629, 1702

CORDA, GIOVANNI

325 Corda, Giovanni. *Dai miei ricordi teatrali*. In Italian. Roma: N.p., 1974. 107 pp.

CORELLI, FRANCO, b. 1921

See item 1563

CORNELIUS, PETER, 1865-1934

326 Skjerne, Godtfred, b. 1880. *Peter Cornelius*. In Danish. København: Nyt Nordisk Forlag, 1917. 48 pp. Illustrated.

A short biographical pamphlet of the famous Danish opera singer, who is *not* the composer of the same name. Like his younger compatriot, Lauritz Melchior, Cornelius also began his career as a baritone, making his debut in Copenhagen in 1892 as Escamillo. His debut as a tenor was as the Steersman in the *Flying Dutchman*. By 1906, the year of his first Bayreuth engagement, he was a well-known *Heldentenor* with an international reputation. The 48-page booklet contains 16 pages of photographs with blank versos; thus the biographical text is brief indeed. PHS

COSMA, LUCIA, 1875-1972

327 Itu, Ion. *Destinul unei artiste: Lucia Cosma*. In Rumanian. Bucureşti: Editura Muzicală, 1976. 143 pp. Illustrated.

COTOGNI, ANTONIO, 1831-1918

328 Angelucci, Nino, 1876-1959. *Ricordi di un artista (Antonio Cotogni)*. In Italian. Roma: Tipografia editrice "Roma," 1907. 131 pp. Illustrated. Repertory, pp. 123-128.

The only book written about the celebrated baritone with a vast repertory. The memoirs recall the principal events of his long career as a singer and a singing teacher, and his encounters with the stellar personalities of the theater world. RT

See also items 1569/A, 1680

329 Deleted

CRABBÉ, ARMAND, 1883-1947

330 Crabbé, Armand. *Conversation et conseils sur l'art du chant.
Quelques anecdotes et souvenirs de 25 années de carrière lyrique
internationale.* In French. Bruxelles: Schott, 1931. 76 pp. Illustrated.

CRESPIN, RÉGINE, b. 1927

331 Crespin, Régine. *La vie et l'amour d'une femme.* In French.
Paris: Fayard, 1982. 318 pp. Illustrated. Discography, pp. 313-316. Chronology of Performances, pp. 287-311.

A candid autobiography that reveals more about the person than
about the artist. Crespin talks openly about the men she loved,
with a degree of sensitivity and understanding that only a few women
possess. She treats the highlights of her career with objectivity,
neither flaunting nor diminishing with false humility her many successes. The book is well written; if it is all her own writing she
is to be complimented for her literary flair. There is a sketchy
chronology lacking many important data (casts, dates) and an equally
superficial discography.

See also item 1788

CRISTOFOREANU, FLORICA, 1887-1960

332 Cristoforeanu, Florica. *Amintiri din cariera mea lirica.* In
Rumanian. Bucureşti: Editura Muzicală, 1964. 361 pp. Illustrated.

CROIZA, CLAIRE, 1882-1948

333 Abraham, Hélène, b. 1890. *Un art de l'interprétation: Claire
Croiza; les cahiers d'une auditrice, 1924-1939.* In French. Paris:
Office de centralisation d'ouvrages, 1954. 367 pp. Illustrated.

A listener's collection of notes and observations on Claire Croiza's
performances, recitals, meetings, day-to-day encounters, etc. There
is an interesting observation about Gigli's May 24, 1934, recital:
"Comme il est malheureux ... comme le chanteur est toujours malheureux!" (p. 268).

CROUCH, ANNA MARIA (PHILLIPS), 1763-1805

334 Young, Mary Julia. *Memoirs of Mrs. Crouch. Including a Retrospect of the Stage, During the Years She Performed.* London: J.
Asperne, 1806. 2 vols.

CRUVELLI, SOPHIE, 1826-1907

335 Favre, Georges. *La Vicomtesse Vigier; Sophie Cruvelli: 1826-1907, une grande cantatrice niçoise.* In French. Paris: A. et J.

Picard, 1979. 109 pp. Illustrated. Bibliography, pp. 105-106.
Index.

See also item 1612

CUÉNOD, HUGUES, b. 1902

336 Spycket, Jérôme. *Un Diable de musicien: Hugues Cuénod.* In
French. Lausanne: Payot, 1979. 231 pp. Illustrated. Discography,
pp. 226-229.

CUNELLI, GEORGES

337 CUNELLI, GEORGES. *Voice No Mystery: Half a Century of Recollections in the Arts of Singing and Speaking.* With a preface by Paul
Robeson. London: Stainer and Bell, 1973. xiii, 160 pp. Illustrated.

A curious book of recollections, with many misspelled names and
some factual errors, the possible result of memory lapses and careless
editing. It contains a fascinating chapter on Titta Ruffo.

CUZZONI SANDONI, FRANCESCA, 1700-1770

See item 1597

D

DALLA RIZZA, GILDA, 1892-1975

338 Rizzi, F.G. *Gilda Dalla Rizza; verismo e bel canto.* In Italian.
Venezia: Edizioni Tipografia Commerciale, 1964. 142 pp. Illustrated.
Repertory, pp. 127-129.

A simple narrative of the career of soprano Gilda Dalla Rizza,
to which is appended a brief biography of her husband, tenor Agostino
Capuzzo. Her biography includes hitherto unpublished letters from
Puccini who, apparently, held her in high esteem.

DAL MONTE, TOTI, 1898-1975

339 Dal Monte, Toti. *Una voce nel mondo.* In Italian. Il Cammeo,
v. 165. Milano: Longanesi, 1962. 381 pp. Illustrated. Dal Monte's
date of birth is given in the various reference sources as 1893,
1896, 1898, 1899.

Exhaustive autobiography of Dal Monte, née Antonietta Meneghel.
The wit and naturalness of the writing makes this book a pleasant
reading. RT

See also items 1544, 1811

DALMORÈS, CHARLES, 1871-1939

See item 1581

D'ALVAREZ, MARGUERITE, 1886?-1953

340 D'Alvarez, Marguerite. *All the Bright Dreams, an Autobiography.* New York: Harcourt, Brace, 1956. 313 pp. Illustrated.

This book was first published in London in 1954 under the title *Forsaken Altars* (q.v.).

340-a ———. *Forsaken Altars; Autobiography of Marguerite d'Alvarez.* London: R. Hart-Davis, 1954. 305 pp. Illustrated.

This book of posthumous recollections first appeared in London, and two years later in the United States under the title "All the Bright Dreams." Those who did not know her might wonder why it was ever published at all. This great hulk of a woman was a true enigma: while neurotic and quixotic, she was still exotic and curiously attractive. When she walked, or perhaps one should say waddled, into a room, all eyes were on her and all conversation stopped: her delightful banter and absolutely magnificent use of simile and metaphor commanded full attention. Some of this comes across in her book. She was a highly emotional person, given to exaggeration which would make Baron Münchausen gasp, and this too comes across. She was ludicrous: her account of Oscar Hammerstein's romantic advances can be nothing but that. Her sheer mass was a constant frustration which was overcome to some degree by her magnificent and sumptuous voice, but resulted in her having a more prominent career as a concert singer. Neurosis aside, there is much poetry in the book, and many frank comments about her fellow artists. WRM

See also items 1541, 1565

DANCO, SUZANNE, b. 1911

341 *Abozzo per la nuova edizione delle testimonianze per Suzanne Danco.* In Italian. Roma: Il Povero Bibliofilo, 19??. 24 pp.

Contains 27 recital programs and all the non-operatic vocal music in her repertory. There are also excerpts from Italian and French press notices. RT

342 *Interpretazioni d'opera di Suzanne Danco, 1949-1950.* In Italian. Roma: Il Poverino Bibliofilo, 1949. 55 pp. Illustrated. Repertory.

A small booklet almost certainly produced by her agent, it lists all of her operatic roles. It contains tributes from Serafin, Scherchen, Perlea, Britten, Poulenc, Gui and others.

DARCLÉE, HARICLEA, 1863-1938

343 Sbârcea, George, and Ion Hartulari-Darclée. *Darclée.* In Rumanian. Bucureşti: Editura Muzicală, 1961. 261 pp. Illustrated. The

birth and death dates are given by the Library of Congress. Harold
Rosenthal gives 1868(?)-1939. Péter Várnai gives the same dates
without the question mark. Kutsch-Riemens gives 1860-1939.

DAVID, LÉON, 1867-1962

344 David, Léon. *La vie d'un tenor.* In French. Fontenay-le-Comte:
P. & O. Lussaud, 1950. viii, 405 pp. Illustrated.

DAVIES, BEN, 1858-1943

See item 1647

DAVIES, DAVID THOMAS FFRANGÇON-, 1855-1918

345 Davies, David Thomas Ffrangçon-. *David Ffrangçon-Davies: His
Life and Book.* With an introduction by Ernest Newman. London: John
Lane, 1938. xxi, 192 pp. Illustrated.

Part I (pp. 1-65) is a biography of the singer, born David Thomas
Davies at Bethesda, in Caernarvonshire, by his daughter, Marjorie.
He was ordained deacon in the Church of England February 18, 1883,
after graduating from Oxford in 1881. He obtained a curacy in
London, which enabled him to study singing with William Shakespeare
and undertake musical studies at Guildhall School. He was encouraged
to embark on a singing career by Clara Novello. His debut in opera
was as the Herald in *Lohengrin* in 1890 with the Carl Rosa Company,
and he later sang with the Augustus Harris Opera Company at Drury Lane
such roles as Alfio in *Cavalleria rusticana.* He created the role of
Cedric in Sullivan's *Ivanhoe* (1891). In later years he was best
known as a concert and oratorio singer, and highly thought of in
Europe and America, as well as England. Extensive correspondence
with Sir Edward Elgar is reproduced. Part II (pp. 77-185) consists
of a revised and abridged edition of the author's *The Singing of the
Future* (q.v.). WRM

346 ————. *The Singing of the Future.* With a preface by Sir Edward
Elgar. London: J. Lane, 1905. xxiii, 269 pp.

346-a ————. *The Singing of the Future.* With a preface by Sir
Edward Elgar. Twentieth Century Masterworks on Singing, Vol. 3.
Champaign, Ill.: Pro Musica Press, 1968. xxiii, 276 pp. Judging
from the pagination, this must be a reprint of the 1905 edition by
J. Lane, London and New York (q.v.).

DAWSON, PETER, 1882-1961

347 Dawson, Peter. *Fifty Years of Song.* London: Hutchinson, 1951.
239 pp. Illustrated.

Although he appeared briefly at Covent Garden as Schwarz in *Meistersinger* (in 1909), Dawson was known principally as a concert and

oratorio singer. A pupil of Sir Charles Santley, Dawson's first singing lessons took place in his hometown of Adelaide, South Australia. As a young singer in London, he found a way to supplement his income by making phonograph records, beginning in 1904 making cylinders for Edison Bell. He was one of the most prolific recorders in the history of sound recording, having made more than 1300 recordings between 1904 and 1958. These were frequently made under assumed names such as Hector Grant, Will Danby, Will Strong, James Osborne, George Welsh, Victor Graham, David Peters, Charles Handy, Arthur Walpole, Walter Wentworth, Fred Davies, Mr. Miles and possibly others. For a time he appeared in English music halls in disguise as a Scottish comedian, Hector Grant. He made many concert tours in England, South Africa and especially in Australia. He apparently never sang in the United States. His book is a breezy one, filled with anecdotes about other artists, told with a considerable sense of humor. There is a great deal about the history of the recording industry and its personalities, of which he was a very important part. WRM

DE ANGELIS, NAZZARENO, 1881-1962

348 De Angelis, Nazzareno. *Er Teatro de la vita e la vita der teatro* [sic]. *Sonetti romaneschi*. In Italian. Roma: N.p., 1922. 224 pp. Source of citation: British Museum General Catalogue.

DE CASTRO, CONSUELO ESCOBAR, b. 1895

See item 1631

DE GARMO, TILLY, b. 1888

See item 1743

DE GOGORZA, EMILIO, 1872-1949

See item 1581

DEL CAMPO, SOFIA, 1882-1964

349 Moran, William R. "Sofia del Campo: A Biographical Progress Report." *The Record Collector* 24, nos. 3 and 4 (March 1978), 86-95. Illustrated. Discography, pp. 90-92.

The career of Chilean soprano Sofia del Campo, known for her Victor recordings of 1927-1929, has always been somewhat of a mystery. Although she was born to a socially prominent family in Chile that did not approve of a career on the stage, del Campo nevertheless did appear in opera in Santiago, Philadelphia and elsewhere, and reviews are cited showing a repertory of at least five roles. The author cites material from the archives of the Municipal Theater in Santiago, and from personal interviews of Mme. del Campo.

DELLA CASA, LISA, b. 1919

350 Debeljevic, Dragan, b. 1921. *Ein Leben mit Lisa della Casa: oder, In dem Schatten ihrer Locken.* In German. Zürich: Atlantis-Verlag, 1975. 268 pp. Illustrated.

An entertaining, affectionate chronicle of the quarter of a century author Debeljevic spent "in the shadow of the ringlets" of his beautiful wife, prima donna Lisa della Casa. He keeps the private and artistic sides of their life together in balance, and places the highlights of her successful international career in perspective. A warm-hearted, informative book.

DELLER, ALFRED, 1912-1979

351 Hardwick, John Michael Drinkrow, b. 1924, and Mollie Hardwick. *Alfred Deller: A Singularity of Voice.* With a foreword by Sir Michael Tippett, illustrated by John Ward. London: Cassell, 1968. xii, 204 pp. Illustrated. Discography, pp. 181-190.

Alfred Deller is credited with the revival of interest in the male alto or countertenor voice and the tremendous repertory of music written for it, especially by Purcell, who was himself a countertenor. Deller was discovered and introduced to the concert platform by Sir Michael Tippett, contributor of a brief foreword to this book. The singer came from a working-class background and was largely self-taught. In addition to his accomplishments as a singer he also became a conductor of note. One chapter consists of the transcription of an interview with Deller. As a biography, this work is a straight-forward account, its value considerably enhanced by a good deal of solid information on the history of the male alto voice and the music written for it. There is no reference to Richard José, the American countertenor, whose recordings made early in this century preserved the countertenor voice until Deller's advent in the 1940s. The appendix contains an essay entitled "The Alto or Countertenor Voice" by G.M. Ardran and David Wulstan. WRM

351-a ————. *Alfred Deller: A Singularity of Voice.* With a fore-word by Sir Michael Tippett. Illustrated by John Ward. New York: F.A. Praeger, 1969. xi, 204 pp.

DEL MONACO, MARIO, 1915-1982

352 Del Monaco, Mario. *La mia vita e i miei successi.* In Italian. Milano: Ruscioni, 1982. 137 pp. Illustrated. Repertory, pp. 129-130. Index, pp. 131-137.

Always reserved about his private life, at age 67 Del Monaco decided to write his autobiography. He narrates in a well-flowing style how he first gained success in the difficult times during the war and how he maintained it for thirty years. The spirited pages are full of surprises and curious and entertaining anecdotes. RT

353 Burian, Karel Vladimir. *Mario del Monaco*. In Czech. Praha:
Supraphon, 1969. 57 pp. Illustrated.

With a 7" 33 rpm record in pocket.

354 Chedorge, André, Roland Mancini, and Jean-Louis Caussou. *Mario
del Monaco*. In French. Supplément semestriel au No. 4 d'Opéra 65,
Special No. 3. Paris: SODAL, 1965. Illustrated.

A summary of del Monaco's career up to 1965, the date of publica-
tion of this booklet. It includes an essay on his voice by Roland
Mancini, and a discussion by del Monaco of "Mes Grands Roles": Don
José, Otello, Samson and Lohengrin!

355 Segond, André, b. 1936, and Daniel Sébille. *Mario del Monaco,
ou, Un ténor de légende*. In French. Collection "Orphée." Lyon:
J.M. Laffont, 1981. 263 pp. Illustrated. Bibliography, p. 261.
Discography, pp. 243-254.

DELNA, MARIA, 1875-1932

356 Beaudu, Edouard. *Marie Delna*. In French. Paris, 1908. Illustrated. Bibliographic information taken from a dealer's catalog.

DE LUCA, GIUSEPPE, 1876-1950

See item 1565

DE LUCIA, FERNANDO, 1860-1925

357 Giorgio, Achemenide de. *Fernando de Lucia*. In Italian. Milano:
Capriolo e Massimino, 1897. 14 pp.

A pedantic, boring panegyric, along with a two-page piece entitled
"recent recollections" by the Italian dramaturgist, librettist and
impresario, Carlo D'Ormeville. RT

See also item 1680

DE LUSSAN, ZÉLIE, 1861-1949

See item 1567

DE MURO, BERNARDO, 1881-1955

358 De Muro, Bernardo. *Quand'ero Folco*. In Italian. Milano:
Gastaldi, 1955. 95 pp.

The singer narrates his life from his carefree childhood on to his
debut, with frequent jumps beyond. "Folco," the falconer of *Isabeau*
by Mascagni, was his favorite warhorse. The appendix contains advice
to aspiring singers (pp. 77-95). RT

359 Fresi, Franco. *Bernardo De Muro, una voce, una fiaba*. In Italian. Tempio Pausania: Associazione Turistica Pro Loco, 1981? xvi, 116 pp. Illustrated.

The author is Sardinian; so is the township of Gallura where Bernardo De Muro was born slightly more than 100 years ago and where this book was done to revive his memory. A lively biography, enthusiastic and affectionate, based on documents and on interviews with friends, acquaintances and admirers, studded with colorful local expressions. The book ends with recollections written by the singer's daughter (pp. 105-116). RT

See also item 1833

DE MURO LOMANTO, ENZO, 1902-1952

360 Giovine, Alfredo. *(Tenore) Enzo De Muro Lomanto*. In Italian. Biblioteca dell'Archivio delle tradizioni popolari baresi. Civiltà musicale pugliese. Bari: N.p., 1970. 20 pp. Illustrated. Bibliography, pp. 15-17. Repertory, pp. 18-19. Discography, p. 20.

A short illustrated biography of this Italian tenor, whose fame rests on a handful of recordings and the first complete recording of *Lucia di Lammermoor*, curiously omitted from the discography. The little that is known today about his career is ably presented in this booklet, based in part on passages from the autobiography, item 339 above, of Toti dal Monte, who was briefly married to him.

DENS, MICHEL, b. 1914

361 Caussou, Jean-Louis, and Roland Mancini. *Michel Dens*. In French. Paris: SODAL, 1964. 32 pp. Illustrated. Discography.

DE PASQUALI, BERNICE, 1880-1925

See item 1581

DERMOTA, ANTON, b. 1910

362 Dermota, Anton. *Tausendundein Abend; mein Sängerleben*. In German. Wien: Neff, 1978. 358 pp. Illustrated. Repertory, pp. 340-342. Index, pp. 353-358. Discography, pp. 343-352.

Dermota's life story in his own words, ending with the publication date. He discusses performances and productions in which he sang and compares his colleagues to each other. The photographs, especially those in costume, are excellent; several recent pictures are also included, even one of a 1977 performance of *Palestrina*. The discography by Jürgen E. Schmidt includes 78s, LPs, and non-commercial recordings, giving recording dates and the number of first issue and some subsequent issues. HCS

DERZHINSKAIA, KSENIIA GEORGIEVNA, 1889-1951

363 Grosheva, Elena Andreevna. *K.G. Derzhinskaia.* In Russian.
Mastera Bol'shogo teatra. Moskva: Gos. muz. izd-vo, 1952. 118 pp.
Illustrated.

See also item 1708

DESTINN, EMMY, 1878-1930

364 Destinn, Emmy. *Bibliotéka Emmy Destinnové. 1. cást. Aukce 2.,
3., 4. kvetna 1934 v paláci Clam-Gallasu v. Praze.... Vente aux
enchères de la bibliothèque Emmy Destinn (curiosités, sciences
occultes, facéties, etc.) le 2, 3, 4 mai 1934 au Palais Clam-Gallas,
à Prague....* In Czech and French? Praha: O. Pysvejc, 1934. 89 pp.

365 ————. *Sturm und Ruhe. Gedichte.* In German. Berlin: C.
Duncker, 1902. 91 pp.

366 ————. *Ve stínu modré ruze; román zašlých vašní.* Napsala Ema
Destinnová. In Czech. Praha: Druzstvotisk, 1924-1925. 3 vols. in 4.

367 Bajerová, Marie. *O Emě Destinnové.* In Czech. Praha: Vyšehrad,
1979. 143 pp. Illustrated. Bibliography, p. 143.

368 Brieger, Lothar, b. 1879. *Emmy Destinn. Maria Labia.* In German.
Persönlichkeiten, Vol. 9. Berlin, Charlottenburg: Virgilius Verlag,
1908. 32 pp. Illustrated.

369 Holzknecht, Vaclav. *Ema Destinnová. Ve slovech i obrazech.*
Translated by Adolf Langer (German), Karel and Věra Hudec (English).
In Czech, English, German. Praha: Panton, 1972. 306 pp. Illustrated.
Discography, pp. 283-297.

A trilingual biography of the famous Czech soprano. Each page is
divided into two columns; one full column contains the original text
in Czech, the other, divided in half, gives the English and German
translations. Accordingly, the translations are incomplete and the
one in English quite elementary. It is hard to evaluate this book;
it is certainly better than nothing. Profusely illustrated; with a
chronology of Destinn's life (Czech only); a good discography in
German but grouped under Czech headings, seemingly complete but
omitting dates of recording, matrix numbers and takes; and a list of
illustrations in three languages.

370 Martinková, Marie, b. 1886. *Stražska černa pani.* In Czech.
Plzeň, 1940. Information taken from the footnote to the Destinn
article in the *Enciclopedia dello Spettacolo.*

371 ————. *Život Emy Destinnové.* In Czech. 2nd ed. Pramen, sv. 2.
Plzeň: E. Kosnar, 1946. 171 pp. Illustrated. First edition could
not be located.

372 Pospíšil, Miloslav. *Veliké srdce. Život a umení Emy Destinnové.*
In Czech. Praha: Supraphon, 1974. 175 pp. Illustrated. Bibliography, pp. 173-174. Discography, pp. 158-172.

373 Rektorys, Artus. *Ema Destinnová*. In Czech. Praha: Girgal,
1936. Information taken from the footnote to the Destinn article in
the *Enciclopedia dello Spettacolo*.

DIJCK, ERNEST VAN, 1861-1923

374 Curzon, Henri de, 1861-1942. *Une gloire belge de l'art lyrique:
Ernest van Dijck, 1861-1923*. In French. Bruxelles: Librairie
nationale d'art et d'histoire, 1933. 202 pp. Illustrated.

DI MURSKA, ILMA, 1836-1889

See item 1658

DIPPEL, ANDREAS, 1866-1932

See item 1581

DI STEFANO, GIUSEPPE, b. 1921

375 Eggers, Heino. *Giuseppe di Stefano*. In German. Rembrandt-
Reihe, Bd. 56. Berlin: Rembrandt-Verlag, 1967. 64 pp. Illustrated.
Discography, pp. 30-32.

   Brief biographical essay, recounting the highlights of the tenor's
life and career up to 1966. The excellent selection of photographs
(30 pages) show the singer from age 16 through adulthood, on and off
stage. The discography is selective.

D'OISLY, EMILE MAURICE, 1883-1949

See item 1594

DOLUKHANOVA, ZARA, b. 1918

376 *Lenin Prize Winners. Soviet Stars in the World of Music*. Compiled by Alexander Lipovsky. Translated by Olga Shartse. Moscow:
Progres Publishers, 1966? 287 pp. Illustrated.

   A collection of articles about Lenin Prize winning Soviet musicians,
formerly published in Soviet magazines and books. The only vocalist
in the volume is mezzo-soprano Zara Dolukhanova. Recipient of the
Lenin Prize in 1966, she is represented by three short articles: one
written by her, the others by Aram Khachaturian, the composer, and
Irina Tsarikovskaia (pp. 278-287).

377 Mikhailovskaia, Noemi Mikhailovna. *Zara Dolukhanova*. In Russian.
Muzykanty-ispolniteli. Moskva: Gos. muzykal'noe izd-vo, 1958. 123 pp.
Illustrated.

DOMINGO, PLÁCIDO, b. 1941

378 Domingo, Plácido. *My First Forty Years*. New York: Alfred A. Knopf, 1983. 256 pp. Illustrated. Index, pp. 243-256. Discography, pp. 237-241. Chronology of Performances, pp. 221-235.

Domingo is said to be a gentle, kind, sociable individual, full of cheerful optimism, bursting with creative energy, the possessor of a wide range of musical talent and uncommon good looks. All these enviable traits come across in various degrees from the simple, unpretentious narrative of the first forty years of his life. He is generous with praise and often commendably candid about colleagues, associates, opera houses, audiences, himself. If Domingo's luck and robust good health lasts, his second forty years will be no less successful. The precise dates of all of his appearances (although incomplete for 1968) are a researcher's dream come true.

378-a ———. *My First Forty Years*. London: Weidenfeld & Nicolson, 1983. 256 pp. Illustrated. Index, pp. 243-256. Discography, pp. 237-241. Chronology of Performances, pp. 221-235.

See also items 1563, 1654

DONALDA, PAULINE, 1882-1970

379 Brothman, Ruth C. *Pauline Donalda: The Life and Career of a Canadian Prima Donna*. Montreal: Eagle Pub., 1975. xvii, 125 pp. Bibliography, pp. 124-125. Discography, pp. 112-114.

A well-organized, straightforward biography of one of the lesser stars of opera in the first quarter of the twentieth century. Donalda, born of Russian immigrant parents in Montreal, studied in Paris and made her debut on December 30, 1904, in Nice. She subsequently sang extensively in Europe; her seasons at Covent Garden included many performances opposite Caruso. Following retirement she opened an opera studio in Paris. Upon her return to Montreal before World War II, she founded the Opera Guild of Montreal. The author makes extensive use of contemporary reviews. The Appendix contains a cast list of operas produced by the Opera Guild Inc. of Montreal between 1942 and 1969 under the artistic direction of Pauline Donalda.

DONETS', MIKHAILO IVANOVICH, 1883-1941

380 Stefanovich, Mykhailo Pavlovich. *Mikhailo Ivanovich Donets'*. In Russian. Kiev: Mistetstvo, 1965. 39 pp. Illustrated.

Brief biography with illustration of the Russian bass, Donets'. His roles included Tsar Saltan, Taras Bul'ba, Ivan Susanin.

DONINELLI, ALDA, b. 1898

381 Reyes Calderón, Consuelo. *Alda Doninelli: prima donna siempre, artista de Guatemala*. In Spanish. Washington, D.C.: C. Reyes Calderón, 1980. 47 pp. Illustrated.

DORUS-GRAS, JULIE, 1805-1896

See item 1601

DRAGONETTE, JESSICA, 1904-1980

382 Dragonette, Jessica. *Faith Is a Song; the Odyssey of an American Artist.* New York: McKay, 1951. 322 pp. Illustrated.

Born in India of American parents and orphaned at an early age, Jessica Dragonette was raised by nuns from whom she learned the articles of her faith which sustained her throughout her career. She completed her vocal training with Estelle Liebling in New York, and first came to public notice as the Angel Voice in Max Reinhardt's *Miracle.* She made her radio debut shortly after the organization of the National Broadcasting Company in 1927 and thereafter devoted her singing career to broadcasting and concert work. The book contains much first-hand information for those interested in the history of broadcasting in the United States. Unfortunately, dates are seldom given. WRM

382-a ————. *Faith Is a Song; the Odyssey of an American Artist.* Paterson, N.J.: St. Anthony Guild Press, 1967. 322 pp. Illustrated.

383 ————. *Your Voice and You.* Emmaus, Pa.: Rodale Books, 1966. 243 pp. Illustrated.

One of the first "serious" artists to have continuous and sustaining programs on radio, Jessica Dragonette literally grew up with the industry. After some 22 years in radio and on concert tours, the singer turned lecturer. This book was written from her lecture material. In it she discusses the human voice from all aspects, stressing the use of the speaking voice as a vehicle for the projection of personality. She analyzes such things as pauses between words, using as an example Hamlet's "To be or not to be" as spoken by Sir John Gielgud and Sir Lawrence Olivier. WRM

DRAGULINESCU-STINGHE, ELENA

384 Dragulinescu-Stinghe, Elena. *Amintiri.* In Rumanian. Bucureşti: Editura Muzicală, 1965. 189 pp. Illustrated.

DRAMBUSKAITE, ANTANINA

385 Kalckreuth, Johannes V. *Antanina Drambuskaite.* In English, German, Lithuanian. München: F. Bruckmann, 1949. 70 pp.

DUFFEYTE

386 *Biographie de M. Duffeyte, premier ténor au Grand-Théâtre de Lyon, suivie d'une ode adressée par cet artiste à la reine des Pays-Bas, de la réponse de Sa Majesté et d'une lettre du prince d'Orange.* In French. Lyon: Imprimerie de L. Perrin, 1844. 20 pp.

DUGAZON, ROSE LOUISE (LEFÈVRE), 1755-1821

387 Le Roux, Hugues, 1860-1925, and Alfred Le Roux. *La Dugazon.* In French. Paris: F. Alcan, 1926. vii, 139 pp. Illustrated. Edition limited to 100 copies.

388 Olivier, Jean-Jacques. *Madame Dugazon de la Comédie-Italienne (1755-1821).* In French. Paris: Société Française d'Imprimerie et de Librairie, 1917. 129 pp. Illustrated. Bibliography, pp. 107-112. Repertory, pp. 91-99.

An interesting biography of the one-time star of the Opéra-Comique, based on exhaustive research. The scholarly apparatus is outstanding, the annotations are extensive and the sources identified. The bibliography and an annotated iconography add value to the book.

See also items 1596, 1738

DUPREZ, GILBERT LOUIS, 1806-1896

389 Duprez, Gilbert Louis. *L'art du chant.* In French. 2nd ed. Paris: Brandus, 18?? 212 pp. First edition could not be located.

390 ———. *Le mélodie; études complémentaires vocales et dramatiques de l'Art du chant.* In French. Paris: Heugel, 18?? xxiv, 221 pp. Illustrated.

391 ———. *Récréations de mon grand age.* In French. Paris, 1888.

392 ———. *Souvenirs d'un chanteur.* In French. Paris: Calman Lévy, 1880. 280 pp.

393 ———. *Sur la voix et l'art du chant, essai rimé.* In French. Paris: Tresse, 1822. 24 pp.

394 Elwart, Antoine Aimable Élie, 1808-1877. *Duprez, sa vie artistique; avec une biographie authentique de son maître, Alexandre Choron.* In French. Paris: V. Magen, 1838. 219 pp.

See also items 1601, 1745

DURIGO, ILONA, 1881-1943

395 Weidenmann, Jakobus, b. 1886. *Ilona Durigo, 1881-1943. Rede gehalten an der Gedenkfeier für Ilona Durigo am 30. Januar 1944 in Zürich.* In German. St. Gallen: Buchdruckerei H. Tschudy, 1944. 21 pp. Illustrated.

DVOŘÁKOVÁ, LUDMILA, b. 1923

396 Jirásková, Jiřina. *Ludmila Dvořáková.* In Czech. Praha: Supraphon, 1978. 58 pp. Illustrated.

Published with a 7" 33 rpm record in pocket.

E

EAMES, EMMA, 1865-1952

397 Eames, Emma. *Some Memories and Reflections*. New York: D. Appleton, 1927. ix, 310 pp. Illustrated.

The name of Emma Eames is found in the "great casts" of the 1890s and early 1900s in Paris, London and New York, and she rightly deserved her place beside Calvé, Melba, Nordica, the de Reszke brothers, Plançon and others of the times. G.B. Shaw admired her voice, but commented, "As an actress Miss Eames is intelligent, lady-like, and somewhat cold and colorless," an opinion shared by most critics. Eames never overcame her breeding and background of a strict New England family, and her book reflects a certain stiffness and remoteness. From their student days in the École Marchesi in Paris, Eames's principal rival was Melba, whose name is not mentioned in her book, although she makes it completely clear that she refers to Melba, whom she accuses of treachery, cunning and intrigue. Eames was married twice, first to the artist Julian Story, whom she divorced in 1907. Story figures frequently in the book, but there is only passing reference to her second husband of some twenty years, baritone Emilio de Gogorza, although the book contains a portrait labeled "Emma Eames de Gogorza." The book is important for the many references to the operatic scene during her heyday, her personal contacts with Gounod and other composers with whom she studied, and for her account of the San Francisco earthquake and the adventures of the Metropolitan Opera Company artists during the event. It must be read with some knowledge of Eames's many prejudices and foibles. WRM

397-a ———. *Some Memories and Reflections*. With a discography by W.R. Moran. Opera Biographies. New York: Arno Press, 1977. ix, 310 pp. Illustrated.

Reprint of the 1927 edition published by Appleton, New York (q.v.). The discography by William R. Moran was prepared for this edition.

398 Lawrence, Edward. *A Fragrance of Violets. The Life and Times of Emma Eames*. New York: Vantage Press, 1973. 186 pp. Illustrated.

Surely this book must qualify as one of the worst biographies ever attempted! The work has every evidence of having been printed directly from a *very* rough draft without one whit of editorial supervision or proofing. Not only is the book filled with typographical errors, distortions of fact and the most incongruous statements, but it also abounds in incomplete groupings of words which pass for sentences, incorrect grammar and just plain bad writing, not to mention a general sprinkling of malapropisms. Singers' names are misspelled and interchanged: i.e., Giuseppe de Luca (1876-1950) is confused with Fernando de Lucia (1860-1925). The author has Gigli and Pinza singing at the Metropolitan in 1915 although their debuts were in 1921 and 1926 respectively, and so on. The book might serve as a parlor game to see who can spot the most errors: participants' scores will be astronomical as the howlers must average two or three per page. WRM

See also items 1567, 1581, 1615, 1803, 1804, 1805

EASTON, FLORENCE, 1884-1955

See items 1541, 1565, 1581, 1695

EGGERTH, MARTA, b. 1912

399 Brinker, Käthe. *Das Martha Eggerth-Buch.* In German. Berlin:
H. Wendt, 1935. 52 pp. Illustrated.

The wife of the Polish tenor Jan Kiepura, Eggerth made several
films with and without her husband, some of them of operatic interest.
Her voice was mostly of operetta caliber, as were most of her stage
appearances. She did appear in *Les Contes d'Hoffmann* and *Hänsel und
Gretel* in Budapest.

See also item 688

EIZEN, ARTUR

See item 1732

EKBERG, EINAR

400 Ekberg, Einar. *Han vård om mig tar; en sångares minnen.* In
Swedish. Stockholm: Förlaget Filadelfia, 1953. 159 pp. Illustrated.

401 ———. *På estrad och autostrada; genom U.S.A. som sångare.*
In Swedish. Stockholm: Förlaget Filadelfia, 1947. 151 pp. Illustrated.

402 ———. *Ur mitt liv som sångare; minnen och intryck.* In
Swedish. 2nd ed. Stockholm: Förlaget Filadelfia, 1941. 192 pp.
Illustrated. First edition could not be located.

403 Svendlund, Karl Erik. *Einar Ekberg, en furste bland sångare.*
In Swedish. Stockholm: Förlaget Filadelfia, 1961. 139 pp. Illustrated.

ELLEVIOU, JEAN, 1769-1842

404 Curzon, Henri de, 1861-1942. *Elleviou.* In French. Paris:
F. Alcan, 1930. 121 pp. Illustrated.

See also item 1738

ELLIS, KENNETH, 1891-1972

405 Ellis, Kenneth. *Singing and Living*. Bristol: Q.E.D., 1973. 177 pp. Illustrated.

ELLIS, MARY, b. 1900

406 Ellis, Mary. *Those Dancing Years; an Autobiography*. London: John Murray, 1982. 182 pp. Illustrated. Index, pp. 176-182.

Opera alone could not satisfy Mary Ellis's versatility as a performer. She spent three successful seasons at the Metropolitan, where she made her debut in the world premiere of Puccini's *Trittico*. She was the Tsarevitch in whose arms Chaliapin used to die as Boris, and the Giannetta who passed her handkerchief to a hemorrhaging Caruso in that fateful performance of *L'Elisir d'amore*. It was David Belasco who lured her away and she had many decades of success on the legitimate stage, both in acting and singing roles, including the female lead in the world premiere of Friml's *Rose Marie*.

The book is a grab-bag of recollections of an outspoken old lady who admits to her occasional memory gaps. The interesting highlights of her active life sustain interest and, in the process, provide a fine self-portrait.

ELWES, GERVASE, 1866-1921

407 Elwes, Winefride (Feilding), and Richard Elwes. *Gervase Elwes: The Story of His Life*. London: Grayson & Grayson, 1935. vii, 319 pp. Illustrated.

ELY, SALLY FROTHINGHAM (AKERS), 1873?-1917

408 Ely, Sally Frothingham (Akers). *A Singer's Story*. Privately printed by Leonard W. Ely. Stanford University: The University Press, 19?? 151 pp.

ERB, KARL, 1877-1958

409 Müller, Maria (Gögler), b. 1900. *Karl Erb. Das Leben eines Sängers*. In German. Offenburg: Franz Huber, 1948. 190 pp. Illustrated.

See also item 1711

ERNSTER, DEZSÖ, 1898-1981

410 Fábián, Imre. *Ernster Dezsö*. In Hungarian. Nagy magyar előadómüvészek, 9. Budapest: Zenemükiadó, 1969. 47 pp. Illustrated. Repertory, pp. 46-47.

The only book devoted to the late Dezsö Ernster. The biographical section is somewhat rushed, the chronology is detailed only from 1923 to 1944. Two 7" 33 rpm records inserted in a pocket at the end of the book give a fair idea of Ernster's voice.

ERSHOV, IVAN VASIL'EVICH, 1867–1943

411 Bogdanov-Berezovskii, Valerian Mikhailovich. *Ivan Ershov.* In Russian. Zamechatel'nye russkie muzykanty. Moskva: Gos. muzykal'noe izd-vo, 1951. 73 pp.

412 IAnkovskii, Moisei Osipovich, b. 1898, editor. *Ivan Vasil'evich Ershov; stat'y, vospominaniia, pis'ma.* Sostaviteli S.V. Akimova-Ershova i E.E. Shvede. In Russian. Leningrad: Iskusstvo, 1966. 397 pp. Illustrated.

F

FAGOAGA, ISIDORO DE, 1895–1976

413 Fagoaga, Isidoro. *Domingo Garat, el defensor del Biltzar.* In Spanish. Biblioteca de cultura vasca, 37. Buenos Aires: Editorial Vasca Ekin, 1951. 242 pp. Illustrated. Bibliography, pp. 239–242.

An erudite historical biography of the famous French statesman and lawyer, Domingo Garat (1736–1799), defender of the ancient rights and rules of his native Basque land during the French Revolution and against Napoleon. His son, Pierre (or Pedro), was a fine opera singer, to whom Fagoaga devoted another biographical volume (see item 508). AM

414 ———. *La musique représentative Basque.* In French. Bayonne: La Presse, 1944. 26 pp. "Extrait du *Bulletin* de la Société des sciences, lettres et arts de Bayonne, no. 48, avril–juin 1944."

415 ———. *La opera vasca.* In Spanish. San Sebastián: Real Sociedad Vascongada de los Amigos del País, 1968. 20 pp.

416 ———. *Los poetas y el país vasco.* In Basque. Colección Ensayo, 4. San Sebastián: Sociedad Guipuzcoana de Ediciones y Publicaciones, 1969. 184 pp.

417 ———. *Retablo vasco: Huarte, Ravel, Paoli, Gayarre y Eslava.* With a foreword by José de Arteche. In Spanish. Zarauz: Editorial Icharopena, 1959. 203 pp. Illustrated.

418 ———. *Retablo vasco: Huarte, Ravel, Paoli, Gayarre, Eslava*; Prólogo de José de Arteche. In Spanish. Bilbao: Editorial La Gran Enciclopedia Vasca, 1975. 118 pp.

419 ———. *El teatro por dentro....* In Basque. Colección Reportaje-documento, 10. Bilbao: La Gran Enciclopedia Vasca, 1971. 271 pp.

420 ———. *Unamuno a orillas del Bidasoa, y otros ensayos.* In Spanish. Colección Auñamendi, 39. San Sebastián: Editorial Auñamendi, 1964. 194 pp. Illustrated.

421 ————. *Lo vasco en la vida y la obra de Cervantes.* In Spanish.
San Sebastián: Real Sociedad Vascongada de los Amigos del País, 1964.
Reprinted from the *Boletin* of the Real Sociedad Vascongada de los
Amigos del País, año 20, cuaderno 3.

See also item 508

FALCON, CORNÉLIE, 1814-1897

422 Bouvet, Charles, b. 1858. *Cornélie Falcon.* In French. Paris:
F. Alcan, 1927. ii, 151 pp. Illustrated.

FARINELLI, CARLO BROSCHI, called, 1705-1782

423 Bouvier, René. *Farinelli, le chanteur des rois.* In French.
Paris: A. Michel, 1943. 284 pp. Illustrated. Bibliography, pp.
277-281.

424 Crudeli, Tommaso, 1703-1745. *In lode del Signor Carlo Broschi
detto Farinello, musico celebre*, ode di Tommaso Crudeli. In Italian.
Firenze: A.M. Albizzini, 1734. 18 pp. Illustrated.

425 Desastre, Jean. *Carlo Broschi; kuriose Abenteuer eines
Sopranisten.* In German. Zürich, 1903. Information taken from the
Farinelli article in the *Enciclopedia dello Spettacolo.*

426 Giovine, Alfredo. *Perchè Carlo Broschi di Andria e non napole-
tano era soprannominato Farinelli?* In Italian. Biblioteca dell'-
archivio delle tradizioni popolari baresi. Bari, 1971. 16 pp.
Illustrated.

427 Haböck, Franz, d. 1921. *Die Gesangkunst der Kastraten. Erster
Notenband: A. Die Kunst des Cavaliere Carlo Broschi Farinelli.
B. Farinellis berühmte Arien.* Eine Stimmbiographie in Beispielen aus
Handschriften und frühen Drucken gesammelt und für den Studien- und
Konzertgebrauch bearbeitet und erläutert von Franz Haböck. In German.
Wien: Universal-edition, 1923. lvii, 227 pp. Illustrated.

This work was projected to comprise two volumes of text and two of
music. The text, left unfinished at the author's death, was published
in one volume under the title: *Die Kastraten und ihre Gesangkunst*
(q.v.).

428 ————. *Die Kastraten und ihre Gesangkunst, eine Gesangphysiolo-
gische, kultur- und musikhistorische Studie.* In German. Stuttgart:
Deutsche Verlags-anstalt, 1927. xvii, 510 pp. Illustrated.

This is the unfinished portion of a work which was to comprise two
volumes of text and two of music. One volume, completed before the
author's death, appeared under the title *Die Gesangkunst der Kastraten*
(q.v.). The two works are included in this bibliography because of
the many references to the art of Farinelli. In fact, half of *Die
Gesangkunst* is devoted to that singer.

429 Ricci, Corrado, b. 1858. *Burney, Casanova e Farinelli in Bologna*. In Italian. Milano: G. Ricordi, 1890. 44 pp. Illustrated.

430 Sacchi, Giovenale, 1726-1789. *Vita del cavaliere Don Carlo Broschi*. In Italian. Vinegia: Coleti, 1784. 48 pp.

431 Scribe, Augustin Eugène, 1791-1861. *Carlo Broschi*. In French. Bruxelles: Miline, Cans, 1839. 236 pp.

432 Vallejo Nágera, Juan Antonio, b. 1926. *Locos egregios*. In Spanish. Madrid: Dossat, 1977. 421 pp. Illustrated.

This remarkable book by a noted professor of psychology analyzes the close relationship of genius and mental disorders. An indicator of its quality and interest is shown by the fact that it reached 14 editions within five years after it was first published. The subjects include such notable personalities as Machiavelli, Mozart, Goya, Van Gogh, Nijinsky and Rudolf Hess. Of operatic interest are the two castrati best known to posterity: Farinelli and Caffarelli. Despite the relative brevity of the chapters devoted to these singers every researcher deserves to be guided to these analytical studies. AM

FARRAR, GERALDINE, 1882-1967

433 Farrar, Geraldine. *The Autobiography of Geraldine Farrar: Such Sweet Compulsion*. New York: Da Capo Press, 1970. xii, 303 pp. Illustrated.

Reprint of the 1938 Greystone Press, New York, edition (q.v.) published under its main title *Such Sweet Compulsion*. The alternate title was possibly chosen because the book was also reprinted in the same year by the Books for Libraries Press (q.v.)--a rather infantile promotional gimmick.

434 ————. *Geraldine Farrar; the Story of an American Singer, by Herself*. Boston: Houghton Mifflin, 1916. ix, 114 pp. Illustrated. Publication in book form of a series of articles which first appeared in the *Ladies Home Journal* from November 1915 through March 1916.

Carl Van Vechten opens his chapter on Farrar in his book *Interpreters* (1917--see item 1795 below), with the comment: "The autobiography of Geraldine Farrar is a most disappointing document; it explains nothing, it offers the reader no insights. Given the brains of the writer and the inexhaustibility of the subject, the result is unaccountable...." Perhaps critic Van Vechten expected too much from the idol of the Metropolitan Opera House who was in the midst of becoming an idol of the silver screen or, perhaps, he was too close to the scene. Viewed today, the book is interesting as much for what it does not tell as for what it tells, especially as compared with her 1938 biographical effort, *Such Sweet Compulsion* (q.v.). One aspect of the publication of this work was totally unexpected. It appeared before America had entered World War I, but at a time when public sentiment had definitely begun to crystalize with respect to Germany. Farrar, who had strong ties with Germany, in all innocence expressed her affection for much that was German in her book. Quite a public fuss was raised, and copies were withdrawn from many public libraries! No doubt this was after the original dust jacket had been removed, for this showed Miss Farrar swathed in the American flag as "Columbia." WRM

435-T ———. *Memoiren.* Translated by Adelina Sacerdoti-Thomin. In German. Mainz: Zaberndruck-Verlag, 1928. viii, 251 pp. Illustrated.

The German translation of *Geraldine Farrar; the Story of an American Singer* (q.v.).

436 ———. *Such Sweet Compulsion: The Autobiography of Geraldine Farrar.* New York: The Greystone Press, 1938. xii, 303 pp. Illustrated. Repertory, pp. 289-294. Index, pp. 297-303.

Geraldine Farrar's second attempt at autobiography takes its title from Milton, and appears in a rather novel format: in an attempt to free herself of some of the constraints of autobiography, Miss Farrar adopted the device of having alternate chapters supposedly written by her mother (who died in 1923). While the use of "Mother's Chapters" does in a way free Miss Farrar's pen in some respects, both Mother and Daughter are overly decorous throughout this book, considering the subject. We are reading the words of a rather mellowed, retired lady whose times of excitement and youthful exuberance are in the dim and distant past, and whose image, at the time of writing, was the better for leaving them there. The book should be read in conjunction with Miss Farrar's earlier (1916) work, *Geraldine Farrar; the Story of an American Singer* (q.v.), for they complement each other, although both together do not tell the whole story. All told, *Such Sweet Compulsion* is a straightforward, honest, but tame, account of a very exciting life which still deserves to be recounted. The listing of the singer's operatic roles is taken directly from Wagenknecht's *Geraldine Farrar: An Authorized Record of Her Career* (1929) (q.v.). WRM

436-a ———. *Such Sweet Compulsion: The Autobiography of Geraldine Farrar.* Freeport, N.Y.: Books for Libraries Press, 1970. xii, 303 pp. Illustrated.

Reprint of the 1938 Greystone Press, New York, edition, published as *The Autobiography of Geraldine Farrar: Such Sweet Compulsion* (q.v.).

437 *Carmen*; based on Prosper Mérimée's story, illustrated from the Jesse L. Lasky photo-play, released through the Paramount picture corporation, produced under the direction of Cecil B. De Mille and acted by Geraldine Farrar. New York: A.L. Burt, 1915. xii, 189 pp. Illustrated.

438 Humiston, William Henry, 1869-1923. *Farrar.* Little Biographies, Series 1: Musicians. New York: Breitkopf & Härtel, 1921. 18 pp. Illustrated.

A brief, but accurate, account of Farrar's life, drawn largely from the singer's 1916 autobiography, but also from Henry T. Finck's *Success in Music and How It Is Won* (see item 1615 below).

439 Nash, Elizabeth. *Always First Class: The Career of Geraldine Farrar.* Washington, D.C.: University Press of America, 1981. ix,

281 pp. Illustrated. Bibliography, pp. 249-276. Index.

This almost overly scholarly work gives a very factual account of Geraldine Farrar's career as drawn exclusively from published data, including the singer's two autobiographies and material covered in the 28-page "selected bibliography." A great deal of use has been made of Miss Farrar's voluminous scrapbooks, now housed in the Library of Congress, much from clippings (many unidentified as to source) and from publicity oriented articles. Thus no new light is shed on a number of minor mysteries connected with Miss Farrar's personal life. Nearly every sentence is documented as to source by means of notes: of the 247 pages of text, 45 are devoted to some 676 notes. Nearly every new role at the Metropolitan, from 1906 to 1922, is covered by a review of the plot (which seems unnecessary in a book of this kind) and quotations from contemporary reviews (which are of great value). Miss Farrar's motion picture career (1915-1920) is well documented. Her concert activities (1927-1932) are covered in one sentence, and the final 32 years of retirement in one paragraph. Her recordings are briefly mentioned twice; there is no discography. A final chapter, entitled "Theory and Practice," is devoted to the singer's philosophical approach to her roles and their preparation. Since this book was printed in facsimile type-script, there is no excuse for having used a machine not properly equipped with exponent type: every one of the 676 "footnote" references is set in full scale type above the line in such a way that each partially overprints the preceding line, a source of constant annoyance to the reader. WRM

440 Tellegen, Lou, b. 1883. *Women Have Been Kind; the Memoirs of Lou Tellegen*. New York: Vanguard Press, 1931. xiii, 305 pp. Illustrated.

Tellegen was an exceptionally handsome and virile ladies' man, actor and model. He was the male model for Rodin's Eternal Spring, the leading man and lover of Sarah Bernhardt, and husband to Geraldine Farrar. The marriage didn't last but it left indelible memories for both parties. Tellegen devotes a chapter (pp. 287-297) to Farrar.

440-a ————. *Women Have Been Kind; the Memoirs of Lou Tellegen*. London: Jarrolds, 1932. 288 pp. Illustrated.

441 Wagenknecht, Edward Charles. *Geraldine Farrar, an Authorized Record of Her Career*. Seattle: University Book Store, 1929. 91 pp. Illustrated. Bibliography, pp. 89-91. "This book is published in a limited edition of three hundred and fifty copies."

Pages 19 to 46 of this little book are in the form of "An Appreciation" by the author. This is followed (pp. 49-55) by a complete listing of the singer's operatic roles in Berlin, Monte Carlo, Warsaw, Paris and New York, with dates of first performances and casts. There follows a chronology of Miss Farrar's operatic appearances in New York, and (pp. 67-69) a listing of Farrar's 14 silent motion pictures, with dates, directors, casts, and one-line summaries of the plots. The discography is incomplete (no catalog numbers, no matrix numbers, no playing speeds, and dates by year only; no recognition of repeated takes). The work concludes with six typical concert programs (from 1913, 1919, 1922 and 1928) and a selected bibliography.

See also items 1565, 1581, 1615, 1695, 1792, 1795, 1796, 1803, 1805

FARRELL, EILEEN, b. 1920

See items 1654, 1758

FAURE, JEAN-BAPTISTE, 1830-1914

442 Faure, Jean Baptiste. *Une année d'études; exercises et vocalises avec théorie. Édition pour baryton ou basse.* In French. Paris: Heugel, 190? 127 pp.

443-T ————. *Un año de estudios: ejercicios y vocalizaciones con teoría, sacados del tratado La voz y el canto.* In Spanish. Paris: Heugel y cía, 1901. 2 vols.

444 ————. *Aux jeunes chanteurs, notes et conseils. Extraits du traité pratique La voix et le chant.* In French. Paris: Au Ménestrel, H. Heugel, 1890. 83 pp.

445 ————. *La voix et le chant; traité pratique.* In French. Paris: Au Ménestrel, H. Heugel, 1886. 255 pp. Illustrated.

446 Curzon, Henri de, 1861-1942. *Une gloire française de l'art lyrique: J.-B. Faure, 1830-1914.* In French. Paris: Fischbacher, 1923. 180 pp. Illustrated. Repertory, pp. 179-180.

See also item 1588

FAVART, MARIE JUSTINE BENOITE (DURONCERAY), 1727-1772

447 Dumoulin, Maurice, 1862-1911. *Favart et Madame Favart; un ménage d'artistes au XVIIIe siècle.* In French. Paris: Louis-Michaud, 1902. 191 pp. Illustrated. Bibliography, p. 6.

448 Pougin, Arthur, 1834-1921. *Madame Favart, étude théâtrale, 1727-1772.* In French. Paris: Fischbacher, 1912. 62 pp. Illustrated.

See also item 1596

FAVERO, MAFALDA, 1903-1981

449 Buscaglia, Italo. *Mafalda Favero nella vita e nell'arte.* In Italian. Milano: Ed. Italiana, 1946. 95 pp. Illustrated. Repertory, pp. 93-94.

A good biography of this famous soprano, it traces her career with affectionate admiration and obvious interest without being excessively laudatory or particularly distinguished by depth of research. The narrative ends with the years of recovery following World War II. RT

FENTON, LAVINIA, 1708-1760

See item 1597

FERRI, BALDASSARE, 1610-1680

450 Conestabile della Staffa, Giovanni Carlo, 1824-1877. *Notizie biografiche di Baldassare Ferri, musico celebratissimo*. In Italian. Perugia: Tip. Bartelli, 1846. 46 pp.

FERRIER, KATHLEEN, 1912-1953

451 Cardus, Neville, b. 1889, editor. *Kathleen Ferrier, a Memoir*. With contributions by Sir John Barbirolli, Benjamin Britten, Neville Cardus, Roy Henderson, Gerald Moore and Dr. Bruno Walter. London: Hamish Hamilton, 1954. 122 pp. Illustrated. Discography, pp. 120-122. "All proceeds from the sale of this book will be devoted to the Kathleen Ferrier Memorial Scholarship."

A memorial testimonial by her friends, the six separate articles are largely biographical but, of course, unrelated. The work was published less than a year after the singer's death, and thus is chronologically the first of three books published about the lamented artist who died in the very prime of her expanding career. The discography gives the catalog numbers but no other physical details of Ferrier's Decca and Columbia recordings published to the date of the book's issue. WRM

451-a ———. *Kathleen Ferrier, 1912-1953; a Memoir*. With contributions by Neville Cardus and others. New York: Putnam, 1955. 125 pp. Illustrated. Discography, pp. 120-125.

452 Ferrier, Winifred. *Kathleen Ferrier; Her Life*. And: *A Memoir*, edited by Neville Cardus. London: Penguin Books, 1959. 319 pp. Illustrated. Repertory, pp. 307-314. Discography, pp. 315-319.

Republished version in a Penguin paperback of Winifred Ferrier's book about her sister, originally published under the title *The Life of Kathleen Ferrier* (q.v.); bound with the work first published as *Kathleen Ferrier, a Memoir* (q.v.), edited by Neville Cardus.

453 ———. *The Life of Kathleen Ferrier*. By her sister, Winifred Ferrier. London: Hamish Hamilton, 1955. 191 pp. Illustrated. Repertory, pp. 185-191.

A sensitive, intimate and personal biography by the singer's sister, written two years after Kathleen Ferrier's death from cancer at the age of 41. Winifred and Kathleen were apparently very close to one another; when Kathleen was away on tour, she was a frequent correspondent, and her letters were filled with accounts of her daily experiences in the musical world. Winifred has shared many of these letters with the reader. Under the circumstances, one would hardly expect this book to be an unbiased and critical biographical work, and this it certainly is not. Stress is given to Kathleen's musical development and artistic triumphs. The fact that she had an unsuccessful marriage is merely hinted: her husband's first name is never mentioned. Still we are thankful for the view we do have, one-sided though it may be. An appendix is headed: "Taken from her own notebooks, here is a list of what she sang." Items which were recorded are so marked, without recordings details. WRM

454 Lethbridge, Peter. *Kathleen Ferrier*. Red Lion Lives, 3. London: Cassell, 1959. 121 pp. Illustrated.

455 Ramberg, Ruth, b. 1905. *Kathleen Ferrier: fra 14 år gammel ykeskvinne til sanger av verdensformat*. In Norwegian. Oslo: N.p., 1974. 191 pp. Illustrated. Discography, pp. 188-191.

456 Rigby, Charles, b. 1894. *Kathleen Ferrier; a Biography*. London: R. Hale, 1955. 198 pp. Illustrated.

A professional and apparently competent, straightforward and conventional biography by the biographer of Sir John Barbirolli and Sir Charles Hallé. Some (all?) copies have a tipped-in page between pages viii and ix, which reads: "Since this biography by the late Charles Rigby was printed, a biography by her sister, Winifred Ferrier, has been published. It is evident that in many instances the late Charles Rigby's manuscript contains errors of fact and expressions of opinion which are clearly wrong. These errors can be explained because the author, in the first place, did not have access to Kathleen Ferrier's personal papers, nor an opportunity for a thorough revision of his manuscript before his death. The publishers would, however, like to draw to readers' attention certain of these errors which, if they stood uncorrected, might give rise to a misleading impression...." There follow page references to nine corrections, the first of which refers to a page of "Acknowledgements and Sources" and states: "Dr. Bruno Walter, Dame Myra Hess and the Liverpool Philharmonic Society have been included inadvertently." It is not hard to read between the lines: one can speculate that this obviously "unauthorized" biography caused a stir, which was further complicated by the necessity of the embarrassing insertion on the part of the publisher. In spite of the admitted "errors," this book makes a makes a good supplementary volume to Winifred Ferrier's *The Life of Kathleen Ferrier* (q.v.). WRM

See also items 1702, 1711, 1744

FIELDS, GRACIE, b. 1898

457 Fields, Gracie. *Sing as We Go ...; Autobiography*. London: F. Muller, 1960. 203 pp. Illustrated.

458 ————. *Sing as We Go; the Autobiography of Gracie Fields*. New York: Doubleday, 1961. 216 pp. Illustrated.

FIGNER, MEDEIA IVANOVNA (MEI), 1859-1952

459 Figner, Medeia Ivanovna (Mei). *Moi vospominaniia*. In Russian. S.-Peterburg, 1912. 44 pp. Illustrated.

FIGNER, NIKOLAI N., 1857-1919

460 Figner, Nikolai N. *Vospominaniia. Pis'ma. Materialy*. In Russian. Leningrad: Muzyka, 1968. 191 pp. Illustrated. Bibliography, pp. 178-181. Index, pp. 182-190. Discography, pp. 176-177.

FINKENSTEIN, JETTKA, b. 1860-61

461 Wilda, Oscar, b. 1862. *Jettka Finkenstein, grossherzogliche hessische Kammersängerin; eine biographische skizze zum 25 jährigen Künstlerjubiläum*. In German. Breslau: Schletter'sche Buchhandlung, 1906. 31 pp. Illustrated.

FISCHER-DIESKAU, DIETRICH, b. 1925

462 Fischer-Dieskau, Dietrich. *Auf den Spuren der Schubert-Lieder; Werden, Wesen, Wirkung*. In German. Wiesbaden: F.A. Brockhaus, 1971. 371 pp. Illustrated. Bibliography, pp. 356-357.

A remarkable study by a remarkable interpreter of Schubert's entire song literature. Fischer-Dieskau unites in himself the best qualities of interpreter, musician and scholar. In this book he presents the reader with the essence of his erudition and experience. He appropriately recognizes the inseparability of the composer's life experiences, the poetry that sparked his imagination and the music. Giving nearly equal weight to each component, Fischer-Dieskau goes on to discuss the matter of interpretation, devoting an entire chapter to the interpreters of Schubert, from his nineteenth-century contemporaries to the present. The depth of Fischer-Dieskau's familiarity with his subject is formidable, and his statements carry the weight and authority that only the most knowledgeable specialist could challenge.

463 ————. *Das deutsche Lied, ein Hausbuch*. In German. Stuttgart: Deutscher Bücherbund, 1968. 495 pp. "Originaltitel: *Texte deutscher Lieder, ein Handbuch*" (q.v.).

464-T ————. *A Schubert-dalok nyomában. Születésük, világuk, hatásuk*. Translated by Dezsö Tandori. In Hungarian. Budapest: Gondolat, 1975. 425 pp. Illustrated. Bibliography, pp. 376-378. Index, pp. 379-396. Checklist of Schubert Songs, pp. 397-423.

The Hungarian translation of *Auf den Spuren der Schubert-Lieder; Werden, Wesen, Wirkung* (q.v.).

465 ————. *Texte deutscher Lieder. Ein Handbuch*. In German. DTV Taschenbücher 3091. München: Deutscher Taschenbuch-Verlag, 1968. 474 pp.

466 ———. *Wagner und Nietzsche: der Mystagoge und sein Abtrünniger*. In German. Stuttgart: Deutsche Verlags-Anstalt, 1974. 310 pp. Illustrated. Bibliography, pp. 303-305. Index.

467 Demus, Jörg, b. 1929. *Dietrich Fischer-Dieskau*. Von Jörg Demus u.a. In German. Berlin: Rembrandt, 1966. 88 pp. Illustrated. Repertory, p. 82. Discography, pp. 83-88.

The text of this book consists of four short articles. Only the first, a "Conversation with Dietrich Fischer-Dieskau," contains biographical material; the others discuss his artistry and interpretation. More than half of the book is taken up by 67 excellent photographs. The discography, with a cut-off date of 1966, is hopelessly obsolete.

468 Florent, François. *Dietrich Fischer-Dieskau*. In French. Paris: SODAL, 1967. 32 pp. Illustrated. Discography, pp. 28-32.

469 Herzfeld, Friedrich, b. 1897. *Dietrich Fischer-Dieskau*. In German. Rembrandt-Reihe, 10. Berlin: Rembrandt, 1958. 63 pp. Illustrated.

470 Whitton, Kenneth S. *Dietrich Fischer-Dieskau, Mastersinger; a Documented Study*. New York: Holmes and Meier, 1981. 342 pp. Illustrated. Bibliography, pp. 291-294. Index, pp. 295-309. Discography, pp. 313-342.

"The present book is not intended to be a 'biography'.... This 'Documented Study' attempts to put his career since his debut in 1947 into perspective by documenting his achievements and delineating those aspects of his art which make him not only unique, but, in the opinion of most good judges, a musical phenomenon.... It attempts ... to document his stage and concert appearances and his recordings by examining his work in three main musical areas: oratorio, opera and the solo song" (pp. 7-8).
The book systematically explores Fischer-Dieskau's work in the genres listed above, analyzing his approach. It includes musical examples. The discography is in alphabetical order by composer and gives the recording date, the number of first issues, and the numbers of some reissues. There are photographs of Fischer-Dieskau in costume and street clothes. HCS

470-a ———. *Dietrich Fischer-Dieskau, Mastersinger*. London: Oswald Wolff, 1981. 342 pp. Illustrated. Bibliography, pp. 291-294. Index, pp. 295-309. Discography, pp. 313-342.

See also item 1702

FLAGSTAD, KIRSTEN, 1895-1962

471 Flagstad, Kirsten, and Louis Biancolli. *The Flagstad Manuscript*. New York: Putnam, 1952. xix, 293 pp. Illustrated. Repertory, pp. 282-283. Index, pp. 285-293.

An autobiography taken down by Biancolli from Flagstad's dictation, it has the merit of being the singer's story in her own words, from her point of view, and with her biases; this is the one place where Flagstad tells her side of what happened to her in Norway during and after World War II and explains her troubles in getting her career restarted. The coverage of the years before 1935 is also better here than in any other English-language source. Internal evidence suggests that Flagstad dictated the last chapters in the early months of 1952; she projects her schedule for the rest of that year through the end of 1953, saying she is positive her last public appearance will be on December 12, 1953. Thus there is nothing here about the last decade of her life. HCS

471-a ———. *The Flagstad Manuscript*. New York: Arno Press, 1977. xix, 293 pp. Illustrated. Repertory, pp. 282-283. Index, pp. 285-293.

Reprint of the 1952 edition published by Putnam, New York (q.v.).

472 Flagstad, Kirsten, and Torstein Gunnarson. *Remember Me: utsyn over en kunstnergjerning*. Kirsten Flagstad i radiosamtale med Torstein Gunnarson i Norsk rikskringkasting 29. desember 1961. In Norwegian and English. Oslo: Gyldendal, 1975. 44 pp. Illustrated.

473 McArthur, Edwin. *Flagstad; a Personal Memoir*. New York: A.A. Knopf, 1965. xvi, 343, ix pp. Illustrated. Repertory, pp. 340-343. Index, pp. i-ix.

This biography of Kirsten Flagstad, written by her accompanist, covers the years from 1935 to the end of her life more fully than the years before 1935; this is natural, since McArthur did not meet Flagstad till after her debut at the Metropolitan Opera. It is valuable for the details it contains about the Flagstad-Melchior feud, her troubles in Norway immediately after World War II, the reprints of McArthur's letters to the Norwegian authorities and his testimony to the Norwegian court. The list and chronology of repertoire is almost identical to that in Biancolli's *Flagstad Manuscript* (q.v.). Appendix A, pp. 311-339, contains letters McArthur wrote to the Norwegian authorities to try to clear Flagstad's name after the war and some of his testimony to the Norwegian court. Errata sheet laid in after p. 300. HCS

473-a ———. *Flagstad: A Personal Memoir*. Da Capo Press Music Reprint Series. New York: Da Capo Press, 1980. xvi, 343, ix pp. Illustrated. Repertory, pp. 340-343. Index, pp. i-ix.

Reprint of the 1965 edition published by A.A. Knopf, New York (q.v.).

474 Rein, Aslaug. *Kirsten Flagstad*. In Norwegian. Oslo: Ernst G. Mortensen Forlag, 1967. 287 pp. Illustrated. Bibliography, p. 268. Repertory, pp. 269-271. Index, pp. 278-287. Discography, pp. 272-277.

The only Flagstad biography so far that traces her life to its conclusion but was not written by anyone closely associated with her during the years in which she was internationally famous. Especially valuable for photographs, not reproduced elsewhere, of Flagstad's activities in Scandinavia both early and late in her career and of her family. The discography is incomplete and inaccurate. HCS

475 Schäfer, Jürgen. *Kirsten Flagstad.* In German. Sammlung Jürgen Schäfer. Hamburg: Jürgen Schäfer, 1972. Discography. Unverified; data obtained from secondary literature.

See also items 1545, 1606, 1607, 1608, 1623, 1716, 1719, 1792, 1822

FLETA, MIGUEL, 1893-1938

476 Torres, Luís, and Andrés Ruiz Castillo. *Miguel Fleta; el hombre, el "divo", y su musa.* In Spanish. Zaragoza: El Heraldo de Aragón, 1940. 282 pp. Illustrated.

FODOR, JOSEPHINE

See Mainvielle-Fodor, Josephine

FØNSS, JOHANNES, b. 1884

477 Fønss, Johannes. *Bagom breve.* In Danish. København: Chr. Erichsens Forlag, 1962. 186 pp. Illustrated.

478 ———. *Ham, der leder efter operaen.* In Danish. Aarhus: Soren Lunds Forlag, 1958. 182 pp. Illustrated.

479 ———. *Kvaerulantens Klagesange.* In Danish. København: Privat Tryk, 1959. 70 pp. Illustrated.

480 ———. *Med den KGL Thespiskerre.* In Danish. København: Chr. Erichsens Forlag, n.d. 144 pp. Illustrated.

481 ———. *Mennesker, musikfolk- og minder; fra kirken til teatrene.* In Danish. København: C. Erichsen, 1960. 177 pp. Illustrated. Index, pp. 173-176.

Twenty short memoirs and incidental essays on a variety of topics. Two deal with Covent Garden (one was written for the theater's 100th anniversary), one with opera in England, four concern Richard Strauss (one on *Rosenkavalier*, one on *Ariadne auf Naxos*), one is about demonstrations against German music (e.g., Wagner) in Italy during World War I, another concerns Dorothy Larsen (the Danish dramatic soprano), one is about Frida Leider, Melchior and Slezak, and another about Frida Leider. For the most part they are quite short. There is a great deal of personal recollection and much recounting of casts and dates of performances (e.g., the first performance of *Tristan* in Denmark was on 14 February 1914; the first *Parsifal* was on 9 April 1915). An interesting, entertaining small volume. PHS

482 ———. *Saerlig husker jeg; erindringer om politikere og andre personligheder.* In Danish. København: C. Erichsen, 1950. 112 pp. Illustrated. Index, pp. 114-115.

Fønss, sometime bass with Covent Garden and elsewhere, met many important people before turning impresario and writer. None of the

sketches in this volume are of musicians, though there is an interesting memoir of Max Reinhardt, and a few itemizations of individual
performances Fønss attended (e.g., Reinhardt's production of *Fledermaus*,
which premiered on 6 April 1930). On the whole, a well-written book,
with only occasional material about operas, singers and productions.
PHS

FOHSTRÖM-VON RODE, ALMA EVELINA, 1856-1936

483 Rode, V. von. *Alma Fohström*, kirjoiitanut Paul Ervé (pseud.).
Tekijän käsikirjoituksesta suomentanut Toivo Haapanen. In Finnish.
Helsingissä: Kustannusosakeyhtiö Otava, 1920. 123 pp. Illustrated.

FOLESCU, GHEORGHE

484 Buescu, Corneliu. *Gheorghe Folescu*. In Rumanian. Bucureşti:
Editura Muzicală, 1966. 139 pp. Illustrated.

FORMES, KARL JOHANN FRANZ, 1815-1889

485 Formes, Karl Johann Franz. *Aus meinem Kunst- und Bühnenleben;
Erinnerungen des Bassisten*. Bearbeitet von Wilhelm Koch. In German.
Köln: Gehly, 1888. 122 pp. Illustrated.

486 ————. *Karl Formes' Method of Singing for Soprano and Tenor*.
San Francisco, 1885. 165 pp.

487-T ————. *My Memoirs*. Autobiography of Karl Formes. San Francisco: J.H. Barry, 1891. 240 pp. Illustrated.

FORNIA, RITA, 1878-1922

488 Moran, William R. "Rita Fornia." *The Record Collector* 10, nos.
10-11 (September-October 1956), 216-237. Illustrated. Discography,
pp. 232-233.

The San Francisco-born soprano (née Regina Newman), pupil of Emil
Fischer, Sofia Scalchi and Selma Nicklass-Kemper, was for many years
a well-known and admired figure at the Metropolitan, where she made
her debut in 1907, after her initial career in Europe. She was especially admired in the role of Suzuki in *Madama Butterfly*. She sang
both soprano and mezzo-soprano roles, once substituting at short
notice for Marcella Sembrich as Rosina in the *Barber*, again for Eames
in *Il Trovatore* and for Gadski in *Don Giovanni*. She created roles in
Mme. Sans-Gêne and *Suor Angelica*. Material for the article was
supplied by members of the Newman family, as well as Geraldine Farrar
and other personal friends.

FORSELL, JOHN, 1868-1941

489 Ljungberger, Erik. *John Forsell*. In Swedish. Stockholm: H.W. Tullberg, 1916. 43 pp. Illustrated.

490 Stockholm. Kungliga Teatern. *Boken om John Forsell; utgiven av Operan på John Forsells 70-årsdag den 6 nov. 1938*. Edited by Folke Gustavson. In Swedish. Stockholm: P.A. Norstedt & söner, 1938. 112 pp. Illustrated.

See also item 1617

FRANCILLO-KAUFMANN, HEDWIG, 1878-1948

491 Francillo-Kaufmann, Hedwig. *Von Caruso zu dir; Gesangstechnisches aus der Praxis und für die Praxis*. Redigiert und bearbeitet von Eugen Gottlieb-Hellmesberger. In German. Wien: Universal-Edition, 1935. 55 pp. Index, p. 55.

FRANKLIN, DAVID, 1908-1973

492 Franklin, David. *Basso cantante: An Autobiography*. London: Duckworth, 1969. 232 pp. Illustrated. Index, pp. 228-232.

David Franklin's operatic career began at Glyndebourne before World War II. He became a member of Covent Garden after the war, but had to give up singing at mid-career when the aftereffects of a thyroid operation impaired his voice. Out of desperation he launched a second career and became a successful lecturer, radio and television commentator and program host. The book is an intelligent recapitulation of his experiences, trials, successes, failures and reemergence, told with candor and a fine sense of understated humor.

FRASCHINI, GAETANO, 1816-1887

See item 1129

FREMSTAD, OLIVE, 1868-1951

493 Cushing, Mary Fitch (Watkins). *The Rainbow Bridge*. New York: Putnam, 1954. 318 pp. Illustrated. Quotation from letter to W.R.M. from Mrs. Cushing, dated January 12, 1955: "Olive Fremstad was born in Stockholm on *February 16, 1868*. I have seen her birth certificate. Her baptismal name was ANNA OLIVIA."

This book should at least be subtitled "The Story of Seven Intimate Years with Olive Fremstad" for that is exactly what it is from beginning to end. Mary Fitch Watkins was a seventeen-year-old schoolgirl when, in 1911, she first saw and heard Fremstad as the Walküre Brünnhilde. She was so entranced by the great singing-actress, she devised a means of meeting her. Fremstad was so pleased that she offered her the position of companion, secretary and general "buffer" as she liked to call her, and took Miss Watkins to Europe with her in the summer of 1911. For the next seven years, until Mary Watkins joined the women's motor corps and went to France in the Spring of 1917, she was Fremstad's constant companion, secretary, dresser, whipping-girl, and above all, devoted defender. This, then, is a detailed biography of seven years in the life of the singer. The few facts about her early life are incidental; what the author has to say about Fremstad during the last thirty-three years of her life is said in the final two-and-one-half pages. A fascinating and important book. WRM

493-a ———. *The Rainbow Bridge*. With a discography by W.R. Moran. New York: Arno Press, 1977. 318, vi pp. Illustrated. Discography, pp. i-vi.

Reprint of the 1954 edition published by Putnam, New York (q.v.). The discography by William R. Moran was prepared for this edition.

See also items 1795, 1796

FRENI, MIRELLA, b. 1935

494 Chédorge, André. *Mirella Freni*. In French. Les Trésors de l'Opéra, no. 5. Paris: Opéra International, 1979. 64 pp. Illustrated. Discography, pp. 61-64.

A somewhat biased summary of Freni's career, nonetheless interesting and informative. The discography seems to be complete up to the time of publication; surprisingly, it includes a Rome radio broadcast of *I Puritani* "hors catalogue," which is the French way of saying it is a private recording.

FRICK, GOTTLOB, b. 1906

495 Hey, Hans. *Gottlob Frick*. In German. München: Harald Herbrecht, 1968. 35 pp. Illustrated.

FRIEDLEIN, CHRISTINE

496 Friedlein, Christine. *Erinnerungsblätter*. *Erinnerungen einer Hofopernsängerin*. In German. Karlsruhe: C.F. Müller, 1923. 59 pp.

FUENTES, JOVITA, 1895-1978

497 Hernandez Chung, Lilia. *Jovita Fuentes; a Lifetime of Music*. Manila: Jovita Fuentes Musical Society, 1978. 184 pp. Illustrated. Bibliography, p. 183.

FUGÈRE, LUCIEN, 1848-1935

498 Fugère, Lucien, and Raoul Duhamel. *Nouvelle méthode pratique*

de chant français par l'articulation. In French. Paris: Enoch et cie, 1929. xii, 90 pp. Illustrated.

499 Boschot, Adolphe, b. 1871. *Chez les musiciens (du XVIIIe siècle à nos jours).* In French. Paris: Plon-Nourrit, 1922. 285 pp.

The only chapter about a singer deals with Lucien Fugère; the other biographees are mostly composers.

500 Duhamel, Raoul. *Lucien Fugère, chanteur scénique français.* Préface de Sacha Guitry. In French. Paris: B. Grasset, 1929. 203 pp. Illustrated.

See also item 1588

FUJIWARA, YOSHIE, 1898-1976

501 Fujiwara, Yoshie. *Ruten shichijugonen* [A biography of 75 years]. In Japanese. Tokyo, 1974. 255 pp.

FUOCO, SOFIA, d. 1916

502 Rivalta, Camillo, b. 1876. *Il tramonto di una diva (Sofia Fuoco). Note di storia teatrale faentina.* In Italian. Faenza: Tip. Novelli e Castellani, 1916. 15 pp.

G

GABRIELESCU, GRIGORE, 1859-1915

503 Massoff, Ioan. *Glorioasa existenţă a tenorului Grigore Gabrielescu.* In Rumanian. Bucureşti: Editura muzicală, 1974. 148 pp. Illustrated.

GABRIELLI, CATARINA, 1730-1796

See items 1597, 1612

GADSKI, JOHANNA, 1872-1932

See item 1581

GAGLIARDI, CECILIA

See item 1731

GALEFFI, CARLO, 1882-1961

504 Celletti, Rodolfo. *Carlo Galeffi e La Scala.* In Italian. Milano: Teatro alla Scala, Electa, 1977. 102 pp. Illustrated. Index,

pp. 99-100. Discography, pp. 96-97. Chronology of Performances, pp. 91-95.

Celletti's book complements an earlier volume about Galeffi by Marchetti (q.v.) that was published in 1973. While that book merely set into a narrative the facts of his career, Celletti attempts to write a traditional biography. He tries to find answers to questions posed at the beginning of his work: what made Galeffi a unique interpreter, how did his work reflect the musical inheritance of his predecessors and, more significantly, who was Carlo Galeffi the man? The large number of excellent photographs, surprisingly, do not duplicate the ones in the equally well-illustrated Marchetti book. Anyone interested in the life and career of this singer should be familiar with both works.

505 Guimarães, Beatriz Leal. *A deslumbrante carreira do célebre barítono Carlo Galeffi.* In Portuguese. Rio de Janeiro: Iguassú, 1962. 74 pp. Illustrated.

506 Marchetti, Arnaldo. *Carlo Galeffi: una vita per il canto.* Prefazione di Franco Abbiati. In Italian. Roma: Staderini, 1973. 108 pp. Illustrated. Index, pp. 103-108. Discography, pp. 99-101.

The brief biographical section of the first chapter makes use of Galeffi's own autobiographical attempt left in manuscript. Unfortunately, he abandoned the project and the existing two hundred pages cover his life story only up to the beginning of his career. Marchetti acknowledges the help he received from others, particularly from Riccardo Galeffi, nephew of the singer. The memorabilia placed at his disposal is the main source for the bulk of the book, which is nothing more than an engagement-by-engagement recounting (complete with casts) of his long career of five decades. This is, then, more a narrative of his appearances than a biography in the conventional sense. As such it complements the work by Celletti (q.v.) published four years later. The simple discography, apparently complete, includes matrix numbers. Beautifully printed, generously illustrated.

GALLI-CURCI, AMELITA, 1882-1963

507 Le Massena, Clarence Edward, b. 1868. *Galli-Curci's Life of Song.* New York: The Paebar Company, 1945. 336 pp. Illustrated. Repertory, p. 331. Discography, pp. 333-336.

The only Galli-Curci biography to date, written with her knowledge and approval, and with assistance given "in supplying data and material" by her second husband, Homer Samuels. In addition, the author acknowledges that Samuels read the manuscript and made "suggestive modifications," a somewhat unfortunate choice of words. Not surprisingly, the author views the events of the diva's life from her vantage point and he is generous with praise whenever possible. This does not detract from the overall value of the book; the basic facts are all there, and the lady has scored enough international successes to allow her biographer to exploit them without the distortion of truth. It is only with respect to the events toward the end of her career where the author juggles words to cast the best possible light on some unfortunate events, including the disastrous Budapest engagement of 1930 and the comparably ill-advised Chicago *La Bohème*, an unsuccessful attempt at a comeback in 1936.

The final chapter, "1938 and Beyond," is a short statement about her life in retirement. Despite its slight bias an interesting, informative biography. The rather elementary discography that completes the book is incomplete and inaccurate.

507-a ————. *Galli-Curci's Life of Song*. An Opera Classics Book. Beverly Hills, Calif.: Monitor Book Co., 1978. 280 pp. Illustrated. Index, pp. 275-280. Discography, pp. 267-273.

This is a newly typeset edition, with some supplementary material, of the first edition (1945) of Le Massena's book (q.v.). It replaces the concluding chapter with another short summary of her retirement years until her death by William Seward. There is also appended an interview with Galli-Curci conducted by Seward. Other new features are a chronology of her performances at the Metropolitan and with the Chicago Opera, both with casts; and a good discography (minus take numbers) of her 78 rpm records with cross-references to the major LP transfers. An index has been prepared for this edition; it enhances the usefulness of the book.

See also items 1541, 1565, 1581, 1588, 1695, 1792, 1803, 1807

GALLI-MARIÉ, CELESTINE, 1840-1905

See item 1588

GARAT, PIERRE JEAN, 1762-1823

508 Fagoaga, Isidoro, 1895-1976. *Pedro Garat, "el Orfeo de Francia."* In Spanish. Buenos Aires: Editorial Vasca Ekin, 1948. 280 pp. Illustrated. Bibliography, pp. 275-277.

509 Lafond, Paul, b. 1847. *Garat, 1762-1823*. In French. Paris: Calmann Lévy, 1899. 363 pp. Illustrated.

510 Miall, Bernard. *Pierre Garat, Singer and Exquisite, His Life and His World (1762-1823)*. New York: C. Scribner's Sons, 1913. 364 pp. Illustrated.

510-a ————. *Pierre Garat, Singer and Exquisite; His Life and His World (1762-1823)*. London: T.F. Unwin, 1913. 364 pp. Illustrated.

511 Deleted

GARCIA, EUGÉNIE (MAYER), 1818-1880

See item 1601

GARCIA, MANUEL, 1805-1906

512 Garcia, Manuel. *The Art of Singing*; Part I. Boston: Ditson,
18?? 43 leaves.

512-a ———. *The Art of Singing*. Philadelphia: O. Ditson, T.
Presser distributor, 194?

513-T ———. *Complete School of Singing*. Boston: Ditson, n.d.

514-T ———. *École de Garcia: traité complet de l'art du chant*.
Translated by Wilhelm Mangold, C. Wirth. In French and German.
Mayence: B. Schott, 1847. 2 vols.

515-T ———. *Garcia's Complete School of Singing in Which the Art
Is ... Developed in a Series of Instructions and ... Examples*. London: Cramer, n.d. 66 pp.

516-T ———. *Garcia's New Treatise on the Art of Singing. A Compendious Method of Instruction, with Examples and Exercises for the
Cultivation of the Voice*. Revised ed. Boston: C.H. Ditson & Co.,
18??

The English translation of his *Nouveau traité de l'art du chant*
(q.v.).

516-T-a ———. *Garcia's New Treatise on the Art of Singing. A
Compendious Method of Instruction, with Examples and Exercises for
the Cultivation of the Voice*. London: Leonard & Co., 18?? 82 pp.
Illustrated.

The English translation of his *Nouveau traité de l'art du chant*
(q.v.).

517-T ———. *Garcia's Treatise on the Art of Singing. A Compen-
dious Method of Instruction, with Examples and Exercises for the
Cultivation of the Voice*. Edited by Albert Garcia. London: Leonard
& Co., 1924. 75 pp.

518-T ———. *Hints on Singing*. Translated by Beata Garcia. London:
E. Ascherberg & Co., 1894. vii, 75 pp. Illustrated.

518-T-a ———. *Hints on Singing*. Introduction by Byron Cantrell.
Canoga Park: Summit Pub. Co., 1970.

519 ———. *Mémoire sur la voix humaine, présenté à l'Académie des
sciences en 1840*. Réimpression augmentée de quelques observations
nouvelles sur les sons simultanés et suivie du rapport de la commission de l'Académie des sciences du 12 avril 1841. In French.
Paris: E. Duverger, 1847. 39 pp.

520 ———. *Nouveau traité sonnaire de l'art du chant*. In French.
Paris: M. Richard, 1856. 100 pp.

521-T ———. *Observaciones sobre la voz humana. Contribución a la
historia de la laringoscopia*. Translated by Servando Taio y Calvo.
In Spanish. Madrid: R. Fé, 1889. 16 pp.

522 ———. *Observations physiologiques sur la voix humaine.* In French. Paris: Masson, 1855. 16 pp.

523-T ———. *Scuola di Garcia; trattato completo dell'arte del canto.* Translated by Alberto Mazzucato. In Italian. Milano: G. Ricordi, 1849? 2 vols. in 1.

524 ———. *Traité complet de l'art du chant.* In 2 parts. In French. Paris, 1831.

525 Mackinlay, Malcolm Sterling, b. 1876. *Garcia the Centenarian and His Times; Being a Memoir of Manuel Garcia's Life and Labours for the Advancement of Music and Science.* Edinburgh: W. Blackwood and Sons, 1908. xii, 335 pp. Illustrated.

526 Richard, Paulin. *Notice sur l'invention du laryngoscope, ou miroirs du larynx (Garcia's Kehlkopfspiegel du Dr. Czermak), servant d'introduction à la seconde édition des observations physiologiques sur la voix humaine.* Traduction française d'un mémoire publié dans les *Proceedings of the Royal Society,* London, vol. vii, no. 13, 1855. In French. Paris: J. Claye, 1861. 36 pp.

527 Tapia, A.G. *Manuel Garcia. Su influencia en la laringologia y en el arte del canto.* In Spanish. Madrid, 1905. vii, 228 pp.

See also items 1643, 1681, 1682, 1689, 1745

GARCIA, MANUEL DEL POPOLO VICENTE, 1775-1832

528 Garcia, Manuel del Popolo Vicente. *340 exercises, thèmes variés et vocalises,* composés pour ses élèves par Manuel Garcia (père). In French. 4th ed. Paris: Heugel, 1868. 101 pp. The first edition could not be located.

See also items 1562, 1681, 1682, 1689, 1745

GARDEN, MARY, 1877-1967

529 Garden, Mary, and Louis Biancolli. *Mary Garden's Story.* New York: Simon and Schuster, 1951. xii, 302 pp. Illustrated.

During her long and exciting career Mary Garden left a trail of stories and anecdotes, surely not all of them apocryphal! Yet few of them, and certainly none of the sensational ones, find their way into this rather tame and disappointing book. If indeed Mary Garden was the model for the character of Easter Brandes in critic James Gibbons Huneker's shocking 1919 novel, *Painted Veils* (as it is generally supposed that she was), one would never guess it from *Mary Garden's Story.* While the book is disappointing for what it omits, there is much of value once the reader accepts the fact that this is a very much watered-down version of only the professional life of an important artist. WRM

529-a ———. *Mary Garden's Story*. London: Michael Joseph, 1952. 276 pp. Illustrated. Index, pp. 273-276.

530 Huneker, James Gibbons, 1857-1921. *Bedouins*. New York: Scribner, 1920. vii, 271 pp. Illustrated. The first 44 pages of the book are a chapter devoted to Mary Garden.

531 Kahn, Otto Hermann, 1867-1934. *Of Many Things; Being Reflections and Impressions on International Affairs, Domestic Topics and the Arts*. New York: Boni & Liveright, 1926. 437 pp.

This book, dealing mostly with finance, economic conditions domestic and foreign, also contains some addresses and essays by the powerful chairman of the Metropolitan Opera Board. There is a chapter on the Met, one on Antonio Scotti and one on Mary Garden. Considering the scarcity of material about Scotti, this book deserves to be included.

See also items 1541, 1581, 1615, 1792, 1795, 1796, 1803, 1807

GARRISON, MABEL, 1886-1963

See item 1695

GASTÉ, JACQUELINE (ENTÉ), b. 1928

532 Gasté, Jacqueline (Enté). *Bonsoir mes souvenirs*; by Line Renaud (pseud.). In French. Paris: Flammarion, 1963. 252 pp.

GATES, LUCY, 1885-1951

See item 1541

GAUVADAN FAMILY

See item 1738

GAY, MARIA, 1879-1943

See item 1731

GAYARRE, JULIÁN, 1844-1890

533 Arredondo, Máximo de. *Julián Gayarre! Estudio critico-biografico*. In Spanish. Madrid: Edición Minuesa de los Rios, 1890. 75 pp. Illustrated.

534 Beramendi, E.F. *Julián Gayarre y Pablo Sarasate*. In Spanish. Buenos Aires: "Centro Navarro," 1944. 182 pp. Illustrated.

535 Carmena y Millán, Luis, 1845-1890. *Cosas del pasado. Música, literatura y tauromaquia.* In Spanish. Madrid: Imprenta Ducazal, 1904. xv, 281 pp.

Pages 3-18 of this book are a chapter entitled "El tenor Gayarre."

536 Castro y Serrano, José de, 1829-1896. *Julián Gayarre.* In Spanish. Madrid, 1890. Entry taken from the article on Gayarre in the *Enciclopedia Universal Ilustrada Europeo-Americana* (Espasa-Calpe).

537 *Centenario de Sarasate y Gayarre. Articulos varios.* In Spanish. Pamplona, 1944. Entry obtained from secondary literature.

538 Enciso, Julio, 1849-1922. *Memorias de Julián Gayarre*; escritas por su amigo y testamentario, Julio Enciso. In Spanish. Madrid: Enrique Rubiños, 1891. 374 pp. Illustrated.

538-a ————. *Memorias de Julián Gayarre*; escritas por su amigo y testamentario, Julio Enciso. In Spanish. Colección Ipar, 3. Pamplona: Editorial Gómez, 1955. 273 pp. Illustrated.

539 Gimeno, Amalio Gimeno y Cabanas, conde de, 1852-1936. *La laringe de Gayarre.* In Spanish. Madrid, 1935. Entry obtained from secondary literature.

540 González, Anselmo. *Gayarre.* In Spanish. Vida anecdótica los grandes artistas liricos y dramáticos. Paris: Casa editorial franco-ibero-americana, ca. 1930. 213 pp. Illustrated.

541 Hernández Girbal, Florentino, b. 1902. *Julián Gayarre, el tenor de la voz de ángel.* In Spanish. Barcelona: Ediciones Lira, 1955. 606 pp. Illustrated. Bibliography, pp. 605-606. Repertory, p. 599. Index, pp. 600-604. Chronology, pp. 571-573. Another edition by the same publisher was issued in 1970.

541-a ————. *Julián Gayarre, el tenor de la voz de ángel.* In Spanish. Opera Biographies. New York: Arno Press, 1977. 606 pp. Illustrated. Bibliography, pp. 605-606. Repertory, p. 599. Index, pp. 600-604. Chronology, pp. 571-573.

Reprint of the 1955 edition published by Ediciones Lira, Barcelona (q.v.).

542 ————. *Una vida triunfal: Julián Gayarre, biografia novelesca.* In Spanish. Vidas extraordinarias del siglo XIX. Madrid: Biblioteca Atlántico, 1931. 356 pp. Repertory, p. 356.

543 Horcajada, Romulo. *Vida y gloria de Gayarre.* In Spanish. Barcelona: Ediciones G.P., 1963. Illustrated.

544 Muñoz, Matilde. *Julián Gayarre. Suplemento de "Lecturas."* In Spanish. N.d. Entry obtained from secondary literature.

545 Peña y Goñi, Antonio, 1846-1896. *Arte y patriotismo. Gayarre y Masini.* In Spanish. Madrid: Impr. E. Minuesa, 1878. Entry obtained from secondary literature. 2nd edition of 1883 has 40 pages.

546 Perillan y Buxo, Eloy, 1848-1889. *Historia artistica y apuntes biograficos del eminente tenor español Julián Gayarre*. In Spanish. Habana, 1890. Entry obtained from secondary literature.

547 Sanjuan Urmeneta, José María, 1937-1968. *Gayarre*. In Spanish. Navarra: Temas de Cultura Popular, no. 9. Pamplona: Diputación Foral de Navarra-Dirección de Turismo, Biblioteca y Cultura Popular, 1968. 31 pp. Illustrated.

See also items 417, 418, 1620, 1680, 1756, 1757

GAZZANIGA, MARIETTA, 1824-1884

548 *Un recuerdo a Marietta Gazzaniga*. In Spanish. La Habana: La Habanera, 1858. 16 pp.

GEDDA, NICOLAI, b. 1925

549 Gedda, Nicolai. *Gavan är inte gratis*; Nicolai Gedda berätter sitt liv för Aino Sellermark. In Swedish. Stockholm: Bonnier, 1977. 227 pp. Illustrated. Repertory, pp. 213-219. Index, pp. 225-228. Discography, pp. 219-224.

Sellermark is a Swedish journalist and this is a straightforward, well-written journalistic biography. It is narrated in the first person, but it is unlikely that Gedda had much to do with the actual writing. There are a few personal anecdotes, but most of the work is friendly, uncritical and harmless. The repertory is arranged by the nationality of composers; the disorganized discography is mostly chronological, lacking casts and record numbers. PHS

GERHARDT, ELENA, 1883-1961

550 Gerhardt, Elena. *Recital*. With a preface by Dame Myra Hess. London: Methuen, 1953. x, 183 pp. Illustrated. Index, pp. 181-183. Discography, pp. 172-180.

An unpretentious autobiography, concentrating on the highlights of a distinguished career that was launched with the active assistance (as piano accompanist) of the great conductor Arthur Nikisch. He accompanied her on many more occasions, in Germany and elsewhere, and Gerhardt gives due recognition to her artistic benefactor. Nikisch was also the conductor on the occasion of her operatic debut in the title role of Mignon, in 1905, two years after her concert debut. Her operatic career was short, as she soon turned exclusively to recital work. Mention of nonmusical matters of her life are minimal. The book contains an essay ("Elena Gerhardt and the Gramophone") and a discography by Desmond Shawe-Taylor. The discography is in need of revision.

550-a ————. *Recital*. With a preface by Dame Myra Hess. St. Clair Shores, Mich.: Scholarly Press, 1972. x, 183 pp. Illustrated.

Reprint of the 1953 edition by Methuen, London (q.v.).

See also item 1702

GERSTER, ETELKA, 1855-1920

551 Gerster, Etelka. *Stimmführer. Guida vocale....* In German, Italian, French, English. Berlin, 1907. 41 pp. Information taken from a dealer's catalog.

GERVILLE-RÉACHE, JEANNE, 1882-1915

552 McPherson, James B., and William R. Moran. "Jeanne Gerville-Réache." *The Record Collector* XXI, nos. 3 & 4 (July 1973), 51-84. Illustrated. Discography, pp. 73-76. Includes a special appendix (pp. 79-83) on the performances of the National Opera Co. of Canada, 1913-1914.

This article on the great French contralto, together with a selection from reviews of a number of performances, seems to be the only extensive biographical work available. She is considered by many of today's record collectors to have been one of the greatest contraltos to have made recordings. Unfortunately, her untimely death in her thirty-second year cut short a career which might have proved to be one of the great ones in opera and concert. The authors had assistance from the singer's relatives in preparing the article. The discography is by W.R. Moran.

GHIAUROV, NIKOLAI GEORGIEV, b. 1929

553 Grenèche, Philippe. *Nicolai Ghiaurov.* In French. Les trésors de l'Opéra, no. 3. Paris: Opéra International, 1979. 64 pp. Illustrated. Discography, pp. 59-62.

A short, sketchy biography, barely more than the highlights of his career, set in an easy-flowing narrative. Some of his important roles are discussed in detail. The discography seems complete for Western commercial recordings, but excludes the ones made in the U.S.S.R. early in his career.

554 Kazaka, Teniu. *Nikolai Ghiaurov. Otkrandnati migove.* In Bulgarian. Sofiia: Nar. mladezh, 1972. 156 pp. Illustrated.

GHIUSELEV, NIKOLA, b. 1936

555 Abadzhiev, Aleksandur Marinov. *Nikola Giuzelev: biogr. ocherk.* In Bulgarian. Sofiia: Muzika, 1979. 90 pp. Illustrated. Bibliography. Discography.

GIANNINI, DUSOLINA, b. 1902

556 Moran, William R. "Dusolina Giannini and Her Recordings." *The Record Collector* IX, no. 2 (February 1954), 26-51. Illustrated. Discography. Record reviews are quoted from *The Gramophone.*

The Philadelphia-born soprano, Dusolina Giannini, was the daughter of Ferruccio Giannini, one of the first operatic tenors to make re-

cordings. Mme. Giannini was a pupil of Marcella Sembrich, and made
her debut in concert in 1923. Her operatic debut was in Hamburg in
1925 as Aida. She sang at the Berlin Opera, La Scala, Covent Garden,
and the Metropolitan, and was much admired as a concert artist in
Australia and New Zealand. This article was an "authorized" one,
having been written after several interviews with the singer, who
reviewed and approved the text before publication.

See also item 1811

GIAUROV, NIKOLAI

See Ghiaurov, Nikolai

GIGLI, BENIAMINO, 1890-1957

557-T Gigli, Beniamino. *Atminas.* Translated by A. Birzeniece. In
Latvian. Riga: Liesma, 1967. 242 pp. Illustrated.

  Latvian translation of his *Memorie* (q.v.).

558 ———. *Confidenze.* In Italian. Roma: De Carlo, Consorzio
editorial italiano, 1942. 212 pp.

  Written as a series of interviews with Italo Toscani. Gigli "talks"
about a variety of subjects, some of them only obliquely autobiographical.
He discusses music, art, singing, sports, film making, fans, politics,
etc. An important forerunner of his second autobiographical effort
completed near the end of his life.

559-T ———. *Memoirs.* Translated by Darina Silone. London:
Cassell, 1957. x, 277 pp. Illustrated. Repertory, pp. 230-231.
Index, pp. 271-277. Discography, pp. 233-270.

  This is the English translation—and a very good one—of Gigli's
Memorie (q.v.). It agrees with the original textually, but the book
differs in three important aspects: it has 48 illustrations instead
of the 8 in the Italian edition, Gigli's repertory has been added,
and there is an excellent discography (minus take numbers) by Mark
Ricaldone prepared for this edition. The discography lists commercial
recordings only; thus the passage of time that saw the release of
many off-the-air and pirated material, along with numerous LP transfers,
has rendered the discography incomplete.

559-T-a ———. *The Memoirs of Beniamino Gigli.* Translated by
Darina Silone. Opera Biographies. New York: Arno Press, 1977. x,
277 pp. Illustrated. Repertory, pp. 230-231. Index, pp. 271-277.
Discography, pp. 236-270.

  The reprint edition of the 1957 Cassel edition (q.v.).

560 ———. *Memorie.* In Italian. "Le Scie." Milano: A. Mondadori,
1957. 354 pp. Illustrated.

  Gigli's second autobiographical effort, published in the year of
his death. The Italian- and English-language editions appeared

simultaneously. It is a superb book; it not only narrates his initial struggles in great detail and touches on all the highlights of
his consistently successful career without a trace of distasteful
conceit, but his writing also presents the portrait of an essentially
simple man singled out by fate as the possessor of one of the outstanding lyric tenor voices of the twentieth century. "I was born
with a voice and very little else: no money, no influence, no other
talents" is the opening statement, and recurring theme, of the book.
It is a fine self-portrait of a great singer, aware of the distance
he had traveled from his hometown, Recanati, to world fame. Surprisingly, the fine discography by Mark Ricaldone, published in the
English edition, is missing from the Italian original. Yet another
mystery of editorial wisdom.

560-a ————. *Memorie.* In Italian. Recanati: Micheloni, 1979.
357 pp. Illustrated.

Reprint of the 1957 edition published by Mondadori, Milan (q.v.).

561-T ————. *Pamietniki.* In Polish. Muzyka moja milosc. Kraków:
Polskie Wydawn. Muzyczne, 1973. 333 pp. Illustrated.

Polish translation of his *Memorie* (q.v.).

562 ————. *La verità sul mio "caso."* In Italian. Roma: Società
Tipografia Editrice Italiana, 1945. 35 pp.

After World War II Gigli was accused of having collaborated with
the Germans. The accusations were largely groundless, but in the end
an Honor Court was convened. Gigli was acquitted, but the Court
observed that he, "like many other artists, is unaware that some of
his actions may take on a political aspect." During the trial and
the events leading up to it the press refused to print many letters
that Gigli wrote in self-defense. Wanting to bring his "case" to a
close, he had printed 50,000 copies of this booklet at his own ex-
pense, presenting his side of the story, the evidence presented to
the Honor Court and the Court's deliberations and verdict. A fascinating document in every respect.

563 *Beniamino Gigli.* In Italian. Quaderni del casanostra, no. 1.
Recanati: Comune di Recanati, 1962. 60 pp. Illustrated.

A booklet containing four discourses (pp. 9-48) by four expert
musicologists delivered in consecutive years between 1959 and 1962
in the Aula Magna of Recanati, birthplace of Gigli. A guide to the
Beniamino Gigli museum (pp. 51-60) completes the volume. The museum,
set up by the town, preserves the artistic memorabilia of Gigli
donated to the community by the heirs of the tenor. RT

564 Calderón, Elda. *Gigli explica su triunfo.* In Spanish. Buenos
Aires: Editorial Mundo Moderno, 1952. 158 pp. Illustrated.

565 Flamini, Luigi. *Beniamino Gigli: è la sua gente che parla.* In
Italian. Recanati: Micheloni, 1979. 277 pp. Illustrated.

566 Foschi, Franco. *Primavera del tenore. Il giovane Beniamino
Gigli.* In Italian. Milano: Micheloni Editore, 1978? 191 pp. Illustrated. Repertory, pp. 109-131.

Accompanied by a slender biography, the book consists of many sharp reproductions of the memorabilia preserved in the Beniamino Gigli museum in Recanati. The author too was born in Recanati; he was a councilman and later became the mayor of the city. The organizer of the museum is now (1982) a member of parliament. RT

567 Hahn, Herbert, b. 1890. *Un'anima cantava, eine Seele sang. Begegnungen mit Beniamino Gigli*. In German. Stuttgart: Mellinger, 1966. 144 pp. Illustrated. The Library of Congress cataloging card states: "Continuation of the author's *Heute wird es nicht regnen-- es singt ja Gigli*" (q.v.).

A continuation of the same author's *Heute wird es nicht Regnen--es singt ja Gigli* (q.v.), this is a German-language biography by a friend. It begins around 1944 and continues until the end of the singer's life, consisting largely of reminiscences of performances by, and conversations with, Gigli. Very few dates are mentioned, thus making it difficult to establish chronological relationships. The photographs are of Gigli in and out of costume. HCS

568 ————. *Heute wird es nicht regnen--es singt ja Gigli*. In German. Stuttgart: Waldorf Verlag, 1940. This citation was found in the preface of *Un'anima cantava, eine Seele sang* (q.v.) by the same author. No library copy located.

569 Herbert-Caesari, Egon F. *Tradition and Gigli, 1600-1955; a Panegyric*. London: Robert Hale, 1958. 160 pp. Illustrated.

This is a treatise on the tradition of singing, whose last exponent, in the author's opinion, was the late Beniamino Gigli. "Gigli's voice and Gigli's production were together a living symbol of the one and only Tradition, the one and only School--one and only because completely natural." The author, a pupil of Riccardo Daviesi (1827-1921) and a voice teacher as well, believes that the old school of singing, true bel canto singing, no longer exists because there is no one to teach it. The book's concluding chapter (there are an Epilogue and a Postscript) extols the artistry of Gigli. The author also manages to weave into the discussion of vocal art his views about art in general, the vanishing standards of composition, singing and graphic arts. It is up to the reader to decide whether Herbert-Caesari is right or not in expecting music to have melody, harmony and rhythm, or a statue of a human being to have parts of his anatomy where nature put them. The second edition, issued by the same publisher in 1963, has no illustrations.

570-T Rensis, Raffaello de, 1880-1970. *Beniamino Gigli, sein Leben, seine Kunst, seine Persönlichkeit*. Translated by Ivo Striedinger, b. 1868. In German. München: H. Hugendubel, 1936. 149 pp. Illustrated.

The German translation of *Il cantore del popolo, Beniamino Gigli*, published in Rome by the Società editrice di "Novissima" in 1933 (q.v.).

571 ————. *Il cantore del popolo, Beniamino Gigli*. In Italian. Roma: Società editrice di "Novissima," 1933. 239 pp. Illustrated. Index, pp. 233-239. List of Benefit Performances, pp. 229-232.

The first major Gigli biography, written by the noted Italian musicologist, Raffaello de Rensis, who is Tito Gobbi's and Boris

Christoff's father-in-law. The bulk of the book is a fair summary of Gigli's path from the tiny village of Recanati to world fame. A good biography, worth reading, with excellent photographs not reproduced elsewhere.

572 Rosner, Robert. *Benjamino Gigli und die Kunst des Belcanto*. In German. Wien: C. Haslinger qdm. Tobias, 1929. 29 pp.

573 Rovigo, Italy (Province). [*Beniamino Gigli*.] A cura dell'Ente provinciale per il turismo di Rovigo con la collaborazione della direzione del Teatro sociale. In Italian. Rovigo: Tip. Ist. padano di arti grafiche, 1951. 43 pp. Illustrated.

574 Silvestrini, Domenico. *Beniamino Gigli e l'anima delle folle*. In Italian. Bologna: Tipografia Aldina editrice, 1937. 94 pp.

See also items 183, 1544, 1617, 1680, 1811

GIORGI, MARIA (BRIZZI), 1775-1812

575 Bacchetti, Antonio. *Elogio funebre di Maria Brizzi Giorgi, detto nella Chiesa delle Muratelle in Bologna nel giorno de'suoi funerali, 22 gennajo, 1812, dal dottore Antonio Bacchetti*. In Italian. Bologna: Tipografia Masi e comp., 1812? vi, 40 pp.

GIUGLINI, ANTONIO, 1827-1865

See item 1562

GIUZELEV, NIKOLA

See Ghiuselev, Nikola

GLOVER, WILLIAM

576 Glover, William. *The Memoirs of a Cambridge Chorister*. London: Hurst and Blackett, 1885. 2 vols.

GLUCK, ALMA, 1884-1938

577 Davenport, Marcia (Gluck), b. 1903. *Too Strong for Fantasy*. New York: Scribner, 1967. 483 pp. Illustrated.

The subtitle on the book jacket, "A Personal Record of Music, Literature, and Politics in America and Europe Over Half a Century," accurately describes the book's contents. Marcia Davenport is the daughter of soprano Alma Gluck and step-daughter of violinist Efrem Zimbalist. The first part deals with the distinguished novelist and biographer's childhood and, intentionally or not, is the best biographical reference work on the career of Alma Gluck. There is much information about the musical scene, both concert and opera, especially in New York, from 1909 to 1918. The author was a great admirer and personal friend of Arturo Toscanini, and there are many references to the conductor. The last part of the book gives a moving account of the crisis in Czechoslovakia, the Communist takeover and the death of Jan Masaryk. WRM

See also item 1581

GMIRIA, BORIS ROMANOVICH, 1903-1969

578 Gmiria, Boris Romanovich. *Statti, listi, spogadi*. In Ukrainian. Kiev: Muzichna Ukraina, 1975. 230 pp. Illustrated.

579 Kyrychenko, T. *Boris Romanovich Gmiria*. In Ukrainian. Kiev: Derzh. vid-vo obrazotvorchogo mistetstva i muzichnoi lit-ri URSR, 1958. 14 pp. Illustrated.

580 Stebun, Illia Isakovich, b. 1911. *Boris Romanovich Gmyria, narodnyi artist SSSR*. In Ukrainian. Kiev: Derzh. vid-vo obrazotvorchogo mistetstva i muzichnoi lit-ri URSR, 1960. 38 pp. Illustrated.

GNATIUK, DMITRO MIKHAILOVICH, b. 1925

581 Stefanovych, Mykhailo Pavlovych. *Dmitro Mikhailovich Gnatiuk, narodnii artist SRSR*. In Russian. Kiev: Derzh. vid-vo obrazotvorchogo mistetstva i muzichnoi lit-ri URSR, 1961. 21 pp. Illustrated.

GOBBI, TITO, 1913-1984

582-T Gobbi, Tito, and Ida Cook. *Életem*. Translated by Zsuzsa Sarlós. In Hungarian. Budapest: Zeneműkiadó Vállalat, 1980. 230 pp. Illustrated.

The Hungarian translation of *My Life* (q.v.). Unfortunately, this edition is without an index or a discography, both of which were present in the English-language original.

583 ———. *My Life*. London: Macdonald and Jane's. 1979. 217 pp. Illustrated. Index, pp. 211-217. Discography, pp. 201-210.

The joint effort of an exceptionally intelligent singing-actor and an exceptionally gifted writer produced this remarkable autobiography. With the aid of ghost-writer Ida Cook, Tito Gobbi narrates his life story in an easy-flowing, interesting, readable manner. He dwells on all aspects and periods of his artistic and private life just marginally too briefly; one always wishes he would tell more: more facts in greater detail. Analyzing *his* conception of his major roles should be instructive to young singers. A major musical biography of one of the outstanding performers of the post-World War II period. The discography was compiled by John Steane, the section on the 78 rpm records by Bryan Crimp includes matrix numbers and takes. For LP records both the American and British catalog numbers are given.

583-a ————. *My Life*. New York: Doubleday, 1980. 229 pp. Illustrated. Index, pp. 221-229. Discography, pp. 203-220.

This is the American edition of Gobbi's autobiography published in London a year earlier. The discography by John Steane incorporates a few elusive items omitted from the discography in the British edition; it is now complete.

583-b ————. *My Life*. London: Futura Publications, 1980. 286 pp. Illustrated. Index. Discography. Originally published in 1979 by Macdonald and Jane's, London.

584 *Costumi per un museo. Tito Gobbi e la sua città*. In Italian. Bassano: Lions Club, 1980. 46 pp. Illustrated.

An important lecture given by Professor Remo Schiavo in 1980 (pp. 9-24) and a detailed list of the costumes Tito Gobbi donated to Bassano, his native city (pp. 25-44). The costumes are on exhibit at the Museo Civico of Bassano. RT

See also item 1544

GOLOVKINA, SOF'IA NIKOLAEVNA

See item 1708

GOMPERZ-BETTELHEIM, CAROLINE VON

585 *Caroline von Gomperz-Bettelheim; biographische Blätter*. In German. Wien: Carl Fromme, 1915. 41 pp. Illustrated.

GONZÁLEZ, MARUJA

586 Ramirez L., Arturo. *El canto de la alondra; reportaje de una trayectoria artistica*. In Spanish. Habana: Editorial Lex, 1957. 130 pp.

GORDON, JEANNE, 1893-1952

See item 1541

GRANFORTE, APOLLO, 1886-1975

587 Delicata, A.A.G. "Apollo Granforte." *The Record Collector* XII, nos. 8 & 9 (November-December 1959), 172-194. Illustrated. Discography, pp. 180-187.

This appears to be the only source for biographical information on the career of this Italian singer, so well known to record collectors from his work as the principal baritone in the "complete" HMV recordings of *Otello, Tosca, Il Trovatore* and *Pagliacci* in the early days of electrical recording. His youth was spent in the Argentine, where he later created the title role in Boero's opera *El Matrero*. He was a member of the Melba Opera Company in Australia in 1922, and well known at La Scala, Covent Garden, etc. The singer assisted the author with material for this article.

GRASSINI, GIUSEPPINA, 1773-1850

588 Gavoty, André, b. 1894. *La Grassini, première cantatrice de S.M. l'Empereur et Roi*. In French. Collection "Lenôtre," 8. Paris: B. Grasset, 1947. 255 pp. Illustrated. Bibliography, pp. 241-249.

589 Jeanne, René, b. 1887. "La chanteuse de l'empereur." *Les Oeuvres libres*, Nouvelle série no. 34 (1949), 131-196. In French.

590 Pougin, Arthur, 1834-1921. *Une cantatrice "amie" de Napoléon. Giuseppina Grassini, 1773-1850*. In French. Paris: Fischbacher, 1920. 73 pp. Illustrated.

591 Rensis, Raffaello de, 1880-1970. *La cantante dell'imperatore*. In Italian. Collezione Fonte viva, n. 9. Roma: Fratelli Palombi, 1948. 240 pp. Illustrated.

GRAVEURE, LOUIS, 1888-1965

592 Graveure, Louis. *"Super-Diction"; Twelve Studies in the Art of Song*. Music settings by Bryceson Treharne. High voice (original).... Schirmer's Scholastic Series, vol. 53. New York: G. Schirmer, 1918. 63 pp.

See also item 1811.

GREENE, HARRY PLUNKET, 1865-1936

593 Greene, Harry Plunket. *From Blue Danube to Shannon*. London: P. Allan, 1934. vii, 179 pp. Illustrated.

A miscellany, mostly from the writings of bass Harry Plunket Greene, famous as an interpreter of songs and author of *Interpretation in Song* (q.v.). These essays and sketches were originally written for *Music and Letters* (1923, 1926, 1928 and 1932); *The Times* (no date), *Royal College of Music Magazine* (1917) and the author's lecture at the Royal Institute (1930). Some of the sketches tell of visits to Canada; one deals with a concert in Ireland. The book also includes a chapter on Hubert Parry's songs by Charles L. Graves from that author's book, *Hubert Parry* (1926). Greene was Parry's son-in-law, which may be the reason why he has included someone else's views of Parry's compositions. WRM

594 ————. *Interpretation in Song*. New York: Macmillan, 1912. xii, 307 pp. Illustrated. Index, pp. 301-307.

Harry Plunket Greene made his debut as a bass in 1888, and first sang at Covent Garden in 1890. Later he changed to a baritone, and confined his work to concerts and oratorio. Vocal deterioration came early, but he had established such a reputation as an interpreter of song, especially in the Lieder of Brahms and Schumann, and in old English songs, that he continued with a distinguished career. He taught at the Royal College of Music. This book is considered a classic in its field. The author stresses three basic rules: "Never stop the *March* of a Song"; Unbroken continuity: "Sing mentally through your rests"; and "Sing as you Speak" (Purity of diction, Sense of prosody and metre, Identity of texture in the sound of the spoken and the sung word). These he elaborates on at length, with musical examples. He also has a section on the making of programs, and how to study a song. WRM

594-a ———. *Interpretation in Song*. London: Macmillan & Stainer and Bell, 1912. xii, 323 pp. Illustrated. Index. The book went through many editions.

595 ———. *Where the Bright Waters Meet*. London: P. Allan & Co., 1924. viii, 253 pp. Illustrated.

The subject of this book is trout fishing.

GREVILLE, URSULA

See item 1695

GRISHKO, MIKHAILO STEPANOVICH, b. 1901

596 Kozak, Sergii Davidovich, b. 1921. *Mikhailo Grishko; biografichna povist'*. In Ukrainian. Seriia biografichnikh tvoriv. vypusk 40. Kiev: Molod', 1978. 198 pp. Illustrated.

Biography of the Russian baritone Grishko. The illustrations show him in his best roles: Igor, Germont, Scarpia, Rigoletto, Amonasro and others. Grishko also appeared in Russian films.

597 Stebun, Illia Isakovich, b. 1911. *Mikhail Stepanovich Grishko, narodnyi artist SSSR*. In Ukrainian. Kiev: Derzh. vid-vo obrazotvorchogo mistetstva i muzichnoi lit-ri URSR, 1960. 37 pp. Illustrated.

GRISI, GIULIA, 1811-1869

598 Mirecourt, Eugène de, 1812-1880. *Julia Grisi, Clémence Robert*. In French. Les contemporains, 115. Paris: Librairie des Contemporains, 1871. 62 pp. Illustrated.

See also items 1562, 1597, 1601, 1612, 1694, 1745

GROZĂVESCU, TRAIAN, 1894-1927

599 Demeter Grozăvescu, Mira, and I. Voledi. *Traian Grozăvescu*. In Rumanian. Bucureşti: Editura Muzicală, 1965. 266 pp. Illustrated. Bibliography, pp. 266-267.

GUASCO, CARLO, 1813-1876

600 Gualerzi, Giorgio, b. 1930. *Carlo Guasco, tenore romantico fra mito e realtà*. Foreword by Francesco Sottomano (Mayor of Solero, Guasco's birthplace). In Italian. Alessandria: Cassa di Risparmio di Alessandria, 1976. 21 pp. Illustrated. Bibliography, pp. 17-19. Repertory, p. 21.

GUBELLINI, PIETRO, b. 1877

601 Biagi, Enzo Marco. *È di scena Pietro Gubellini*. In Italian. Bologna: Testa Editore, 1939. 81 pp.

The Bolognese tenor, Gubellini, sang in Italy, Russia, other European countries, Egypt and South America, in good theaters and with famous colleagues. He was active until the twenties and ended his life in poverty and forgotten. The author never heard him sing, but had long conversations with the singer who recalled the details of his unfortunate life. These recollections were written as a humane gesture of amends offered to Gubellini. RT

GÜNTHER, CARL, 1885-1958

602 Wiese, Eberhard von. *Nach den Sternen muss man griefen; vom Kupferschmied zum Kammersänger. Erinnerungen des Kammersängers Carl Günther von der Hamburgischen Staatsoper*. In German. Hamburg: H. Christian, 1956. 238 pp.

GUERRABELLA, GINEVRA

See Ward, Genevieve

GUERRINI, ADRIANA, 1907-1970

603 Feliciotti, Giorgio. *Adriana Guerrini, una voce che ritorna*. In Italian. Bologna: Bongiovanni, 1980. 111 pp. Illustrated. Repertory, pp. 101-104. Index, pp. 107-109. Discography, pp. 105-106. Chronology of Performances, pp. 75-100.

An exhaustive, precise biography. The author was fortunate to have access to the reliable documentation preserved and catalogued by the soprano's sister. Adriana Guerrini made her debut in 1935 and retired in 1960. The biography concentrates on these twenty-five years of artistic activities spent, almost exclusively, in Italy. RT

See also item 1545

GUERRINI, VIRGINIA, b. 1872

604 *Recuerdo dedicado a la eminente artista Virginia Guerrini por sus admiradores. (Juicios de la prensa madrilena)*. In Spanish. Madrid,

1900. 72 pp. At head of title: Teatro Real de Madrid. Temporada de 1899 a 1900.

GULBRANSON, ELLEN, 1863-1947

605 Elsta, Fanny, b. 1899. *Boken om Ellen Gulbranson*. Oslo: Cammermeyer, 1950. 190 pp. Illustrated.

GULIAEV, IURII, b. 1930

See item 1732

GURA, EUGEN, 1842-1906

606 Gura, Eugen. *Erinnerungen aus meinem Leben*. In German. Leipzig: Breitkopf und Härtel, 1905. 124 pp. Illustrated.

GURJEV, VIKTOR, b. 1914

607 Heinapuu, Uno. *Viktor Gurjev*. In Estonian. Tallinn: Eesti Raamat, 1974. 55 pp. Illustrated. At head of title: Eesti NSV Teatriühing.

GUTHEIL-SCHODER, MARIE, 1874-1935

608 Gutheil-Schoder, Marie. *Erlebtes und Erstrebtes*. In German. Veröffentlichungen des Verlages der Museumfreunde in Wien. Wien: Krey, 1937. 58 pp.

609 Rie, Therese (Herz), b. 1879. *Marie Gutheil-Schoder*. By Andro L. (pseud.). In German. *Die Wiedergabe*. Reihe 2, Bd. 10. Wien: Wiener literarische Anstalt, 1923. 31 pp. Illustrated. Information taken from *Deutsche Bücherverzeichnis*.

H

HAGMAN, SOPHIE, 1761-1826

610 Forsstrand, Carl Wilhelm, 1854-1928. *Sophie Hagman och hennes samtida; några anteckningar från det gustavianska Stockholm*. In Swedish. Stockholm: Wahlström & Widstrand, 1911. 211 pp. Index, pp. 197-211.

HAHN, REYNALDO, 1875-1947

611 Hahn, Reynaldo. *Notes (journal d'un musicien)*. In French. Paris: Plon, 1933. 293 pp.

612 Bendahan, Daniel. *Reynaldo Hahn: su vida y su obra*. In Spanish.

Caracas: Italgrafica, 1973. xvi, 113 pp. Illustrated. Bibliography, pp. 103-104. Index.

612-a ———. *Reynaldo Hahn: su vida y su obra*. In Spanish. Caracas: Monte Avila Editores, 1979. 176 pp. Illustrated. Bibliography, pp. 173-176.

613 Gavoty, Bernard. *Reynaldo Hahn*. In French. Paris: Buchet Chastel, 1978. 320 pp. Illustrated.

HAMLIN, GEORGE JOHN, 1868-1923

614 Hamlin, Anna M. *Father Was a Tenor*. Hicksville, N.Y.: Exposition Press, 1978. 96 pp. Illustrated.

Partly based on father George Hamlin's diaries and partly on daughter Anna's recollections, this book is a succession of vignettes and commentary about the greats and near-greats of the music world, loosely held together by the sketchy life story of the Hamlins. Anna, too, was a singer, yet the reader does not get a coherent picture of her career and not much more of her father's. A good source work for a more scholarly biography.

615 Trott, Josephine, b. 1874. *George Hamlin, American Singer, 1868-1923; a Resume of His Career*. Denver: Nelson, 1925. 53 pp. Illustrated.

An uneven, sketchy outline of George Hamlin's career. It tries to capture, with limited success, his personality and his artistic importance as the foremost American Lieder and oratorio tenor of his time. Richard Aldrich's objective introduction puts Hamlin's voice and artistry in the proper perspective. Hamlin is remembered today for his many Victor and few Edison recordings and as the pioneer interpreter in the United States of Richard Strauss's songs.

HAMMOND, JOAN, b. 1912

616 Hammond, Joan. *A Voice, a Life; Autobiography*. London: Gollancz, 1970. 264 pp. Illustrated. Repertory, pp. 246-248. Index, pp. 259-264. Discography, pp. 249-256.

An unembellished, simple recounting of the major events of her life, including early struggles, poverty, disappointments and a disproportionate amount of bad luck. Born in Christchurch, New Zealand, and raised in Sydney, Hammond was on her way to a career as a violinist when a bicycle accident severely damaged her left arm and forced her to reorient her musical ambitions. She turned her attention to singing and gave her first concert in Sydney in 1931. She continued her vocal training in Vienna and later in London with Dino Borgioli. *Two days* before her La Scala debut as Mimi she was ordered to leave the country on account of Italy's impending entry into World War II. Her career blossomed after the war but ended abruptly in 1964 when she suffered a heart attack, after which she retired in Australia. WRM

See also item 1545

HASSE, FAUSTINA (BORDONI), 1693-1781

617 Hoegg, Margarete. *Die Gesangskunst der Faustina Hasse und das Sängerinnenwesen ihrer Zeit in Deutschland.* In German. Königsbrück; 1931. 95 pp. Illustrated.

618 Niggli, Arnold, 1843-1927. *Faustina Bordoni-Hasse.* In German. Leipzig, 1880. 58 pp. Bibliography. A monographic reprint with double pagination: its own and the pagination of its source: *Sammlung musikalischer Vorträge*, ed. by Paul graf Waldersee. Leipzig, 1879-98. Neue Reihe, no. 21-22 (1880), 261-318. "Quellen," p. 318.

619 Polko, Elise (Vogel), 1823-1899. *Faustina Hasse, musikalischer Roman.* In German. Leipzig: Schlicke, 1860. xii, 586 pp. 2 vols. in 1. 2nd ed.: 1870; 3rd ed.: 1884; 4th ed.: 1895.

620 Urbani de Gheltof, Giuseppe Marino. *La Nuova Sirena e il Caro Sassone; note biografiche.* In Italian. Venezia: M. Fontana, 1890. 81 pp.

See also items 1597, 1612

HAUK, MINNIE, 1852-1929

621 Hauk, Minnie. *Memoirs of a Singer.* Collated by Captain E.B. Hitchcock, preface by A.M. Williamson. London: A.M. Philpot, 1925. 295 pp. Illustrated.

A typical prima donna's biography, offering enough details about 19th-century musical life to hold the reader's interest. Born in New York, Hauk made her debut in Brooklyn in *La Sonnambula* at the age of sixteen. Considered one of the foremost dramatic sopranos of her time, she describes her adventures at Covent Garden, the Royal Opera in Berlin, Budapest, Vienna and the United States. Even though Hauk makes herself the center of the musical world, this world is populated by the great and near-great of the last third of the period. Her account of her meetings with Bizet, Liszt, Wagner, and other composers and performers are of historical interest, especially the details of Wagner's fund raising concerts in Budapest.

621-a ―――. *Memoirs of a Singer.* Opera Biographies. New York: Arno Press, 1977. 295 pp. Illustrated.

Reprint of the 1925 edition published by A. Philpot, London (q.v.).

See also items 1567, 1694

HAYES, CATHERINE, 1825-1861

622 *Memoir of Miss Catherine Hayes, "The Swan of Erin,"* by a contributor to the Dublin University Magazine. London: Cramer, 1852? 40, 9 pp. Illustrated.

See also item 1562

HAYES, ROLAND, 1887-1976

623 Harris, Charles J. *Reminiscences of My Days with Roland Hayes.*
Orangeburg, S.C.: N.p., 1944. 27 pp. Illustrated.

The recollections of pianist Charles Harris, who was Hayes's accompanist on his engagements between 1912 and the spring of 1917. It
was the period of Hayes's emergence from obscurity on his way to
national renown. These reminiscences are written with affection and
the permissible bias of an author who is too close to his subject.
An interesting supplementary reading to Mackinley Helm's biography of
Hayes (q.v.).

624 Helm, Mackinley, b. 1896. *Angel Mo' and Her Son, Roland Hayes.*
Boston: Little, Brown and Company, 1942. viii, 289 pp. Illustrated.

A remarkable biography of a black singer, who had to fight the
handicap of deep-rooted blind prejudice in his native United States
and artistic chauvinism abroad, all the way to world fame and even
beyond. Thanks to his intelligence, talent and determination, and
most of all to the love and spiritual guidance of his mother, he became a first rank recitalist. Hayes was the first black singer to
reap great critical acclaim in that area of music that before him
was strictly the white artist's domain. He conquered a hostile
Berlin audience with German Lieder, he sang Schubert songs in Vienna,
and gave a command performance in Buckingham Palace to King George V
and Queen Mary. His story carries a message that goes far beyond the
limits of the narrative of a musical career.

See also item 1744

HELMRICH, DOROTHY ADELE, b. 1889

625 Carell, Victor, and Beth Dean. *On Wings of Song: Dorothy Helmrich and the Arts Council.* Sydney: Alternative Publishing Cooperative, 1982. 146 pp. Illustrated. Contains "A Personal Account of
the Arts Council Development and History" by Gordon Horswell (pp. 87-
110) and "Arts Council Anecdotes" (pp. 117-129).

Dorothy Adele Helmrich led two lives which overlapped in her native
Australia. Her first career, that of a distinguished Lieder singer,
began with her training at the New South Wales Conservatorium in
Sydney as a pupil of Stefan Mavrogodato, and was continued as a student
at the Royal College of Music in London, where she studied with Sir
Hugh Alen. During this period she also became a pupil of Sir George
Henschel, who accompanied her at her London debut at Wigmore Hall.
Through the mid-1920s into the 1940s she was a popular figure at the
Promenade concerts of Sir Henry J. Wood, and was often heard in
oratoria with the well-known conductors of the period. She made a
number of concert tours throughout England and on the continent, and
was heard in many B.B.C. concerts. She was called back to Australia
for a series of concerts sponsored by the Australian Broadcasting
Commission in 1936, and again in 1941, when she joined the staff of
the N.S.W. Conservatorium. Having worked with the Arts Council of
Great Britain, she established a similar organization in Australia,
soon becoming its president and chief guiding light. This organization

has grown to be of tremendous importance in bringing concerts, opera, ballet and theater to outback Australia. This book was designed as a tribute to Dorothy Helmrich: part biographical and part the history of the Arts Council. Its authors were closely associated with the Council, and major emphasis has been placed on this portion of the book. The best portions of the text are long quotations from Miss Helmrich herself; joining these together has often been poorly accomplished. One of the reviews appended is of one of Miss Helmrich's recordings, serving to call to the attention of the reader the serious omission of a discography. WRM

HEMPEL, FRIEDA, 1885-1955

626 Hempel, Frieda. *Mein Leben dem Gesang; Erinnerungen.* In German. Berlin: Argon, 1955. 319 pp. Illustrated. Repertory, pp. 309-310. Index, pp. 313-319.

A panoramic autobiography, rich in detail, lacking in continuity. Hempel covers the highlights of her career in an easy, conversational style, but of greater significance and value are her vignettes of the many prominent musicians, singers in particular, who played an important part in her artistic life. The preface is signed and dated September 1955. Since Hempel died on October 7, 1955, this is indeed an artist's overview of her entire life's experiences. Yet another book that deserves to be translated.

See also items 1541, 1565, 1581, 1695, 1803

HENKE, WALDEMAR, 1876-1945

See item 1743

HENSCHEL, GEORGE, 1850-1934

627 Henschel, George. *Musings and Memories of a Musician.* London: Macmillan, 1918. 400 pp. Illustrated. Index, pp. 399-400.

These are the musical--rather than personal--reminiscences of one of the outstanding musicians of the 19th century. Henschel was an accomplished singer, mostly active in oratorio and Lieder recitals, a successful composer, a good pianist and an excellent conductor. He studied voice with Goetze, the first Lohengrin, and piano with Ignaz Moscheles, Beethoven's pupil. He sang Hans Sachs in the first concert performance of *Die Meistersinger* in Leipzig and Wotan's Farewell from the newly published score with Liszt at the piano at the latter's house in Weimar. In his song recitals he was often his own accompanist. According to the testimony of some rare 78s made in 1928, he preserved his voice into old age. He was also the founding conductor of the Boston Symphony (at age 31!) and the founder of the London Symphony. An interesting account of a fascinating life spent in the golden century of music.

627-a ———. *Musings and Memories of a Musician.* New York: Macmillan, 1919. 400 pp. Illustrated.

628 ————. *Personal Recollections of Johannes Brahms, Some of His Letters to and Pages from a Journal Kept by George Henschel.* Boston: Richard G. Badger, 1907.

629 Henschel, Helen Henriette. *When Soft Voices Die, a Musical Biography.* London: J. Westhouse, 1944. 216 pp. Illustrated. Index, pp. 209-216.

A brief, well-written autobiography by the daughter of Sir George Henschel and his first wife, soprano Lillian Henschel. While the autobiographical portions focus on her own life, there are many references to the parents. Parts III and IV contain father George's observations on singing and interpretation and his personal recollections of Brahms. A fine companion volume to Henschel's autobiography.

629-a ————. *When Soft Voices Die; a Musical Biography.* London: Methuen, 1949. 180 pp. Illustrated.

See also item 1566

HENSCHEL, LILLIAN JUNE (BAILEY), 1860-1901

See items 627, 629

HERFORD, JOHANN JOSEPH, 1771-1829

630 Grunwald, Fritz. *Aus dem Leben des Tilsiter Cantors Johann Joseph Herford.* In German. Koenigsberg i. Pr.: K. Jüterbock & Co., 1934. 90, lx pp. Illustrated. Bibliography, pp. xliii-xlvii.

HÉRITTE-VIARDOT, LOUISE PAULINE MARIE, 1841-1918

631 Héritte-Viardot, Louise Pauline Marie. *Memories and Adventures.* Translated from the German manuscript and arranged by E.S. Buchheim. London: Mills and Boon, 1913. xiii, 271 pp. Illustrated. "These recollections ... have not been published in any other country."

Daughter of famed singer Pauline Viardot-Garcia, Louise Héritte-Viardot was a famous singing teacher at the Petrograd Conservatory, and in Frankfurt, Heidelberg and Berlin. She sang opera in Russia, and devotes a good part of her book to her adventures in that country. There is much about her celebrated mother and her operatic associates, Grisi, Mario and others of the period. Appendices are devoted to an essay on the discovery of the laryngoscope (by her uncle, Manuel Garcia, brother of Pauline) and an article on her aunt, Maria Malibran. WRM

632 ————. *Die Natur in der Stimmbildung, für Redner und Sänger.* In German. Heidelberg: O. Petters, 1906. 29 pp.

See also item 1643

HEROLD, VILHELM, 1865-1937

633 Ipsen, Arne, b. 1941. *Sangeren fra Hasle: folkebog om Vilhelm Herold og hans bornholmske barndomsby i 1870'erne.* In Danish. Rønne: Bornholmeren, 1979. 63 pp. Illustrated. Bibliography, p. 63.

634 *Vilhelm Herold 1893-1915.* In Danish. København: Erslev & Hasselbalch, 1915. 16 unnumbered leaves. Illustrated.

Contains a short biography of the Danish tenor and a large number of photographs showing Herold in his many roles.

HINES, JEROME, b. 1921

635 Hines, Jerome. *Great Singers on Great Singing.* Garden City, N.Y.: Doubleday, 1982. 356 pp. Illustrated. Glossary, pp. 353-356.

Interviews conducted by Jerome Hines with forty of the most important singers of the present day and recent past on vocal technique. There are also interviews with Morton Cooper, a voice pathologist, and Leo P. Reckford, M.D., Hines's physician. There are illustrations of musical exercises and an occasional diagram of the vocal apparatus itself. The interviews vary in detail, but mostly contain revealing, insightful comments on the art of singing. HCS

636 ————. *This Is My Story, This Is My Song.* Westwood, N.J.: Fleming H. Revel, 1968. 160 pp. Illustrated.

After six years' academic training as a chemist, mathematician and physicist, and well into a successful operatic career, a series of religious experiences made Jerome Hines restructure his life. He claims to have had quasi-dialogues with God which helped him find the way to serve the Lord in religious work away from the stage and fortified him in the face of all odds as a singer. The incidents he relates are too numerous and too unusual to be mere coincidences; the readers will have to draw their own conclusions. The operatic side of the story falls short of expectations; what is left out could literally fill a volume. Only the remarkable first Russian tour is discussed in detail and even that focuses on the series of near-disasters averted through his faith in divine intervention. The book ends on the eve of the Cuban blockade. The author, still active in his sixth decade, owes his public the rest of his story.

HÖNGEN, ELISABETH, b. 1906

637 Wurm, Ernst, b. 1906. *Elisabeth Höngen. Ein Künstlerbild.* In German. Wien: Österreichischer Bundesverlag, 1966. 71 pp. Illustrated. Discography.

HOFFMANN, BAPTIST, 1864-1937

638 Hoffmann-Kusel, Georg. *Baptist Hoffmann; ein Leben für die Kunst.* In German. Berlin: Afas-Musikverlag, 1949. 75 pp. Illustrated.

HOLLÓSY, KORNÉLIA, 1827-1890

639 Barna, János, editor. *Hollósy Kornélia emlékalbum.* Bevezetéssel ellátta Diósszilágyi Sámuel. In Hungarian. Makó, 1927. 47 pp. Illustrated.

640 Diósszilágyi, Sámuel. *Amikor a "Magyar csalogány" dalolt Bécsben. (Hollósy Kornélia bécsi vendéqszereplése).* In Hungarian. Makó: The author, 1938. 18 pp.

641 ———. *Hollósy Kornélia és a magyar opera a szabadságharc éveiben.* In Hungarian. Makó: The author, 1935. 22 pp.

HOLM, EMIL, b. 1867

642 Holm, Emil. *Erindringer og Tidsbilleder fra Midten af forrige Aarhundrede til vor Tid.* In Danish. København: Berlingske Forlag, 1938. Illustrated.

HOLTZEM, LOUIS ALPHONSE EDMOND

643 Holtzem, Louis Alphonse Edmond. *Bases de l'art du chant; traité théorique et pratique et guide spécial à l'usage des jeunes chanteurs et des amateurs.* In French. Paris: Girod, 1865. x, 246 pp.

644 ———. *Une vie d'artiste. Souvenirs de théatre et de voyages.* In French. Lyon: Chez l'Auteur, 1885. 392 pp. Illustrated.

HOMER, LOUISE DILWORTH (BEATTY), 1871-1947

645 Homer, Anne. *Louise Homer and the Golden Age of Opera.* New York: W. Morrow, 1973. 439 pp. Illustrated. Bibliography, pp. 432-434. Index, pp. 435-439.

The author arrived on the Homer family scene in 1907, seven years after her mother's Metropolitan Opera debut. She was not yet in her teens when mother Louise left the Met for the first time, in 1919, and barely in her twenties during the singer's final three seasons in the house, from 1927 to 1930. Thus despite her obvious access to family documents and lore, she does not write about much of her mother's career from personal experience, and the reader has the feeling of a recital of researched facts rather than original material. There is considerable evidence that Anne Homer was never very close to music by choice; for instance, one enmeshed in music affairs would surely know that both Henri Scott and Chaliapin were basses, not baritones. The book also fails in some respects where it should be best: much of the family life of the Homers and their six children is excellent, but all too often one is introduced to a new member of the family and left hanging.... They seem to just disappear, never to be mentioned again. In many respects this book supplements that of her father Sidney, *My Wife and I* (q.v.). WRM

646 Homer, Sidney, 1864-1953. *My Wife and I; the Story of Louise and Sidney Homer.* New York: Macmillan Company, 1939. xii, 269 pp. Illustrated.

A warm and gentle book about an amazing American family: the father a composer, the mother a distinguished opera singer who somehow managed to raise six children. The work has a theme of devotion, mutual respect and family pride. Obviously Louise did not have time for petty opera squabbles. The book leaves no doubt that she made her place in the famous casts of which she was an important part by hard work and always being prepared when an opportunity came along. The book combines charm and factual accuracy, and offers an interesting parallel to the autobiographies of some of Homer's contemporaries who often sang in the same performances but made different use of their spare time. WRM

646-a ————. *My Wife and I; the Story of Louise and Sidney Homer.* Da Capo Press Music Reprint Series. New York: Da Capo Press, 1977. xii, 269 pp. Illustrated.

Reprint of the 1939 edition published by Macmillan, New York (q.v.).

647 Vermorcken, Elizabeth (Moorhead). *These Two Were Here: Louise Homer and Willa Cather.* Pittsburgh: University of Pittsburgh Press, 1950. 62 pp.

647-a ————. *These Two Were Here: Louise Homer and Willa Cather.* Norwood, Pa.: Norwood Editions, 1977. 62 pp.

Reprint of the 1950 edition published by the University of Pittsburgh Press (q.v.).

See also items 1565, 1695

HOPPE, HEINZ, b. 1924

648 Hoppe-Linzen, Carla. *Willst du dein Herz mir schenken ...: mein Leben mit Heinz Hoppe.* In German. Emsdetten: Lechte, 1972. 152 pp. Illustrated. Discography, pp. 137-151.

HORNE, MARILYN, b. 1934

649 Horne, Marilyn, and Jane Scovell. *Marilyn Horne, My Life.* New York: Atheneum, 1983. 258 pp. Illustrated. Index, pp. 247-258. Discography, pp. 241-245.

650 Dodge, Emelie Ruth. *Marilyn Horne.* New York: Gloria Enterprises, 1979. 10 unnumbered leaves. Illustrated.

Brief biography on three pages, followed by a fine selection of photographs, showing Horne on and off stage, beginning with childhood pictures.

See also item 1758

HOTTER, HANS, b. 1909

651 Wessling, Berndt Wilhelm, b. 1935. *Hans Hotter*. In German.
Bremen: Schünemann, 1966. 138 pp. Illustrated. Bibliography, pp.
140-141.

HOWARD, KATHLEEN, 1873-1956

652 Howard, Kathleen. *Confessions of an Opera Singer*. New York:
A.A. Knopf, 1918. 273 pp. Illustrated.

Kathleen Howard "confessed" too soon! She sang at the Metropolitan
for a full ten years after her book was published, and went on to a
distinguished career in Hollywood where she appeared in some 24 films
between 1934 and 1950. Her book, of course, deals with her early
career. Among her voice teachers was Jean de Reszke. Her account
of her early years, learning a repertory and gaining experience in
small German opera houses (she lists 68 roles, many of which she sang
in four languages), presents a classic description of operatic affairs
in Germany before World War I. WRM

652-a ————. *Confessions of an Opera Singer*. London: K. Paul,
1920. 273 pp. Illustrated.

HUARTE, MANUEL, 1861-1942

See items 417, 418

I

IBOS, GUILLAUME, b. 1860

653 Loiseau, Georges, b. 1888. *Notes sur le chant*. In French.
Neuilly: Georges Loiseau, 1947. 192 pp. Illustrated.

The book contains the autobiography of Ibos (pp. 15-56), creator
of the role of Werther, entitled "Quelques souvenirs d'Ibos."

INFANTINO, LUIGI, b. 1921

See item 1544

ISAAC, ADELE, 1854-1915

See item 1588

ISLANDI, STEFAN, b. 1907

654 Indrithi G., Thorsteinsson. *Áfram veginn: sagan um Stefán Islandi*.
In Icelandic. Akureyri: Björnsson, 1975. 264 pp. Illustrated.
Index, pp. 253-264. Discography, pp. 251-252.

A biography of the Icelandic tenor. Contains facsimiles of reviews arranged as a collage and several illustrations of the singer on and off stage. As some readers may want to examine this book even though not familiar with the language, to facilitate access to the only recorded copy in the United States, at the Library of Congress, the call number is ML 420.I 87 I 6; the LC card number 76-511878. (Icelandic orthography may render this all but unlocatable without the data given here.)

ISTRATTY, EDGAR

655 Istratty, Ella. *De vorbă cu Edgar Istratty.* In Rumanian. Bucureşti: Editura Muzicală, 1969. 192 pp. Illustrated.

IVANOV, ALEKSEI PETROVICH, b. 1904

656 Ivanov, Aleksei Petrovich. *Ob iskusstve geniia.* In Russian. Moskva: Profizdat, 1963. 102 pp. Illustrated.

657 Moscow. Gosudarstvennyi akademicheskii Bol'shoi teatr. *Aleksei Petrovich Ivanov.* In Russian. Moskva: Iskusstvo, 1953. 16 pp. Illustrated.

A brief appreciation of the singer followed by a large number of illustrations. The quality of the reproductions is poor.

See also item 1708

IVOGÜN, MARIA, b. 1891

See items 1695, 1811

J

JACOBS, ESTHER

658 Jacobs, Esther. *Love and Law. A Story of Joy and Woe in a Singer's Life.* New York: G.W. Dillingham, 1895. vi, 243 pp.

JANACÓPULOS, VERA, 1892-1955

659 França, Eurico Nogueira. *Memorias de Vera Jancópulos.* In Portuguese. Rio de Janeiro: Ministéro da Educaçao e Cultura, Serviço de Documentação, 1959. 83 pp. Illustrated.

JÉLIOTTE, PIERRE, 1713-1797

660 Pougin, Arthur, 1834-1921. *Un ténor de l'Opéra au XVIIIᵉ siècle. Pierre Jélyotte et les chanteurs de son temps.* In French. Paris: Fischbacher, 1905. 235 pp. Illustrated.

JENKINS, FLORENCE FOSTER

661 Bendiner, Milton, b. 1908. *Florence Foster Jenkins*. New York:
The Melotone Recording Studio, 1946. 11 pp. Reprinted in *The Record
Collector* 8, no. 9 (September 1953).

There have been good singers and bad singers, and there was Florence
Foster Jenkins, in a class all by herself. Those who know her voice
from her justly celebrated Melotone recordings will realize that no
bibliography, biographical dictionary or musical encyclopedia could
be considered complete without mentionng her, without an enlightening
discussion of her unique artistry. The editor was pleased to have
been able to locate this valuable booklet, which contains all that is
known today about the life and career of this remarkable lady.

JERITZA, MARIA, 1887-1982

662 Jeritza, Maria. *Sunlight and Song; a Singer's Life*. Translated
by Frederick H. Martens. New York: D. Appleton and Company, 1924.
viii, 261 pp. Illustrated. The German edition of this book (if
there was one) could not be located.

Considering Jeritza's fame and artistic stature, this is a most
disappointing autobiography. It is unforgivable of a singer, for
whom composers like Korngold and Richard Strauss wrote lead roles, to
spend nearly one-fourth of her memoirs on political name dropping
and lengthy discussions of the various members of the Hapsburg family.
By contrast, she has little to say about the world premieres of
Ariadne auf Naxos (she was a member of the cast of both versions) and
Die Frau ohne Schatten. She devotes a whole chapter to her mother-
in-law, Blanche Marchesi, without ever mentioning her husband, Baron
von Popper. Most of her writing focuses on the trivial and superficial, substantiating Strauss's outburst of "dumme Ganz," which he
once called her during a rehearsal.

The book was published in 1924 when Jeritza was thirty-seven. She
threatened to write another one thirty years later. It is to be regretted she didn't; age must have brought her wisdom. There are two
conspicuous factual errors: Piccaver was born in England and raised
in the United States, thus he was not "American"; Albert Niemann could
not have sung in the Metropolitan Opera House in 1866, eighteen years
before it opened (p. 50).

662-a ———. *Sunlight and Song; a Singer's Life*. Translated by
Frederick H. Martens. New York: Arno Press, 1977. viii, 261 pp.
Illustrated.

Reprint of the 1924 edition published by D. Appleton, New York (q.v.).

663 Decsey, Ernst, b. 1870. *Maria Jeritza*. In German and English.
Wien: J. Fischer-Verlag, 1931. 25 pp. Illustrated.

664 Müller-Guttenbrunn, Roderich, 1892-1956. *Bagage; Reigen um eine
Sängerin*. In German. Wien: Fiba-Verlag, 1931. 348 pp. Author's
pseudonym, Dietrich Arndt, at head of title.

665 Nagy, István. *A Jeritza, a Saljapin, meg a Biller. Egy ujságiró jegyzetei a szinházi világbõl.* In Hungarian. Budapest: Szekulesz, 1928. 146 pp. Only copy located held in the Széchenyi Library, Budapest.

666 Werba, Robert. *Primadonna des Verismo: Maria Jeritza.* In German. Vienna: Österreichischer Bundesverlag, 1981. 186 pp. Illustrated. Bibliography, pp. 175-184. Repertory, pp. 171-174.

667 Wymetal, Wilhelm. *Marie Jeritza.* In German. Wien: "Wila," 1922. 51 pp. Illustrated.

See also items 1541, 1695, 1803

JOACHIM, AMALIE, 1839-1899

668 Plaschke, Olga. *Amalie Joachim; Blätter der Erinnerung, dem Freundes- und Schülerkreise der verewigten Meisterin*, gewidmet von Olga Plaschke. In German. Berlin: "Harmonie" Verlagsgesellschaft, 1899. 39 pp. Illustrated.

JOHNSON, EDWARD, 1878-1959

669 Mercer, Ruby. *The Tenor of His Time: Edward Johnson of the Met.* With a discography by J.B. McPherson and W.R. Moran. Toronto: Clarke, Irwin, 1976. xv, 336 pp. Illustrated.

A generally competent, well-researched account of the singer's life. Chapters bracket specific years of his career, which is helpful. The degree of accuracy obtained is largely due to the meticulous editing of Jim McPherson. Space restrictions by the publisher forced the discographers to list the details of published takes only. WRM

670 Simon, Robert Edward, b. 1914. *Be Your Own Music Critic. The Carnegie Hall Anniversary Lectures by Olin Downes, Edward Johnson, Yves Tinayre and others....* Garden City, N.Y.: Doubleday, Doran and Co., 1941. xiv, 300 pp.

See also item 1565

JONES, GWYNETH, b. 1936

671 Mutafian, Claude. *Gwyneth Jones.* In French. Les Trésors de l'Opéra. Paris: Opéra International, 1980. 63 pp. Illustrated. Discography, p. 60. Chronology, pp. 48-59. Filmography, p. 61.

A heavily illustrated, short biography of the Welsh soprano. It summarizes her career, concentrating on her successes, but not ignoring her long spell of vocal difficulties caused by a displaced vertebra, the result of a car accident. The condition wasn't diagnosed properly and remained uncorrected for seven years. The discography seems complete up to the date of publication; the recording companies are identified but record numbers are not given.

JORDAN, JULES, 1850-1927

672 Jordan, Jules. *The Happenings of a Musical Life.* Providence: Palmer Press, 1922. 195 pp. Illustrated.

The reminiscences of a singer, teacher, conductor and composer. Possessor of a fine tenor voice but short in stature, he declined an operatic career but was active as a concert and oratorio singer. He sang the title role in the first American performance of *La Damnation de Faust* at Steinway Hall under the baton of Leopold Damrosch. He gives a fairly detailed account of his life, devoting long passages to Campanari, Melba, Nordica, Kellog and Christine Nilsson.

JOURNET, FRANÇOISE, 1675-1722

673 Vallas, Léon, b. 1879. *"Les Lyonnais dignes de mémoire."* I. La *véritable histoire de Françoise Journet, chanteuse d'opéra (1675-1722).* II. J.-B. Prin et son Mémoire sur la trompette marine (1742). In French. Lyon: Imprimerie réunies, 1912. 41 pp.

The first paper, relating to Françoise Journet, appeared in the *Revue d'histoire de Lyon*, November-December 1911. It constitutes the first 28 pages of this booklet.

JOVICZKY, JÓZSEF, b. 1918

See item 1740

JURINAC, SENA, b. 1921

674 Tamussino, Ursula. *Sena Jurinac.* In German. Augsburg: Schroff-Druck Verlagsgesellschaft, 1971. 214 pp. Illustrated. Chronology, pp. 195-206.

This biography, concentrating almost exclusively on the artistic--as opposed to private--life of the singer gives a fair account of her career. The book is enhanced by a good chronology and a superb collection of photographs; the design and printing are excellent.

See also item 1788

K

KANAWA, KIRI TE

See Te Kanawa, Kiri

KASCHMANN, GIUSEPPE, 1847-1925

See items 1620, 1680

KASHKIN, NIKOLAI DMITRIEVICH, 1839–1920

675 IAkovlev, Vasilii Vasil'evich, 1880–1957. *N.D. Kashkin.* In
Russian. Zamechatelnye russkie muzykanty. Moskva: Gos. muzykal'noe
izd-vo, 1950. 59 pp. Illustrated.

KATKINŠ, ADOLFS, b. 1885

676 Katkinš, Adolfs. *Dzives opera; atminu telojumi.* Redigejis
Edgars Andersons. In Latvian. Stockholm: Daugava, 1965. 261 pp.
Illustrated.

KATUL'SKAIA, ELENA KLIMENT'EVNA, 1888–1966

677 Grosheva, Elena Andreevna, editor. *Elena Kilment'evna Katul'skaia.*
Sbornik. In Russian. Deiateli muzykal'nogo teatra. Moskva: Sov.
kompozitorov, 1973. 325 pp. Illustrated.

678 ———. *Katul'skaia.* In Russian. Moskva: Gos. muzykal'noe
izd-vo, 1957. 236 pp. Illustrated.

KELLOGG, CLARA LOUISE, 1842–1916

679 Kellogg, Clara Louise. *Memoirs of an American Prima Donna*, by
Clara Louise Kellogg (Mme. Strakosch). New York: G.P. Putnam's Sons,
1913. xiii, 382 pp. Illustrated. Index.

  Clara Louise Kellogg (named after the famous soprano Clara Novello,
1818–1908) was a contemporary and personal friend of Adelina Patti.
Her husband, Carl Strakosch, was the nephew of Maurice Strakosch,
teacher and manager of Adelina, and Max Strakosch, husband of Amelia
Patti. Kellogg was the first American singer to achieve truly international fame. She had a repertory of over forty roles; she was the
first Marguerite in Gounod's *Faust* in America (New York, 26 November
1863), as well as the first American Mignon and Senta. Her book is
remarkably frank in her opinions of her peers (she thought Carlotta
Patti "a more satisfactory singer to Adelina") and is an important
reference work for information about the state of opera in Europe and
America during the last quarter of the 19th century. WRM

679-a ———. *Memoirs of an American Prima Donna.* Da Capo Press
Music Reprint Series. New York: Da Capo Press, 1978. xiii, 382 pp.
Illustrated. Index.

  Reprint of the 1913 edition published by Putnam, New York (q.v.).

See also item 1694

KELLY, MICHAEL, 1764?–1826

680 Kelly, Michael. *Reminiscences of Michael Kelly, of the King's
Theatre; Including a Period of Nearly Half a Century; with Original*

Anecdotes of Many Distinguished Persons, Political, Literary, and Musical. London: N.p., 1825. 2 vols.

Singer, composer, impresario, man of the theater, Michael Kelly completed his autobiography near the end of his life and it first appeared shortly before his death. Kelly, being a raconteur rather than a writer, his publisher, Henry Colburn, saw fit to engage a ghost writer, Theodore Hook. The full extent of Hook's contribution cannot be ascertained, the tongue-in-cheek style can be as much his as the vain and witty Irishman's. The life story is rich in detail, populated by a large number of famous people of all walks of theatrical, literary and musical life. Of special interest are the numerous references to Sheridan and Mozart; Kelly created the role of Don Basilio and Don Curzio in the first performance of *The Marriage of Figaro* at the composer's invitation.

680-a ───────. *Reminiscences of Michael Kelly of the King's Theatre and Theatre Royal Drury Lane.* New introduction by A. Hyatt King. Da Capo Press Music Reprint Series. New York: Da Capo Press, 1968. 2 vols.

Reprint of the 1825? edition, printed in London (q.v.).

680-b ───────. *Reminiscences of Michael Kelly.* Compiled by Theodore Edward Hook. New York: B. Blom, 1969. xv, 424 pp.

680-c ───────. *Reminiscences*; edited with an introduction by Roger Fiske. Oxford English Memoirs and Travels. London: Oxford University Press, 1975. xx, 396 pp. Illustrated. Index, pp. 373-396.

680-d ───────. *Solo Recital: The Reminiscences of Michael Kelly*; edited and with a biographical index by Herbert van Thal; introduction by J.C. Trewin. Abridged ed. London: Folio Society, 1972. 372 pp. Illustrated. Index.

681 Ellis, Stewart Marsh. *The Life of Michael Kelly, Musician, Actor, and Bon Viveur, 1762-1826.* London: V. Gollancz, 1930. 400 pp. Illustrated.

682 Jacob, Naomi Ellington, b. 1889. *The Irish Boy, a Romantic Biography.* London: Hutchinson, 1955. 288 pp.

KEMP, BARBARA, 1881-1959

683 Bie, Oskar, b. 1864. *Barbara Kemp.* Der Schauspieler, nr. 8. In German. Berlin: E. Reiss, 1921. 47 pp. Illustrated.

See also item 1742

KESTEREN, JOHN VAN, b. 1921

684 Kesteren, John van. *Notities van een 'notekraker.'* In Dutch. Nieuwkoop: Heuff, 1978. 83 pp. Illustrated.

KHANAEV, NIKANDR SERGEEVICH

685 Moscow. Gosudarstvennyi akademicheskii Bol'shoi teatr. *Nikandr Sergeevich Khanaev.* In Russian. Moskva: Iskusstvo, 1953. Unpaged. Illustrated.

A brief appreciation of the singer, followed by many illustrations. The quality of reproduction is poor. Khanaev was a tenor of the Bol'shoi; his roles included Sadko, Hermann, Otello, Raoul, Radames, Dimitrii, Faust, Shuiskii.

KHOKHLOV, PAVEL AKINFIEVICH, 1854-1919

686 IAkovlev, Vasilii Vasil'evich, 1880-1957. *P.A. Khokhlov.* In Russian. Moskva: Gos. muzykal'noe izd-vo, 1950. 47 pp. Illustrated.

KIEPURA, JAN, 1902-1966

687 Hernicz, Roman. *Mozg i krtan. Opowies o Jane Kiepurze.* In Polish. Wieden, 1931. 111 pp. Information taken from the British Museum General Catalogue.

688 Ramage, Jean. *Jan Kiepura.* In French. Collection "Spécial Opéra." "Supplément semestriel au no. 71 d'OPÉRA." Paris: SODAL, 1969. 32 pp. Illustrated.

A fine short biography of the best-known Polish tenor of the century and his Hungarian-born wife of thirty years, Marta Eggerth. They appeared together in several films and countless productions of musicals and operetta in the United States and Europe. This booklet presents the highlights of his rich career on both sides of the Atlantic and both sides of Broadway: The Metropolitan Opera and musicals.

689 Waldorff, Jerzy. *Jan Kiepura.* In Polish. Krakow: Polskie Wydaw. Muzyczne, 1976. 93 pp. Illustrated.

KINGSTON, MORGAN, 1881-1936

See item 1565

KIRKBY-LUNN, LOUISE, 1873-1930

See item 1635

KIRSTEN, DOROTHY, b. 1915

690 Kirsten, Dorothy, and Lanfranco Rasponi. *A Time to Sing.* Garden City, N.Y.: Doubleday and Company, 1982. xiv, 247 pp. Illustrated. Index, pp. 241-247. Discography, pp. 235-239. Awards, Degrees, Citations, p. 233.

One of the most successful, best-balanced autobiographies by a prima donna in recent years. It is a frank, unpretentious piece of writing, a literary entity just like Kirsten's career is a musical whole. The omission of her repertory is but a minor flaw. The discography by Stanley A. Bowker includes 78 rpm records and seems complete, except for the complete 1949 Met *Faust* the editor saw and heard in his youth on four (or five?) 14" LP records. Anyone know the whereabouts of that set?

See also items 1654, 1792

KLAFSKY, KATHARINA, 1855-1896

691 Ordemann, Ludwig. *Aus dem Leben und Wirken von Katharina Klafsky.* In German. Hameln: T. Fuendeling, 1903. vii, 90 pp. Illustrated.

See also item 1658

KNOTE, HEINRICH, 1870-1953

692 Wagenmann, Josef Hermann, b. 1876. *Der sechzigjährige deutsche Meistersänger Heinrich Knote in seiner stimmbildnerischen Bedeutung und im Vergleich mit anderen Sängern.* In German. München: E. Hecht, 1931. 257 pp. Illustrated. Advertising Matter, pp. 254-257.

KÖTH, ERIKA, b. 1927

693 Adam, Klaus. *Herzlichst! Erika Köth.* In German. Darmstadt: Justus von Liebig Verlag, 1969. 295 pp. Illustrated.

KOLLO, RENÉ, b. 1937

694 Fabian, Imre. *René Kollo.* In German. Zürich: Orell Füssli Verlag, 1982? 172 pp. Illustrated.

KOROLEWICZ-WAYDOWA, JANINA, 1875-1957

695 *Janina Korolewicz-Waydowa, 35-lecie dzialalności.* In Polish. Warszawa: Druk "Monolit," 1935. 61 pp. Illustrated.

696 Korolewicz-Waydowa, Janina. *Sztuka i zycie; mój pamietik.* Text opracowal, przedmowa i komentarzem opatrz. A. Gozdawa-Reutt. In Polish. Wroclawa: Narodowy im Ossolinskich, 1958.

The Polish soprano offers an interesting overview of theatrical life at the end of the 19th century and the first half of the 20th. She describes her meetings with many singers, some of whom are regarded today as the pillars of the history of lyric art. Profusely annotated with helpful notes, there is also an extensive biographical section (pp. 324-399) of the personages mentioned in the book. RT

697 ————. *Zhizn' i iskusstvo; vospominaniia opernoi pevitsy.*
Translated by M. Malkova. In Russian. Leningrad: Iskustvo, 1965.
344 pp. Illustrated. Index, pp. 332-341. Notes, pp. 298-331.

The Russian translation of her autobiography published in Warsaw
under the title *Sztuka i zycie; mój pamiętik* (q.v.).

KOSCHAT, THOMAS, b. 1845

698 Krobath, Karl, b. 1875. *Thomas Koschat der Sänger Kärntens,
seine Zeit und sein Schaffen.* In German. Leipzig: F.E.C. Leuckart,
1912. 135 pp. Illustrated.

KOZLOVSKII, IVAN SEMENOVICH, b. 1900

699 Kuznetsova, Anna Sergeevna. *Narodnyi artist; stranitsy zhizni
i tvorchestva I.S. Kozlovskogo.* In Russian. Moskva: Sovetskaia
Rossiia, 1964. 204 pp. Illustrated.

700 Moscow. Gosudarstvennyi akademicheskii Bol'shoi teatr. *Ivan
Semenovich Kozlovskii.* In Russian. Moskva: Iskusstvo, 1953. Unpaged. Illustrated.

A brief appreciation of the singer containing many well-selected
illustrations, but their reproduction is of poor quality.

701 Sletov, V. *I. Kozlovskii.* In Russian. Mastera Bol'shogo
teatra. Moskva: Gos. muzykal'noe izd-vo, 1951. 47 pp. Illustrated.

KRÁSOVÁ, MARTA, 1901-1970

702 Solin, Vladimir. *Marta Krásová.* In Czech. Umelci Narodniho
divadla, sv. 1. Praha: Panton, 1960. 39 pp. Illustrated.

KRAUSS, GABRIELLE, 1842-1906

703 Charnacé, Guy de, 1825-1909. *Gabrielle Krauss.* In French.
Les étoiles du chant, 3 livr. Paris: H. Plon, 1869. 28 pp. Illustrated.

See also items 1573, 1588

KRAVEISHVILI, BATU IRAKLIEVICH

704 Kraveishvili, Batu Iraklievich. *Nezabyvaemoe. Zapiski pevtsa.*
Translated by A. Tsulukidze. In Russian. Tbilisi: Merani, 1970.
292 pp. Illustrated.

KRÜGER, EMMY

705 Krüger, Emmy. *Der Weg einer deutschen Künstlerin.* In German.
München: C. Wolf und Sohn, 1940. 127 pp. Illustrated.

KRUSZELNICKA, SALOMEA, 1872-1953

706 Golovashchenko, Mikhaila, editor. *Solomiia Krushel'nits'ka;
spogadi, materiali, listuvannaia.* In Ukrainian. Kiev: Muzichna
Ukraina, 1979. 2 vols. Illustrated. Repertory, Vol. 2, pp. 383-384.
Discography, Vol. 2, pp. 163-167. Library of Congress catalogs this
work under its title.

An outstanding collection of reminiscences about Kruszelnicka,
written by more than a hundred individuals. The second volume contains newspaper and magazine articles, and interviews (translated into
Ukrainian) about her international appearances, including an article
from *The New York Times* (1928) and one from *Hobbies* (1939). Additional
documentary materials include 170 letters written to and by the
singer. The book is generously illustrated. This being the only
work about this important singer, and Ukrainian one of the less accessible languages, the book certainly deserves to be translated.

KURZ, SELMA, 1875-1933

707 Goldmann, Hermann. *Selma Kurz, der Werdegang einer Sängerin.*
In German. Bielsko?: Im Selbstverlage des Herausgebers, 1934. 78 pp.
Illustrated.

708 Halban, Dési, and Ursula Ebbers. *Selma Kurz; die Sängerin und
ihre Zeit.* In German. Stuttgart: Belser, 1983. 224 pp. Illustrated.
Bibliography. Repertory. Index.

Published by the daughter of Selma Kurz, herself a singer, to com-
memmorate the fiftieth anniversary of the death of her mother. Most
of the material is taken from original correspondence, as well as
notes dictated to Halban during Kurz's last illness. An outstanding,
beautifully illustrated book.

L

LABÁN, EUGENIO, 1843-1910

See item 1756

LABIA, MARIA, 1880-1953

See items 368, 1823

LABLACHE, LUIGI, 1794-1858

709-T Lablache, Luigi. *Complete Method of Singing*; ... Translated from French. Boston, 1830.

709-T-a ————. *A Complete Method of Singing for the Bass Voice* ... *with Illustrative Examples, Exercises and Progressive Studies in Vocalization.* Boston: O. Ditson, 1894. 88 pp.

710 ————. *Exercises pour mezzo-soprano ou contralto*; revus par Max Friedländer. In French. Leipzig: Peters, n.d. 24 pp.

711 ————. *Exercises pour voix de soprano ou tenor avec accompagnement de piano....* En 2 suites.... In French. Mayence: B. Schott, 1844. 2 vols. in 1.

712 ————. *XIV Vocalises; a Selection of Useful Solfeggi for Soprano or Tenor.* Cleveland: Brainard, n.d. 31 pp.

713 ————. *Lablache's Complete Method of Singing: or, A Rational Analysis of the Principles According to which the Studies Should Be Directed for Developing the Voice* ... *with Examples for Illustration, and Progressive Vocalizing Exercises.* New York: S.T. Gordon, 18?? 102 pp.

714 ————. *Méthode complète de chant avec exemples démonstratifs, exercises et vocalises gradués. No. 1, pour soprano ou tenor.* In French and German. Mayence: B. Schott, 1840. 101 pp.

715 ————. *Méthode complète de chant; ou, Analyse raisonnée des principes d'après lesquels on doit diriger les études pour développer la voix, la rendre légère et pour former le goût, avec exemples démonstratifs, exercises et vocalises graduées.* In French. Paris: Canaux, 1840. 90 pp. Illustrated.

716-T ————. *Metodo completo di canto; ossia, Analisi ragionata di principi sui quali diriger gli studi per isviluppar la voce, renderla pieghevole e formar il gusto, con esempi dimostrativi, esercizi e vocalizzi graduati.* In Italian. Milano: G. Ricordi, 18??. 95 pp.

717-T ————. *New Instructions on the Art of Singing: Comprising Directions for the Formation and Cultivation of the Voice, after the Methods of the Best Italian Masters; also a Series of Progressive Lessons ... Chiefly Selected from Lablache.* Arranged and edited by Edward F. Rimbault. London: Chappell, 185? 81 pp.

718 Blaze, François Henri Joseph, called Castil-Blaze, 1784-1857. *Biographie de Lablache.* In French. Paris. 1850.

719 *Onori alla memoria di Luigi Lablache.* In Italian. Napoli: Teodoro Cottrau, 1858. 85 pp.

A collection of commemorative articles, contributed by various authors (including his son-in-law, Thalberg), published shortly after his death.

720 Widén, Gust. *Lablache, en bild från sångens guldålder; några anteckningar vid hundraårsminnet af Luigi Lablache*. In Swedish. Music Lovers' Series. Göteborg: W. Zachrissons boktrychkeri, 1897. xiii, 184 pp. Illustrated.

See also items 1562, 1601, 1620, 1680, 1745

LABORDE, ROSINE, b. 1824

721 Jahyer, Félix. *Rosine Laborde*. In French. Paris: Bouchy, 1908. 16 pp.

LAGET, AUGUSTE, 1821-1902

722 Laget, Auguste. *Le chant et les chanteurs*. In French. Paris: Heugel, 1874. 364 pp. Sequel: *Le monde artiste* (q.v.).

723 ———. *Le monde artiste*. In French. Paris: Heugel, 1883. 336 pp. Sequel to his: *Le chant et les chanteurs* (q.v.).

LAMPERTI, FRANCESCO, 1811-1892

See item 789

LANGDON, MICHAEL, b. 1920

724 Langdon, Michael, and Richard Fawkes. *Notes from a Low Singer*. London: Julia MacRae, 1982. 205 pp. Illustrated. Index, pp. 197-205.

The double-pun of the title foreshadows the tone of the book: it is written with insight, healthy objectivity and the right touch of understated humor. Langdon is the quintessential Covent Garden product and his life story is populated with the artistic and administrative luminaries of the house. He gives credit where it is due; at the same time he is not afraid to recognize artistic--or human--failures, including his own. The book reads well; it informs, educates and entertains.

LANZA, MARIO, 1921-1959

725 Bernard, Matt. *Mario Lanza*. New York: Macfadden-Bartell Corp., 1971. 224 pp.

The sensationalism of this book impairs whatever other values it may have. It concentrates excessively on the ugly side of Lanza's life and character, and dwells overlong on his sexual exploits. If the latter were part of a larger, longer, more complete biography, it would not be such a distracting, disproportionate component of the story. There is a fascinating hour-by-hour narrative of the Las Vegas disaster. If it is accurate--and it sounds accurate--it only accentuate's Lanza's desperate need of psychiatric help.

The book tells nothing of its author or his sources; it would have been a helpful guide in trying to determine the book's reliability. However, there is a wealth of details concerning episodes that could be known only by someone quite close to the singer. There is no index, notes or illustrations.

726 Callinicos, Constantine, and Ray Robinson. *The Mario Lanza Story*. New York: Coward-McCann, 1960. 256 pp. Illustrated. Discography, pp. 251-256.

The first Lanza biography, written within a year of the singer's death by his accompanist and orchestra conductor on many of his records. Although imperfect in many ways, this biography succeeds in making the reader understand that it takes a strong, secure, balanced individual to cope with sudden fame and fortune, and Mario Lanza had none of these qualities. He was erratic, paranoid, insecure. The self-made crises of his private and professional life prevented him from attaining the artistic excellence for which he was predestined, as much by his musicality, physique and exceptional good looks as by his voice, whose inborn qualities ranked with those of the greatest singers of the century. The writing and structure of the book is good, without being distinguished. The discography, current as of 1960, seems to be complete up to that date. Only catalog numbers and selection (or album) titles are given. Lanza recorded for RCA Victor only.

727 Hausner, Hermann Maximilian, b. 1935. *Mario Lanza; Tragödie einer Stimme*. In German. München: Dokumenten Verlag, 1962. 135 pp. Illustrated. Bibliography, pp. 134-135.

728 Strait, Raymond, and Terry Robinson. *Lanza, His Tragic Life*. Englewood Cliffs, N.J.: Prentice-Hall, 1980. 181 pp. Illustrated. Index, pp. 177-181. Discography, pp. 173-175.

This is chronologically the third Lanza biography and, in different ways, just as unsatisfactory as its predecessors. It recounts the events of Lanza's life as it became known to his physical fitness coach, coauthor Terry Robinson. Initially it was Robinson's job to train with Lanza and bring his weight down for each motion picture to make him fit to face the cameras; he soon became Lanza's closest friend and confidant. As the authors are apparently not qualified to discuss music and singing, they wisely don't. They mention a few of Lanza's sexual escapades which, considering the singer's reported preoccupation with them, is not inappropriate. But on the whole the book remains a shallow collection of loosely knit details from his private life that do not add up to a total picture. The late Mrs. Lanza's contention that Mario was killed in his hospital bed by the Mafia, in revenge for a cancelled concert, makes one wonder as to its veracity. As the other biographies, this too adds something to the Lanza story while it remains incomplete. The discography lists only LP albums, but none of the 45 rpm singles nor the 78s.

LASSALLE, JEAN, 1847-1909

See item 1588

LAURI-VOLPI, GIACOMO, 1892-1979

729 Lauri-Volpi, Giacomo. *A viso aperto*. In Italian. Milano: "Corbaccio": dall'Oglio, 1953. 482 pp. Illustrated.

730 ———. *Cristalli viventi*. In Italian. Roma: Atlantica, 1948. 311 pp. Illustrated.

731 ———. *L'equivoco (così è, e non vi pare)*. In Italian. 2nd ed. Milano: Edizioni Corbaccio, 1939. 441 pp. Illustrated. First edition could not be located.

Lauri-Volpi had an unusually long career, from his debut in 1919 well into the 1970s when he made his last recording. This volume covers the events of the first portion of that career, until 1938. It makes fascinating reading with a wealth of detail, not only about the tenor's career, but also about his fellow artists, impresari, and the world of opera in general for the period it covers. The large amount of factual information makes this book particularly valuable. TGK

731-a ———. *L'equivoco*. In Italian. Bologna: Bongiovanni, 1979. 265 pp. Illustrated.

732 ———. *Incontri e scontri*. In Italian. Le Carte Nascoste, no. 1. Roma: Bonavita, 1971. 414 pp.

733 ———. *Misteri della voce umana*. In Italian. Milano: Dall'Oglio, 1957. 361 pp.

734 ———. *Parlando a Maria*. In Italian. Roma: Trevi editore, 1972. 312 pp. Illustrated. Index.

Concerns María Asunción de Aguilar Ros.

735 ———. *La voce di Cristo*. In Italian. Roma: Tip. della Pace, 1971. 261 pp.

736-T ———. *Voces paralelas*. Translated by Manuel Torregrosa-Valero. In Spanish. Colección Universitaria de Bolsillo "Punto Omega," Sección Arte, no. 174. Madrid: Ediciones Guadarrama, 1974. 252 pp.

Spanish translation of the second edition of his *Voci parallele* (q.v.). There is a biographical sketch of Lauri-Volpi at the end of the volume, a chronological account of his career and a list of his books. WRM

737 ———. *Voci parallele*. In Italian. Milano: Aldo Garzanti, 1955. 253 pp.

The premise of this book is to give the reader the benefit of the author's long experience by comparing the voices of the older and younger generations of singers. Lauri-Volpi emphasizes in the preface that these comparisons are indeed parallels drawn for their instructive value and not to exalt or denigrate any of the subjects. Many of the comparisons are successful, some forced, a few invalid. But most of Lauri-Volpi's observations are of interest as they come from a successful, experienced, knowledgeable—if somewhat opinionated—singer who expresses his ideas with clarity and insight.

737-a ————. *Voci parallele*. In Italian. 2nd revised ed. Milano: Garzanti, 1960. 279 pp.

This is the "second revised, updated and enlarged" edition first published in 1955 by the same publisher (q.v.). The observations made of that work apply to this one also.

737-b ————. *Voci parallele*. In Italian. 3rd revised ed. Bologna: Bongiovanni, 1977. 238 pp.

738-T ————. *La voz de Cristo*. Translated by Andrés Travesí. In Spanish. Colección "Los Tres Dados." Madrid: Editorial Prensa Española, 1969. 222 pp.

Spanish translation of *La voce di Cristo* (q.v.).

739 Bragaglia, Leonardo, b. 1932. *La voce solitaria: cinquanta personaggi per Giacomo Lauri-Volpi. Con venti lettere autografe inedite di Lauri-Volpi a Bragaglia*. In Italian. Roma: Bulzoni, 1982. 253 pp. Illustrated. Bibliography, p. 240. Discography, pp. 242-253.

739/A Gustarelli, Andrea, b. 1884. *Chi è Giacomo Lauri-Volpi*. In Italian. Collana biografica dei grandi artisti lirici italiani. Milano: Edizioni "L'Attuale," 1932. 70 pp. Illustrated.

Born out of a polemic, the book begins with the difficult childhood, moves on to his distinguished military service in World War I and concludes with a short summary of his career from his debut to his great successes. The author's name is absent from the title page; it appears only as a signature at the end of the book. RT

See also items 1569/A, 1834

LAWRENCE, MARJORIE, 1909-1979

740 Lawrence, Marjorie. *Interrupted Melody; the Story of My Life*. New York: Appleton-Century-Crofts, 1949. 307 pp. Illustrated. Index.

Melbourne-born Marjorie Lawrence studied in Paris with Cecile Gilly and made her debut in Monte Carlo, in 1932. She appeared at the Paris Opera until 1935, when she made her debut at the Metropolitan, singing there until 1941. During a season in Mexico City in that year she contracted poliomyelitis, which left her paralyzed in both legs. With an heroic effort and after much hard work and therapy she returned to the concert stage, and eventually appeared in a few operatic performances, as Venus in *Tannhäuser*, Amneris in *Aida*, and in a concert performance of *Elektra*. She narrates all this in unembellished prose, with much emphasis and credit to her husband and "Sister" Elizabeth Kenny who stood by her during her illness and whom she credits with her recovery. WRM

740-a ———. *Interrupted Melody; the Story of My Life.* London: Falcon Press, 1952. 286 pp. Illustrated.

This edition contains fewer and different illustrations than those in the U.S. edition (q.v.). However, there is an additional chapter here called "Australian Music" (pp. 64-67).

See also item 1608

LAWSON, WINIFRED

741 Lawson, Winifred. *A Song to Sing-O!* London: M. Joseph, 1955. 238 pp. Illustrated.

The autobiography of a D'Oyly Carte prima donna who sang all the major Gilbert and Sullivan soprano roles to great critical acclaim, in Great Britain and internationally. She also sang Marguerite in *Faust*, though her operatic appearances were of little consequence. She made acoustic and electric recordings of Sullivan's music for HMV.

LÁZARO, HIPÓLITO, 1887-1974

742 Lázaro, Hipólito. *El libro de mi vida.* In Spanish. La Habana: Editorial Lex, 1949. 897 pp. Illustrated.

Surely one of the most egotistical autobiographies ever written! From the dedication, "A mis admiradores" (To my admirers), to a final 41 pages of carefully selected press reviews, the book is absolutely filled with self-adulation and praise. Throughout, the author carries a broad chip on his shoulder--one might say a log: a curious mixture of bragging and blame heaped upon managers and others for lack of appreciation for his great art. He tells about driving down the streets of Havana, and hearing his voice from his recordings pouring from windows on all sides, yet, he claims that he was never paid royalties for those recordings. He tells of a season (1915) at the Colón in Buenos Aires when the "three aces of the season were Caruso, Lázaro and Ruffo." It would have been difficult, he says, to have found a company which could compete with us! He goes on to say, however, that there existed no sincere friendship among the majority of the company, and that many of the artists must have had "sick livers" because they behaved like cats and dogs. "The only person who paid the consequences was I, for I believed in the sincere friendship which Caruso demonstrated, in spite of the actions which he demonstrated at the Metropolitan to the contrary, as we shall see later on. This was because he said: 'Ah!, if I only had the voice of Lázaro!'" (¡Ah, si yo tuviese la voz de Lázaro!). WRM

742-a ———. *El libro de mi vida.* In Spanish. 3rd ed. Madrid: Editora Nacional, 1968. xvi, 691 pp. Illustrated. Dedication: "A mis admiradores" (To my admirers).

743 ———. *Mi método de canto.* Preface by Frank Marshall. In Spanish. Barcelona: Agustín Núñez (for the author), 1947. 179 pp. Illustrated. "Lecciones de vocalización" (music): pp. 49-118.

From the title, one would assume this was a book of instruction, and after some ten pages of introduction which recite the qualifications of the author, it begins. There is the text for 12 lessons, some filling less than one page. From pages 51 through 118, musical exercises are given, sometimes brief examples from well-known operatic arias. From page 119 to the end of the book, we have a chapter entitled "Consejos" (Advice) which makes suggestions for a singer's diet but soon wanders into personal reminiscences, a brief section of "Enfermedades" (Illness) and finally extensive quotations from the press praising the work of the author as a singer. The work concludes with a list of the opera houses wherein Lázaro has sung. Scattered throughout the text are some 18 portraits of the author. WRM

See also item 1543

LEAR, EVELYN, b. 1930

See item 1654

LEBLANC, GEORGETTE, 1869-1941

744-T Leblanc, Georgette. *The Choice of Life.* Translated by Alexander Teixera de Mattos. New York: Dodd, Mead, 1914. 287 pp. Illustrated.

745 ———. "D'Annunzio au Vittoriale; souvenirs inédits." *Les Oeuvres libres* (Paris) 203 (1938), 111-126. In French.

746-T ———. *The Girl Who Found the Blue Bird.* Translated by Alexander Teixeira de Mattos. London: Hodder and Stoughton, 1914. 159 pp. Illustrated.

English translation of *Le miracle des hommes: Helen Keller.*

747 ———. *La machine à courage; souvenirs.* Préface de Jean Cocteau. In French. Paris: J.B. Janin, 1947. 230 pp. Illustrated. Bibliography, p. 226.

748-T ———. *Maeterlinck and I.* Translated by Janet Flanner. London: Methuen, 1932. 215 pp. Illustrated. The American edition by Dutton was published under the title *Souvenirs; My Life with Maeterlinck* (q.v.).

Sister of author Maurice Leblanc (1864-1941), one of the two important French writers of detective fiction of the first quarter of the twentieth century (and creator of Arsène Lupin), and mistress of the Belgian poet, Maurice Maeterlinck from about 1899 until his marriage to a teen-age girl in 1919. Georgette Leblanc was better known as an actress than a singer. She had created the role of Françoise in Bruneau's *L'Attaque du Moulin* at L'Opéra-Comique in 1893, Ariane in Dukas's *Ariane et Barbe-Bleue* (Comique, 1907), and had sung Fanny in Massenet's *Sapho* as well as the title roles of *Thaïs*, *La Navarraise* and *Carmen*. Maeterlinck tried to force Debussy into accepting Leblanc to create the role of Mélisande, which of course went instead to Mary Garden. She did sing Mélisande, however, in Boston in the season of 1911-12. For a hilarious description of this event, as well as the singer's Carmen, see Quaintance Eaton's *The Boston Opera Company* (Appleton-Century, 1965), pp. 130-144, in a chapter entitled "L'Affaire Maeterlinck."

The present book is a highly emotional exposé of the singer's life with the poet, in which she delights in the role of the injured woman. Unfortunately for any reputation which she may have had as a singer, she left four recordings for Columbia from her 1912 visit; they had disappeared from the catalog by 1916. WRM

749-T ————. *Maeterlinck's Dogs.* Illustrated with drawings by the author. Translated by Alexander Teixeira de Mattos. London: Methuen, 1919. xvi, 176 pp. Illustrated.

Translation of *Nos chiens* (q.v.).

749-T-a ————. *Maeterlinck's Dogs.* Illustrated with drawings by the author. Translated by Alexander Teixeira de Mattos. New York: Dodd, Mead, 1919. xvi, 179 pp. Illustrated.

Translation of *Nos chiens* (q.v.).

750 ————. "Mes conversations avec Éléonora Duse; choses vues." *Les Oeuvres libres* (Paris) 66 (1926), 305-324. In French.

751 ————. *Nos chiens.* Illustré par l'auteur. In French. Paris: Charpentier et Fasquelle, 1919. 117 pp. Illustrated.

752 ————. *Un pélerinage au pays de Madame Bovary.* In French. Paris: Sansot, 1913. 106 pp. Bibliography, pp. 103-106.

753 ————. *Souvenirs (1895-1918).* Précédé d'une introduction par Bernard Gasset. In French. Paris: Bernard Gasset, 1931. xiii, 344 pp.

754-T ————. *Souvenirs; My Life with Maeterlinck.* Translated by Janet Flanner. New York: E.P. Dutton, 1932. 352 pp. Illustrated.

The American edition of *Maeterlinck and I*, published in 1932 by Methuen, London (q.v.).

LEHMANN, LILLI, 1848-1929

755-T Lehmann, Lilli. *How to Sing* [Meine Gesangkunst]. Translated by Richard Aldrich and Clara Willenbücher. New, revised and supplemented ed. New York: Macmillan, 1929. xi, 303 pp. Macmillan re-issued this book several times, the most recent edition as late as 1960.

This is the English translation of Lehmann's *Meine Gesangkunst* (q.v.) by the distinguished music critic of the *New York Times*, Richard Aldrich. Approaching the end of her distinguished career, Lilli Lehmann attempted in this book to explain in easily accessible terms the art and science of singing. "Science understands too little of singing, the singer too little of science" she writes in her preface. Her own formidable technique and competency as a singer lends authority to her statements. Her intelligence and erudition, with the aid of numerous diagrams, surmounts the difficulty of putting into words the skill, craft and art of voice production that can be best expressed by aural means.

755-T-a ————. *How to Sing* [Meine Gesangkunst]. Translated by Richard Aldrich. Northbrook, Ill.: Whitehall, 1972. ix, 281 pp. Illustrated.

756 ————. *Mein Weg*. In German. Leipzig: S. Hirzel, 1913. vii, 309, 280 pp. Illustrated. *Deutsche Bücherverzeichnis*, the source of this citation, does not specify two volumes, as it normally would. The double pagination possibly means two volumes in one.

757 ————. *Meine Gesangkunst*. In German. Berlin: Verlag der Zukunft, 1902. 45 pp. Illustrated. *Kayser*, where this information was located, gives the pagination thus: "45 Seite mit 31 Tafeln un Bildnis," i.e., the total pagination would be 76, one page less than given by the Library of Congress for the 1961 Bote and Bock edition (q.v.). Thus probably the correct number of pages is 76, not 45.

757-a ————. *Meine Gesangkunst*. In German. Berlin: Bote and Bock, 1961. 75 pp. Illustrated.

758 ————. *My Path Through Life*. Translated by Alice Benedict Seligman. New York: G.P. Putnam's Sons, 1914. xiii, 510 pp. Illustrated. Repertory, pp. 489-495. Index, pp. 497-510.

The English translation of her *Mein Weg* (q.v.). Lilli Lehmann, who began her career as a florid lyric soprano of the old Italian school of Bellini and Donizetti and who became one of the greatest of all Brünnhildes and Isoldes, produced this monumental and very Germanic autobiography in her 65th year. It is a strictly chronological account of her life, with much first-hand information on Wagner and the first *Ring* production at Bayreuth in which she sang the very first lines as one of the Rhinemaidens. Her repertory included more than 170 roles in 115 operas. After 35 years on the operatic stage she became a famous voice teacher, numbering among her pupils, Olive Fremstad and Geraldine Farrar. Her book is a perfect goldmine of historical information, with only very seldom a tiny glint of humor. WRM

758-a ————. *My Path Through Life*. Translated by Alice Benedict Seligman. New York: Arno Press, 1977. xiii, 510 pp. Illustrated. Repertory, pp. 489-495. Index, pp. 497-510.

Reprint of the 1914 edition published by G.P. Putnam's Sons, New York (q.v.).

759 ————. *Studie zu Tristan und Isolde*. In German. Wittenberg: Herrose & Ziemsen, 1927. 43 pp. Illustrated.

760 Rie, Therese (Herz), b. 1879. *Lilli Lehmann ... by L. Andro* (pseud.). In German. Moderne Musiker. Berlin: "Harmonie" verlagsgesellschaft für Literatur und Kunst, 1907. 40 pp. Illustrated.

761 Wagenmann, Josef Hermann, b. 1876. *Lilli Lehmanns Geheimnis der Stimmbänder*. In German. Moderne Gesanglehrer. Ebd.?, 1905. 97 pp. Published in: *Allgemeine Bücher-Lexikon* XXXIV (XIV. Supplement, vol. 2).

761-a ─────. *Lilli Lehmann's Geheimnis der Stimmbänder*. In German. 2nd revised ed. Wagenmannbücher, Vol. 2. Leipzig: A. Felix, 1926. 131 pp. First edition published in 1905 as a critical review of Lilli Lehmann's *Geheimnis der Stimmbänder*, which appeared in *Die Woche*, Nov. 1903, and of her treatise, *Meine Gesangkunst*, first published in 1902.

See also items 985-T, 1565, 1615, 1658, 1803, 1804, 1805

LEHMANN, LIZA, 1862-1918

762 Lehmann, Liza. *The Life of Liza Lehmann*. New York: E.P. Dutton, 1918. xii, 232 pp. Illustrated. Index, pp. 229-232.

Liza Lehmann--unrelated to either of her celebrated namesakes--was a concert singer, composer, voice teacher, and the pupil of Jenny Lind. Her social position, both through her husband and her father, a well-known portrait painter and miniaturist, enabled her to associate with prominent artists, writers, musicians of her times. This included frequent visits to the paternal home by Liszt, Browning, Brahms and numerous others. She also attended with her parents a private dinner at the Verdis' home in Genoa, Boito being the other invited guest. After dinner young Liza sang Scottish songs for the composer. The polished style of Lehmann shows erudition and her graceful prose lends distinction to the simple narrative of her life.

762-a ─────. *The Life of Liza Lehmann*. London: T.F. Unwin, 1919. xii, 232 pp. Illustrated. Index, pp. 229-232.

762-b ─────. *The Life of Liza Lehmann*. Da Capo Press Music Reprint Series. New York: Da Capo Press, 1980. xii, 232 pp. Illustrated. Index, pp. 229-232.

Reprint of the 1920 edition published by E.P. Dutton, New York (q.v.).

763 ─────. *Practical Hints for Students of Singing*. London: Enoch, 19?? 117 pp.

LEHMANN, LOTTE, 1888-1976

764 Lehmann, Lotte. *Anfang und Aufstieg*. *Lebenserinnerungen*. In German. Wien, 1937. 237 pp.

765-T ─────. *Eternal Flight*. Translated by Elsa Krauch. New York: G.P. Putnam's Sons, 1937. 265 pp.

The English translation of *Orplid, mein Land*. *Roman* (q.v.). It is a romantic novel about an opera singer and the world of opera.

766 ─────. *Eighteen Song Cycles: Studies in Their Interpretation*; with a foreword by Neville Cardus. London: Cassell, 1971. xiii, 185 pp. Dedicated to the memory of Paul Ulanowsky.

An introduction (pp. 1-7) discusses "Interpretation," much of which is taken word-for-word from the Introduction to the same author's

More Than Singing (1945, q.v.). The discussions of *An die ferne Geliebte*, *Die Winterreise*, *Die schöne Müllerin*, *Dichterliebe* and *Frauenliebe* are also taken from the earlier work. The balance of the text is new. An index to the first lines and titles of the individual songs of the eighteen cycles discussed is very helpful. Lehmann's fame as an interpreter of the German Lied was well justified; the discussions of these songs was developed during the years in which she taught "Master Classes" in interpretation in Santa Barbara, California. WRM

767 ———. *Five Operas and Richard Strauss*. Translated by Ernst Pawel. New York: Macmillan, 1964. ix, 209 pp. Illustrated. Index, pp. 207-209. The 1964 H. Hamilton, London, edition was published under the title: *Singing with Richard Strauss* (q.v.).

Detailed discussions, including a review of the plots, as well as personal reminiscences of singing under the composer's direction, of *Ariadne auf Naxos*, *Die Frau ohne Schatten*, *Intermezzo*, *Arabella* and *Der Rosenkavalier*. In a "First Postscript" she says: "These five Strauss operas in which I was chosen to sing the main roles comprise but a small part of my very extensive opera repertoire, but they have always loomed as milestones. Among them, in turn, the Marschallin stands out by herself. Long after I had given up most of my other roles in obedience to the inexorable command of time, I still was being recalled to the stage to re-create this, my favorite role. And whenever I sang it, I felt caught up in the sheer joy of it, swept away by its magic, the words and music streaming out as though they were truly part of myself and created by me. And whenever I closed the door on Sophie and Octavian to leave them to their bliss, I always felt as though I were closing the door upon part of my own life, taking leave with a smile." In a second postscript, Lehmann discusses directing *Der Rosenkavalier* at the Metropolitan Opera in New York. WRM

768-T ———. *Midway in My Song, the Autobiography of Lotte Lehmann*. Translated by Margaret Ludwig. Indianapolis: Bobbs-Merrill, 1938. ix, 250 pp. Illustrated. Index, pp. 247-250. "First published in England and as interim copyright established under the title *Wings of Song*" (q.v.).

The English translation of *Anfang und Aufstieg* (q.v.). The author states in her Foreword: "Perhaps it is too early to write my memoirs.... This book represents to me a restful pause for breath--a looking back into the valley. I want to go on. Ahead of me I know lies still a goodly climb...," and in a postscript, dated May 1938, she adds: "This book of my memoirs was written before Germany annexed Austria. My blood is German, my whole being is rooted in the German soil. But my conception of art is different from that of my country. I cannot serve politics. I can only serve that which has always been and still is the mission of my life.... I want to be an artist-- nothing else.... And I who was born a German, and who was bound to Austria with the bonds of deepest love--I stand now at the door of America. I want to become an American citizen. I am sure I shall find my third home here, and that I shall not again need to wander. I want to become a good American. But that which was my beloved Homeland will live on for me in my songs." Later works detail the

accomplishment and fulfillment of her wishes. The book is a sym-
pathetically written, rather nostalgic account of the singer's life,
beginning with childhood recollections, emphasizing her early training and finding of her artistic home in Vienna with her debut as
Agathe in *Der Freischütz* in 1914. There is much of interest about
opera in Vienna and elsewhere in Europe during this period and later,
when Lehmann created the Dyer's Wife in *Die Frau ohne Schatten* (1919)
and took part in the first performance of Strauss's *Intermezzo*
(Dresden, 1924). WRM

768-T-a ———. *Midway in My Song; the Autobiography of Lotte
Lehmann*. Translated by Margaret Ludwig. Freeport, N.Y.: Books for
Libraries Press, 1970. xi, 250 pp. Illustrated. Index, pp. 247-250.

Reprint of the 1938 edition of The Bobbs-Merrill Company, Indianpolis
(q.v.). This is the English translation of her *Anfang und Aufstieg*
(q.v.).

768-T-b ———. *Midway in My Song; the Autobiography of Lotte
Lehmann*. Translated by Margaret Ludwig. Westport, Conn.: Greenwood
Press, 1970. ix, 250 pp. Illustrated. Index, pp. 247-250.

Reprint of the 1938 edition of The Bobbs-Merrill Company, Indianapolis (q.v.). This is the English translation of her *Anfang und Aufstieg*
(q.v.).

769-T ———. *More than Singing, the Interpretation of Songs*.
Translated by Frances Holden. New York: Boosey and Hawkes, 1945.
192 pp. Illustrated.

The book contains, in addition to an introductory letter from Bruno
Walter, a "Foreword" by Lehmann explaining the overbalance of the
contents of the book to German Lieder, followed by an Introduction
(pp. 10-17) in which the author explains her meaning of "Interpretation." The main text of the book discusses the meaning and the interpretation of six songs by Schubert, six by Schumann, eighteen by
Brahms, three by Mendelssohn, ten by Wolf, ten by Strauss, three by
Mahler. The Song Cycle is discussed, with examples from Beethoven,
Schubert amd Schumann. The book concludes with further discussion
of 25 songs from the French, Italian and Russian literatures. WRM

769-T-a ———. *More than Singing: the Interpretation of Songs*.
Translated by Frances Holden. Westport, Conn.: Greenwood Press,
1975. 192 pp.

Reprint of the 1945 edition published by Boosey and Hawkes, New York.

770-T ———. *My Many Lives*. Translated by Frances Holden. New
York: Boosey and Hawkes, 1948. 262 pp. Illustrated.

In a five-page introduction, Mme. Lehmann tells how she once lived
for opera, and that now (i.e., 1948) her life has become even richer
"through a deeper penetration into the boundless realm of the Lied."
She continues, "I am glad to have this opportunity to tell of my
experience in opera. It made me very happy to be asked after the
appearance of my book on interpretation of Lieder, *More Than Singing*
[1945, q.v.] to write of my ideas, experiences and conception of
opera roles which I have sung." The chapters which follow do just

that, and are titled: Elsa, Elisabeth, Eva, Sieglinde, Leonore, Manon Lescaut, Marguerite, Tatjana, and the Marschallin. Interspersed are chapters entitled "Along the Road to an Opera Career" (pp. 54-68), "Singing in Salzburg" (pp. 88-95), "Glimpses of Latin Operas" (pp. 163-175), "Singing with Strauss" (pp. 194-200), and there is a final chapter. One of the great charms of this book are the reminiscences of performances in which the singer took part, and her fellow artists. There are stories about Slezak, comments about roles such as Tosca, Mimi, Suor Angelica, Turandot, and even lengthy remarks about Santuzza, a role she never sang. WRM

770-T-a ———. *My Many Lives*. Translated by Frances Holden. Westport, Conn.: Greenwood Press, 1974. 262 pp. Illustrated.

Reprint of the 1948 edition published by Boosey and Hawkes, New York (q.v.).

771 ———. *Orplid, mein Land; Roman*. In German. Wien: H. Reichner, 1937. 252 pp.

772-T ———. *Singing with Richard Strauss*. Translated by Ernst Pawel. London: H. Hamilton, 1964. xi, 188 pp. Illustrated. The 1964 edition published by Macmillan, New York, was published under the title: *Five Operas and Richard Strauss* (q.v.).

Same text and illustrations as the American and Canadian editions, but without an index.

773-T ———. *Wings of Song, an Autobiography*. Translated by Margaret Ludwig. London: K. Paul, Trench, Trubner, 1938. vi, 251 pp. Illustrated. The 1938 Bobbs-Merrill, Indianapolis, edition was published under the title: *Midway in My Song, the Autobiography of Lotte Lehmann* (q.v.).

This is the English translation of her *Anfang und Aufstieg* (q.v.).

774 Eustis, Morton Corcoran, 1905-1944. *Players at Work; Acting According to the Actors; with a Chapter on the Singing Actor by Lotte Lehmann*. New York: Theater Arts, 1937. 127 pp. Illustrated.

The chapters of this book are written by actors, actresses and dancers (Helen Hayes, Lunt and Fontanne, Nazimova, Fred Astaire, etc.) and one vocalist: Lotte Lehmann. Her short ten-page chapter, "The Singing Actor," briefly covers the topic implied by the title.

775 Osborne, Charles, b. 1927, editor. *Opera '66*. London: A. Ross, 1966.

The first and only volume of a new opera annual, it contains a wide selection of excellent articles on a variety of subjects of interest to readers of operatic literature. Particularly noteworthy are the two articles written by Lotte Lehmann (pp. 63-80 and 187-199) and Clifford Elkin's essay about, and entitled, "The Negro Singers" (pp. 200-208).

776 Stefan-Gruenfeldt, Paul, b. 1879. *Bruno Walter, mit Beiträgen von Lotte Lehmann, Thomas Mann, Stefan Zweig*. In German. Wien: H. Reichner, 1936. 76 pp. Illustrated.

777 Wessling, Berndt Wilhelm, b. 1935. *Lotte Lehmann ... mehr als eine Sängerin.* In German. Salzburg: Residenz Verlag, 1969. 209 pp. Illustrated. Bibliography, p. 193. Discography, pp. 194-203.

See also items 1606, 1607, 1608, 1623

LEIDER, FRIDA, 1888-1975

778 Leider, Frida. *Das war mein Teil, Erinnerungen einer Opernsängerin.* In German. Berlin: F.A. Herbig, 1959. 232 pp. Illustrated. Index, pp. 230-232.

779-T ————. *Playing My Part.* Translated by Charles Osborne. New York: Meredith Press, 1966. 217 pp. Illustrated. Index, pp. 215-217. Discography, pp. 211-214.

English translation of her *Das war mein Teil* (q.v.). Leider was considered the greatest Wagnerian soprano of the interwar years. She made her debut in 1915 as Venus and began her climb through the provincial opera houses in Germany. She was also a famous Fidelio and sang many roles in the Italian repertory. Her story encompasses two wars and tells much of her association with conductors and other artists of the 1920s and '30s. There is an excellent discography by Harold Burros, not found in the original German edition. WRM

See also items 1743, 1811

LEISNER, EMMI, 1885-1958

See item 1811

LEMESHEV, SERGEI IAKOVLEVICH, 1902-1977

780 Lemeshev, Sergei IAkovlevich. *Put' k iskusstvy.* In Russian. Moskva: Iskusstvo, 1968. 312 pp. Illustrated. Bibliography, pp. 286-302.

An excellent autobiography of this outstanding Russian tenor. The book is profusely illustrated, showing him in his many roles: Gerald, Almaviva, Indian Guest, Rodolfo, Vladimir, Duke of Mantua, Lenskii, Romeo, Werther, and others; it also contains photographs of his family, teachers, etc. The quality of the reproductions is poor.

781 L'vov, Mikhail L'vovich, 1887-1957. *S. IA. Lemeshev.* In Russian. Laureaty Stalinskoi premii. Moskva: Muzgiz, 1947. 51 pp. Illustrated.

782 Moscow. Gosudarstvennyi akademicheskii Bol'shoi teatr. *Sergei IAkovlevich Lemeshev.* In Russian. Moskva: Iskusstvo, 1953. Unpaged.

A brief appreciation of the singer, followed by many photographs, well selected but the reproduction is of poor quality.

See also item 1686

LENDVAI, ANDOR, 1901-1964

783 Lendvai, Andor. *Két felvonás között.* In Hungarian. Budapest: Baross Könyvkiadóvállalat, 1942. 192 pp. Illustrated.

Lendvai was a student at the Academy of Music in Budapest before he had the opportunity to perfect his technique and study roles with Fritz Feinhals. He began his career in Munich (1928-33). When Hitler came to power, he was dismissed because he was Jewish. He made his debut in 1934 with the Royal Opera House in Budapest as Alfio. In 1939 he was dismissed again for reasons of religion. Silenced by the government, he then wrote his autobiography with the evocative title "Between Two Acts." As he explains, he feels like a singer between acts: ready to sing but without the opportunity to do so. His autobiography ends in 1942. After the war he returned to the Opera House and later became a teacher at his alma mater, the Academy of Music in Budapest. He made some records for His Master's Voice; they were issued on a special cream-colored label.

LEONOVA, DAR'IA MIKHAILOVNA, 1829-1896

784 IAkovlev, Vasilii Vasil'evich, b. 1880. *D.M. Leonova.* In Russian. Moskva: Gos. muzykal'noe izd-vo, 1950. 30 pp. Illustrated.

LEVIK, SERGEI IUREVICH, b. 1883

785 Levik, Sergei IUr'evich. *Chetvert' veka y opere.* In Russian. Moskva: Iskusstvo, 1970. 536 pp. Illustrated.

Autobiography of the celebrated Russian baritone. An outstanding Beckmesser, he also sang Tonio, Klingsor, Amonasro, Tomskii, Valentin, etc. Generously illustrated, the quality of reproduction is fair.

786 ———. *Zapiski opernogo pevtsa; iz istorii russkoi opernoi stseny.* In Russian. Moskva: Iskusstvo, 1955. 472 pp. Illustrated.

The first of two editions containing critical discussions of Russian opera singers.

786-a ———. *Zapiski opernogo pevtsa.* In Russian. 2nd revised, enlarged ed. Moskva: Iskusstvo, 1962. 711 pp. Illustrated.

Detailed, critical appraisal of all major opera singers of tsarist and Soviet Russia and those who sang extensively in Russia. The space devoted to each subject varies according to his or her importance in operatic history; accordingly, Chaliapin gets nearly a hundred pages. Very well indexed; deserves to be translated into English.

LEWIS, MARY, 1897-1941

787 Dougan, Michael B. "Mary Lewis, an Arkansas Girl in Grand Opera." *The Record Collector* 23, nos. 7 & 8 (December 1976), 171-191. Illustrated. Discography, pp. 184-191. Includes "The Recordings of Mary Lewis" by W.R. Moran.

Apart from Mary Lewis's reminiscences, published under the title

"From the Slums to the Follies, to Grand Opera" in the *Ladies Home Journal*, May and June 1927, practically nothing has been published about the rags-to-riches career of this Arkansas girl who made her operatic debut under Weingartner in Vienna in 1923, and arrived at the Metropolitan by way of Monte Carlo, London and Paris. For a time, one of her husbands was German bass Michael Bohnen, who was replaced by a millionaire oil company executive. Her career was meteoric at both ends, tragically fueled too often by alcohol. A well-researched piece of biographical work. WRM

LIEBLING, ESTELLE, 1884-1970

788 Liebling, Estelle. *The Estelle Liebling Vocal Course for Coloratura Soprano, Lyric Soprano, and Dramatic Soprano.* Edited by Bernard Whitefield. New York: Chappell, 1956. 68 pp. Illustrated.

The pupil of Mathilde Marchesi, Liebling made her debut in Dresden, later sang at the Paris Opera and appeared at the Metropolitan between 1901 and 1904. Following her retirement she became a voice teacher. She is best remembered today as the only teacher of Beverly Sills, but she also coached such celebrities as Göta Ljunberg, Max Lorenz, Maria Müller and, supposedly, Titta Ruffo.

789 Lamperti, Francesco, 1811-1892. *Vocal Studies in Bravura, Provided with Explanatory Text of a Pedagogical Nature by Estelle Liebling.* New York: G. Schirmer, 1942. 48 pp.

Based on Lamperti's *Studi di bravura, in chiave di sol* (Milano: Ricordi, 1870). However, since the original work was in three volumes (in one), the present work cannot be more than excerpts from the original.

LIND, JENNY, 1820-1887

790 Lind, Jenny. *Jenny Lind utom scenen*; förtoliga brev till hennes förmyndare H.M. Munthe, i urval och med kommentarier utgivna av Lotten Dahlgren. In Swedish. Stockholm: Wahlström & Widstrand, 1928. 415 pp. Illustrated. Index, pp. 405-413.

This is an immensely valuable collection of letters (with brief introductions) from Jenny Lind to her legal guardian, H.M. Munthe, members of the Munthe family and others. The letters begin on 16 August 1843 (reproduced in holograph) and go through 15 June 1880. They originate from nearly every place in Scandinavia and abroad where Lind travelled and performed, and include England, Germany and the United States. The reader obtains a number of insights of the singer's family life, her own views of her performances and her views of many artists, impresarios and others. The introductory remarks are brief and to the point, and the notes, where necessary, are informative. There is an illustration of almost every person of relevance to this correspondence. The index is satisfactory but, quite remarkably, none of the letters contains any reference to Verdi. At least the introduction to the group written from the British Isles in 1847-48 ought to have mentioned her participation in the world premiere of *Masnadieri* under the baton of the composer. This book should be translated into a more accessible language. PHS

791 ————. *The Lost Letters of Jenny Lind*. Translated from the German and edited with commentaries by W. Porter Ware and Thaddeus C. Lockard, Jr. London: Victor Gollancz, 1966. 159 pp. Illustrated.

Charming, spontaneous and warm-hearted correspondence from Lind to her lifetime friend, Amalia Wichmann, covering the period from 1845 to 1874. Most of the letters are published here for the first time. Extracts from some of them were published by Holland and Rockstro (q.v.), and these are keyed in the appendix. The letters themselves are interspersed with informative notes. WRM

792 Aldrich, Richard, 1863-1937. *Musical Discourse from the New York Times*. London: Oxford University Press, 1928. 304 pp. Illustrated.

A collection of writings by the *New York Times* music critic. The volume has two chapters of operatic interest: "Jenny Lind and Barnum" and "Adelina Patti in America."

792-a ————. *Musical Discourse; from the New York Times*. Freeport, N.Y.: Books for Libraries Press, 1967. 304 pp. Illustrated.

Reprint of the 1928 edition published by Oxford University Press, London (q.v.).

793 Barnum, Phineas Taylor, 1810-1891. *Autobiography of Barnum*. New York, 1854. 160 pp.

793-a ————. *The Autobiography of P.T. Barnum, Clerk, Merchant, Editor and Showman; with His Rules for Business and Making a Fortune....* London: Ward and Lock, 1855. 160 pp.

794 ————. *Here Comes Barnum*; P.T. Barnum's Own Story Collected from His Books and Introduced by Helen Ferris; Illustrated by Franz A.R. Dobias. New York: Harcourt, Brace, 1932.

795 ————. *The Life of Barnum, the World-Renowned Showman....* Philadelphia: Globe Bible Publishing Company, n.d. 520 pp.

796 ————. *The Story of My Life. A Personal Narrative Covering a Period of Seventy-Five Years (1810 to 1885)....* To Which is Added, *The Art of Money Getting....* San Francisco: A.L. Bancroft, 1886. 503 pp. Illustrated.

797 ————. *Struggles and Triumphs: or, Forty Years' Recollections of P.T. Barnum*. Hartford: J.B. Burr and Company, 1869. xxiv, 780 pp. Illustrated.

In his entertaining autobiography the "World's Greatest Showman" devotes six chapters (XVII through XXII) to his triumphal management of the "Swedish Nightingale," with a fascinating account of travels and adventures on the tour. Statistics of the tour are tabulated in detail: there were 95 non-charity concerts, of which 35 were in New York, 12 in New Orleans, 8 in Philadelphia, 3 in Havana, etc. Gross receipts from the tour were $712,161.34, the singer's net earnings

were $176,675.09. In addition there were numerous concerts the re-
ceipts from which were donated to local charities. Written with
brilliance and flair, candor and humor, Barnum's story reflects the
personality and zeal of its author. WRM

798 Bayley, Frederic William Naylor, 1808-1853. *The Souvenir of the
Season. The Wake of Extacy, a Memory of Jenny Lind.* London: Willoughby
and Co., 1848. 67 pp. Illustrated. Poems.

799 Becher, Alfred Julius, 1803-1848. *Jenny Lind. Eine Skizze ihres
Lebens und ihrer Künstler-Laufbahn bis auf die neueste Zeit.* In
German. 2nd revised ed. Wien: Jasper'sche Buchhandlung, 1846. 48 pp.
Illustrated.

800 Benét, Laura. *Enchanting Jenny Lind.* New York: Dodd, Mead,
1939. ix, 452 pp. Illustrated. Bibliography, pp. 451-452.

The author states that her desire was not to write a fictional
account but an authentic biography of Jenny Lind's first thirty years.
She admits to drawing heavily on Holland and Rockstro. Perhaps the
only contribution of this volume is the inclusion of material referring to Mme. Lind from Hans Christian Anderson's *Story of My Life*
and his *Swedish Pictures*, Bayard Taylor's *Northern Travel* and E.T.
Cook's *The Life of John Ruskin*, from which incidents have been reported. Otherwise, the usual sources have been used extensively.
Unfortunately, there are no notes, and the sources for much of the
material used, including reported conversations, are not specified.
WRM

801 Brancato, Bernice Grace Sanborn, b. 1908. *Jenny Lind: A Col-
lection of Childhood Activities and Adventures in Her Birthplace, the
Gold-Mining Town of Jenny Lind in the Motherlode Country.* N.p.:
B.G.S. Brancato, 1981. 128 pp. Illustrated. Index.

802 Bulman, Joan. *Jenny Lind, a Biography.* London: J. Barrie,
1956. 326 pp. Illustrated.

803 Bunn, Alfred, 1796(?)-1860, plaintiff. *The Case of Bunn versus
Lind, Tried at the Court of Queen's Bench, Guildhall, City, before
Mr. Justice Erle and a Special Jury, on Tuesday, February 22nd, 1848,
Given in Full, from Short-Hand Notes Taken at the Time, with a Series
of Letters from Plaintiff and Defendant, Produced Thereat, with
Others from Both, Now for the First Time Published. To Which Are
Added, Notes Explanatory and Critical.* London: W.S. Johnson, 1848.
73 pp.

"Mr. Bunn, for many years lessee of Drury Lane theatre, seeks com-
pensation for the breach of a contract entered into with him by the
celebrated singer, Jenny Lind" (p. 19).

804 Cavanah, Frances. *Jenny Lind and Her Listening Cat.* Illustrated
by Paul Frame. New York: Vanguard Press, 1961. 158 pp. Illustrated.
Juvenile literature.

805 Cavanah, Frances. *Jenny Lind's America.* Philadelphia: Chilton
Book Company, 1969. xvi, 227 pp. Illustrated. Juvenile literature.

Written by the author of two books for children about Jenny Lind

(*Two Loves for Jenny Lind* and *Jenny Lind and Her Listening Cat*, q.v.), this volume was produced to mark the 150th anniversary of Lind's birth. A popular account, obviously written for popular consumption, emphasis is on Jenny Lind the person, rather than the artist. There appears to be nothing new in this account which cannot be found in more detail elsewhere. The book contains a list of American museums where collections of Lind memorabilia can be found. WRM

806 ————. *Two Loves for Jenny Lind.* Philadelphia: Macrae Smith, 1956. 207 pp. Musical fiction.

807 Dorph, Sven Wilhelm, b. 1864. *Jenny Lind's triumftag genom Nya Världen och senare levnadsckorder.* In Swedish. Uppsala: J.A. Lindblad, 1918. 439 pp. Illustrated. Information taken from a dealer's catalog.

807-a ————. *Jenny Lind's triumftag genom Mya Världen och övriga levnadsöden.* In Swedish. 2nd ed. Uppsala: J.A. Lindblad, 1918. 464 pp. Illustrated.

This is a straightforward piece of adulation, focused principally on Jenny Lind's trip to America and her conquest of the New World. Like Dorph's subsequent work published a year later (*Jenny Lindiana...*, q.v.) this work, too, is lacking a scholarly apparatus, bibliography, etc. Passages of interest include an accounting in dollars of the benefit concerts Lind gave under P.T. Barnum's management, one of Barnum's most powerful publicity devices that took permanent hold of the imagination of the American public. In reference to an earlier remark (p. 396) Dorph reprints the scores for a number of Lind's cadenzas in the final chapter (three from *Beatrice di Tenda*, and one each from Pamina's Act II aria from *Zauberflöte*, *La Somnambula* [sic], I.A. Berg's *Herdegossen*, and *Norsk Fjällsång*). PHS

808 ————. *Jenny Lindiana till hundraårsminnet.* In Swedish. Uppsala: J.J. Lindblat, 1919. 351 pp. Illustrated.

Published in anticipation of the centenary of Jenny Lind's birth, this is an excellent chronologically ordered biography, full of newspaper reviews, personal letters, poems dedicated to Lind, and a variety of illustrations. Unfortunately, there is no bibliography and no scholarly apparatus, but this omission does not diminish the value and interest of the narrative. It can be regarded as a companion volume to Dorph's 1918 book, *Jenny Linds triumftag* (q.v.), as it complements the contents of that work. PHS

809 Dunlop, Agnes Mary Robertson. *Girl with a Song*; the story of Jenny Lind by Elisabeth Kyle. London: Evans Brothers, 1964. 189 pp. Illustrated. Juvenile literature.

810 ————. *The Swedish Nightingale: Jenny Lind*, by Elisabeth Kyle. New York: Rinehart and Winston, 1965, c1964. 224 pp. Bibliography, p. 224.

A biography written specifically for young adults. The suggested "Books for Further Reading" on page 224 are neither well chosen nor suggestive of the author's adequate familiarity with the subject.

811 Elmblad, Sigrid Agneta Sofia (Petterson), b. 1860. *Jenny Lind;*
en livsstudie. In Swedish. Uppsala: J.A. Lindblads, 1920. 192 pp.
Illustrated.

Without bibliography or notes, this is a concise, readable biography, giving all the basic facts of Jenny Lind's life and career.
There are some useful and interesting passages, like the entries for
Louise Johanson's diary for February 10 through June 20, 1847 (pp.
91-102) relating to Lind's four-month "season" in Vienna. By and
large, however, the apparatus and source materials are designed for
the "fan," not the scholar or historian. PHS

812 Foster, George G., d. 1850. *Memoir of Jenny Lind*. Compiled
from the most authentic sources, and edited by G.G. Foster.... New
York: Dewitt and Davonport, 1850. 64 pp. Illustrated.

813 Franzén, Nils Olof. *Jenny Lind: en biografi*. In Swedish.
Stockholm: Bonniers, 1982. 298 pp. Illustrated. Bibliography, pp.
291-292. Index.

814 Gleason, F. & Co., Publishers, Boston. *Jenny Lind*. Boston,
n.d. 4 pp. A 4-page newspaper, giving sketches of the famous
singer, her songs and poems dedicated to her.

815 Goldschmidt, Otto, 1829-1907. Diaries. [London], 1872-1878,
& 1887. 10 vols. In the collection of the New York Public Library.

816 ———. *Jenny Lind adenser i urval*, utgifna af O. Goldschmidt.
In Swedish. Stockholm, 1891. 22 pp.

817 Headland, Helen. *The Swedish Nightingale; a Biography of Jenny
Lind*. Illustrated by the author. Rock Island, Ill.: Augustana Book
Concern, 1940. 145 pp. Illustrated. Juvenile literature.

818-T Holland, Henry Scott, 1847-1918, and W.S. Rockstro. *Jenny Lind.*
Ihre Laufbahn als Künstlerin. 1820 bis 1851. Nach Briefen, Tagebüchern
und andern von Otto Goldschmidt gesammelten Schriftstücken. Translated by Hedwig J. Schoell. In German. Leipzig: F.A. Brockhaus,
1891. 2 vols. Illustrated.

819 ———. *Jenny Lind the Artist, 1820-1851. A Memoir of Madame*
Jenny Lind Goldschmidt, Her Art-Life and Dramatic: from Original
Documents, Letters, Ms., Diaries, etc., Collected by Mr. Otto Gold-
schmidt. New and abridged ed. London: J. Murray, 1893. xix, 473 pp.
Illustrated.

820 ———. *Memoir of Madame Jenny Lind-Goldschmidt: Her Early Art-*
Life and Dramatic Career, 1820-1851. From Original Documents, Letters,
Ms. Diaries, etc., Collected by Mr. Otto Goldschmidt. London:
J. Murray, 1891. 2 vols. Illustrated.

The most famous and well-known Lind biography, this "official and
authorized" work was written with access to original documents, letters
and diaries, with the collaboration of Otto Goldschmidt, Mme. Lind's
husband. The work is scholarly and well documented, with sources of
materials identified. Emphasis is on the singer's professional rather

than private life. Different chapters were written separately by the two authors; those by Canon Holland are especially Victorian. Without doubt this is the principal source for all subsequent books written about Lind's career. This work ends with Lind's departure for America. Her adventures in the New World are covered by a number of authors, none in a more entertaining fashion than by P.T. Barnum in his auto-biography (q.v.). The music compiled and edited by Otto Goldschmidt contained in the appendix includes cadenzas and "other ornaments" used by Lind. WRM

821 Holmström, Maria. *Jenny Lind, som konstnärinna och manniska.* In Swedish. Göteborg: Ahlén & Akerlund, 1914. 267 pp. Illustrated. Bibliography, p. 6.

A popular, highly derivative biography. Holmström draws heavily on the work of Holland and Rockstro (q.v.), and cites eight other works (p. 6) as her sources. There is no real documentation, nor are there any revelations or illuminations of a musical or personal nature. PHS

822 ———. *Jenny Lind.* In Swedish. Studentföreningen verdandis smaskrifter, 236. Stockholm: A. Bonnier, 1920. 40 pp. Illustrated.

823 Horn, Vivi (Ankarcrona), b. 1877. *Jenny Lind 1820-1920: studier utgivna av Svenska Samfunder för Musikforskning.* In Swedish. Stock-holm, 1920.

824 ———. *På sångens vingar, Jenny Linds levnadssaga.* In Swedish. Stockholm: Wahlström & Widstrand, 1940. 351 pp. Illustrated.

824-a ———. *På sångens vingar. Jenny Linds romantiska levnadssaga.* In Swedish. Stockholm: Wahlström, 1945. 386 pp. Illustrated. Index, pp. 380-384.

While containing a wealth of scholarly detail (dates, sailings, contracts, accompanists, sums of money), this is a "popular" biog-raphy, without footnotes, and with only the sparsest bibliographical references. Though Horn acknowledges use of the police and provincial archives in Uppsala and Stockholm and a number of private collections of letters and memorabilia, she never identifies the sources where items of interest can be found. Many letters are quoted *in extenso*, and are most illuminating as to contemporary attitudes towards theaters (e.g., Gustav III's opera house) and eminent artists' views of Jenny Lind (e.g., Felix Mendelssohn-Bartholdy and Hans C. Anderson). There is a good deal of space devoted to personalia, to Lind's husband (Otto Goldschmidt) and sons, to the minutiae of everyday life. Unfortunately, there is little concerning her singing, style or actual performances. The Verdi premiere in London, for example, is not even mentioned. The biography primarily concerns the singer's private life, not her music. There are few citations from contemporary reviews, save on Jenny Lind's triumphal American and German tours, and her concert appearances in England towards the end of her career. The index is both detailed and useful; the illustrations are well chosen and re-produced. PHS

825 *Incidents in the Life of Jenny Lind, the Noblehearted Swede....* New York: Mark H. Newman and Co., 1851. 24 pp. Illustrated.

826 *Jenny Lind Association, New York*. Brooklyn: Paragon Press, 1923.
64 pp. "The Jenny Lind Centennial Celebration."

827 Jenny Lind Centennial Celebration Committee. *Press Comments on the Jenny Lind Centennial Celebration, October Sixth, 1820-1920*.
New York, 1920. 2 vols. Illustrated.

828 *Jenny Lind Comic Almanac, 1851*. New York: Elton, 1850 or 51.
24 pp. Illustrated.

829 *Jenny Lind, die schwedische Nachtigall; eine biographische Skizze*. In German. Hamburg: B.S. Berendsohn, 1845. 16 pp. Illustrated.

830 *Jenny Lind: Skildring of hennes leinad*. In Swedish. Stockholm:
Lundberg & Comp., 1848. 46 pp.

831 Keil, Doris Parkin. *The Ploughboy and the Nightingale*. Toronto:
Copp Clark, 1958. 304 pp.

832 Kielty, Bernardine. *Jenny Lind Sang Here*. Illustrated by
Douglas Gorsline. North Star Books, 14. Boston: Houghton Mifflin,
1959. 179 pp. Illustrated.

833 *Lindiana. An Interesting Narrative of the Life of Jenny Lind*.
With a portrait by Linton. Arundel, Sussex: J. Thomas, 1847. 52 pp.
Illustrated.

834 Lisei, Cesare, 1848-1888. *Jenny Lind; note biografiche*. In
Italian. Milano: G. Ricordi, 1888. 21 pp. Illustrated.

835 Lyser, Johann Peter Theodor, 1803-1870. *Giacomo Meyerbeer. Jenny Lind. Fragmente aus dem Tagebuche eines alten Musikers. Für Freunde der Tonkunst*. In German. Wien: M. Kuppitsch, 1847. 32 pp.

836 Maude, Jenny Maria Catherine (Goldschmidt). *The Life of Jenny Lind, Briefly Told by Her Daughter, Mrs. Raymond Maude, O.B.E.*
London: Cassell, 1926. 222 pp. Illustrated.

Jenny Lind's daughter, the author of this book, felt a need for a
current memoir of her mother in 1926, the Holland & Rockstro work then
being out of print. "In view of the still constant reference to, and
use of her name, I have compiled this little book, in a lighter vein
than the old Memoir, from many documents in my possession, aided by
my own recollections." A personal memoir of considerable charm and
interest, it emphasizes the private life of the singer, and thus is
supplemental to the Holland & Rockstro work. It also deals with the
singer's life after leaving America in 1852 (pp. 176-218). A tabulated list of her roles with the total number of performances appears
on p. 114. It shows that her 677 operatic appearances (418 of these
in Stockholm) took place in the time span of eleven years, and all of
it before she was 29 years old! WRM

836-a ————. *The Life of Jenny Lind*. New York: Arno Press, 1977.
222 pp. Illustrated.

Reprint of the 1926 edition published by Cassell, London (q.v.).

837 *Memoir of Jenny Lind....* London: J. Ollivier, 1847. 20 pp.
Illustrated.

838 Munthe, Curt Fredrik, b. 1900. *Jenny Lind och sångens Beateberg.*
In Swedish. Stockholm: Natur och kultur, 1960. 204 pp. Illustrated.

839 Norlind, Tobias, b. 1879. *Jenny Lind; en minnesbok till hundra-*
årsdagen. In Swedish. Stockholm: Wahlström & Widstrand, 1919. 251 pp.
Illustrated. Bibliography, pp. 244-247. Index, pp. 248-251.

An excellent biography in brief compass arranged in eight distinc-
tive chapters ("Youth," "Paris," "Sweden," "Germany," "England,"
"America," "Home Life," "Jenny Lind as an Artistic Personality").
There is a brief list of references. In addition to the usual photographs and engravings, there are the scores for several solfeggi (pp.
231-232) which may be of interest to the voice student. PHS

840 Pergament, Moses, b. 1893. *Jenny Lind.* In Swedish. Stockholm:
P.A. Norstedt, 1945. 325 pp. Illustrated. Index, pp. 321-325.

A profusely illustrated, glossy, coffee-table type biography. The
text is well written but relatively uninformative when compared with
other Lind biographies. Most of the illustrations are engravings
with a few photographs; there are no references and no bibliography.
PHS

841 *Programme of Mademoiselle Jenny Lind's Concert for Monday Evening,*
June 9, 1851, at the National Theatre, Containing the Words of the
Songs in English, German, Italian and Swedish. New York, 1851. 32 pp.
Contains a sketch of "Jenny Lind in America" (pp. 28-32).

842 Reach, Angus Bethune, 1821-1856. *Jenny Lind at Last; or, the*
Swedish Nightingale. *An Apropos Bagatelle, in One Act.* Barth, Vol.
VII, no. 10. London: Barth, 1847? 16 pp.

842-a ———. *Jenny Lind at Last; or, the Swedish Nightingale.* *An*
Apropos Operatic Bagatelle, in One Act. Spencer's Boston Theatre,
iv. 5, n.s., no. 33. Boston: W.V. Spencer, 1856. 16 pp.

842-b ———. *Jenny Lind at Last; or, the Swedish Nightingale.* *An*
Apropos Operatic Bagatelle in One Act.... To Which are Added a
Description of the Costume-Cast of the Characters ... and the Whole
of the Stage Business. As Now Performed at the Principal English and
American Theatres. French's Minor Drama. The Acting Edition, no.
CLXXXIX. New York: S. French, 1864? 12 pp.

843 *A Review of the Performances of Mademoiselle Jenny Lind, During*
her Engagement at Her Majesty's Theatre, and Their Influence and Effect
upon our National Drama; with a Notice of Her Life. London: J. & L.
Dickinson, 1847. 36 pp. Illustrated. Cover title reads: A serious
review....

844 Rockstro, William Smyth, 1823-1895. *Jenny Lind; a Record and*
Analysis of the "Method" of the Late Madame Jenny Lind-Goldschmidt;
Together with a Selection of Cadenze, Solfeggi, Abellimenti, etc., in
Illustration of Her Vocal Art, ed. by Otto Goldschmidt. London:

Novello and Company, 1894. 20, xxvii pp. Illustrated. "All those portions of the following pages which have already been published are here reprinted from the work entitled *Jenny Lind, the Artist* by Rev. H.S. Holland and W.S. Rockstro" (q.v.).

845 Rootzén, Kajsa Wilhelmina, b. 1904, and T. Meyer. *Jenny Lind, den Svenska näktergalen*. In Swedish. Stockholm: Lindfors, 1945. 135 pp. Illustrated. Bibliography, p. 135. Repertory, pp. 133-134.

846 Rosenberg, Charles G. *Jenny Lind: Her Life, Her Struggles, and Her Triumphs*. New York: Stringer and Townsend, 1850. 82 pp. Illustrated.

847 ———. *Jenny Lind in America*. New York: Stringer and Townsend, 1851. 226 pp. Illustrated.

A detailed contemporary account of the Barnum tour by a musically knowledgeable Englishman who was a member of the tour party. Descriptions of Lind's voice, comparisons with such singers as Grisi, program details, and a sometimes amusing account of travel, with numerous anecdotes about Lind, Barnum, Julius Benedict and others make this an important first-hand source book. WRM

848 Schirmer, Adolf. *Jenny Lind und die Hamburger, oder ein Ständchen im Jungfernstieg*. Genrebild von Snüffelmann (pseud.). In German. Hamburg: Berendsohn, 1845. Illustrated.

849 Schultz, Gladys Denny. *Jenny Lind, the Swedish Nightingale*. Philadelphia: J.B. Lippincott, 1962. 345 pp. Illustrated. Index, pp. 339-345.

A detailed biography capitalizing on the access to rare documents in private collections and the Jenny Lind literature that predates this book. The dialogues as invented by the author are not inappropriate and as they are used sparingly, they facilitate the progression of the story. She wisely restricts her discussion of Lind's voice to quoting the commentary of others. The overwhelming portion of the book deals with the first 32 years of her life and is especially concerned with her career; the remaining 35, from 1852 to 1887, is compressed into a 20-page chapter entitled "After America." Considering the breadth of coverage the reader misses a bibliography and listing of documents. Even so, this is one of the important English-language biographies of the "Swedish Nightingale."

850 Spongberg, Ernest Albert, b. 1881. *The Life of Jenny Lind, October 6, 1820-November 2, 1887. A Compilation from Various Sources, in Commemoration of Her Birth*. Minneapolis, 1920. 79 pp. Illustrated.

851 Svenska samfundet för musikforskning. *Jenny Lind, 1820-1920*. Studier utgivna av Svenska samfundet för musikforskning. In Swedish. Stockholm: Wahlström & Widstrand, 1920. 149 pp. Illustrated.

852 Thorp, Roderick. *Jenny and Barnum; a Novel of Love*. Garden City, N.Y.: Doubleday, 1981. 375 pp. Fictionalized biography.

853 Wagenknecht, Edward Charles, b. 1900. *Jenny Lind*. Boston: Houghton Mifflin, 1931. xix, 231 pp. Illustrated. Bibliography, pp. 189-202. Index.

One of the most scholarly treatments of Jenny Lind's life, the author states in his preface that the book "is not a biography in the usual sense; it is a portrait, a psychograph," which he calls "a new craft." The author states that he attempted a study of Jenny Lind the woman, in her art life and in her personal life. "My aim has been to show her as she was, so far as can be accomplished at this date, without disparagement and without eulogy. The book contains no 'new,' in the sense of hitherto unpublished, material." The author has, on the other hand, drawn on many 19th-century reminiscences and biographies for supplemental information, many of which are not generally associated with the life of the singer. Whatever the fate of the modish "psychograph," this work remains an excellent biography. The excellent bibliography contains some 150 titles. WRM

853-a ————. *Jenny Lind*. Da Capo Press Music Reprint Series. New York: Da Capo Press, 1980. xix, 230 pp. Illustrated. Bibliography, pp. 189-202. Index.

Reprint of the 1931 edition published by Houghton, Mifflin Company, Boston (q.v.).

854 ————. *Seven Daughters of the Theater: Jenny Lind, Sarah Bernhardt, Ellen Terry, Julia Marlowe, Isadora Duncan, Mary Garden, Marilyn Monroe*. Norman: University of Oklahoma Press, 1964. x, 234 pp. Illustrated. Bibliography, pp. 217-224. Index, pp. 225-234.

An intelligent summary of the primary literature about Lind (pp. 1-49) and Garden (pp. 159-179). The Jenny Lind essay was published in book form in 1931 (q.v.) and 1959.

855-T Wallace, Irving, b. 1916. *El fabuloso empresario; la vida y la época de P.T. Barnum*. Translated by Amparo Garcia Burgos. In Spanish. Barcelona: Ediciones Grijalbo, 1968. 259 pp. Illustrated. Bibliography, pp. 253-259.

Translation of *The Fabulous Showman* (q.v.).

856 ————. *The Fabulous Showman; the Life and Times of P.T. Barnum*. New York: Knopf, 1959. 317 pp. Illustrated.

A retelling, without the flare of the original, of the material contained in Barnum's autobiographical writings. Pages 119-147 contain the passages that deal with Jenny Lind. The book went through several American and British editions. WRM

857 Ware, William Porter, b. 1904, and Thaddeus C. Lockard, Jr. *P.T. Barnum Presents Jenny Lind: The American Tour of the Swedish Nightingale*. Baton Rouge: Louisiana State University Press, 1980. xiv, 204 pp. Illustrated. Bibliography, pp. 197-200. Index.

858 Wilkens, Cornelius August, b. 1829. *Jenny Lind. Ein Cäcilienbild aus der evangelischen Kirche*. In German. Gütersloh, C. Bertelsmann, 1894. 66 pp.

858-a ————. *Jenny Lind. Ein Cäcilienbild aus der evangelischen Kirche*. In German. 2nd enlarged ed. Gütersloh: C. Bertelsmann, 1895. 128 pp.

858-b ————. *Jenny Lind. Ein Cäcilienbild aus der evangelischen Kirche.* In German. 5th ed. Gütersloh: C. Bertelsman, 1915. xvii, 241 pp. Illustrated.

859-T ————. *Jenny Lind, cantatrice chrétienne, 1820-1887.* Translated by Julia Jequier. In French. Genève: J.H. Jeheber, 1896. 235? pp. Illustrated.

860 Willis, Nathaniel Parker, 1806-1867. *Memoranda of the Life of Jenny Lind.* Philadelphia: Robert E. Peterson, 1851. 238 pp.

The author declares his purpose in writing this book to be "the collecting together such material as there is, for knowledge of her life and its incidents, thus far, and such data as are within our reach for a fair and critical estimate of her powers." He further states, "It is, of course, far too early, in the life of such a woman, to be time for a biography. She adds a new chapter to it every day." A contemporary account, spawned by the singer's visit to America, the book has value for its many personal anecdotes, letters, personal impressions of the singer and press quotations.

See also items 1562, 1597, 1612, 1615, 1621, 1669, 1694, 1745, 1792

LINDBERG, HELGE, 1887-1928

861-T Vehanen, Kosti, b. 1887. *Mästersångaren Helge Lindberg; personliga minnen.* In Swedish. Helsingfors: Holger Schildts, 1929. 97 pp. Illustrated.

Swedish translation of his *Mestarilaulaja Helge Lindberg: henkilökohtaisa muistelmia* (q.v.).

862 ————. *Mestarilaulaja Helge Lindberg: henkilökohtaisa muistelmia.* In Finnish. Helsinki: Kustannusosakeyhtiö Kirja, 1929. 90 pp. Illustrated.

A biography containing memorial articles by several authors, published within a year after the singer's death. Lindberg, a baritone, was considered a fine Lieder singer, who died in mid-career, at the early age of forty-one. Kosti Vehanen was his accompanist from 1921 to 1924 and toured with him in Scandinavia, France and England. Lindberg recorded for Polyphon. WRM

LISITSIAN, PAVEL GERASIMOVICH, b. 1911

863 Moscow. Gosudarstvennyi akademicheskii Bol'shoi teatr. *Pavel Gerasimovich Lisitsian.* In Russian. Moskva: Iskusstvo, 1953. 16 pp. Illustrated.

A brief appreciation of the singer, followed by many photographs; the quality of reproduction is poor.

See also item 1708

LITTA, stage name of MARIE EUGENIA VON ELSNER, 1856-1883

864 Scott, John M., 1824-1898. *Litta, an American Singer; a Sketch of Marie Eugenia von Elsner.* Bloomington, Ill., 1897. 160 pp. Illustrated.

LITVINENKO-VOL'GEMUT, MARIIA IVANIVNA, 1895-1966

865 Isachenko, Il'ia Isaakovich. *Mariia Ivanovna Litvinengo-Vol'gemut, narodnaia artistka SSSR.* In Russian. Kiev: Derzh. vid-vo obrazotvorchogo mistetstva i muzichnoi lit-ri URSR, 1960. 29 pp. Illustrated.

866 Shvachko, Tetiana Oleksiivna. *Mariia Litvinenko-Vol'gemut.* In Ukrainian. Maistri mistetstv Ukraini. Kiev: Muzichna Ukraina, 1972. 182 pp. Illustrated. Bibliography.

LITVINNE, FÉLIA, 1860-1936

867 Litvinne, Félia. *Ma vie et mon art; souvenirs.* Préface de Charles Widor. In French. Paris: Plon, 1933. iv, 292 pp. Illustrated. Repertory, pp. 283-296.

867-a ———. *Ma vie et mon art; souvenirs.* Préface de Charles Widor. Opera Biographies. New York: Arno Press, 1977. iv, 292 pp. Illustrated. Repertory, pp. 283-286.

Reprint of the 1933 edition published by Plon, Paris (q.v.).

868-T ———. *Moia zhizn' i moe iskusstvo....* Vstupit. stat'ia i red. per. A. Gozenpuda. In Russian. Leningrad: "Muzyka," 1967. iv, 164 pp. Illustrated.

The Russian translation of her *Ma vie et mon art* (q.v.).

869 ———. *School of Singing: Exercises and Counsels.* Paris: Au Ménestrel, 1924. iii, 33 pp. Illustrated.

870 Quincey, Alain. *Félia Litvinne.* In French. Les Trésors de l'Opéra, no. 3. Paris: Opéra International, 1979. 64 pp. Illustrated. Repertory, pp. 61-62.

The first half of this booklet, the biographical portion, is based on Litvinne's own memoirs; the second half is excerpts from it. Since it was written in French, Quincey was spared even the trouble of translation. The illustrations are also reproduced from her *Ma vie et mon art* (q.v.).

See also item 1835

LIUTSKANOV, MIKHAIL, b. 1900

871 Liutskanov, Mikhail. *Moiat put kum opernata stsena: spomeni.* In Bulgarian. Sofiia: Muzyka, 1976. 150 pp. Illustrated.

LLERA, FELIPE, 1887-1942

See item 1631

LOEFFEL, FELIX, 1892-1981

872 *Felix Loeffel; eine Freundesgabe zum siebzigsten Geburtstag.* Edited by Hans Würgler und Arthur Loosli. In German. Bern: Francke, 1962. 109 pp. Illustrated.

A Festschrift prepared for Felix Loeffel on the occasion of his 70th birthday. Loeffel was a voice teacher and a former singer, whose roles included Sarastro, Gurnemanz, Marke, Rocco, the Commendatore—the last named he sang with Klemperer in Berlin.

LORENZ, MAX, 1901-1975

873 Herrmann, Walter. *Max Lorenz*. In German. Wien: Österreichische Bundesverlag, 1976. 48 pp. Illustrated. Bibliography, p. 48. Discography, pp. 41-47.

874 Schäfer, Jürgen. *Max Lorenz*. In German. Sammlung Jürgen Schäfer. Hamburg: Jürgen Schäfer, 1973. 15 pp. Discography, pp. 6-15.

See also item 1811

LUBIN, GERMAINE, 1890-1979

875 Casanova, Nicole, b. 1934. *Isolde 39*. In French. Paris: Flammarion, 1974. 251 pp. Illustrated. Discography, pp. 249-250.

An informative biography of France's prominent Wagnerian soprano of the interwar years who enjoyed unqualified success at Bayreuth. The personal endorsement and unconcealed admiration of Hitler and his top officials brought her in close association with the high ranking Nazis of the Third Reich. After the war she was labeled a collaborator and was briefly imprisoned. The book generally sides with the biographee. Nicole Casanova tries to justify and explain, excuse and re-interpret all of Lubin's actions with the singleminded fanaticism of a crusader. Apart from this apparent bias and a "slick" style, the book can be recommended as much for its overview of this prominent singer's career as for the revealing details of how politics can intertwine with the performing arts and its practitioners.

LUCCA, PAULINE, 1841-1908

876 Jansen-Mara, Anna, and Dorothea Weisse-Zehrer. *Die Wiener Nachtigall; der Lebensweg der Pauline Lucca*. In German. Berlin: O. Petters, 1935. 216 pp. Illustrated. Fictionalized biography.

See also items 1597, 1615, 1658, 1694

LUCCIONI, JOSÉ, 1903-1978

877 Mancini, Roland. *José Luccioni*. In French. Monstres sacrés--
Les cahiers d'Opéra, no. 5. Paris: SODAL, 1966. 32 pp. Illustrated.
Discography, p. 3.

878 ———. *José Luccioni*. Préface par Mario del Monaco. Les
Trésors de l'Opéra, no. 1. Paris: Opéra International, 1978. 64 pp.
Illustrated. Discography, p. 2.

A slightly partisan biography of this famous French tenor whose
long career was limited to France and Italy, with some South American
and Mexican engagements. The discography gives a simple listing of
his records on 78 and 33rpm. This is, presumably, a reworking of the
same author's work published in the 1960s as a special supplement to
Opéra. The earlier edition could not be located for examination.

LUDWIG, CHRISTA, b. 1924

879 Lorenz, Paul, b. 1893. *Christa Ludwig, Walter Berry*. In German.
Wien: Bergland-Verlag, 1968. 127 pp. Illustrated.

LYNN, OLGA

880 Lynn, Olga. *Oggie; the Memoirs of Olga Lynn*. London: Weidenfeld
and Nicolson, 1955. 160 pp. Illustrated. Index, pp. 155-160.

The somewhat rambling memoirs of a concert singer and voice teacher,
who learned her craft with Herman Klein and Jean de Reszke. Her
diminutive stature precluded an operatic career. The loosely knit
story line is enlivened by anecdotes and vignettes about the de Reszke
brothers, Patti, Melba, Chaliapin and others.

M

MAASIK, ELSA, b. 1908

881 Paalma, Vilma. *Elsa Maasik*. In Estonian. Tallinn: Eesti
Raamat, 1973. 50 pp. Illustrated. Bibliography.

McCORMACK, JOHN, 1884-1945

882 McCormack, John. *John McCormack, His Own Life Story*, transcribed
by Pierre V.R. Key. Boston: Small, Maynard and Company, 1918. 444 pp.
Illustrated. Index, pp. 435-444. A photographic reproduction of a
handwritten letter from John McCormack addressed to the publishers is
included following the title page. It reads in part: "I am writing
to remind you that I wish it clearly to be made known that this is my
one and only authorized biography...."

The long-standing mystery of the genesis of this book became known
in 1940 upon the publication of the memoirs of American impresario,
Charles Wagner. In his *Seeing Stars* (New York: Putnam, 1940, pp. 159-

160) Wagner says: "In the spring of 1918, I felt a book based on Mc-Cormack's unusual rise to artistic heights would be a sort of homeopathic dose of press agentry--a sugarcoated publicity stunt--and had faith enough to believe his friends would buy it. The plan was to title it, 'The Story of John McCormack--Told to Me to Tell to Others', and I interested Pierre V.R. Key to become the author. Publication arrangements were made and Key began his daily interviews and visits to John's summer home in Noroton, Connecticut. Then two things happened. First, a newspaper man began publication of an unauthorized life of McCormack in one of the Boston papers. Second, Bishop Michael Curley of Baltimore, his schoolmate and lifelong friend, visited John at this time and came in for consultation. As a result, the entire idea was altered. What was intended to be an authentic story turned out to be a very sentimental and unreal account. No one ever had greater regard for John than this splendid churchman, but the work was packed with oversentimental expressions that sounded quite absurd on paper. Key was obliged to change his writing style and the bishop edited the copy for John. I remained silent. The book was published, and damned with faint praise; John bought off the publishers and withdrew the entire edition. Key did his work in good faith and since I had gotten him into it, we settled with him for $5,000, of which I paid $1,000...." The book was reprinted in facsimile in 1973, with a lengthy introduction which expands the above account in some respects. See the notes for this reprint edition. WRM

882-a ————. *John McCormack, His Own Life Story*, transcribed by Pierre V.R. Key. New York: Vienna House, 1973. xliv, 444 pp. Illustrated. Index, pp. 435-444.

A reprint edition of the 1918 publication by Small, Maynard & Co. of Boston (q.v.), with a new introduction by John Scarry, a page of references to notes in the introduction, a page of "addenda and corrigenda" and a detailed index. This edition has replaced the original photographic illustrations with a new collection of photographs, some taken as late as 1938. In his introduction, Scarry repeats the Charles Wagner story (given in this work in the annotation for the original edition), and adds a few details to the story. He also adds several pages by way of biographical fill-in. The text of the book has not been altered. WRM

883 Beddington, Frances Ethel (Homan-Mulock) ("Mrs. Claude Beddington"). *All that I Have Met*. London: Cassell, 1929. xii, 286 pp. Illustrated.

A society lady's reminiscences with one chapter of operatic interest and one other devoted to John McCormack.

884 Foxall, Raymond. *John McCormack*. Foreword by Sir Compton Mackenzie. London: R. Hale, 1963. 185 pp. Illustrated.

Chronologically, the fourth biography of John McCormack, written 17 years after the singer's death. In his Preface, the author states: "This biography is an attempt to present for the interest of two generations--his own and the one that came after--a serious and detailed study of the world famous tenor ... who for millions of the former is a well-remembered idol, and whose name for the latter is synonymous with the very beginning (sic) of the gramophone.... Apart from my research, which has been as exhaustive as possible, my only qualification for writing this book is that as one who never heard him sing in person I am more likely to present a cool and dispassionate picture than the warmer judgement—either in praise or criticism—that might be given by a biographer who was one of his own contemporaries." Bold words and worthy ambition, but unfortunately, words not well realized. This turns out to be a very pedestrian work at best, re-counting many incidents lifted from earlier books. There is little new added, and much of importance omitted. Many small slips indicate that the author was often on unfamiliar ground, like making Carmen Melis a Chilean! WRM

884-a ———. *John McCormack.* Foreword by Sir Compton Mackenzie. Staten Island, N.Y.: Alba House, 1964. 185 pp. Illustrated.

885 Hume, Ruth (Fox), b. 1922, and Paul Hume. *The King of Song: The Story of John McCormack.* Illustrated by Irene Murray. Credo Books, 23. New York: Hawthorne Books, 1964. 185 pp. Illustrated.

McCormack's life story retold for young adults; juvenile literature.

886 Ledbetter, Gordon T. *The Great Irish Tenor.* London: Duckworth, 1977. 160 pp. Illustrated. Bibliography, p. 157. Index, pp. 158-160.

The fifth and latest biography of John McCormack is best described as a "pictorial biography" as there is at least one photograph or illustration on nearly every page. The work starts with a "Prelude" titled "The Talking Machine," a history of the machine so wide-ranging (pages 8 through 34) that one wonders how the author will manage to get back to the supposed subject of his book! (It is, for the most part, an accurate history, with one serious blooper: Eldridge R. Johnson most certainly did not use shellac "as the medium of recording.") When we finally get to the main subject of the book, the second sentence confers Polish birth on Prague-born Ernestine Schumann-Heink! Such slips are unfortunate, as the author does bring a new approach to our view of John McCormack. In a sense the biographical aspect takes a back seat to extended discussions of the singer's early recordings, bits and pieces of relevant quotations and excellent illustrations from record labels to concert and opera programs. The work displays an immense amount of research, with the bringing together for the first time much McCormack memorabilia. Record collectors will delight in the continued joining of the McCormack story with his recordings. Far from conventional biography, the book might well be described as a highly researched scrapbook, and one worthy of a place on any Mc-Cormack lover's bookshelf. WRM

886-a ———. *The Great Irish Tenor.* New York: Scribner, 1978. 160 pp. Illustrated. Bibliography, p. 157. Index.

887 McCormack, Lily (Foley). *I Hear You Calling Me.* With "A Mc-Cormack Discography" by Philip F. Roden. Milwaukee: Bruce Pub. Co., 1949. 201 pp. Illustrated. Discography, pp. 190-201.

A sentimental and personal account of the singer's life by his devoted wife of nearly 40 years. Her recollections of McCormack's student days in Italy, and incidents of his early career when he was first becoming established, first as a concert singer and then at Covent Garden, are fondly told. Lily accompanied her husband on concert tours throughout his career, so many of the incidents she recalls could only be told by her. While the book is hardly a definitive biography, it is certainly an important part of the Mc-Cormack heritage. The discography, by Philip F. Roden, was excellent for its day. Only published recordings (to 1949) are listed, and unfortunately no matrix numbers or takes are given. For a more complete discography, see McDermott Roe (1972) (q.v.). WRM

887-a ———. *I Hear You Calling Me*. London: W.H. Allen, 1950. 232 pp. Illustrated. The paperback, "A Pinnacle Book," edition by the same publisher has 192 pages.

887-b ———. *I Hear You Calling Me*. Westport, Conn.: Greenwood Press, 1975. 201 pp. Illustrated. Discography, pp. 190-201.

Reprint of the 1949 edition published by Bruce Publishing Co., Milwaukee (q.v.).

888 Roe, Leonard F.X. McDermott. *John McCormack, the Complete Discography*. London: Charles Jackson, 1956. 93 pp. Illustrated. Discography, pp. 31-92. The cover lists both a "popular edition" (spiral bound, hard covers) and a "library edition" (presumably cloth bound). The latter was never issued.

The first 20 pages of this work are more or less biographical, with emphasis on his recording career. The final 17 pages are devoted to photographs of the singer. The discography was a bold effort at accuracy and completeness. Lack of matrix numbers and takes, however, lead to innumerable errors, most of which were corrected in a subsequent volume by the same author, *The John McCormack Discography* (Oakwood Press, 1972, q.v.). WRM

888-a ———. *The John McCormack Discography*. Lingfield, Surrey: The Oakwood Press, 1972. 93 pp. Discography, pp. 2-93.

Unlike the previous (1956) edition, this volume contains no biographical material but instead confines itself entirely to the Mc-Cormack discography. It is vastly improved over the earlier edition. Matrix numbers and takes are given, as well as recording dates. The author is still just a little too pleased with his work, which he introduces by saying "Every recording made by the tenor is shown ... a complete listing!" While by far the best McCormack discography yet published, it is by no means without error or omission. There has been no attempt to include listings of non-commercial or off-the-air recordings, many of which have appeared on long playing discs. WRM

889 Strong, Leonard Alfred George, b. 1896. *John McCormack, the Story of a Singer*. New York: The Macmillan Company, 1941. x, 301 pp. Illustrated. Discography, pp. 297-301.

Chronologically, the second biography of John McCormack, and like Key's 1918 work, it was written "in collaboration" with the singer. Published only four years before his death, it is complete as far as McCormack's career is concerned. Strong lets McCormack speak for himself throughout the book, and the reader feels that the occasional quotation directly from the singer, as for example his frank comments about Melba, are probably accurate. There is much detail in the book which could only have come from the singer. The author has an annoying way of interrupting the flow of his story with discussions, comments or stories which are out of place chronologically, no doubt intentionally done to attempt to get into the book more of the personality of the singer. The book's serious fault derives from the fact that its author was too close to his subject, so some of the more unpleasant events in the singer's life are carefully avoided or are brushed by very lightly. The disastrous 1921 tour of Australia, for example, receives but one sentence.

The discography is badly arranged, and very incomplete. The lack of an index is a serious omission, and makes it difficult to compare specific incidents recorded in the book with other versions of the same incidents. With all its faults, this probably remains the best single McCormack biography to date. An appendix (pp. 273-296) contains a few lines about each of the singers mentioned in the book, from Ackté to Zerola, with a few comments on specific recordings by each singer. WRM

889-a ———. *John McCormack, the Story of a Singer.* London: Methuen, 1941. x, 291 pp. Illustrated. Discography, pp. 271-292.

See also items 1541, 1702, 1807, 1824

McCRACKEN, JAMES, b. 1926

890 McCracken, James, and Sandra Warfield. *A Star in the Family; an Autobiography in Diary Form by James McCracken and Sandra Warfield.* Edited by Robert Daley. New York: Coward McCann and Geoghegan, 1971. 388 pp. Illustrated.

This book is the product of one year's taped reminiscences by the operatic husband-and-wife team whose career and marriage is one of the rare success stories. Editor Robert Daley's role was to organize and clean up the transcribed tapes, "repairing the broken sentences where necessary," in short: to turn the co-authored text into a book. On the whole he has done a creditable job and the end result is more than satisfactory. Interweaving current events with reminiscences may occasionally hinder continuity, but by the end of the book the reader is on familiar terms with the singers and knows all about their lives. The immediacy of the narrative is never broken and the presence of the narrators is felt throughout. The story ends in 1970. The McCrackens owe their public a sequel.

MacDONALD, JEANETTE, 1907-1965

890/A Stern, Lee Edward. *Jeanette MacDonald.* New York: Jove Publications, 1977. 159 pp. Illustrated. Bibliography, p. 149. Index. Filmography, pp. 151-154.

MacEWAN, SYDNEY, b. 1909

891 MacEwan, Sydney. *On the High C's: (a Light-Hearted Journey): An Autobiography.* Glasgow: J. Burns, 1973. 326 pp. Illustrated. Discography, pp. 324-326.

A tenor turned priest--yet another, in addition to José Mojica. He kept on singing after having been ordained; made records for Parlophone. The book is light-hearted indeed. It contains several references to John McCormack, who advised MacEwan to pursue a singing career.

MAINVIELLE-FODOR, JOSEPHINE, 1789-1870

892 Mainvielle-Fodor, Joséphine. *Réflexions et conseils sur l'art du chant.* In French. Paris: Perrotin, 1857. 15 pp.

This is a short textbook on singing technique. A brief introduction gives some background about the author, setting her up as an example. There follow short chapters on formation of the lips, pronunciation, the importance of the vowel on which one vocalizes, deep breathing, swelling and diminishing the tone, avoidance of fatigue and moderation in ornaments. HCS

893 Unger, Johann Karl, b. 1771. *Joséphine Mainvielle Fodor.* Précis historique, publié par Jean Charles Unger. In French and German. Vienne: C.F. Beck, 1823. 24 pp. Illustrated.

MAJORANO, GAETANO

See Caffarelli

MAKEDONSKI, STEFAN, 1885-1952

894 Tikholov, Petko. *Stefan Makedonski; zhivot i deinost.* In Bulgarian. Sofiia: Nauka i izkustvo, 1956. 183 pp. Illustrated.

MAKSAKOVA, MARIIA PETROVNA, b. 1902

895 L'vov, Mikhail L'vovich, 1887-1957. *M.P. Maksakova.* In Russian. Laureaty Stalinskoi premii. Moskva: Gos. Muzykal'noe izd-vo, 1947. 47 pp. Illustrated.

See also items 1686, 1708

MALIBRAN, MARIA FELICITA, 1808-1836

896 Barbieri, Gaetano. *Notizie biografiche di M.F. Malibran,* raccolte e pubblicate de Gaetano Barbieri. In Italian. Milano: A.F. Stella, 1836. 54 pp. Illustrated.

897 Bériot, Charles August de, 1802-1870. *A Contribution Towards an Accurate Biography of Charles August de Bériot and Maria Felicità Malibran Garcia; Extracted from the Correspondence of the Former.* By Edward Heron-Allen. London: Printed for the author by J.W. Wakeham, 1894. 24 pp. Illustrated. "This edition is limited to 20 copies." Reprinted from *The Violin Times*.

The contents of this booklet originally appeared in *The Violin Times*. The letters are given in the original French and in English translation.

898 Bielli, Domenico. *Maria Malibran nel centenario della sua morte (23 sett. 1836-23 sett. 1936).* In Italian. I grandi maestri e i grandi artisti del teatro lirico, no. 1. Casalbordino: N. de Arcangelis, 1936. 46 pp. Illustrated.

899 Bürkli, Johann Georg, 1793-1851. *Züge aus dem Leben der brühmten Sängerin Maria Malibran-Garcia.* In German. Zürich: Orell, Füssli und compagnie, 1840. 16 pp. Illustrated.

900 Bushnell, Howard. *Maria Malibran: A Biography of the Singer;* foreword by Elaine Brody. University Park, Pa.: Pennsylvania State University Press, 1979. xix, 264 pp. Illustrated. Bibliography, pp. 253-257. Repertory, pp. 241-244. Chronology of Performances, pp. 238-240. Index, pp. 259-264.

This scholarly and thoroughly researched biography of Malibran eclipses all previous studies of this singer's career. It could well serve as a model for any future works on the great figures of the nineteenth-century lyric stage. Supported by scholarly apparatus, it rests on the critical examination of available monographic and periodical literature, correspondence and memorabilia. The bibliography is exhaustive; the index is thorough. The volume's overall excellence would have been further enhanced by a more detailed chronology of performances with dates, casts, number of performances. As it stands it is a perfunctory job, not without errors. TGK

901 Calmann, Ludwig. *Homoeopathy no Humbug; or, a Refutation of Dr. James Johnson ... Containing letters to and from that gentleman; translation of letters from ... the King of Prussia, etc.; a few cases pronounced incurable by eminent medical men and cured by homoeopathy; an answer to Satis superque; Malibran.* London: James Leath, 1843. 48 pp.

902 Crump, Phyllis Eirene. "Musset et Malibran; an Episode in the Literary Career of Alfred de Musset." *A Miscellany of Studies in Romance Languages and Literatures Presented to Leon E. Kastner* (Cambridge) (1932), pp. 162-171.

903 Desternes, Suzanne, b. 1896, Henriette Chandet, and Alice Viardot. *La Malibran et Pauline Viardot.* In French. Paris: Fayard, 1969. 277 pp. Illustrated. Bibliography, p. 273.

904 Escudier, Léon, d. 1881. *Aus dem Leben Paganini's. Von Léon Escudier, nebst einer Biographie der Malibran.* In German. Leipzig: J.A. Bergson-Sonenberg, 1862. 102 pp.

Translation of *Vie anecdotique de Paganini* and *Mme Malibran* in *Vie et aventures des cantatrices célèbres, précédées de Musiciens de l'empire* (q.v.) by M.P.Y. and Léon Escudier, Paris, 1856.

905 Flament, Albert, b. 1877. *L'enchanteresse errante, la Malibran.* In French. Paris: E. Flammarion, 1937. 286 pp. Fictionalized biography.

906 ———. *Une étoile en 1830, La Malibran.* In French. Il y a cent ans. Paris: P. Lafitte, 1928. 126 pp.

907 Giusti, Giuseppe, 1809-1850. *In morte della Malibran de Bériot. Poema con appendice.* In Italian. London: W. Smith, Son and Co., 1837. 64 pp.

908 *In morte di M.F. Malibran de Bériot, cantata de eseguirsi all'I.R. Teatro alla Scala, la sera del 17 marzo 1837.* In Italian. Milano: L. di Giacomo Pirola, 1837. 26 pp. Illustrated.

Libretto. Note on page 5: "La poesia è del sig. Antonio Piazza, la musica dei signori ... Gaetano Donizetti ... Giovanni Pacini ... Saverio Mercadante ... Pietro Antonio Soppola ... Nicola Vaccaj."

909 Lanquine, Clément. *La Malibran.* In French. Les écrits et la vie anecdotique et pittoresque des grands artistes. Paris: Société des éditions Louis-Michaud, 1912. 192 pp. Illustrated.

910 Larionoff, P., and F. Pestellini. *Maria Malibran e i suoi tempi.* In Italian. Firenze: R. Bemporad, 1935. 250 pp. Illustrated.

910-a ———. *Maria Malibran e i suoi tempi.* In Italian. 2nd ed. Firenze: Casa editrice Marzocco, 1943. 250 pp. Illustrated. Bibliography.

A broad historical setting which brings the personality of the celebrated singer well into focus. RT

911-T ———. *María Malibrán y su época.* Translated by María Sandiumenge. In Spanish. Colección grandes biografías. Barcelona: Editorial Juventud, 1953. 224 pp. Illustrated. Bibliography, p. 223.

Spanish translation of *Maria Malibran e i suoi tempi* (q.v.).

912 Legouvé, Ernest, 1807-1903. *Maria Malibran.* In French. Études et souvenirs de théâtre. Les initiateurs. Paris: Hetzel, 1880. 48 pp.

913 Lorenzi de Bradi, Michel, b. 1869. *La brève et merveilleuse vie de la Malibran.* In French. Paris: J. Tallandier, 1936. 251 pp. Illustrated.

The fictionized life story of Malibran told in a romanticized, fluid and pleasant style. RT

914 "Madama Malibran-Garcia a Milano nel 1834." *Galleria teatrale d'Italia.* Milano: Editore Carlo Canadelli, 1835. 143 pp. Illustrated.

The main chapter (pp. 5-47) of a small almanac, quite rare and unusual, edited by the man of letters and librettist Felice Romani and
bearing the title *Galleria teatrale d'Italia*. He comments in grand-
iloquent style on the appearances of Malibran at La Scala in May
1834, in *Norma* and Rossini's *Otello*. The almanac reviews other performances of the 1834 season of La Scala (pp. 48-75) and of other
major Italian theaters (pp. 76-119); there is an exulting ode devoted
to Malibran (pp. 120-124); finally, an appendix contains reviews from
the provincial houses (pp. 125-143). There are five simple etchings,
one of Malibran as Norma, with Marini as Oroveso. RT

915 *Madame Malibran, biographische Skizze.* Nach der Englisch von
A. von Treskow. In German. Quedlinburg: Basse, 1837.

916 Malherbe, Henry, b. 1886. *La passion de la Malibran.* In French.
Paris: A, Michel, 1937. 255 pp.

917 *Memoirs, critical and historical, of Madame Malibran de Bériot
and Monsieur de Bériot. To which is appended a brief biographical
notice of Señor Garcia.* By an Amateur. (The memoir of M. de Bériot,
by the editor of the "Memoirs" signed: W.H.O.) London: Cookes and
Ollivier, 1836. 81 pp. Information taken from the British Museum
General Catalogue.

918 *Memoirs of the Public and Private Life of the Celebrated Madame
Malibran, etc.* Lambeth: J. Thompson, 1836. 8 pp. Information taken
from the British Museum General Catalogue.

919 Merlin, Maria de las Mercedes Santa Cruz y Montalvo, comtesse de,
1789-1852. *Madame Malibran.* In French. Bruxelles: Société
Typographique Belge, 1838. 2 vols. in 1. Lettres de Maria, Vol. 2,
pp. 243-288.

920-T ————. *Memoirs and Letters of Madame Malibran. With Notices
of the Progress of the Musical Drama in England.* Philadelphia: Carey
and Hart, 1840. 2 vols.

920-T-a ————. *Memoirs of Madame Malibran, by the Countess de
Merlin, and other Intimate Friends. With a Selection from Her Cor-
respondence, and Notices of the Progress of the Musical Drama in
England.* London: H. Colburn, 1840. 2 vols. Illustrated.

921 Minarêl, Camell. *Per la Malibran.* Bulôgna: Voulp, 183? 12 pp.
In verse; signed: D'Camell Minarêl.

922 Myers, Henry. *The Signorina.* New York: Crown Publishers, 1956.
311 pp. Fictionalized biography.

923 Nathan, Isaac, 1792-1864. *Memoirs of Madame Malibran de Beriot.*
2nd ed. London: J. Thomas, 1836. 72 pp.

924 Parkinson, Richard, 1797-1858. *A Sermon on Isaiah XXIV. 8-11
Preached on the Second Day of October 1836, Being the Day After the
Funeral of the Late Mme Malibran de Beriot in the Collegiate Church
of Manchester.* Manchester, 1836. Information taken from the British
Museum General Catalogue.

925 Pasquier, Marguerite. *La véritable histoire de la Malibran*;
illustré de André Harford. In French. Paris: La Caravelle, n.d.
24 pp. Illustrated. Contains: "Stances à la Malibran," par Alfred
de Musset.

926 Pougin, Arthur, 1834–1921. *Marie Malibran. Histoire d'une
cantatrice.* In French. Paris, 1911. 284 pp. Information taken from
the British Museum General Catalogue.

927-T ————. *Marie Malibran; the Story of a Great Singer.* Paris:
Plon, 1911. 284 pp. Illustrated. Bibliography. Repertory.

927-T-a ————. *Marie Malibran: The Story of a Great Singer.* London: E. Nash, 1911. x, 323 pp. Illustrated. Bibliography. Repertory.

928 Reparaz, Carmen de. *Maria Malibrán, 1808–1836: estudio biográfico*; prólogo de Pedro Lain Entralgo. In Spanish. Madrid:
Servicio de Publicaciones del Ministerio de Educación y Ciencia,
1976. 269 pp. Illustrated. Bibliography, pp. 267–269. Index.

A fine book on La Malibran. It is profusely illustrated, the
bibliography is exhaustive, and there is a Garcia family tree.

929-T ————. *Maria Malibran, la diva romantique.* In French.
Paris: Editions Perrin, 1980? 286 pp.

French translation of her *Maria Malibrán, 1808–1836: estudio
biográfico* (q.v.).

930 *The Star of La Scala; or, Recollections of Madame Malibran, in
the Autumn of 1835.* By an amateur. London: Seguin's Subscription
Library, 1837. 34 pp.

931 Teneo, Martial. "La Malibran d'après des documents inedits."
Sämmelbande der Internationalen Musikgesellschaft, Jahrgang 7.
In French? Leipzig: Breitkopf & Härtel, 1906?

932 Trebbi, Oreste, 1872–1931. *Nella vecchia Bologna; cronache e
ricordi*, con prefazione di Alfredo Testoni. In Italian. Bologna:
N. Zanichelli, 1924. xiii, 229 pp. Illustrated.

Contains a chapter relating to Malibran, entitled "Il primo sog-
giorno di Maria Malibran a Bologna (1832)."

See also items 1426, 1562, 1597, 1612, 1615, 1620, 1621, 1643, 1668,
1669, 1680, 1681, 1682, 1689, 1694, 1745

MALTEN, THERESE, 1855–1930

See item 1658

MAMMADOVA, SHOVKAT, b. 1897

933 Danilov, Daniil Khristoforovich. *Shevket Mamedova.* In Russian.
Baku: Ishyg, 1976. 98 pp. Illustrated.

MANCINI, GIOVANNI BATTISTA, 1716-1800

934 Mancini, Giovanni Battista. *L'art du chant figuré de J.B. Mancini*. Translated by M.A. Desaugiers. In French. Paris: Cailleau, 1776. viii, 64 pp.

French translation of his *Pensieri, e riflessione pratiche sopra il canto figurato* (q.v.), published in Vienna in 1774.

935 ———. *Lettera di Giambattista Mancini, maestro di canto dell'imperiale, e real corte di Vienna diretta all'illmo. fig. conte N.N.* In Italian. Vienna: M.A. Schmidt, 1796. 48 pp.

936 ———. *Metodo per ben insegnare ed apprendere l'arte del cantare, o siano Osservazioni pratiche su questa nobile e difficile arte, utili ai professori ed agli studenti della medesima.* In Italian. Firenze: Stamperia del Giglio, 1807. 81 pp.

Although according to its preface this purports to be a new work, it is in fact extracted from the author's *Riflessioni pratiche sul canto figurato* (q.v.).

937 ———. *Pensieri, e riflessioni pratiche sopra il canto figurato.* In Italian. Vienna: Ghelen, 1774. 188 pp. Illustrated.

938-T ———. *Practical Reflections on the Figurative Art of Singing.* Translated by Pietro Buzzi. Boston: R.G. Badger, 1912. 104 pp. Illustrated.

939-T ———. *Réflexions pratiques sur le chant figuré....* Traduites sur la 3. éd. italienne. Translated by J.M. Gérard de Rayneval. In French. Paris: Du Pont, 1796.

940 ———. *Riflessioni pratiche sul canto figurato.* Riv., corr., ed. aumentate. In Italian. 3rd ed. Milano: G. Galeazzi, 1777. 259 pp. Illustrated.

The same edition also published as part of *Canto e bel canto* by Andrea della Corte (q.v.).

941 Corte, Andrea della, b. 1883, editor. *Canto e bel canto.* In Italian. Biblioteca di cultura musicale, no. 5. Torino: G.B. Paravia, 1933. 274 pp.

In addition to an essay by the editor entitled "Vicende degli stili del canto dal tempo di Gluck al '900," the book contains two other works on singing: the 1723 edition of *Opinioni de' cantore antichi e moderni* by Pietro Francesco Tosi (see item 1786) and the 1777 edition of *Riflessioni pratiche sul canto figurato* by the castrato Giovanni Battista Mancini (q.v.).

MANN, JOSEF, 1883-1921

See item 1742

MARA, GERTRUD ELISABETH (SCHMELING), 1749-1833

942 Anwand, Oskar Paul Wilhelm, b. 1872. *Die Primadonna Friedrichs des Grossen; Roman*. In German. Berlin: R. Bong, 1930. 332 pp. Illustrated.

943 *Authentische Notizen über die kunstr. Sängerinnen Mara und Catalani*. 2 Theile. A.u.d.T.: *Das Leben der Künstlerin Mara*, von G.C. Grossheim (1823). *Angelica Catalani-Valabregue*, vom Freiherrn E--d von W--e. In German. Cassel: Luckhardt, 1825.

944 Bürkli, Johann Georg, 1793-1851. *Biographie der Sängerin Mara, geborne Gertrud Elisabeth Schmäling*. In German. Neujahrstück der Allgemeinen Musikgesellschaft in Zürich, 23. Zürich, 1835. 12 pp. Illustrated.

945 Grosheim, Georg Christoph, 1764-1847. *Das Leben der Künstlerin Mara*. In German. Cassel: Luckhardt'schen Hofbuchhandlung, 1823. 72 pp.

946 Kaulitz-Niedeck, Rosa, b. 1881. *Die Mara; das Leben einer berühmten Sängerin*. In German. Heilbronn: E. Salzer, 1929. 233 pp. Illustrated. Bibliography, pp. 223-233.

947 Niggli, Arnold, 1843-1927. "Gertrud Elisabeth Mara. Eine deutsche Künstlerin des 18. Jahrhunderts." *Sammlung musikalischer Vorträge*, Leipzig, 1879-98, 3. Reihe, nr. 30 (1881), 163-208. In German. Double pagination.

See also items 1597, 1615, 1668, 1669

MARCHESI, BLANCHE, 1863-1940

948 Marchesi, Blanche. *The Singer's Catechism and Creed.... Here I Lay Down the Truth about Two Hundred and Twenty Years of Teaching by One Method*. London: J.M. Dent and Sons, 1932. xxvi, 168 pp. Illustrated.

949 ————. *Singer's Pilgrimage*. London: Grant Richards, 1923. 304 pp. Illustrated. Index, pp. 300-304.

   Daughter of the famous singing master, Mathilde Marchesi, and thus the logical recipient of the hallowed cloak of Manuel Garcia and his children: Manuel II, Pauline Viardot Garcia and Maria Felicità Malibran, Blanche opens her autobiography with tributes to her fore-bears. She then introduces some of her mother's famous pupils, pulling no punches in her frank opinions. Blanche herself was trained by her mother and had a brief operatic career, followed by a success-ful career as a concert artist and an even more distinguished one as a teacher of singing. She is outspoken and at times amusing, and generously mixes advice on singing with anecdotal stories about the great who passed through her mother's studio, as well as her own contemporaries. WRM

949-a ————. *Singer's Pilgrimage*. Boston: Small, Maynard, 1923. 304 pp. Illustrated. Index, pp. 300-304.

949-b ————. *Singer's Pilgrimage*. With a discography by W.R. Moran. Opera Biographies. New York: Arno Press, 1977. 304, 3 pp. Illustrated. Index, pp. 300-304. Discography, pp. 1-3.

Reprint of the 1923 edition published by G. Richards, London (q.v.). The discography by William R. Moran was prepared for this edition.

949-c ————. *Singer's Pilgrimage*. Da Capo Press Music Reprint Series. New York: Da Capo Press, 1978. 304 pp. Illustrated. Index, pp. 300-304.

Reprint of the 1923 edition published by Small, Maynard, Boston (q.v.).

See also item 1825

MARCHESI, LUIGI, 1755-1829

950 *Lodi caratteristische del celebre cantore Signor Luigi Marchesi.* In Italian. Siena: V.P. Carli e figli, 1781. x pp.

MARCHESI, MATHILDE (GRAUMANN), 1821-1913

951 Marchesi, Mathilde (Graumann). *Aus meinem Leben*. In German. Düsseldorf, F. Bagel, 1888. viii, 246 pp. Illustrated. First published in Vienna in 1877 under the title: *Erinnerungen aus meinem Leben* (q.v.).

952 ————. *Erinnerungen aus meinem Leben*. In German. Wien: C. Gerold's Sohn, 1877. vi, 104 pp. Illustrated.

953 ————. *Marchesi and Music*. *Passages from the Life of a Famous Singing Teacher*; with an introduction by Massenet. New York: Harper, 1897. xiv, 301 pp. Illustrated.

954 ————. *Theoretical and Practical Vocal Method*. With a new introduction by Philip L. Miller. Dover Books on Music. New York: Dover Publications, 1970. xviii, 108 pp. "Unabridged republication of the work originally published by Enoch and Sons, ltd., London."

MARCHISIO, BARBARA, 1833-1919

955 Gorin Marchisio, Emma. *Le sorelle Marchisio*, ricordi di Emma Gorin Marchisio. In Italian. Milano: Gli amici del Museo teatrale alla Scala, 1930. 300 pp. Illustrated. "Edizione fuori commercio di n. 300 esemplari numerati."

This book gives a fascinating insight into the world of opera in the third quarter of the 19th century. The two sisters constituted one of the best-known operatic sister acts, singing together from 1856 to 1871. Carlotta died in childbirth at the age of 36 in 1872.

Barbara kept on singing by herself for several years and upon retirement from the stage became a voice teacher. Her best known pupils were Rosa Raisa and Toti dal Monte.

This volume, written with affection by Carlotta's(?) daughter, goes into an unusual amount of detail about the personal lives and careers of the two artists, and follows them from season to season as they toured Europe. It is particularly valuable for the insight that it gives into operatic life in the Spanish provinces, where the sisters sang so often. TGK

MARCHISIO, CARLOTTA, 1835-1872

See item 955

MARCONI, FRANCESCO, 1853-1916

See item 1680

MARDONES, JOSÉ, 1868-1932

956 Val, Venancio del. *José Mardones, el mejor bajo-cantante del mundo.* In Spanish. Vitoria: Diputación Foral de Alava, Consejo de Cultura, 1972. 57 pp. Illustrated. Some sources give the author's name as Venancio del Val de Sosa.

This superb Spanish artist with the dark bass voice deserves a much better biography than this little volume, full of factual (over sixty) and typographical errors. The illustrations are poorly reproduced. The only merit of the booklet lies in the information it gives about his childhood and early years as a church and zarzuela singer. AM

MARÉCHAL, HÉLÈNE, b. 1893

957 Maréchal, Hélène. *Hélène Maréchal, een leven van zang en toneel.* In Dutch. Gent: Begijnhofdries 18, 1968. 79 pp. Illustrated.

MARINESCU, EMIL, b. 1897

958 Marinescu, Emil, and Melanie Schmidt. *Amintiri.* In Rumanian. Bucureşti: Editura Muzicală, 1977. 293 pp. Illustrated.

MARIO, GIOVANNI, CAVALIERE DI CANDIA, 1810-1883

959 Beale, Thomas Willert, 1828-1894. *The Light of Other Days Seen Through the Wrong End of an Opera Glass,* by Willert Beale (Walter Maynard). London: R. Bentley and Son, 1890. 2 vols.

On Mario and Giulia Grisi.

960 Benaglio, Ines (Castellani Fantoni), 1849-1897. *Mario. Romanzo.*

[By] Memini. Edizione postuma con prefazione di Neera. In Italian. Milano, 1906. Fictionalized biography.

961-T Pearse, Cecilia Maria (de Candia), and Frank Hird. *Le roman d'un grand chanteur (Mario de Candia) d'après les "Souvenirs" de sa fille, Madame Cecilia Pearse, et la version française de Mademoiselle Ethel Duncan.* Translated by Ethel Duncan. In French. Paris: E. Pasquelle, 1912. 274 pp.

The French translation of *The Romance of a Great Singer* (q.v.).

962 ————. *The Romance of a Great Singer; a Memoir of Mario.* London: Smith, Elder, 1910. ix, 309 pp. Illustrated. Repertory, p. 306. Index, pp. 307-309.

962-a ————. *The Romance of a Great Singer; a Memoir of Mario.* New York: Arno Press, 1977. ix, 309 pp. Illustrated. Repertory, p. 306. Index, pp. 307-309.

Reprint of the 1910 edition published by Smith, Elder, London (q.v.).

963-T ————. *Il romanzo di un celebre tenore; ricordi di Mario (Giovanni dei marchesi de Candia) raccolti dalla figlia Cecilia Pearse de Candia.* In Italian. Firenze: Successori Le Monnier, 1913. ix, 232 pp.

The Italian translation of *The Romance of a Great Singer; a Memoir of Mario* (q.v.).

See also items 1562, 1599, 1615, 1680, 1745

MARIO, QUEENA, 1896-1952

964 Mario, Queena. *Death Drops Delilah.* New York: E.P. Dutton, 1944. 206 pp. Illustrated.

965 ————. *Murder in the Opera House.* A Dutton Clue Mystery. New York: E.P. Dutton, 1934. 286 pp. Illustrated.

966 ————. *Murder Meets Mephisto.* New York: E.P. Dutton, 1942. 244 pp.

MARTINELLI, GIOVANNI, 1885-1969

See item 1565

MARTON, EVA, b. 1943

967 Wilkens, Carol. *Eva Marton.* In German, English, Italian. Hamburg: Floria Verlag, 1982. 80 pp. Illustrated. Repertory, pp. 77-79. Chronology of Performances, pp. 61-75.

This trilingual book, with German, English, Italian in parallel columns, gives a concise summary of Marton's rapid rise to international stardom along with a short chapter on her student years and first professional experience in her native Hungary. The tone and approach is excessively flattering, to the point of sounding like a publicity agent's hard sell. Yet all the nice things said about the artist, the woman, the voice and the career are supported by evidence, in and out of the book. Marton may just be one of those hard-working, conscientious singers who reaps in full her well-earned rewards. With a 45 rpm disc in pocket.

MASINI, ANGELO, 1844-1926

968 Forlì, Italy. Comitato Cittadino per le Onoranze ad Angelo Masini nel Quarantesimo della Morte. *Angelo Masini, il tenore angelico. Forlì, 28 settembre 1966.* In Italian. Forlì, 1966. 96 pp. Illustrated.

969 *Angelo Masini, il tenore angelico.* Comitato cittadino per le onoranze ad Angelo Masini nel quarantesimo della morte. Forlì, 28 settembre 1966. In Italian. Forlì: Comitato cittadino ..., 1966. 95 pp. Illustrated. Bibliography, pp. 89-92. Repertory, pp. 59-60. Index, pp. 93-94.

Articles by Michele Raffaelli, Giovanni Borelli, Antonio Mambelli, Antonio Stanghellini and Walter Vichi. (Same as item 968?) AM

970 *Atti del Convengo su Angelo Masini. Ottobre 1976.* In Italian. Forlì: Comune di Forlì, 1977. 57 pp. Illustrated. Bibliography, pp. 53-56.

Contains articles by Fernando Battaglia, Giorgio Gualerzi, Rodolfo Celletti and Walter Vichi. AM

See also items 545, 1680, 1757

MASINI, GALLIANO, b. 1902

971 Calvetti, Mauro. *Galliano Masini. La vita e la carriera artistica del celebre tenore.* In Italian. Livorno: O. Debatte e Figli, 1979. 113 pp. Illustrated. Repertory, pp. 108-109. Discography, pp. 109-110.

In his preface Gianfranco Pierucci confirms that, in addition to patient research and documentation, this biography is permeated by information taken from the author's notes hastily jotted down during the many hours he had spent in the company of the cantankerous extroverted tenor. As a result, the life and career of the singer, painted in broad brush strokes, emerge with pleasing spontaneity. Both repertory and discography are sketchy and insignificant. RT

MASSARDI, ROMARINA

972 Massardi, Romarina. *Una artista lírica; anécdotas, descripción de paises, teatros, ciudades, costumbres, la enseñanza del canto, meditaciones y vida de Rina Massardi.* Recopiladas y editadas por

Alba Luz Massardi. In Spanish. Montevideo: N.p., 1957. 98 pp. Il-lustrated.

MASSARY, FRITZI, 1882-1969

973 Bie, Oskar, 1864-1938. *Fritzi Massary*. In German. Berlin: E. Reiss, 1920. 47 pp. Illustrated.

974 Schneidereit, Otto. *Fritzi Massary. Versuch eines Porträts.* Mit einem Nachwort von R.F. Schmiedt. In German. Berlin: Lied d. Zeit, 1970. 144 pp. Illustrated.

MATERNA, AMALIE, 1844-1918

See item 1658

MATEU Y NICOLAU, FRANCISCO, 1847-1913

975 Aris Garcia, José. *Francisco Mateu (Uetam), hijo ilustre de Mallorca. Memoria biográfica escrita por encargo del Excmo. Ayuntamiento de Palma y leída en la Sala de sesiones de esta Cor-poración el día 21 de Diciembre.* In Spanish. Palma de Mallorca: José Tous, 1914. 18 pp.

This booklet offers the printed text of a lecture given by the author in the Ayuntamiento (City Council) of Palma in honor of the singer who had passed away seven months before. Until the full-length biography by Julio Sanmartin appeared in 1952 (q.v.), this was the main source of information about this distinguished singer. AM

976 Sanmartín Perea, Julio. *Uetam el mejor bajo cantante de su tiempo; biografia.* Ilustraciones de "Xam." Fotos: J. Vila y A. Llompart. In Spanish. Palma de Mallorca: Gráficas Miramar, 1952. 279 pp. Illustrated.

977 Vidal Isern, José. *Hombres de ayer: 30 semblanzas.* In Spanish. Palma de Mallorca: Imprenta Sagrados Corazones, 1961. 151 pp. Illus-trated.

This book presents short biographies of 30 personalities from Mallorca. Chapter VII (pp. 29-33) is devoted to Spanish bass Francisco Mateu ("Uetam") who was born there. AM

See also item 1756

MATUROVÁ, RŮŽENA, b. 1869

978 Rektorys, Artus. *Růžena Maturová.* S úvodem Zdeňka Nejedlého. In Czech. Praha: O. Girgal, 1936. 135 pp. Illustrated.

MAUREL, VICTOR, 1848-1923

979 Maurel, Victor. *Appreciation de la presse parisienne sur Victor Maurel dans Don Juan à l'Opéra-Comique.* In French. Paris: Warmont, 1896. iii, 19 pp.

980 ————. *À propos de la mise en scène de Don Juan; réflexions et souvenirs.* In French. Paris: P. Dupont, 1896. viii, 81 pp.

981 ————. *À propos de la mise en scène du drame lyrique Otello; étude précédée d'aperçus sur la théâtre chanté en 1887.* In French. Rome: Impr. editrice romana, 1888. 183 pp.

982 ————. *Le chant rénové par la science.* In French. Paris: A. Quinzard, 1892. 71 pp. "Conférence faite à Milan le 2 juin 1892."

983 ————. *Dix ans de carrière, 1887-1897.* Préface de Léon Kerst. In French. Paris: Imprimerie P. Dupont, 1897. xv, 419 pp. Illustrated.

An interesting book from the pen of this cultured singer of broad experience and great successes. His views, at times, are uttered in a tone of finality that would border on arrogance were they not made by an artist who sang lead roles in the world premieres of *Otello* and *Falstaff.* His long chapters about the production of these works and his character analyses reflect the authority of someone handing down the composer's conceptions to future generations. Maurel also discusses *Don Giovanni* and how it should be produced; he even includes a step-by-step blocking of the first act duel as obtained from a fencing master familiar with the rules prevalent in Spain at the time of the action. Other chapters contain his thoughts about exercises for singers, the conservatory, lyric art, etc.
The book announces three more works to appear shortly by Maurel; the editor has been unable to trace them in libraries or bibliographies: *Le Théâtre et l'Art du Chant*; *Préliminaires Scientifiques de l'Enseignement de l'Art Vocal*; *Enseignement de la Technique du Chant et de la Scène.* Were they ever published?

983-a ————. *Dix ans de carrière.* Préface de Leon Kerst. In French. Paris: Villerelle, 1897. xv, 419 pp.

983-b ————. *Dix ans de carrière, 1887-1897.* Préface de Léon Kerst. In French. Opera Biographies. New York: Arno Press, 1977. xv, 419 pp. Illustrated.

Reprint of the 1897 edition published by P. Dupont, Paris (q.v.).

984 ————. *Un problème d'art.* In French. Paris: Tresse et Stock, 1893. vii, 314 pp.

985-T ————. *Zehn Jahre aus meinem Künstlerleben 1887-1897.* Vorrede und Übersetzung von Lilli Lehmann-Kalisch. Translated by Lilli Lehmann. In German. Berlin: Raabe & Plothow, 1899. iii, 284 pp. Illustrated.

This is the German translation of his *Dix ans de carrière* (q.v.) by none other than the great Lilli Lehmann herself. Since the two artists were said to be romantically involved around the time of publication of the book, Lehmann's gesture could well have been as much a tribute from one great singer to another as a labor of love.

986 Maurel, Berty. *Victor Maurel--ses idées--son art*. In French. Paris: N.p., n.d. 80 pp. Illustrated.

987 Wicart, Alexis. *Le chanteur*. Préface de M. Albert Carré. In French. Paris: P. Ortiz, 1931. 2 vols. Illustrated.

See also items 1565, 1588, 1615

MAYR, RICHARD, 1877-1935

988 Holz, Herbert Johannes. *Richard Mayr*. In German. Die Wiedergabe, Reihe 2, Bd. 6. Wien: Wiener Literarische Anstalt, 1923. 33 pp. Illustrated.

989 Kunz, Otto, b. 1880. *Richard Mayr. Weihe, Herz un Humor in Bassschlüssel*. Foreword by Lotte Lehmann. In German. Graz: Das Bergland-Buch, 1933. 205 pp. Illustrated.

MAZARIN, MARIETTE

See items 1795, 1796

MAZEIKA, JUOZAS, b. 1907

990 Yla, Stasys, b. 1908. *Juozas Mazeika*. In Lithuanian. Vilnius: Lietuvos TSR teatro draugija, 1968. 70 pp. Illustrated.

MAZUROK, IURII, b. 1931

See item 1732

MEGANE, LEILA, 1891-1960

991 Lloyd-Ellis, Megan. *Hyfrydlais Leila Megane*. In Welsh. Llandysul: Gwasg Gomer, 1979. 140 pp. Illustrated.

MEI-FIGNER, MEDEA, 1858-1952

992 Figner, Medeia Ivanova (Mei). *Moi vospominaniia*. In Russian. Sankt-Peterburg: N.p., 1912. 44 pp.

MELBA, NELLIE, 1861-1931

993 Melba, Nellie. *Melba Method. Part One, Breathing and Other Exercises, Examples, and My Daily Exercises; Part Two, Vocalises for*

Low and High Voice. London: Chappell and Co., 1926.

994 ———. *Melodies and Memories*. London: T. Butterworth, 1925.
335 pp. Illustrated. Published serially in the United States
in *Liberty Magazine* (1925-26), then in book form in the United States
by George H. Doran Co. in 1926 (q.v.) with different illustrations,
in part, than those in the British edition.

This book purports to be the singer's official autobiography. It
was, in fact, written for her in 1924 by the British author, Beverley
Nichols. At the time, Nichols was 23 years of age; Melba was 62.
Nichols has told in his book *All I Could Never Be: Some Recollections*
(London: Jonathan Cape, 1949, pp. 63, 64) how he approached the
singer in London with the avowed purpose of getting the job to write
her memoirs. Eighteen years after the singer's death he gave a perfect description of his plans and purposes:

> Melba, I decided, must write her autobiography, or rather, must
> permit me to write it for her. Her brain was a treasurehouse of
> the sort of material for which editors, as Fleet street had taught
> me, were prepared to pay through the nose. Hers was still a great
> name in England and America; the gossip autobiography was at its
> highest peak of popularity; all I had to do was to take down these
> stories as she told them at the dinner-table, string them together,
> sprinkle them with an appropriate coating of sugar--for it was
> essential, if we were to obtain really large figures for the serial
> rights, that the central figure should be presented, not only with
> a golden voice but also with a golden heart--and then, take them
> into the market to seek the highest bidder.

Nichols accomplished just exactly what he had set out to do. The
fact that the book is filled with inaccuracies, omissions and faulty
chronology shows that Nichols did not do his homework. He apparently
did not even consult the Murphy book, and Melba just didn't want to
be bothered. Nichols sold the serial rights to *Liberty Magazine* in
the United States, and the book rights in New York and London, for
which he received fifty percent of the fees. He moved to a new house,
bought a car, acquired a butler and started writing books, most of
them drawing on his experiences, real or imagined, with Melba. After
the singer's death, he performed the coup de grâce with a nasty novel
called *Evensong* about an old opera singer, which he smugly admitted
owed part of its success to its being a "succès de scandale." So
much for *Melodies and Memories*! WRM

994-a ———. *Melodies and Memories*. New York: George H. Doran
Company, 1926. 339 pp. Illustrated.

994-b ———. *Melodies and Memories*. Freeport, N.Y.: Books for
Libraries Press, 1970. 339 pp. Illustrated.

Reprint of the 1926 edition published by the George H. Doran Company, New York (q.v.).

994-c ———. *Melodies and Memories*. New York: AMS Press, 1971.
339 pp. Illustrated.

Reprint of the 1926 edition published by George H. Doran Company,
New York (q.v.).

994-d ————. *Melodies and Memories*. Introduction and notes by
John Cargher. Melbourne: Thomas Nelson, 1980. xv, 253 pp. Illustrated. Index, pp. 248-253.

This is a newly typeset edition with an introduction and notes
added by John Cargher, specifically prepared for this edition.
The illustrations are different from the ones in previous editions.
The same book marketed in England bears the imprint of Hamish Hamilton,
London.

995-T ————. *Mitt liv som sängerska: en divas minnen och upplevelser*.
Translated by Elisabeth Krey-Lange. In Swedish. Stockholm: Wahlström
& Widstrand, 1927. 302 pp.

Swedish translation of *Melodies and Memories* (q.v.).

996 Casey, Maie, 1892-1983. *Melba Re-Visited*. Melbourne: C.S.
Graphic Reproduction Pty., 1975. 30 pp. Illustrated. Author's full
name: Ethel Marien Sumner Ryan (Lady Richard Gardiner Casey).

A personal essay "written as a tribute to her only grandchild,
Pamela, the Lady Vestey." The author first heard Melba as a child,
and later became a close personal friend. Some of her reminiscences
are of a very personal nature; included is a photograph and a letter
to Melba from Louis-Philippe, Duc d'Orléans, which throws some light
on an interesting and famous romance. The booklet is illustrated
with sketches in black and white and with color reproductions of
paintings by the author and others; also contains photographs. WRM

997 Colson, Percy, b. 1873. *Melba; an Unconventional Biography*.
London: Grayson & Grayson, 1932. x, 278 pp. Illustrated.

Colson produced his biography of Melba in the year of the diva's
death. Colson was a sometime critic, sometime newspaperman who
produced gossipy articles and books, the chief distinction of which
was bounteous name-dropping. His book was obviously rushed into
print and does little more than regurgitate the old stories with
occasional embellishments. The book is particularly deficient in
recounting Melba's activities in Australia, and, in sum, makes little
contribution. WRM

998 Hetherington, John Aikman, b. 1907. *Melba; a Biography*. Melbourne: Cheshire, 1967. 312 pp. Illustrated.

Australian journalist John Hetherington has given us by far the
most definitive biography of Nellie Melba. Here, for the first
time, we have the Australian side of the story well developed through
new research. Melba's husband, Charles Armstrong, is for once not
merely dismissed by casual mention: something is told of his life
and character and his part in the picture. Many gaps in the Melba
story have been filled, but the emphasis is on Melba the person rather
than the artist. The author is not a musician, nor does he have any
strong interest in the artistic side of Melba's life, and from this
standpoint the work is weak. Scant notice is taken of Melba's recordings, and there is no discography. WRM

998-a ————. *Melba; a Biography*. London: Faber & Faber, 1967.
312 pp. Illustrated. Reprinted by the same publisher in 1973.

998-b ——————. *Melba; a Biography*. New York: Farrar, Straus & Giroux, 1968. 310 pp. Illustrated. Bibliography, pp. 297-301.

New edition, with an introduction by the late Francis Robinson, Assistant Manager of the Metropolitan Opera.

999 Jones, Dora Duty, d. 1913. *Lyric Diction for Singers, Actors and Public Speakers; with a Preface by Madame Melba*. New York: Harper, 1913. xv, 341 pp.

1000 *Melba's Gift Book of Australian Art and Literature*. Melbourne: G. Robertson, 1915. 176 pp. Illustrated. "The Entire Profits from the Sale of this Book will be devoted by Madam Melba to the Belgian Relief Fund."

In her introduction, Mme. Melba writes: "There is a personal reason for the appearance of this book. I was born in Australia, and I glory in the land of my birth. But as an artist I was born in Belgium.... I love every stone in Belgium; but now those stones are trodden by invaders.... One lies awake at night thinking of what they have done, and wondering how one can help the victims who still survive.... And that is the purpose of this Australian book." A collection of sketches, stories, poetry, drawings and paintings in the best Australian tradition, contributed for this work of charity. Many color plates, tipped in on art paper. Presumably, most of this work is published here for the first time. Edited by Franklin Peterson. WRM

1000-a *Melba's Gift Book of Australian Art and Literature*. London: Hodder and Stoughton, 1915. iv, 123 pp. Illustrated. "Published on behalf of the Belgian Relief Fund."

1001 Moran, William R., b. 1919, editor. *Melba: A Contemporary Review*. Westport, Conn.: Greenwood Press, 1984? Bibliography. Repertory. Index. Discography.

As one of the greatest singers of her time, Melba had a personality which automatically created news no matter where or in what circumstances she was. Throughout her meteoric career she generated copy not only in the musical press of the world, but also in many areas of current literature; accounts of Melba's activities are found scattered in innumerable memoirs. This work brings together a selection from this wide range of material. It also incorporates Melba's own writings with advice to singers and articles on her own technique. The bibliography is extensive, and the definitive discography by the editor gives complete recording data, including the correct playing speed for every Melba recording. An excellent anthological overview of one of the great operatic personalities and her career.

1002 Murphy, Agnes G. *Melba; a Biography. With Chapters by Madame Melba on the Selection of Music as a Profession & on the Science of Singing*. New York: Doubleday, Page, 1909. xiv, 348 pp. Illustrated.

Chronologically this is the first book-length Melba biography. Few today seem to be aware that its author was Melba's personal secretary and, as the British critic Herman Klein once said, the book is as close to being an autobiography as it could possibly be. While it thus has all the failings of a self-serving work and the author tells us what Melba wanted told about herself, it is nevertheless one of the most important works about the singer. By 1909 Melba's place in the world of music was assured, and she must have felt that it was time to dispel some of the myths, many of which she had deliberately created during her climb to fame. The book was obviously written with full access to source material, scrapbooks, reviews, programs, and letters because performance dates are correct and events are placed in their correct sequence. Those facts that are given are correct; her early singing lessons with Pietro Cecchi are discussed (previously she had always said she had had no other teacher than Marchesi); those reviews that are given (selected, to be sure) are correctly quoted. The book concludes with a correct list of her roles, and two articles from the pen of the singer herself, one on the selection of music as a profession, and the other on the science of singing. All told, the book covers excellently the major events of the singer's public life to 1909. WRM

1002-a ———. *Melba: A Biography, with Chapters by Madame Melba on the Selection of Music as a Profession & on the Science of Singing: Illustrated by Various Portraits, Views, & Autographs.* London: Chatto & Windus, 1909. xiv, 348 pp. Illustrated.

1002-b ———. *Melba: A Biography. With Chapters by Madame Melba on the Selection of Music as a Profession and on the Science of Singing.* Da Capo Press music reprint series. New York: Da Capo Press, 1977. xiv, 348 pp. Illustrated. Index.

Reprint of the 1909 edition (q.v.).

1003 Nichols, Beverley, b. 1899. *25; Being a Young Man's Candid Recollections of His Elders and Betters.* New York: George H. Doran Company, 1926. 256 pp.

Nichols's reminiscences written at the ripe old age of twenty-six. Contains a chapter on Melba. WRM

1003-a ———. *25; Being a Young Man's Candid Recollections of His Elders and Betters.* London: J. Cape, 1926. 256 pp. Illustrated.

1004 Sherman, Paul. *Melba.* Contemporary Australian Plays, 6. St. Lucia, Queensland: University of Queensland Press (Distributed by Prentice-Hall International), 1976. x, 77 pp. Illustrated. Bibliography, p. 77. Dramatized biography of Melba.

A play, first performed at the Brisbane Arts Theater on 22 September 1974. The author states: "This play is essentially a work of drama, not of historical biography. While its origin is an image of a real woman, it does not seek to be factually correct in all respects." Characters in the play drawn from real life include Sarah Bernhardt, Mathilde Marchesi, Charles Armstrong, Beverley Nichols, and two of Melba's protegées, Helen Danies (who sang as Elena Danieli) and Stella Power. WRM

1005 Wechsberg, Joseph, b. 1907. *Red Plush and Black Velvet; the Story of Melba and Her Times.* Boston: Little, Brown, 1961. 372 pp.

Wechsberg's book draws almost entirely on previously published material. Rather than make a contribution to the Melba literature it does a disservice because of its multiple factual errors. WRM

1005-a ———. *Red Plush and Black Velvet; the Story of Melba and Her Times.* London: Weidenfeld & Nicholson, 1962. 376 pp.

1006-T ———. *Roter Plüsch und schwarzer Samt; die grosse Melba und ihre Zeit.* Translated by Kurt Wagenseil. In German. Rororo Taschenbuch Ausgabe, 697. Reinbek bei Hamburg: Rowohlt, 1964. 188 pp.

The German translation of *Red Plush and Black Velvet* (q.v.).

See also items 1541, 1567, 1581, 1615, 1621, 1635, 1647, 1658, 1662, 1663, 1716, 1744, 1792, 1803, 1804, 1805, 1826

MELCHIOR, LAURITZ, 1890-1973

1007 Nually, Jana. *Lauritz Melchior.* Translated by Mette Nissen. In Danish. København: Steen Hasselbachs, 1969. 223 pp. Illustrated.

See also items 1544, 1606, 1607, 1608, 1719

MELCHISSÉDEC, LÉON, 1843-1925

1008 Melchissédec, Léon. *Le chant, la déclamation lyrique, le mécanisme et l'émission de la voix.* In French. Paris: Nilsson, 1925. 207 pp. Illustrated.

1009 ———. *Pour chanter, ce qu'il faut savoir.* In French. Paris: Nilsson, n.d. 242 pp.

MELLISH, MARY (FLANNERY), 1890-1955

1010 Mellish, Mary (Flannery). *Sometimes I Reminisce; Autobiography.* New York: G.P. Putnam's Sons, 1941. 336 pp. Illustrated.

The life story of an intelligent, educated, sensitive woman, blessed with wisdom and a fine literary style. Her accidental acquaintance-ship with Caruso led to her engagement at the Metropolitan that lasted for seven seasons. She writes affectionately about Antonio Scotti also, whom she got to know during her tours with the Scotti Opera Company. The story concentrates on the personal rather than the musical events of her life.

MENTSINSKII, MODEST OMELIANOVICH, 1875-1935

1011 Derkach, Ivan Stepanovich. *Modest Mentsins'kii--geroychnii tenor.* Naris Ivana Derkacha. In Ukrainian. L'viv: "Kameniar," 1969. 83 pp. Illustrated.

MERRILL, ROBERT, b. 1919

1012 Merrill, Robert, and Robert Saffron. *Between Acts; an Irreverent Look at Opera and Other Madness*. New York: McGraw-Hill, 1976. 240 pp. Illustrated.

1013 Merrill, Robert, and Fred G. Jarvis. *The Divas; a Novel*. New York: Simon and Schuster, 1978. 414 pp.

Operatic baritone Merrill's first excursion into the terrain of operatic fiction. One hopes also his last.

1013-a ———. *The Divas; a Novel*. New York: Berkeley Pub. Corp., 1979 (c1978). 359 pp.

1014 Deleted

1015 Merrill, Robert, and Sandford Dody. *Once More from the Beginning*. New York: Macmillan, 1965. 286 pp. Illustrated. Index, pp. 279-286.

A straightforward narrative of the singer's life with the help of Sandford Dody. It contains a magnificent portrait of the "Jewish mother"--the singer's own. The love-hate relationship with his mother, whose powerful personality propelled him towards a career and success, is like a *Leitmotiv* that keeps returning throughout the book. Merrill also talks about the main stops of his career, his colleagues, Tucker, Toscanini, his roles, his marriages. Still, the book is more about his life than his career and artistic concerns.

MESSCHAERT, JOHANNES MARTINUS, 1857-1922

1016 Messchaert, Johannes Martinus. *Eine Gesangstunde; allgemeine Ratschläge nebst gesangstechnischen Analysen von einigen Schubert-Liedern*; hersg. von Franziska Martienssen. In German. Mainz: B. Schott, 1927. 29 pp. Illustrated.

1017 Martienssen-Lohmann, Franziska (Meyer-Estorf), b. 1887. *Die echte Gesangkunst dargestellet an Johannes Messchaert*. In German. 2nd ed. Berlin: B. Behr (F. Feddersen), 1920. 103 pp. Illustrated.

1018 ———. *Johannes Messchaert, ein Beitrag zum Verständnis echter Gesangkunst*. In German. Berlin, 1914.

MIDGLEY, WALTER, 1914-1980

See item 1545

MIKHAILOV, MAKSIM DORMIDONTOVICH, 1893-1971

1019 Kuznetsova, Anna Sergeevna. *Maksim iz Kol'tsovki; povest' o narodnom artiste*. In Russian. Cheboksary: Chuvashskoe izd-vo, 1962. 270 pp. Illustrated.

1020 ————. *Povest' o narodnom artiste.* In Russian. Enlarged ed.
Moskva: Moskovskii rapochii, 1964. 301 pp. Illustrated.

Enlarged edition of *Maksim iz Kol'tsovki* (q.v.).

1021 Moscow. Gosudarstvennyi akademicheskii Bol'shoi teatr. *Maksim Dormidontovich Mikhailov.* In Russian. Moskva: Iskusstvo, 1953. Un-paged. Illustrated.

A short biography of the singer followed by many illustrations of poor quality.

See also item 1686

MILASHKINA, TAMARA, b. 1934

See item 1732

MILDE, HANS FEODOR VON, 1821-1899

See items 1022, 1023

MILDE, ROSA AGTHE VON, 1827-1906

1022 Cornelius, Peter, 1824-1874. *Briefe in Poesie und Prosa von Peter Cornelius an Feodor und Rosa von Milde*; herausgegeben und eingeleitet von Natalie von Milde. In German. Weimar: H. Böhlaus, 1901. 126 pp. Illustrated.

Composer-poet Peter Cornelius maintained a lively correspondence with singers Rosa and Feodor von Milde, sometimes in poetry, other times accompanied by poems. Affection, friendship and a strong attachment radiates from these charming writings of the composer of *Der Barbier von Bagdad*.

1023 Milde, Franz von. *Ein ideales Künstlerpaar, Rosa und Feodor von Milde. Ihre Kunst und ihre Zeit.* In German. Leipzig: Breitkopf & Härtel, 1918. 2 vols.

A biography of the von Mildes by their son. Father Feodor was a baritone, the creator of Telramund in *Lohengrin*; mother, a soprano, was the creator of Elsa in the same performance in Weimar. The bulk of the book is made up of letters written to the von Mildes by everybody who was anybody in the 19th-century musical world.

MILLET, LUIS, 1867-1941

See item 1468

MILNES, SHERRILL, b. 1935

1024 Blackwood, Alan, b. 1932. *The Performing World of the Singer; with a Profile of Sherrill Milnes.* Morristown, N.J.: Silver Burdett

Company, 1981. 113 pp. Illustrated.

An overview of the history of singing, all kinds of singing, written expressly for young adults. Among the three vocalists who are singled out to exemplify the life and career of the singer, Sherrill Milnes (pp. 39-53) and Matthew Best (pp. 93-99) are operatic artists. The Milnes interview was conducted by Frank Granville Barker; the one with Best by Nicholas Robinson. Both are simple summaries of the singers' lives, obviously aimed at encouraging talented youngsters toward a musical career.

See also item 1654

MINGOTTI, REGINA (VALENTINI), 1728-1807

1025 Mingotti, Regina (Valentini). *An Appeal to the Publick*, by Signora Mingotti. London: Printed for the authoress, 1756? 13 pp.

A pamphlet presenting Mrs. Mingotti's side of an extended dispute between her and the impresario Vansecchi in London. More interesting than the wrongs sustained by Mrs. Mingotti at the hand of Vansecchi are her references to prevailing operatic practices of the time, whereby it was customary to "improve" an opera, even if its composer was Metastasio, by the insertion of other compositions of proven popular appeal.

1026 ————. *A Second Appeal to the Publick*, by Signora Mingotti. London: Printed for Signora Mingotti, 1756? 11 pp.

See also item 1597

MIRATE, RAFFAELE, 1815-1885

See item 1620

MIROSHNICHENKO, IEVGENIIA SEMENIVNA, b. 1931

1027 Zotsenko, Mykola Volodymirovich. *IEvgeniia Miroshnichenko. Narodnaia artistka SRSR*. In Ukrainian. Maistri mistetsv Ukraini. Kiev: Muzyka Ukraina, 1972. 107 pp. Illustrated.

1028 ————. *Sribni struni*. In Ukrainian. Kiev: Molod', 1963. 84 pp. Illustrated.

MIURA, TAMAKI, 1884-1946

1029 Miura, Tamaki, and Setouchi Harumi. *Madame Butterfly*. In Japanese. Tokyo: Toyo Publishers, 1969. 250 pp. Illustrated. Title translated from Japanese.

See also item 1695

MÖDL, MARTHA, b. 1912

1030 Schäfer, Walter Erich, b. 1901. *Martha Mödl.* Mit einem Beitrag von Wieland Wagner. In German. Velber b. Hannover: Friedrich Verlag, 1967. 99 pp. Illustrated. Discography, pp. 98-99.

MOJICA, JOSÉ, 1895-1974

1031-T Mojica, José. *I, a Sinner ... Autobiography.* Translated by Fanchon Royer. Chicago: Franciscan Herald Press, 1963. v, 393 pp. Illustrated.

English translation of his *Yo pecador* (q.v.).

1032 ———. *Mi guia y mi estrella.* In Spanish. Chicago: N.p., 1975. 95 pp.

1033 ———. *Yo pecador; autobiografia.* In Spanish. Mexico: Editorial Jus, 1956. 662 pp. Illustrated.

A most unusual autobiography of a poor Mexican boy born out of wedlock who became an acclaimed singer of the Chicago Opera Company, a matinee idol and movie star, and then, following his mother's death, gave up all he had accomplished and became a Franciscan priest. It is Father José Francisco de Guadalupe, O.F.M., who tells his life story with straightforward simplicity and honesty. The passages about Mary Garden, Caruso, Chaliapin are especially revealing.

See also item 1631

MONCRIEFF, GLADYS, b. 1893

1034 Moncrieff, Gladys. *My Life of Song.* Adelaide: Rigby, 1971. 145 pp. Illustrated.

MOODY, FANNY, 1866-1945

See item 1567

MOORE, GRACE, 1898-1947

1035-T Moore, Grace. *Man lever kun een gang, erindringer.* Translated by Erling Mortensen, Adam Nygaard. In Danish. København: Samleren, 1947. 271 pp. Illustrated.

Danish translation of *You're Only Human Once* (q.v.).

1036 ———. *You're Only Human Once.* Garden City, N.Y.: Doubleday, Doran, 1944. 275 pp.

A candid, down-to-earth autobiography of the Tennessee girl who gave up a lucrative Broadway career to become a Met artist. Her voice and physical beauty brought her success, in the United States and internationally, on stage and in film. She was partnered by Lawrence Tibbett in *New Moon* and by Georges Thill in the film version of *Louise*. Moore may have played the prima donna to the hilt in life, but her writing suggests an awareness of her proper position in the galaxy of stars. She writes with admiration about many colleagues, Mary Garden in particular. The book is teeming with people of all walks of life; thus it suffers from the absence of an index. It deserves to be mentioned that Moore wrote her autobiography at the relatively young age of 46. She died in a plane crash three years later.

1036-a ————. *You're Only Human Once.* New York: Arno Press, 1977. 275 pp.

Reprint of the 1944 edition published by Doubleday, Doran, New York (q.v.).

1037 Farrar, Rowena Rutherford. *Grace Moore and Her Many Worlds.* New York: Cornwall Books, 1982. 305 pp. Illustrated. Bibliography, pp. 296-301. Index, pp. 303-312. Discography, pp. 284-291. Metropolitan Opera Appearances, p. 283.

Reducing the many-dimensional Grace Moore to the printed page would try the abilities of any author. Farrar has done an excellent job in presenting the singer's remarkable personality, drive and ambition. She is not quite as successful in establishing her claim that "Miss Moore rose to the top in six categories--musical comedy, opera, concerts, motion pictures, radio and records." While the list in one appendix gives the ten roles she sang at the Metropolitan, some of these are not even mentioned in the text, and some only in passing. Only seven musical comedies in which Miss Moore took part are mentioned in the text; other sources give at least nine. Of the eight films listed in the *New York Times Directory of the Film* only *Louise* is listed in the index, although there is much on the success and importance to Moore's career of the highly acclaimed *One Night of Love*. Only passing mention is made of other films. The author has not consulted Bill Park's excellent discography in the appendix, as textual references to dates and makes of recordings are sometimes inaccurate.

This book has so much to recommend it for its coverage of Grace Moore the person, it is unfortunate that it could not have been rounded out with additional appendix material, such as a chronology of operatic performances in Europe and elsewhere, a complete listing of films with casts and dates, and selected reviews of performances. It is hoped that a second edition may correct the typographical errors. WRM

See also items 1607, 1716, 1719

MORENA, BERTA, 1878-1952

1038 Vogl, Adolf, b. 1873. *Berta Morena und ihre Kunst; zweiunddreissig Gedenkblätter aus dem Leben der Künstlerin, mit einer psychologischen Betractung ihrer Persönlichkeit.* In German. München: Hugo Schmidt, 1919. 72 pp. Illustrated. With 34 mounted portraits. Edition limited to 500 copies.

MORTON, RACHEL, 1888-1982

See item 1827

MÜHLMANN, ADOLF, b. 1867

1039 Mühlmann, Adolf. *A grobber Koll; Erinnerungen von Adolf Mühlmann.* In German. Chicago: Gutenberg Press, 1932. 323 pp. Illustrated. Half-title: A grobber Koll; der Werdegang eines Opernsängers.

MÜLLER, MARIA, 1898-1958

See item 1811

MULLINGS, FRANK, 1881-1953

See item 1629

MUSI, MARIA MADDALENA, called LA MIGNATTA, 1669-1751

1040 Cosentino, Giuseppe, b. 1852. *La Mignatta, Maria Maddalena
Musi, cantatrice bolognese famosa, 1669-1751.* In Italian. Bologna:
N. Zanichelli, 1930. ix, 202 pp. Illustrated.

MUSTAFÀ, DOMENICO, 1829-1912

1041 Angelis, Alberto de, b. 1885. *Domenico Mustafà, la Cappella
Sistina e la Società musicale romana.* In Italian. Bologna: N.
Zanichelli, 1926. 192 pp. Illustrated.

MUZIO, CLAUDIA, 1889-1936

1042 Barnes, Harold Melzar, b. 1913. *Claudia Muzio; a Biographical
Sketch and Discography.* Revised. Austin, Tex., 1947. 18 pp.
Discography, pp. 15-18.

See also item 1565

N

NAIA, LEONARD, 1886-1928

1043 Ionescu-Angel, Stelian. *Astă seară cîntă Leonard.* Prefață de
Victor Eftimiu. Postfață de Tudor Mușatescu. Coperta de Gh. Boțan.
In Rumanian. București: Editura Muzicală, 1970. 260 pp. Illustrated.
Bibliography, pp. 257-258.

NATZKE, OSCAR, 1905-1951

See item 1594

NEGRETE, JORGE, 1911-1951

See item 1631

NESTERENKO, EVGENII, b. 1938

See item 1732

NERI, GIULIO, 1909-1958

1044 Clerico, Cesare, b. 1953. *Giulio Neri; una vita nella voce.*
In Italian. Torino: Scomegna, 1981. ii, 81 pp. Illustrated. Bib-
liography, p. 78. Repertory, pp. 52-54. Discography, pp. 31-33.
Chronology of Performances, pp. 34-51.

A clever, exhaustive biographical essay, punctuated by acidy
polemics in support of this famous bass, nicknamed "il bronza," the
forge, for the enormous resonance of his voice. The preface is by
Giorgio Gualerzi. The appendix is entitled "The Definition of the
Bass Voice." The discography gives full casts and includes commercial
releases only. RT

NEUMANN, ANGELO, 1838-1910

1045 Neumann, Angelo. *Erinnerungen an Richard Wagner.* In German.
2nd ed. Leipzig: L. Staackmann, 1907. 341 pp. Illustrated.

1046-T ————. *Personal Recollections of Wagner; Translated from the
4th German Edition.* Translated by Edith Livermore. New York: Henry
Holt, 1908. 329 pp. Illustrated. Index, pp. 321-329.

This is the English translation of Neumann's *Erinnerungen an Richard
Wagner* (q.v.). These memoirs of a singer-turned-superintendant, deal
exclusively with the author's professional relationship with Richard
Wagner and his music dramas. Neumann's story, rich in important details, is partly narrated by the very extensive quotations from
Neumann's correspondence with Wagner. The book also contains many
references to the Wagner interpreters of the period. An invaluable
source book.

1046-T-a ————. *Personal Recollections of Wagner; Translated from
the 4th German Edition.* Translated by Edith Livermore. London: A.
Constable, 1909. 329 pp. Illustrated.

English translation of his *Erinnerungen an Richard Wagner* (q.v.).

1046-T-b ————. *Personal Recollections of Wagner; Translated from
the 4th German Edition.* Translated by Edith Livermore. New York:

Da Capo Press, 1976. 329 pp. Illustrated. Index, pp. 321-329.
Reprint of the 1908 edition of Henry Holt and Company, New York (q.v.).

1047-T ———. *Souvenirs sur Richard Wagner.* Translated by Maurice Rémon, Wilhelm Bauer. In French. Paris: Calmann-Lévy, 1909.
French translation of his *Erinnerungen an Richard Wagner* (q.v.).

NEVADA, EMMA, 1859-1940

See items 1567, 1733

NEZHDANOVA, ANTONINA VASIL'EVNA, 1880-1950

1048 Nezhdanova, Antonina Vasil'evna. *Antonina Vasil'evna Nezhdanova. Materialy i issledovaniia.* Edited by V.A. Vasina-Grossman (et al.). In Russian. Moskva: Iskusstvo, 1967. 543 pp. Illustrated. Discography, pp. 519-525. At head of title: Vokal'no-tvorcheskii kabinet imeni A.V. Nezhdanovoi.

1049 L'vov, Mikhail L'vovich, 1887-1957. *A.V. Nezhdanova.* In Russian. 2nd ed. Moskva: Gos. muzykal'noe izd-vo, 1952. 222 pp. Illustrated. First edition published in 1946 under title: *Antonina Vasil'evna Nezhdanova* (q.v.).

1050 ———. *A.V. Nezhdanova.* In Russian. Moskva: Gos. muzykal'noe izd-vo, 1955. 47 pp.

1051 ———. *Antonina Vasil'evna Nezhdanova; opyt tvorcheskoi kharakteristiki.* In Russian. Moskva: Muzgiz, 1946. 209 pp. Illustrated.

1052 Polianovskii, Georgii Aleksandrovich. *A.V. Nezhdanova.* In Russian. Popul. monografiia. Moskva: Muzyka, 1970. 144 pp. Illustrated. Bibliography, pp. 139-143.

See also item 1686.

NICULESCU-BASU, GEORGE

1053 Niculescu-Basu, George. *Amintirile, unui artist de operă.* In Rumanian. Bucureşti: Editura Muzicală, 1962. 566 pp. Illustrated.

1054 ———. *Cum am cîntat eu.* In Rumanian. Bucureşti: Editura Muzicală, 1961. 259 pp. Illustrated.

NIEMANN, ALBERT, 1831-1917

1055 Niemann, Albert. *Drei bisher unveröffentliche Briefe an Baron von Perglass ... und Botho von Hülsen.* In German. Berlin?, 1931? 9 leaves.

1056 ————. *Unveröffentliche Briefe von Albert Niemann und Caroline Schlegel*. Mit Genehmigung der Generalintendanz der Staatlichen Schauspiele zu Berlin veröffentlicht und den Teilnehmern am Festmahle der Gesellschaft für Theatergeschichte am 26 april 1931 gewidmet von dr. Georg Droescher und dr. Georg Elsner. In German. Berlin: Graphische Kunstanstalt, 1931. 8 pp. Privately printed, edition limited to 150 numbered copies.

1057 Altmann, Wilhelm, b. 1862, editor. *Richard Wagner und Albert Niemann; ein gedenkbuch mit bisher unveröffentlichen Briefen, besonders Wagners....* Nebst einer Characteristik Niemanns, von dr. Gottfried Niemann. In German. Berlin: G. Stilke, 1924. 263 pp. Illustrated.

1058 Sternfeld, Richard, 1858-1926. *Albert Niemann*. In German. Berlin: Schuster & Loeffler, 1904. 90 pp. Illustrated.

1059 Wagner, Karlheinz, b. 1929. "Albert Niemann als Wagner-Darsteller; eine Studie zur Durchsetzung des musikdramatischen Darstellungsstils." Inaug. Dissertation, München, 1954. In German. 110, v leaves. Bibliography, pp. i-v.

NIKOLAI, ELENA, b. 1905

1060 Karapetrov, Konstantin. *Elena Nikolai*. In Bulgarian. Sofiia: Nauka i izkustvo, 1969. 110 pp. Illustrated.

NIKOLOV, NIKOLA, b. 1925

1061 Karapetrov, Konstantin. *Nikola Nikolov*. In Bulgarian. Sofiia: Nauka i izkustvo, 1967. 79 pp. Illustrated.

NILSEN, ISAK

See item 1151

NILSSON, BIRGIT, b. 1918

1062 Nilsson, Birgit. *Mina minnesbilder*. In Swedish. Stockholm: Bonnier, 1977. 120 pp. Illustrated.

1063-T ————. *My Memoirs in Pictures*. Translated by Thomas Teal. Garden City: Doubleday, 1981. 127 pp. Illustrated. Index, pp. 123-127.

The English translation of her *Mina minnesbilder* (q.v.). A pictorial autobiography; the lengthy annotations appended to each photograph tell the personal and artistic life story of the singer. The celebrated Nilsson humor is in evidence by the inclusion of the 1968 *Playboy* caricature and the illustrated exchange of quips with von Karajan. The text is commendably balanced between an unconcealed awareness of artistic worth and humility.

See also items 1654, 1758

NILSSON, CHRISTINE, 1843-1921

1064 Carlsson, Beyron, b. 1869. *Kristina Nilsson, grevinna de Casa Miranda*; minnen och upplevelser upptecknade av Beyron Carlsson. In Swedish. Stockholm: Åhlén & Åkerlund, 1922. 462 pp. Illustrated.

A fascinating insight into the world of the 19th-century vocalist through the "remembrances" of Kristina Nilsson, "as told to" Carlsson. Blaze de Bury called Nilsson "Lind's true sister," and the later 19th century seems to have seen her as a match for the "Swedish nightingale." Her first great success came in 1865 as the Queen of the Night, and there is a photo of her in that role, and in many others. The anecdotes surrounding the performances are profuse and cover the period up to her death in 1921. PHS

1065 Charnacé, Guy de, 1825-1909. *Christina Nilsson.* In French. His: Les étoiles du chant, 2. livr. Paris: H. Plon, 1869. 28 pp. Illustrated.

1066-T ———. *Christina Nilsson.* Met een portret in lichtdruk naar de beroemde gravure van Morse. In Dutch. Nijmegen, 1876.

Dutch translation of his *Christina Nilsson* originally published in French (q.v.).

1067-T ———. *A Star of Song! The Life of Christine Nilsson.* Translated by J.C.M. and E.C. New York: Press of Wynkoop & Hallenbeck, 1870. 39 pp. Illustrated.

English translation of his *Christina Nilsson* (q.v.).

1068 Franzén, Nils Olof. *Christina Nilsson: en svensk saga.* In Swedish. Stockholm: Bonnier, 1976. 271 pp. Illustrated. Bibliography, pp. 267-268. Index.

1069 Headland, Helen. *Christina Nilsson, the Songbird of the North.* Illustrated by the author. Rock Island, Ill.: Augustana Book Concern, 1943. 173 pp. Illustrated. Favorite Swedish Melodies of Christina Nilsson, pp. 165-171.

A simple, factual narrative of Nilsson's life, written in a style best suited for young adults. The author claims that all the facts given are historically correct; the fictional dialogues are distracting.

1070 Lawson, Evald Benjamin, 1904-1965. "Christina Nilsson's Visit to Brockton, Mass., in November, 1870; Pages from the Early History of the Oldest Swedish Lutheran Church in New England." *Augustana Historical Society Publications* (Rock Island, Ill.) no. 3 (1933), 81-96.

1070-a ———. "Christina Nilsson's Visit to Brockton, Mass., in November, 1870. Pages from the Early History of the Oldest Swedish Lutheran Church in New England." Rock Island, Ill., 1934. 16 pp. Illustrated. Reprinted from *Augustana Historical Society Publications*, no. 3 (q.v.).

1071 Norlind, Tobias, b. 1879. *Kristina Nilsson, grevinna de Casa Miranda, sangerskan och konstnärinnan.* In Swedish. Stockholm: Ahlén & Akerlund, 1923. 300 pp. Illustrated.

See also items 1573, 1588, 1597, 1599, 1615, 1658, 1694

NOORDEWIER-REDDINGIUS, AALTJE, 1868-1949

1072 Schouwman, Hans. *Aaltje Noordewier-Reddingius en haar zangkunst.* In Dutch. Den Haag: Servire, 1958. 119 pp. Illustrated. Index, pp. 116-119.

An excellent brief biography of Noordewier-Reddingius with some photographs, and a very large number of contemporary comments. The second part of the volume is organized topically, with sections on Bach, Handel, Mozart, Haydn, Beethoven, Verdi, Brahms, Diepenbrock, Dutch works, songs and church music. In the third part of the book, there are brief sections on students and the gramophone. PHS

NORDGREN, KARL GÖSTA, b. 1926

1073 Adenby, Torsten. *Boken on Snoddas.* In Swedish. Stockholm: Forum, 1952. 150 pp. Illustrated.

NORDICA, LILLIAN, 1859-1914

1074 Nordica, Lillian. *Lillian Nordica's Hints to Singers, Together with an Account of Lillian Nordica's Training for the Opera, as Told in the Letters of the Singer and Her Mother, Amanda Allen Norton*; transcribed by William Armstrong. New York: E.P. Dutton, 1923. xix, 167 pp. Illustrated.

The title and subtitle tell it as it is. The foreword by Ernestine Schumann-Heink, dated October 14, 1922, states: "Every word Lillian Nordica says in the book is gospel truth--this noble great soul died too soon for all of us. She was the greatest, most wonderful *American* singer--what a voice and what ambition. I shall always worship the memory of the artist, the woman." WRM

1075 Glackens, Ira, b. 1907. *Yankee Diva; Lillian Nordica and the Golden Days of Opera. With Lillian Nordica's Hints to Singers.* New York: Coleridge Press, 1963. xiv, 366 pp. Illustrated. Bibliography, pp. 275-277. Repertory, pp. 279-281. Index, pp. 357-366. Discography, pp. 285-300.

The product of many years' research, this well-written biography has stood the test of time as a definitive work. The "Hints to Singers" is a reprint of the Armstrong transcription first published in 1923 (q.v.). The book contains an essay entitled "Recordings and Lillian Nordica," together with a discography by William R. Moran (pp. 285-300) and a brief note "How to Sing a Ballad," which was dictated by Nordica in 1906 (pp. 301-305). WRM

See also items 1541, 1567, 1615, 1658, 1662, 1663, 1792, 1803, 1804, 1805

NORRIE, ANNA, 1860-1957

1076 Norrie, Anna. *Kärlek måste vi ha....* In Swedish. Stockholm: Wahlström & Widstrand, 1945. 189 pp. Illustrated.

1077 ———. *Pa lyckans tinnar; efterskörd av Anna Norries memoarer,* redigerade av Amanda Stjärna. In Swedish. Stockholm: Wahlström & Widstrand, 1946. 163 pp.

NOURRIT, ADOLPHE, 1802-1839

1078 Nourrit, Adolphe. *Un artiste d'autrefois, Adolphe Nourrit; sa vie et sa correspondance,* par Étienne Boutet de Monvel. In French. Paris: Plon-Nourrit et cie, 1903. ii, 319 pp. Illustrated.

1079 Quicherat, Louis Marie, 1799-1884. *Adolphe Nourrit; sa vie, son talent, son caractère, sa correspondance.* In French. Paris: L. Hachette, 1867. 3 vols. Repertory, Vol. 3, pp. 443-445.

Possibly the most exhaustive, best documented 19th-century work on an opera singer. The first volume (527 pp.) is a biography, the second (547 pp.) is an analytical appreciation of the singer and the third (447 pp.) contains his correspondence, letters written by and to Nourrit. The work is flawed by the author's excessive--and un-necessary--zeal in trying to prove Nourrit's supremacy over his con-temporaries, Duprez in particular.

See also item 1745

NOVELLO, CLARA, 1818-1908

1080 Novello, Clara. *Clara Novello's Reminiscences;* compiled by her daughter, Contessa Valeria Gigliucci, with a memoir by Arthur D. Coleridge. London: E. Arnold, 1910. 216 pp. Illustrated.

This book contains Clara Novello's fragmentary memoirs edited by her daughter, Countess Valeria Gigliucci. The Countess omitted several passages from the manuscript, among them many of those that could have offended persons still living at the time of publication. She successfully improves the continuity of the narrative by her ex-tensive editorial inserts. A meandering introductory memoir by Arthur D. Coleridge is of little value.

1081 Mackenzie-Grieve, Averil. *Clara Novello, 1818-1908.* London: G. Bles, 1955. xiv, 337 pp. Illustrated. Bibliography, pp. 329-330. Index, pp. 331-338.

A thoroughly researched, superbly written biography of this im-portant 19th-century singer. The author had access to family archives, correspondence, his subject's manuscript autobiography and other documentation (including the perusal of Queen Victoria's diary). The results show his interest, dedication and judicious use of his material.

1081-a ———. *Clara Novello, 1818-1908.* Da Capo Press Music Reprint Series. New York: Da Capo, 1980. xiv, 337 pp. Illustrated. Bibliography, pp. 329-330. Index, pp. 331-338.

Reprint of the 1955 edition published by G. Bles, London (q.v.).

NOVELLO-DAVIES, CLARA, 1861-1948

1082 Novello-Davies, Clara. *The Life I Have Loved.* London: W. Heinemann, 1940. x, 323 pp. Illustrated.

Welsh singer, voice teacher, choral conductor and founder of the Royal Welsh Ladies' Choir. She owes her name to her father's enthusiasm for Clara Novello, whom he once heard in concert. Her autobiography is highly personal, full of trivial details meaningful only for her or closest family. Her son, David Ivor Davies, the composer and actor known as Ivor Novello, also gets more than his share of space. Music, always a part of her life, is treated equally with her other concerns.

1083 ———. *You Can Sing.* With a foreword by the Rt. Hon. the Earl of Plymouth. London: Selwyn and Blount, 1928. 238 pp.

O

OBRAZTSOVA, ELENA, b. 1937

1083/A Timokhin, Vsevolod Vasil'evich. *Elena Obraztsova.* In Russian. Moskva: Muzyka, 1978.

See also item 1732

OBUKHOVA, NADEZHDA ANDREEVNA, 1886-1961

1084 Belzy, Igor. *Nadezhda Andreevna Obukhova. Vospominaniia, staty, materialy.* In Russian. Moskva: Vserossiiskoe Teatral'noe Obshchestvo, 1967. 319 pp. Illustrated. Repertory, pp. 298-308. Chronology, pp. 289-297.

1085 Moscow. Gosudarstvennyi akademicheskii Bol'shoi teatr. *Nadezhda Andreevna Obukhova.* In Russian. Moskva: Iskusstvo, 1953. Unpaged. Illustrated.

A short biography of the singer followed by many photographs; the reproduction is poor.

1086 Polianovskii, Georgii Aleksandrovich. *Moi vstrechi s N.A. Obukhovoi.* In Russian. Moskva: Sov. kompozitor, 1971. 100 pp. Illustrated. Bibliography, pp. 107-108.

ÖDMANN, ARVID, 1850-1914

1087 Hård-Ödmann, Alma. *Arvid Ödmann, minnesblad.* In Swedish. Stockholm: Hugo Geber, 1915. 255 pp. Illustrated.

OGNITSEV, ALEKSANDR, b. 1920

See item 1732

OLIN, ELISABETH

1088 Flodmark, Johan, 1837-1927. *Elisabeth Olin och Carl Stenborg; tva gustavianska sangargestalter, bilder fran svenska operans första tider.* In Swedish. Stockholm: Fröléen & Comp., 1903. 201 pp.

ONÉGIN, SIGRID, 1891-1943

1089 Penzoldt, Fritz. *Alt-Rhapsodie: Sigrid Onégin--Leben und Werk.* In German. 3rd ed. Neustadt an der Aisch: Degener, 1953. 342 pp. Illustrated.

1089-a ———. *Sigrid Onégin.* In German. Magdeburg: K.J. Sander, 1939. 326 pp. Illustrated.

See also items 1695, 1811

O'NEILL, ENRIQUE

1090 O'Neill, Enrique. *La voz humana.* In Spanish. Barcelona: Maucci, 1923? 399 pp. Illustrated.

ONOFREI, DMITRIE, b. 1893

1091 Onofrei, Constantin, and Grigore Constantinescu. *Dimitrie Onofrei.* In Rumanian. Bucureşti: Editura Muzicală, 1970. 151 pp. Repertory, p. 149. Discography, p. 148.

ORELIO, JOSEPH, 1854-1925

1092 Orelio, Joseph. *M'n Gedenkschriften voor 't nederlandsche volk opgeschreven door J.M. Orelio naar aanleiding van m'n 40-jarig jubileum als concert- en operzanger (1876-1916).* In Dutch. Amsterdam: Scheltens & Giltay, 1916. 192 pp. Illustrated.

ORGENI, AGLAJA, 1842-1926

1093 Brand, Erna, b. 1895. *Aglaja Orgeni; das Leben einer grossen Sängerin, nach Briefen, Zeitquellen und Überlieferung.* With intro-duction by Dr. Ernst Leopold Stahl. In German. München: Beck, 1931. x, 352 pp. Illustrated.

OROSZ, JULIA, b. 1908

See item 1740

OSVÁTH, JULIA, b. 1908

See item 1740

OTS, GEORG, 1920-1975

1094 Tonson, Helga. *Georg Ots.* In Estonian. Tallinn: Eesti Raamat, 1975. 269 pp. Illustrated. Index.

OZEROV, NIKOLAI NIKOLAEVICH, 1887-1953

1095 Ozerov, Nikolai Nikolaevich. *Opery i pevtsy; vyskazyvaniia, vpechatleniia.* In Russian. Moskva: Vseros. teatral'noe ob-vo, 1964. 208 pp. Illustrated.

Autobiography of a celebrated Russian tenor. His roles included Herman, Sadko, Otello, Canio, Faust, Don José, Dmitri, Raoul, Walther and Radames. The illustrations show him in these and other roles.

1096 Sletov, V. *N.N. Ozerov.* In Russian. Mastera Bol'shogo teatra. Moskva: Gos. muzykal'noe izd-vo, 1951. 62 pp. Illustrated.

P

PACCHIEROTTI, GASPARE, 1744-1821

1097 Pacchierotti, Giuseppe Cecchini. *Ai cultori ed amatori della musica vocale: cenni biografici intorno a Gaspare Pacchierotti.* In Italian. Pamphlets on Music (1821-76). Padova: Coi tipi del Seminario, 1844. 16 pp.

1098 Sassi, Romualdo. *Un celebre musico fabrianese, Gaspare Pacchierotti.* In Italian. Fabriano: Stab. di arte grafiche "Gentile," 1935. 51 pp. Illustrated.

A product of a "Conferenza detta nel circolo gentile di Fabriano, sotto gli auspici della 'Dante Aligheri', il 21 marzo 1935 ... col titolo ... 'Un usignolo nato fra i boschetti del Giano.'"

PAGLIUGHI, LINA, 1907-1980

1099 Cernaz, Bruno. *Lina Pagliughi; ricordi.* In Italian. Gambettola, Forlí: Associazone Amici della Musica "Lina Pagliughi," 1982. 83 pp. Bibliography, p. 83. Discography, pp. 78-82.

PALÁNKAY, KLÁRA, b. 1924

See item 1740

PALET, JOSÉ, 1877-1946

1100 Clopas Batlle, Isidro. *José Palet Bartomeu: leyenda, mito y realidad de un tenor martorellense de fama mundial*. In Spanish. Martorell: Ayuntamiento de Martorell, 1979. 145 pp. Illustrated.

See also item 1543

PALLÓ, IMRE, 1892-1978

1101 Palló, Imre, 1892-1978. *Erinnerungen an Feri (Ferenc Fricsay)*. In German. Berlin: N.p., 1964. 14 pp. Information taken from the copy held in the Széchenyi Library, Budapest.

Reminiscences of the late Ferenc Fricsay by one of the leading baritones of the Hungarian Opera House.

1102 Németh, Amadé. *Palló Imre*. In Hungarian. Nagy magyar elöadómüvészek, 10. Budapest: Zenemükiadó, 1970. 54 pp. Illustrated. Repertory, pp. 51-54.

Imre Palló, one of the truly great baritones of international caliber, spent his exceptionally long career in his native Hungary by choice rather than for a lack of opportunity. When Mascagni conducted his *Cavalleria rusticana* in Budapest in 1925, he invited Palló to join his touring company. Palló sang Alfio and Rigoletto with the Mascagni troup all over Europe. He then spent a year in Milano perfecting his technique with Mario Sammarco and afterwards rejoined the Hungarian Royal Opera House in Budapest. His two other excursions abroad were to the Rome Opera in 1935 and in 1936, singing in Rocca's *Il Dybbuk*. He celebrated his 50th anniversary still as an active singer. After the death of his father he earned a doctorate in Economics, "because I promised it to my old man."
In light of the breadth and length of his distinguished career, this biography remains incomplete, despite the many interesting details. A list of his repertory shows 108 roles. The illustrations are well chosen. As one listens to the ringing high notes and the secure delivery of the selections on the two 7" 33 rpm records in the book's pocket, the hearer must bear in mind that Palló recorded these operatic selections in his early sixties. Palló also recorded for His Master's Voice (plum label) and the Hungarian record company. MHV

See also item 1740

PÁLMAI, ILKA, b. 1860

1103 Pálmai, Ilka. *Emlékeim*. In Hungarian. Budapest: Singer és Wolfner, 1912. 254 pp. Illustrated.

The memoirs of the well-known Hungarian operetta singer of the turn of the century who, in the best operetta tradition, became the Countess Kinsky in real life. Although she was best known for her operetta roles: Saffi, Belle Hélène, Grand Duchesse, she also sang the title role in *Madame Butterfly*. Her foreign credentials included London and New York. Without mentioning her stage name, Joan Hammond writes in her memoirs (*A Voice, a Life*, q.v.) about the Countess in whose palace she stayed during her student days in Vienna.

1103-a ———. *Emlékirataim*. In Hungarian. Modern magyar könyvtár. Budapest: Singer és Wolfner, 194-? 215 pp. Illustrated.

New edition of the singer's reminiscences published in 1912 under the title of *Emlékeim* (q.v.).

1104 Deleted

1105-T ———. *Meine Erinnerungen, von Gräfin Ilka Kinsky-Pálmay*. Translated by Heinrich Glücksmann. In German. Berlin: R. Bong, 1911. viii, 277 pp. Illustrated.

PALMER, BESSIE, b. 1831

1106 Palmer, Bessie. *Musical Recollections*. London: The W. Scott Publishing Co., 1904. vi, 314 pp. Illustrated. Index, pp. 309-314.

A disorganized yet interesting Victorian autobiography of the great English contralto. A frequent partner of Reeves, Santley and Lind, she most often sang in oratorio and recitals, but also appeared in opera. Her extensive comments about her contemporaries are especially valuable since her recollection of performances go back to Mario, Grisi and Viardot whom she heard in her early childhood. The book is full of "fillers," from laudatory poems and ditties of the period to letters of minor interest or relevance. However, the substance that is there makes the book worthwhile reading.

PAMPANINI, ROSETTA, 1896-1973

See item 1680

PANZERA, CHARLES, 1896-1976

1107 Panzera, Charles. *L'amour de chanter*. Préface de Georges Duhamel. In French. Paris: H. Lemoine, 1957. 126 pp.

1108 ———. *L'art de chanter*. Préface d'Arthur Honegger. In French. Paris: Editions littéraires de France, 1945. 120 pp. Illustrated.

1109 ———. *L'art vocal, 30 leçons de chant*. In French. Paris: Librairie théatrale, 1959. 122 pp. Illustrated.

1110 ———. *Votre voix, directives générales*. In French. Paris: Édition musicales transatlantiques, 1967. 32 pp.

1111-T ———. *De kunst van het zingen*, met een voorwoord door Arthur Honegger, en een inleiding van Anthon van der Horst, vertaald door Louise Nehret. Translated by Louise Nehret. In Dutch. 's-Gravenhage: L.J.C. Boucher, 1948. 120 pp. Illustrated.

1112   Fabre, Michel. *Souvenirs de Magdeleine et Charles Panzera.* In French. Pau: M. Fabre, 1972. 19 pp. Illustrated.

PAOLI, ANTONIO, 1873-1946

See items 417, 418

PAREPA-ROSA, EUPHROSYNE, 1836-1874

See items 1562, 1694

PASERO, TANCREDI, 1893-1983

1112/A   Clerico, Cesare, b. 1953. *Tancredi Pasero, voce verdiana.* In Italian. Orizzonti musicali, 2. Torino: Scomegna Casa Editrice Musicale, 1983. ii, 141 pp. Illustrated. Repertory, pp. 97-101. Index, pp. 135-138. Discography, pp. 102-103. Chronology of Performances, pp. 81-96.

A short, affectionate biographical profile built around the description and commentary of the 32 characters interpreted by the singer. The documentation is exhaustive and precise. The preface is by Giorgio Gualerzi. RT

PASTA, GIUDITTA, 1798-1865

1113   Alperti, Celso. *Giuditta Pasta al Carcano. Poema eroi-comico.* In Italian. Milano: G. Pirotta, 1829. 32 pp.

1114   Ferranti, Maria (Giulini), b. 1849. *Giuditta Pasta e i suoi tempi*; memorie e lettere raccolte a cura di Maria Ferranti nob. Giulini. In Italian. Milano: Cromotipia Ettore Sormani, 1935. 221 pp. Illustrated.

A faithful, painstaking reconstruction of the life of this historic soprano. The profuse documentation and samples of correspondence reproduced in full are held together by the editor's measured commentary. (According to editor Ferranti, Pasta was born in 1797.) RT

See also items 1562, 1597, 1612, 1615, 1620, 1745

PATAKY, KÁLMÁN, 1896-1964

1115   Somogyi Vilmos, and Imre Molnár. *Pataky Kálmán.* In Hungarian. Nagy magyar előadóművészek, 3. Budapest: Zeneműkiadó, 1968. 69 pp. Illustrated. Repertory, pp. 67-69.

The only biography of the tenor best remembered today for his elegant Don Ottavio in the Fritz Busch recording of the 1936 Glyndebourne *Don Giovanni.* He made his debut in Budapest where he rose to preeminence and partnered many foreign guests, among them Chaliapin in

Faust. Soon Vienna claimed his services, and later he sang many seasons at the Colón, in Berlin, Salzburg (Florestan under Toscanini) and elsewhere. This overview of his career falls short on facts beyond what is readily available in Hungarian archives. It also fails to mention that deafness prematurely ended his career and he ended his life in great physical discomfort, disease, with an amputated leg. There is a list of Pataky's repertory and two 7" 33 rpm records inserted in a pocket which give a fair idea of his voice and artistry.

PATEY, JANET MONACH

See item 1658

PATON, MARY ANN, 1802-1864

See item 1526

PATTI, ADELINA, 1843-1919

1116 Patti, Adelina. *My Reminiscences*. London, 1909. Unverified; data obtained from bibliography in F. Hernández Girbal's biography of Patti (q.v.).

1117 *Adelina Patti (Baroness Cederström)*. Souvenir libretto. Farewell concerts in the United States and Canada. Season 1903-1904. Under the management of Robert Grau. New York: H.A. Rost Printing & Publishing Co., 1903. 53 pp. Illustrated. A copy of this program is in the collection of the New York Public Library.

1118 Boehme, Hermann. *Adelina Patti in Hamburg. Eine Monographie*. In German. Hamburg, 1863. 8 pp. Information as shown taken from the British Museum National Catalogue.

1119 Cabezas, Juan Antonio, b. 1900. *Adelina Patti, la cantata de la voz de oro*. In Spanish. Cómo fueron, t. 6. Madrid: Ediciones B. Bureba, 1956. 96 pp. Illustrated.

1120 Castán Palomar, Fernando. *Adelina Patti: su vida*. In Spanish. Colección Cibeles, no. 8. Madrid: General Ediciones, 1947. 202 pp.

   A readable account of Patti's life, with some details lacking in Klein's work, especially in relation to European performances. However, the device of unauthenticated quoted conversations is used, and there are no references and few specific dates. Of minor importance to any except the confirmed Patti *aficionado*. WRM

1121 Charnacé, Guy de, 1825-1909. *Adelina Patti*. In French. His: Les étoiles du chant, 1. livr. Paris: H. Plon, 1868. 28 pp. Illustrated.

1122 Dalmazzo, G.M. *Adelina Patti's Life, and her Appearances at*

the *Royal Italian Opera, Covent Garden, with Particular Documents*.
London: Cooper Bros. and Attwood, 1877. 48 pp.

1123 Grave, Théodore de, 1830-1913. *Biographie d'Adelina Patti*.
In French. Paris: Castel, 1865. 36 pp.

1124 Hernández Girbal, Florentino, b. 1902. *Adelina Patti, la Reina
del Canto*. In Spanish. Madrid: Ediciones Lira, 1979. 447 pp. Illustrated. Bibliography, pp. 445-446. Repertory, p. 437. Chronology
of Performances, pp. 441-444.

It must be conceded that to date this is the definitive life of
Adelina Patti. The chronology establishes the singer's whereabouts
for almost every year (sometimes with several entries for a single
year) from Patti's birth until her death. The bibliography points
out some weaknesses: while many rare works are cited, some very important ones are omitted, especially those in the English language.
As a result, there are some gross errors: for example, data on Patti's
recordings are incorrect (her accompanist is cited as Wilhelm Ganz,
whereas in the first session it was Landon Ronald, and in the second,
Ettore Barili). The author has the unfortunate habit of quoting conversations which were never actually recorded; while this makes for
a readable text, it throws some doubt on accuracy. Specific quotations and recitation of various incidents are not referenced to the
bibliography, so the reader has no basis for evaluation of their
authenticity. A chapter (entitled "The First Love") is devoted to
Patti's youthful lover from Puerto Rico, José Rios, to whom she was
engaged for a time: letters which Patti wrote to Rios, which surfaced
in Puerto Rico in 1927, are quoted (for the first time in a biography
of the singer?) extensively. The work presents much that is new, or
at least brings together for the first time in one work the results
of much research. The book deserves wider circulation by means of
translation; if this is attempted, it is hoped that it could undergo
considerable revision to correct its faults. The writer was apparently
unaware of the Woodford collection consulted by Tribble (q.v.). WRM

1125 Klein, Hermann, 1856-1934. *The Reign of Patti*. New York: The
Century Co., 1920. ix, 470 pp. Illustrated. 31 Appendices (pp.
384-459), Articles and Reviews.

Hermann Klein's biography of Adelina Patti will remain the corner-
stone upon which all authors dealing with this singer must build.
Himself a pupil of Manuel Garcia, and a distinguished teacher of
singing in his own right, Klein had heard every great singer appearing
in London, beginning with Jenny Lind; most of them he knew personally,
and he was a close friend of Patti. Patti had asked Klein to be her
collaborateur in preparing an autobiography and he began gathering
material for this book in 1913. It was finished less than two months
after her death. The author admits to lack of access to material
about Patti's early life in New York, and this is a gap which has
been filled through extensive research by other authors (i.e., Tribble
and Hernández Girbal, q.v.). But Klein not only knew the singer on a
personal basis for something like fifty years, he was able to compare
her art and impact on the musical world with three generations of
the world's great singers. While perhaps lacking the objectivity less
intimate association might have provided, the work is a unique testimonial to a unique artist. WRM

1125-a ———. *The Reign of Patti*. London: T. Fisher Unwin, 1920.
ix, 470 pp.

1125-b ———. *The Reign of Patti*. With a discography by W.R.
Moran. New York: Arno Press, 1977. ix, 470, v pp. Illustrated.
Discography, pp. i-v.

Reprint of the 1920 edition by the Century Co., New York (q.v.).
The complete discography and the brief essay "Adelina Patti and the
Gramophone" by William R. Moran were prepared for this edition.

1126-T Lauw, Louisa. *Fourteen Years with Adelina Patti*. Translated
by Clare Brune. London: Remington & Co., 1884. 199 pp.

English translation of *Vierzehn Jahre mit Adelina Patti* (q.v.).

1127-T ———. *Fourteen Years with Adelina Patti, Reminiscences*.
Translated by Jeremiah Loder. New York: N.L. Munro, 1884. 68 pp.

English translation of *Vierzehn Jahre mit Adelina Patti* (q.v.).

1127-T-a ———. *Fourteen Years with Adelina Patti: Reminiscences
of Louisa Lauw*. With a new introduction by James Camner. Translated
by Jeremiah Loder. Plainsboro, N.J.: La Scala Autographs, 1977.
68 pp. Illustrated.

English translation of *Vierzehn Jahre mit Adelina Patti* (q.v.).
Reprint of the 1884 edition published by N.L. Munro, New York (q.v.).

1128 ———. *Vierzehn Jahre mit Adelina Patti*. In German. Wien,
1884. 157 pp.

1129 Leo, pseud. *Les artistes contemporains. Adelina Patti.
Fraschini*. In French. Paris, 1865. 32 pp.

1130 Lyden, Émile Ferdinand Mugnot de, 1815-1894. *Adelina Patti*.
In French. Paris, 1865. Unverified; data taken from the bibliography
in F. Hernández-Girbal's biography of Patti (q.v.).

1131 Mortier, Michel. *Biographical Sketch of Madame Adelina Patti*.
New York?: Steinway & Sons?, 1881? 14 pp. Illustrated.

1132 Saint-Léger, A. *Nos actrices*. Fasc. 3: *Biographie de Adelina
Patti*. In French. Paris: Disdéri, 1874? Illustrated.

1133 Schürmann, Joseph Johan, b. 1857. *Les étoiles en voyage. La
Patti, Sarah Bernhardt, Coquelin*. In French. Paris: Tresse & Stock,
1893.

1134 Strakosch, Moritz, d. 1887, and Joseph Johan Schürmann.
*L'impresario in angustie. Adelina Patti e altre stelle fuori della
leggenda (1886-1893)*. Versione, introduzione e note di Eugenio Gara.
In Italian. Milano: Valentino Bompiani, 1940. 379 pp. Illustrated.

Memorie de un impresario by Moritz Strakosch (pp. 23-269) is a
translation of *Souvenirs d'un impresario* (q.v.); *Le stelle in viaggio,
Adelina Patti, Sarah Bernhardt, Constant Coquelin* by Joseph Johan
Schürmann (pp. 273-372) is a translation of *Les étoiles en voyage* (q.v.).

1135 Strakosch, Moritz, d. 1887. *Souvenirs d'un impresario*. In French. 2nd ed. Paris: P. Ollendorff, 1887. vii, 295 pp. The first edition could not be located.

1136 Vacano, Emil Mario, 1840-1892. *Der Roman der Adelina Patti. Nach spanischen, englischen und mundlichen Quellen*. Mit Federzeich-nungen von Karl Klič. In German. Wien: Klič & Spitzer, 1875. 84 pp. Illustrated.

See also items 792, 1541, 1566, 1573, 1597, 1599, 1615, 1620, 1621, 1658, 1680, 1694, 1828

PATTI, CARLOTTA, 1835-1889

See items 1694, 1792

PATTIERA, TINO, 1890-1966

See item 1743

PAVAROTTI, LUCIANO, b. 1935

1137-T Pavarotti, Luciano, and William Wright. *Io, Luciano Pavarotti*. Translated by Paola Campioli. In Italian. "Le Scie." Milano: A. Mondadori, 1981. 330 pp. Illustrated. Repertory, pp. 307-309. Index, pp. 325-330. Discography, pp. 311-320.

  Italian translation of Pavarotti's *My Story* (q.v.).

1138 ———. *My Own Story*. Garden City: Doubleday and Company, 1981. 316 pp. Illustrated. Index, pp. 309-316. Discography, pp. 291-308. Chronology of Performances, pp. 287-290.

  Pavarotti's first "autobiography" was a popular success that re-ceived undeservedly mixed reviews. The book consists of twelve chap-ters by the singer and fourteen by friends, colleagues, his wife, teacher, manager, accompanist and others. Critics found fault with this structure, but one has great difficulty understanding the reason for it. If there had been a book like this by and about every major vocalist, starting with Caruso and traveling in both directions chronologically, posterity would have been immensely richer for it. The quality of the writings vary, though William Wright's collabora-tion brought a high degree of uniformity of style to the components. For any fan wanting to find in one place a great deal of information about her or his hero, this book is likely to be "it" for a long time. There are a list of Pavarotti's first performances and major appear-ances and an accurate discography, including several private recordings.

1138-a ———. *My Story*. New York: Warner Books, 1982. 319 pp. Illustrated. Repertory, pp. 291-294. Index, pp. 309-319. Discog-raphy, pp. 295-308.

1139 Gatti, Gian Carlo, and Giuseppe Cherpelli, editors. *Luciano Pavarotti; vent'anni di teatro*. In Italian. Modena: Cooperativa

Tipografi, 1981. 92 pp. Illustrated. Discography, pp. 89-91. Chronology, pp. 88-89. TV Performances, p. 92.

Contains six short testimonials and an extensive collection of photographs that spans the tenor's entire career. The quarto size volume is beautifully designed and executed.

1140 Jones, Robert. *Luciano Pavarotti*. New York: Gloria Enterprises, 1978. 10 unnumbered leaves. Illustrated.

A short biographical sketch is followed by a large number of photographs that show the singer from age 3 onward, in and out of costume.

See also item 1563

PEERCE, JAN, b. 1904

1141 Peerce, Jan, and Alan Levy. *The Bluebird of Happiness: The Memoirs of Jan Peerce*. New York: Harper and Row, 1976. 325 pp. Illustrated. Index, pp. 317-325.

In organizing Peerce's memoirs into a book, Alan Levy did a more than creditable job. Retaining the singer's own narrative, he incorporated long statements--the other side of the coin, as it were-- by friends and members of the Peerce family. While the book gives a detailed account of the tenor's life and remarkable career, Peerce emerges from these pages as an opinionated, intolerant, quarrelsome man, bent on publicly settling accounts with everybody from Rudolf Bing to brother-in-law Richard Tucker, tossing darts along the way at everyone who ever earned his displeasure. He is equally generous with his praise for people he likes, yet somehow this fails to balance the scale. The book is all it should be: the reader gets to know the singer and the person, and will probably go on admiring the singer-- only.

See also item 1608

PERALTA, ANGELA, 1845-1883

1142 Cuenca, Augustin F. *Angela Peralta de Castera*. In Spanish. Mexico: Valle Hermanos, 1873. 50 pp.

1143 Maria y Campos, Armando de, b. 1897. *Angela Peralta, el ruiseñor mexicano*. In Spanish. Vidas mexicanas, 15. Mexico: Ediciones Xochitl, 1944. 185 pp. Illustrated.

See also item 1631

PERSIANI, FANNY, 1812-1867

See items 1601, 1612

PERTILE, AURELIANO, 1885-1952

1144 Silvestrini, Domenico. *I tenori celebri: Aureliano Pertile e il suo metodo di canto.* In Italian. Bologna: Aldina, 1932. 198 pp. Illustrated.

The author largely sets down the tenor's words. It is well written, but the biographical matter is terse and one cannot easily form an idea of the tenor's personality or aspects of his life. It would appear that the book would be of undoubted value to singers, as a considerable portion of the book is devoted to Pertile's views on the technique of singing. The physiological processes are set down in detail, with sketches of the vocal process involved. There is a short mention of his recording activities, but no discography. There is little or no mention of artists with whom he appeared, but there is a section devoted to the leading Italian tenors from the late 19th century to the first two decades of the 20th, accompanied by an analysis of salient points of each. This is followed by a listing of the roles Pertile sang, with his views on the interpretation of each and a picture of the artist in the proper costume of the character. GLN

See also item 1620

PETERS, ROBERTA, b. 1930

1145 Peters, Roberta, and Louis Biancolli. *A Debut at the Met.* New York: Meredith Press, 1967. ix, 86 pp.

This book, written in an almost conversational style and in the first person, traces Peters's life from the age of 13, when she first thought about studying voice, up to the evening of her debut at the Metropolitan Opera on November 17, 1950. It discusses her early appearances on kiddie radio programs, her relations with her voice teachers and language and drama coaches, her education by private tutors from age 14 on, and the roles played by Jan Peerce, Sol Hurok, hard work and luck in launching her career. Though the book proper ends with her debut at the Metropolitan Opera, an "epilogue"--actually a reprint from *Who's Who*--briefly covers her career from 1950 to the mid-60s. HCS

PETROV, OSIP AFANAS'EVICH, 1806-1878

See item 1686

PETROV, VASILII RODIONOVICH, 1875-1937

1146 Belza, Igor Fedorovich, b. 1904, editor. *Vasilii Rodionovich Petrov; sbornik statei i materialov.* In Russian. Moskva: Gos. muzykal'noe izd-vo, 1953. 237 pp. Illustrated. Bibliography.

PHILLIPPS, ADELAIDE, 1833-1882

1147 Waterson, Anna Cabot Lowell (Quincy). *Adelaide Phillipps, a Record*. By Mrs. R.C. Waterson. Boston: A. Williams and Company, 1883. 170 pp. Illustrated.

PHILLIPS, HENRY

1148 Phillips, Henry. *Musical and Personal Recollections during Half a Century*. London: Charles J. Skeet, 1864. 2 vols. Illustrated.

PICCHI, MIRTO, 1915-1980

1149 Picchi, Mirto. *E lucevan le stelle*. Prefazione di Luigi Baldacci. In Italian. Bologna: Edizioni Bongiovanni, 1981. 108 pp. Illustrated. Index, pp. 105-106.

The second, posthumous book of reminiscences by Picchi. It consists of short, flavorful chapters written in a free-flowing, critical and witty style. RT

1150 ———. *Un trono vicino al sol*. Prefazione di Luigi Baldacci. In Italian. Ravenna: Edizioni del Girasole, 1978. 208 pp. Illustrated. Repertory, pp. 180-193. Index, pp. 201-205. Chronology, pp. 167-186.

The recollections of a serious, intelligent, cultured, refined artist. His life story covers an international career that spanned twenty-nine years and consisted of a vast international repertory. RT

PICCOLOMINI, MARIETTA, 1834-1899

See item 1694

PIETI, ANTIN

1151 *Brever og sanger under vandringen: dokumentaria till Lyngen-Lestadianismen*. Redigert av Kare Svebak. In Norwegian. Oslo: Luther, 1978. 288 pp. Illustrated. Bibliography, pp. 280-281. Index, pp. 282-287.

A book containing letters written by Antin Pieti and Isak Nilsen while on tour. The last section contains the texts of songs written to pre·existing melodies by Nilsen and others. The photographs show Pieti and Nilsen, and the people to whom they wrote. HCS

PINZA, EZIO, 1892-1957

1152 Pinza, Ezio, and Robert Magidoff. *Ezio Pinza, an Autobiography*. New York: Rinehart, 1958. 307 pp. Illustrated. Repertory, pp. 289-293. Index, pp. 295-307.

Doris Pinza, the singer's widow, narrates in the last chapter how her husband, following the last session with his collaborator, Robert Magidoff, suffered a stroke and died a few days later. Thus the book, published posthumously, contains all that Pinza intended to tell. It contains the important events of his personal life but it falls short of expectations concerning musical matters. He also has too little to say about his many colleagues. Pinza's repertory is included, containing embarrassing typographical errors, as if compiler, printer and proofreader had been unfamiliar with the subject.

1152-a ——————. *Ezio Pinza, an Autobiography.* New York: Arno Press, 1977. xi, 307 pp. Illustrated. Repertory, pp. 289-293. Index, pp. 295-307.

Reprint of the edition published by Rinehart, New York, in 1958 (q.v.).

1153 Sargeant, Winthrop, b. 1903. *Geniuses, Goddesses, and People.* New York: E.P. Dutton, 1949. 317 pp.

Contains biographical sketches of prominent people that were originally published in *Life* magazine. Pinza is the only singer among the biographees; the rest include such notables as Toscanini, Rubinstein, Beecham and Rita Hayworth. The Pinza article is quite exhaustive; the style is quality journalism. It appeared in the December 1, 1947, issue of *Life*.

See also items 1606, 1607, 1608

PIROGOV, ALEKSANDR STEPANOVICH, 1899-1964

1154 Moscow. Gosudarstvennyi akademicheskii Bol'shoi teatr. *Aleksandr Stepanovich Pirogov.* In Russian. Moskva: Iskusstvo, 1953. 16 pp. Illustrated.

A brief biography of the singer, followed by numerous illustrations.

See also items 1686, 1708

PIROGOV, GRIGORII STEPANOVICH, 1885-1931

1155 Remezov, Ivan Ivanovich. *G.S. Pirogov.* In Russian. Mastera Bol'shogo teatra. Moskva: Gos. muzykal'noe izd-vo, 1951. 65 pp. Illustrated.

PISARONI, BENEDETTA ROSAMUNDA, 1793-1872

1156 Pavesi, C. *Benedetta Rosamunda Pisaroni. Cenni.* In Italian. Piacenza, 1872.

PONCHARD, LOUIS ANTOINE ÉLÉONORE, 1787–1866

1157 Méreaux, Amédée, 1802–1874. *Ponchard*. In French. Paris: Heugel, 1866. 31 pp.

PONS, LILY, 1904–1976

See items 1607, 1608, 1719, 1792

PONSELLE, ROSA, 1897–1981

1158 Ponselle, Rosa, and James A. Drake. *Ponselle, a Singer's Life.* Garden City, N.Y.: Doubleday, 1982. xxv, 328 pp. Illustrated. Discography, pp. 248–307.

Ponselle's autobiography, ostensibly in her own words, with corrections, amplifications and commentary by James A. Drake added in footnotes. Drake also supplies an introduction, telling how the book came to be written, and a final chapter, relating her death and funeral. A literate, elegantly written book, it traces Ponselle's life from her birth in Meriden, Connecticut, giving details of her relationships with parents, siblings, husband, teachers, her methods of preparing roles and approaching performances. It also outlines her involvement with the Baltimore Opera and briefly discusses her teaching and students. There are photographs of her in most of her roles. Bill Park's excellent discography lists commercial and noncommercial recordings, includes a list of Ponselle's known radio broadcasts and a Carmela Ponselle discography. HCS

See also items 1541, 1695

PONTI, ERNESTINA

See item 1567

POPOVICI–BAYREUTH, DIMITRIE, 1860–1927

1159 Sbârcea, George. *Dimitrie Popovici-Bayreuth, "Cîntăreul pribeag", 1860–1927*. In Rumanian. Bucureşti: Editura muzicală, 1965. 260 pp. Illustrated.

POULTIER, PLACIDE ALEXANDRE GUILLAUME, 1814–1887

1160 Spalikowski, Edmond, b. 1874. *Quelques souvenirs sur le chanteur Poultier*. In French. Rouen: Imprimerie Lainé, 1938. 12 pp.

PREOBRAZHENSKAIA, SOF'IA PETROVNA, 1904–1966

1161 Trainin, Vladimir IAkovlevich. *Sof'ia Petrovna Preobrazhenskaia. Ocherk zhizni i tvorch. deiatel'nosti*. In Russian. Leningrad: Muzyka, 1972. 72 pp. Illustrated.

PREY, HERMANN, b. 1929

1162 Prey, Hermann, and Robert D. Abraham. *Premierenfieber*. In German. München: Kindlerverlag, 1981. 371 pp. Illustrated. Index, pp. 367-371. Discography, pp. 345-366.

An engaging, lighthearted autobiography, reflecting the charm and warm humanity that comes across in Prey's stage work. The book has its serious sides as well: Prey recalls his close friendship with the late Fritz Wunderlich with affection and sadness; his detailed discussion of *each* song of *Winterreise* should be assigned reading for all aspiring Lieder singers. The discography is adequate but neither exhaustive nor sufficiently detailed; the printing, design and illustrations are of a high quality.

PRICE, LEONTYNE, b. 1927

1163 Lyon, Hugh Lee. *Leontyne Price: Highlights of a Prima Donna*. New York: Vantage Press, 1973. 218 pp. Illustrated. Discography, pp. 215-216.

Although published by a so-called vanity press, this biographical effort by a devoted fan who claims to have collected every scrap of information about his subject deserves much wider circulation than it has received. It is quite well written and appears to be based on solid documentary evidence. It is impossible to locate a copy; the publisher claims not to have any back stock and the author's address the publisher supplied produces no response.

See also items 1654, 1758

PRINTEMPS, YVONNE, 1894-1977

1164 *Yvonne Printemps, 1894-1977*. N.p.: Patrick O'Connor, 1978. 30 pp. Illustrated. Discography, pp. 26-29. "Chronological list of works in which Mlle Printemps appeared," pp. 16-18; "Cinema," pp. 22-25. Edition limited to 300 copies.

Articles about Printemps by Vivian Liff, Ivor Newton and John Gielgud give a brief biographical sketch and personal reminiscences. Liff's article and discography are an expanded version of that originally published in the *Journal* of the British Institute of Recorded Sound; Newton's contribution is excerpted from his *At the Piano*; Gielgud's comes from *Golden Days*. The book is illustrated with many photos of Printemps in and out of costume. The list of her films contains the cast and other credits, and a one-page section called "Yvonne Printemps and her Composers" gives brief biographies of Poulenc, Hahn, Messager, Strauss, Yvain and Willemetz, who wrote works for her. HCS

1164/A *Yvonne Printemps, ou L'impromptu de Neuilly*. 4 actes précédés d'un prologue suivis d'essais et d'extraits de presse. In French. Paris: La Table ronde, 1953. 195 pp. Illustrated.

PROHASKA, JARO, 1891-1965

See item 1811

R

RAAFF, ANTON, 1714-1797

1165 Freiberger, Heinz, b. 1905. *Anton Raaff (1714-1797). Sein Leben und Wirken als Beitrag zur Musikgeschichte des 18. Jahrhunderts....* In German. Hoffnungstahl-Köln: E. Pilgram, 1929. vii, 83 pp. Illustrated. Bibliography, pp. v-vii.

RADFORD, ROBERT, 1874-1933

See item 1629

RAICHEV, PETUR, 1887-1960

1166 Raichev, Petur. *Zhivot i pesei.* In Bulgarian. Sofiia: Nauka i izkustvo, 1951. 244 pp. Illustrated.

1167 Kamburov, Ivan Dimitrov, b. 1883. *Pet'r Raichev; biografichno-kriticheska skitsa po sluzhai 15 godishnata stsenicheska deinost' na artista.* In Bulgarian. Sofiia: Kooperativna pechatnitsa "Tipograf," 1926. 86 pp. Illustrated.

RAISA, ROSA, 1893-1963

See items 1565, 1695

RAIMONDI, RUGGERO, b. 1944

1168 Segalini, Sergio, b. 1944. *Ruggero Raimondi.* In French. Images du chant. Paris: Fayard, 1981. 95 pp. Illustrated. Discography, pp. 94-95. Chronology, pp. 88-93.

An appreciation of Raimondi, the singing-actor, in a short article whose length, style and tone reminds one of French magazines, *Paris Match* in particular. The biographical references are insufficient to qualify the 11-page text as a biographical sketch. The rest of the booklet consists of magnificent photographs showing Raimondi on and off the stage and in film. The lengthy notes accompanying the photographs are informative, but fail to provide the breadth of coverage the subject deserves. The printing and book design are excellent.

RALF, OSCAR GEORG, 1881-1964

1169   Ralf, Oscar Georg. *Tenoren han går i Ringen.*   In Swedish.
Stockholm: Bonnier, 1953.   213 pp.   Illustrated.

The memoirs of Oscar Ralf, a leading Wagnerian tenor of the 1920s
and 30s, are gossipy and clever, but not "heavy-weight." The text
is less interesting than the photographs, which include one of John
Forsell and his wife in Malmö in 1911, one of the young Sigurd
Björling at his debut in 1936 and a number of Ralf in his various
roles.   PHS

RAVOGLI, GIULIA, b. 1866

See items 1567, 1658

RAVOGLI, SOFIA, b. 1865

See item 1567

REDDISH, META

1170   Reddish, Claude. *A Chronicle of Memories.*   Miami: Miami Post
Pub. Co., 1950.   253 pp.   Illustrated.

The biography of a minor singer written by her brother. She had a
successful career in Italy; she and her brother once met Caruso in
London and she was even presented to the King. The illustrations
show her in some of her roles: Violetta, Lucia, Amina, Rosina, Gilda,
Marguerite. The narrative mentions all the important singers and
social figures of the period.

REDONDO, MARCOS, 1893-1976

1171   Redondo, Marcos. *Marcos Redondo, un hombre que se va....*   In
Spanish. Hombre y Época. Barcelona: Editorial Planeta, 1973.   312
pp. Illustrated.

For many years Marcos Redondo was the reigning king of that most
Spanish of all Spanish light operas, the zarzuela. From the 1920s
his recordings have made his excellent baritone voice known to lovers
of this genre of music the world over. Here we have his life story
in a well-written, interesting work. He tells of his debut in 1919
in *Cavalleria rusticana*; the critics compared him favorably with
Ruffo. His official debut at the Grand Teatro de Madrid during the
1919 opera season was as Germont in *Traviata*. Later he went to
Milan for further studies. In 1920 he traveled to Cuba and Mexico,
singing principal roles in grand opera, but it was in the realm of
the zarzuela that he had his lasting fame, and his name is linked to
productions of these delightful works. The book displays a man with
a real sense of humor; it makes enjoyable reading.   WRM

REEVES, JOHN SIMS, 1818-1900

1172 Reeves, John Sims. *My Jubilee; or, Fifty Years of Artistic
Life*; with six plates, and a preface by Thomas Ward. London: London
Music Publishing Co., 1889. 280 pp. Illustrated.

Charles E. Pearce, in his introduction to *Sims Reeves: Fifty Years
of Music in England* (q.v.), said of this book: "Sims Reeves' autobiographical effort, *My Jubilee*, is fragmentary, and owing to the
paucity of dates and for other reasons it cannot be accepted as authoritative. At best it is but a collection of memories, interesting
enough, but falling far short of doing justice to the great services
rendered by Sims Reeves towards the advancement of music in England."
This reviewer can but say, "Ah men!" Strangely enough, Pearce does
not mention the book Reeves wrote and published in 1888: *The Life of
Sims Reeves* (q.v.). WRM

1173 ————. *Sims Reeves, His Life Recollections, Written by Himself*. London: Simpkin, Marshall, 1888. 279 pp. Illustrated.

The definitive work on Sims Reeves is undoubtedly the 1924 biography
by Charles E. Pearce (q.v.). While Pearce has some unkind (but very
true) words to say about Reeves's second book, *My Jubilee* (1889)
(q.v.), he does not mention the autobiography of the previous year.
Strange. Actually, far from being "fragmentary" and unsatisfactory
as was *My Jubilee*, this book is a well-organized, straightforward
autobiography with a generous sprinkling of dates. Mr. Pearce must
have leaned heavily on it for his 1924 work. WRM

1174 ————. *Sims Reeves on "The Art of Singing."* New York: Boosey
and Co., 1900. 46 numbered leaves. Illustrated.

1175 Edwards, Henry Sutherland, 1828-1906. *The Life and Artistic
Career of Sims Reeves*. London: Tinsley, 1881. 80 pp. Illustrated.

1176 Pearce, Charles E. *Sims Reeves; Fifty Years of Music in England*.
London: S. Paul, 1924. 315 pp. Illustrated.

The author considered Reeves "England's greatest singer." Since he
left no recordings, we have to judge his fame by the words of others.
Obviously, this work is not unbiased. It was written with the assistance of the Reeves family, and thus the author had the advantage of
first-hand materials, such as correspondence and other documents.
Although biased, the work is important as musical history embracing
opera, oratorio and ballad concerts in England during most of the
Victorian era. The portion of the book relating to opera is the
least comprehensive. WRM

1176-a ————. *Sims Reeves: Fifty Years of Music in England*. Da
Capo Press Music Reprint Series. New York: Da Capo Press, 1980.
315 pp. Illustrated. Index.

Reprint of the 1924 edition published by S. Paul, London (q.v.).

See also item 1566

REICHER-KINDERMANN, HEDWIG, 1853-1883

See item 1658

REINHARDT, DELIA, 1892-1974

See item 1742

REISSENBERGER-UMLING, ADELE

1177 Jekelius, Ernst. *Adele Reissenberger-Umling; Oratoriosängerin als Bachinterpretin.* In German. Hermannstadt: Honterus, 1933. 20 pp. Illustrated.

REIZEN, MARK OSIPOVICH, b. 1895

1178 Reizen, Mark Osipovich. *Mark Reizen: avtobiograficheskii zapiski, stat'i, vospominaniia.* In Russian. Deiateli muzykal'nogo teatra. Moskva: Sovetskii kompozitor, 1980. 303 pp. Illustrated. Bibliography, pp. 288-298. Repertory, pp. 281-287.

1179 Moscow. Gosudarstvennyi akademicheskii Bol'shoi teatr. *Mark Osipovich Reizen.* In Russian. Moskva: Iskusstvo, 1953. 16 pp. Illustrated.

A short appreciation of the singer followed by several illustrations. The quality of reproduction is poor.

See also items 1686, 1708

RENAUD, MAURICE, 1861-1933

See items 1588, 1615

RESZKE, EDOUARD DE, 1853-1917

See items 1181, 1567, 1662, 1663

RESZKE, JEAN DE, 1850-1925

1180 Hurst, Peter G. *The Age of Jean de Reszke; Forty Years of Opera, 1874-1914.* With a foreword by Lady Hamilton Harty (Agnes Nicholls). London: C. Johnson, 1958. 256 pp. Illustrated.

In his preface the author states that he offers this book "as a factual survey of all opera of an international character that was heard in London from 1874 until the first war." The year 1874 was chosen because that was the first year de Reszke was heard in London. His last appearance there took place in 1900. Hurst heard his first opera in 1903, so he never heard de Reszke. He professes to have gained much information from several old singers, and from singers' memoirs. For several years he wrote about historical recordings for *The Gramophone* where his work was admired by some, but highly criti-cized for personal bias by others. The present work is characteris-tically opinionated. Readers will find it both interesting and ir-ritating, for the author has a tendency to consider his opinions sacrosanct. WRM

1180-a ————. *The Operatic Age of Jean de Reszke; Forty Years of Opera, 1874-1914.* New York: McBride, 1959. 256 pp. Illustrated. First published in 1958 under the title: *The Age of Jean de Reszke* (q.v.).

1181 Leiser, Clara. *Jean de Reszke and the Great Days of Opera*; with a foreword by Amherst Webber. London: G. Howe, 1933. xvi, 367 pp. Illustrated. Bibliography, pp. 351-352.

An excellent biography, well researched, with reference notes and correspondence from and to the singer. The Appendix contains an article entitled "Jean de Reszke's Principles of Singing" by Walter Johnstone-Douglas, and one entitled "Jean de Reszke as Teacher" by so-prano Rachel Morton. The excellence of this work is attested to in the foreword by de Reszke's long-time personal friend, Amherst Webber. The memory and accomplishments of this great singer and teacher are well served by this book. WRM

1181-a ————. *Jean de Reszke and the Great Days of Opera*; with a foreword by Amherst Webber. New York: Minton, Balch, 1934. xiv, 337 pp. Illustrated. Bibliography, pp. 323-324.

1182 Lys, Edith de. *Jean de Reszke Teaches Singing.* San Francisco: N.p., 1979. 79 pp.

See also items 1567, 1615, 1662, 1663

RETHBERG, ELIZABETH, 1894-1976

1183 Henschel, Horst, and Erhard Friedrich. *Elisabeth Rethberg; ihr Leben und Künstlertum.* In German. Schwarzenberg: Städtische Geschichtverein, 1928. 119 pp. Illustrated.

Surprisingly, this is the only book to date devoted to the famous German soprano. The inadequacy of the book is partly due to its early publication date: it came out a decade and a half before the soprano's retirement. The Foreword openly admits a bias in favor of the singer. There are two short chapters about her life and artistry, then come long selections of newspaper reviews from Europe and America. A good source book.

1183-a ————. *Elisabeth Rethberg; ihr Leben und Künstlertum.* In German. Opera Biographies. New York: Arno Press, 1977. 119 pp. Illustrated.

Reprint of the 1928 edition published by the Städtischer Geschicht-verein, Schwarzenberg (q.v.).

See also item 1695

RIDER-KELSEY, CORINNE, 1877-1947

1184   Reed, Lynnel. *Be Not Afraid; Biography of Madame Rider-Kelsey.*
New York: Vantage Press, 1955. 168 pp. Illustrated.

A musician's biography of his late wife, published by a "vanity
press." A fair effort, mostly a tribute to her memory. She made
her Covent Garden debut as Micaëla opposite the Carmen of Maria Gay
in 1908. She also sang oratorio and made concert appearances, some
with her violinist husband. She made some records for Columbia.

ROBESON, PAUL, 1898-1976

1185-T   Robeson, Paul. *Aceasta este pozitia mea.* Translated by L.
Levitchi. In Rumanian. Bucureşti: Editura Politică, 1958. 136 pp.

Rumanian translation of *Here I Stand* (q.v.).

1186   ————. *Forge Negro-Labor Unity for Peace and Jobs.* New York:
Harlem Trade Union Council, 1950. 15 pp.

This publication is the text of an address delivered at a meeting
of the National Labor Conference for Negro Rights, held in Chicago
on June 10, 1950.

1187   ————. *Here I Stand.* New York: Othello Associates, 1958.
128 pp.

This slim booklet is Robeson's political credo written toward the
end of a decade of bitter struggle with the United States authorities
that revoked his passport and kept him captive in his native country.
It is an articulate statement of his social and political views and
a reaffirmation that, beyond being a Negro, he considered himself first
and foremost an American whose aim was to see his country the great
homeland of all its citizens. The book was published simultaneously
in London, New York, Bucharest, Budapest, East Berlin and Moscow.

1187-a   ————. *Here I Stand.* London: Dennis Dobson, 1958. 128 pp.

1187-b   ————. *Here I Stand.* With a preface by Lloyd L. Brown.
Boston: Beacon Press, 1971. xx, 119 pp.

1188-T   ————. *Here I Stand.* Translated by Akira Iwasaki. In
Japanese. Tokyo: Kobunsha, 1959. 205 pp.

1189-T   ————. *Itt állok.* Translated by Endre Gömöri. In Hungarian.
Budapest: Európa, 1958. 191 pp. Illustrated.

The Hungarian translation of *Here I Stand* (q.v.).

1190-T   ————. *Mein Lied--meine Waffe.* Translated by G.F. Alexan.
In German. Berlin: Kongress-Verlag, 1958. 192 pp. Illustrated.

The German translation of *Here I Stand* (q.v.).

1191-T   ————. *Na tom ia stoiu.* Translated by V. Bakaeva and A.
Ul'ianova. In Russian. Moskva: Molodaia gvardiia, 1958. 143 pp.

Russian translation of *Here I Stand* (q.v.).

1191-T-a ———. *Na tom ia stoiu*. Translated by V. Bakaeva, A. Ul'ianova and A. Serbina. In Russian. Biblioteka Ogonek, 32. Moskva: Pravda, 1958. 55 pp.

Russian translation of *Here I Stand* (q.v.).

1192 ———. *Paul Robeson Speaks: Writings, Speeches, Interviews, 1918-1974*. Edited with introduction and notes, by Philip S. Foner. Larchmont, N.Y.: Brunner/Mazel Publishers, 1978. xvii, 623 pp. Illustrated. Bibliography, pp. 587-590. Index, pp. 591-623.

A superb collection of Robeson's written and spoken expression of thoughts and beliefs. The selection, presentation, notes and index are all excellent. An indispensable book for anyone interested in Robeson.

1193-T ———. *Przyszedlem zeby śpiewać*. Translated by Adam Klimowicz. In Polish. Warszawa: Czytelnik, 1960. 142 pp.

Polish translation of *Here I Stand* (q.v.).

1194 Brown, Lloyd L. *Paul Robeson Rediscovered*. New York: American Institute for Marxist Studies, 1976. 23 pp.

A paper delivered by a personal friend of Robeson at the National Conference on Paul Robeson, Purdue University, on April 22, 1976.

1195 Clarke, John Henrik, editor. *Dimensions of the Struggle against Apartheid: A Tribute to Paul Robeson*. Proceedings of Special Meeting of the Special Committee Against Apartheid on the 80th Anniversary of the Birth of Paul Robeson, 10 April 1978. Introduction by Leslie O. Harriman. New York: African Heritage Studies Association, 1979. 90 pp. Bibliography, pp. 85-90.

1196 Davis, Lenwood G. *A Paul Robeson Research Guide. A Selected, Annotated Bibliography*. Westport, Conn.: Greenwood Press, 1983. xxv, 879 pp. Illustrated. Index, pp. 833-879. Discography, pp. 771-795. Filmography, pp. 796-798.

An exhaustive compilation of virtually all material related to Robeson, with excellent, informative annotations. A monumental work of the highest quality.

1197 *Days with Paul Robeson*. Gera: Volkswacht, 1961. 36 pp. Illustrated.

1198 Dean, Phillip Hays. *Paul Robeson*. Garden City, N.Y.: Doubleday, 1978. vii, 81 pp.

A two-act play about Paul Robeson; on stage and television it starred James Earl Jones as Robeson.

1199 Gilliam, Dorothy Butler. *Paul Robeson, All-American*. Washington: New Republic, 1976. 216 pp. Illustrated. Bibliography, pp. 199-206. Index, pp. 207-216.

The first full-length biography of Robeson following his death in 1976, it contains many factual details relating to his personal, professional and political life not found in other sources. The book's major merit is its scholarship and impartiality. The text has a natural flow and the author, with a sure sense of proportion, dwells on each incident or event only as long as the topic merits. The notes, extensive bibliography and the numerous quotations indicate that Gilliam has done her "homework" as well as, or better than, other Robeson biographers.

1200-T Gorokhov, Viktor, and Herbert Schirrmacher. *Ich singe Amerika: ein Lebensbild Paul Robesons*. In German. Berlin: Verlag Neues Leben, 1955. 190 pp. Illustrated. Abbreviated edition.

German translation of *Robson* (q.v.).

1201 Gorokhov, Viktor. *Robson*. In Russian. Moskva: Sovetskii Pisatel', 1952. 357 pp. Illustrated.

1202 Graham, Shirley. *Paul Robeson, Citizen of the World*; foreword by Carl Van Doren. New York: J. Messner, 1946. 264 pp. Illustrated. Bibliography, p. 259. Index, pp. 261-264.

An apparently well-researched, detailed biography that deserves a more scholarly treatment. As it stands it is excellent reading for young adults. Having been published in 1946, it ends before the most controversial period of Robeson's life.

1202-a ————. *Paul Robeson, Citizen of the World*. Foreword by Carl Van Doren. Westport, Conn.: Negro University Press, 1971. 264 pp. Illustrated. Bibliography, p. 259. Index, pp. 261-264.

Reprint of the 1946 edition of J. Messner, New York.

1203 Greenfield, Eloise. *Paul Robeson*. Illustrated by George Ford. New York: Thomas Y. Crowell, 1975. 34 pp. Illustrated.

Short biography written for young adults, covering Robeson's life until his 75th birthday.

1204 Hamilton, Virginia. *Paul Robeson: The Life and Times of a Free Black Man*. New York: Harper and Row, 1974. xvi, 217 pp. Illustrated. Bibliography, pp. 205-209. Index, pp. 213-217.

A biography prompted more by devotion to the subject than by anything materially or analytically new the biographer had to contribute to the life story. When short on source material—like Robeson's stay in East Germany—she skips three years from one sentence to the next. A workmanlike effort that deserves but a modest place in the Robeson literature.

1205 Hoyt, Edwin Palmer. *Paul Robeson, the American Othello*. Cleveland: World Pub. Co., 1967. ix, 228 pp.

A detailed, documented biography of Robeson that makes a sincere effort to present both sides of an issue. Hoyt treats the life story in the social-political context it deserves, recounting the racially and politically motivated actions against Robeson in the paranoia of the fifties, and his decade-long fight against the U.S. State Department. To each event Hoyt gives his own analysis, which drew strong criticism from the singer's friends and associates. Paul Robeson, Jr., wrote that Hoyt "presents a totally false image of my father as a man." Nonetheless the main thrust of the biography is Robeson's quest for freedom, equality and human dignity for all oppressed minorities.

1206 Internationales Symposium über Paul Robeson und den Kampf der Arbeiterklasse und der Afro-Amerikaner in den USA, Berlin, 1971. *Protokoll des Symposiums Paul Robeson und der Kampf der Arbeiterklasse und der schwarzen Amerikaner der USA gegen den Imperialismus, Berlin, am 13. und 14. April 1971.* In German. Akademie der Künste der Deutschen Demokratischen Republik. Arbeitshefte, 10. Berlin: Deutsche Akademie der Künste (Henschelverlag Kunst und Gesellschaft), 1972. 76 pp. Illustrated.

1207-T ————. *Symposium: Paul Robeson and the Struggle of the Working Class and the Afro-American People of the USA against Imperialism, Held in Berlin, April 13 and 14, 1971.* Akademie der Künste der Deutschen Demokratischen Republik. Arbeitshefte 10. Berlin: German Academy of Art, 1972. 69 pp. Illustrated.

English translation of *Protokoll des Symposiums Paul Robeson* (q.v.) by the same corporate author.

1208 Kulikova, I.S. *Pol' Robeson--borets za mir i demokratiiu.* In Russian. Moskva: Znanie, 1952. 30 pp. Illustrated.

1209-T ————. *Paul Robeson, ein Kämpfer für Frieden und Demokratie; Stenogramm eines öffentliches Vortrages der Uniongesellschaft zur Verbreitung politischer und wissenschaftlicher Kenntnisse im Moskau.* Translated by Erhard John. In German. Vorträge zur Verbreitung wissenschaftlicher Kenntnisse, 61. Berlin: Aufbau-Verlag, 1954. 43 pp.

German translation of *Pol' Robeson--borets za mir i demokratiiu* (q.v.).

1210 Miers, Earl Schenck, b. 1910. *Big Ben, a Novel.* Philadelphia: The Westminster Press, 1942. xiii, 238 pp. Illustrated. Author's note: "In spirit, if not always in fact, Big Ben is Robeson's story."

1211 Nazel, Joseph. *Paul Robeson; Biography of a Proud Man.* Los Angeles: Holloway House, 1980. 216 pp. Bibliography, pp. 215-216.

1212 *Paul Robeson.* In German. Berlin: Akademie der Künste der DDR; Paul Robeson-Komitee der DDR, 1973. 18 pp. Illustrated.

A collection of essays published as a Festschrift on the occasion of Paul Robeson's 75th birthday, April 9, 1973.

1213 *Paul Robeson: April 9, 1898-January 23, 1976, for His 80th Birthday.* Published by Brigitte Bögelsack. Akademie der Künste der Deutschen Demokratischen Republik, Heft 30. Berlin: Academy of Arts of the German Democratic Republic, 1978. 65 pp.

1214 Paul Robeson Birthday Committee. *Salute to Paul Robeson; a Cultural Celebration of His 75th Birthday.* New York: Paul Robeson Archives, 1973. 44 pp. Illustrated.

1215 Paul-Robeson-Komitee der Deutschen Demokratischen Republik. *Paul Robeson in unserer Zeit. Herausgegeben aus Anlass des Symposiums zum 73. Geburtstag von Paul Robeson.* In German. Berlin?: Paul-Robeson-Komitee der DDR, 1971. 14 pp.

1216 *Paul Robeson: korrespondierendes Mitglied der Akademie der Künste der Deutschen Demokratischen Republik, Gründungsmitglied des Weltfriedensrates, Lenin-Friedenpreis träger.* Zusammenstellung, Brigitte Bögelsack. In German. Berlin: Akademie der Künste der Deutschen Demokratischen Republik, 1975. 19 pp. Illustrated.

1217 *Paul Robeson: The Great Forerunner.* A Special Issue. New York: Freedomways, 1971. 132 pp. Illustrated. Bibliography, pp. 125-132.

A special issue of *Freedomways* magazine dedicated to Paul Robeson. It contains selections from Robeson's speeches and writings, also some rare photographs of Robeson. It served as the nucleus of the more substantial collection of the same title by the editors of *Freedomways*, item 1217-a.

1217-a *Paul Robeson, the Great Forerunner.* (By) the editors of *Freedomways*. New York: Dodd, Mead, 1978. x, 383 pp. Illustrated. Bibliography, pp. 329-371. Index, pp. 377-383.

An outstanding collection of writings by and about Paul Robeson, headed by an essay by Paul, Jr., who tries to "set the record straight" about his father and, in many ways, succeeds. As is the case with anthologies of this sort, the quality of the writing, the authors' biases, orientation and partiality vary a great deal. The notes are good, the illustrations generous and Ernest Kaiser's bibliography excellent and exhaustive. A work of major significance.

1218 *Paul Robeson, Tributes, Selected Writings.* Compiled and edited for the Paul Robeson Archives by Roberta Yancy Dent; assisted by Marilyn Robeson and Paul Robeson, Jr. New York: Paul Robeson Archives, 1976. 112 pp. Illustrated.

1219 Robeson, Eslanda Goode, 1896-1965. *Paul Robeson, Negro.* New York: Harper and Brothers, 1930. 178 pp. Illustrated.

An intelligent, gently race-conscious biography of the thirty-two-year-old Paul Robeson. The degree of objectivity is especially note-worthy considering that the biographer was Robeson's wife and at the time of writing the couple was on the brink of a major marital crisis. At the same time the somewhat patronizing tone left Robeson with a lasting ill-feeling about the book. The biography is strong on family background and evocative of the Harlem scene of the twenties.

1219-a ————. *Paul Robeson, Negro.* London: Gollancz, 1930. 178 pp.

1220 Robeson, Susan, b. 1953. *The Whole World in His Hands: A Pictorial Biography of Paul Robeson.* New York: Citadel Press, 1981. 256 pp. Illustrated.

Written and compiled by Robeson's granddaughter, this book presents his life in text and pictures, including some rare photographs to which only a family member could have had access.

1221 Salk, Erwin A. *Du Bois, Robeson, Two Giants of the 20th Century; the Story of an Exhibit and a Bibliography.* Chicago: Columbia College Press, 1977. 20 pp. Illustrated. Bibliography.

1222 Schlosser, Anatole I., b. 1937. "Paul Robeson: His Career in the Theatre, in Motion Pictures, and on the Concert Stage." Ph.D. dissertation, School of Education, New York University, 1970, viii, 480 pp. Available from University Microfilms, Ann Arbor, Michigan.

1223 Seton, Marie. *Paul Robeson.* With a foreword by Arthur Bryant. London: Denis Dobson, 1958. 254 pp. Illustrated. Index, pp. 245-254.

A purposeful, race-conscious retelling of the major and minor events in Robeson's life. It is competently wrought, but without particular insight or distinction. The narrative ends with the State Department's revocation of the Robesons' passport; thus the life story is left incomplete. Seton is also prone to overstatement, quite unnecessarily, as the U.S. government's treatment of Robeson was disgraceful enough, moving many foreign governments (including non-communist ones, such as England) to action on his behalf. Although drama critic Seton was a close personal friend of the Robesons, her occasional intrusion into the story in the first person singular is jarring and ill-advised.

1224 Wright, Charles H., b. 1918. *Robeson, Labor's Forgotten Champion.* Detroit: Balamp Publishing, 1975. vii, 171 pp. Illustrated. Bibliography, p. 153. Index, pp. 165-170.

Charles H. Wright, MD, a Robeson scholar (and a practicing obstetrician/gynecologist) traces Robeson's involvement with the labor movement in the United States and Great Britain. The author has spared no effort in his research that took him to such distant locations as the British Museum and the Hawaiian Islands. The result is a substantial collection of documents connected by lucid commentary, showing one of Robeson's lifelong concerns: the lot of the working man.

See also item 37

ROBIN, MADO, 1918-1960

1225 Jacqueton, Henri (?), Jean-Louis Caussou and Roland Mancini. *Mado Robin.* In French. Paris: SODAL, 196? 32 pp. Illustrated.

ROBINSON, ANASTASIA, 1692-1755

See item 1597

RODE, WILHELM, 1887-1959

See item 1811

RÖSLER, ENDRE, 1904-1963

1226 Várnai, Péter. *Rösler Endre.* In Hungarian. Nagy magyar elöadómüvészek, 7. Budapest: Zenemükiadó, 1969. 59 pp. Illustrated. Repertory, pp. 56-59.

A brief, sketchy biography of one of Hungary's important Mozart and oratorio singers. He is said to have acquired his solid schooling with de Luca and Edoardo Garbin and, in spite of his slightly nasal tenor voice, enjoyed lasting successes in Budapest and abroad. He sang the *Psalmus Hungaricus* with Toscanini and the Verdi *Requiem* in La Scala under de Sabata (with Caniglia, Stignani and Pasero), according to the poster reproduced in the book.
The writing is plain, the life story incomplete. The author also commits an immense factual error that makes all other data suspect. He states that Rösler studied with de Luca until March 1927 and by the time he returned to Milan in 1931, de Luca was dead. To cap this grave mistake (de Luca died in 1950) he quotes an excerpt from Rösler's letter, "I took some flowers to the grave of my dear, old maestro, de Luca." The possible explanation could be that the teacher-singer in question was not Giuseppe de Luca but Fernando de Lucia--which already shows alarming ignorance on part of the biographer. If, however, this assumption is correct, and it is likely to be correct, then the author is off with his chronology. De Lucia died on February 21, 1925, thus Rösler had to have studied with him not later than 1924, that being the last year when, after returning home "in March," Rösler could still have written to him. The book has a list of his operatic roles and oratorio repertory, and two 7" 33rpm records in a pocket that give a fair idea of Rösler's stylish singing and nasal voice.

ROGER, GUSTAVE HIPPOLYTE, 1815-1879

1227 Roger, Gustave Hippolyte. *Le carnet d'un tenor*; avec préface de Philippe Gille et Notice biographique par Charles Chincholle. In French. Paris: P. Ollendorf, 1880. xxviii, x, 348 pp.

Roger was one of the great tenors of the Paris Opera in the middle of the nineteenth century. Creator of more than twenty roles in world premieres of operas by French composers, he was the first Jean de Leyden in Meyerbeer's *Le Prophète* opposite Pauline Viardot. It was the most spectacular success of his career. The book, published posthumously, contains a prefatory tribute by Philippe Gille and a brief biographical sketch by Charles Chincholle. The rest of the book consists of Roger's own diary entries from 1847 to 1878. It includes the brief, almost report-like entry about his gun accident that destroyed his right arm which then had to be amputated. Unfortunately, sometimes there are enormous gaps between entries, months in the years 1847-1855 or, after 1855, years. Roger's easy style makes one want to read more about his activities and his colleagues: Lind, Lablache, Viardot and others.

ROGERS, CLARA KATHLEEN (BARNETT), 1844-1931

1228 Rogers, Clara Kathleen (Barnett). *Clearcut Speech in Song.*
Boston: Oliver Ditson Company, 1927. 102 pp. Illustrated. Bibliography, p. 102.

1229 ————. *English Diction. A Practical System for the Improve-
ment of Defective Voices, and the Attainment of Perfect Diction in
Both Speech and Song.* Philadelphia: Oliver Ditson Company, 1912-15.
2 vols. Illustrated.

1230 ————. *English Diction for Singers and Speakers.* Boston:
The author, 1912. ix, 105 pp.

1231 ————. *Journal-letters from the Orient*, edited, with introductory letters and supplementary notes, by Henry Munroe Rogers....
Norwood, Mass.: Priv. printed at the Plimpton Press, 1934. xii, 420
pp. Illustrated. "This Clara Kathleen Rogers memorial edition is
limited to five hundred copies ... for private distribution. No
copies are for sale."

1232 ————. *Memories of a Musical Career.* Boston: Little, Brown,
1919. xviii, 503 pp. Illustrated.

1232-a ————. *Memories of a Musical Career.* Norwood, Mass.:
Priv. printed at the Plimpton Press, 1932. xviii, 503 pp. Illustrated. "This Clara Kathleen Rogers memorial edition is limited to
five hundred copies ... for private distribution. No copies are for
sale."

1233 ————. *My Voice and I, or, The Relation of the Singer to the
Song.* Chicago: A.C. McClurg, 1910. xiv, 265 pp. Illustrated. Bibliography, pp, ix-xii.

1234 ————. *The Philosophy of Singing.* New York: Harper, 1893.
xv, 218 pp. Illustrated.

1235 ————. *The Story of Two Lives; Home, Friends, and Travels,
Sequence to "Memories of a Musical Career."* Norwood, Mass.: Priv.
printed at the Plimpton Press, 1932. xvii, 348 pp. Illustrated.

1236 Harvard University. Library. *The Rogers Memorial Room; an
Account of the Nature, Origin, and Significance of the Memorabilia
Presented to Harvard College in 1930 by Clara Kathleen and Henry
Munroe Rogers.* Boston: Priv. printed, The Cosmos Press, 1935. 31 pp.
Illustrated.

ROLF, ERNST, b. 1891

1237 Hodell, Björn, b. 1885. *Sagan om Ernst Rolf.* Teckningar av
Martin Nilsson. In Swedish. Stockholm: Birgins, 1948. 156 pp.
Illustrated.

ROMERO, MARIA, b. 1903

See item 1631

ROMERO-MALPICA, MANUEL, 1874-1939

See item 1631

RONCONI, GIORGIO, 1810-1890

See item 1562

ROS, MARIA ASUNCIÓN DE AGUILAR, 1899-1970

See item 734

ROSENGREN, MARGIT INGEBORG, b. 1901

1238 Rosengren, Margit Ingeborg. *Oförgätligt glada stunder ... ett livs roman i fa sekunder.* Illustratör: Arne Lindenbaum. In Swedish. Stockholm: C.E. Fritze, 1948. 230 pp. Illustrated.

ROSING, VLADIMIR, 1890-1963

See item 1716

ROSSI-LEMENI, NICOLA, b. 1922

1239 Rossi-Lemeni, Nicola. *Oltrè l'angoscia.* In Italian. Bologna: Cappelli, 1972. 55 pp.
   A volume of poems.

ROSVAENGE, HELGE ANTON, 1897-1972

1240 Rosvaenge, Helge Anton. *Guide Lines for Aspiring Singers.* Translated by J.F.E. Dennis. 2nd enlarged ed. Ipswich: Calver Press, 1977? 32 pp. Illustrated.
   English translation of *Leitfaden für Gesangsbeflissene* (q.v.).

1241 ————. *Lache bajazzo; Ernstes und Heiteres aus meinem Leben.* In German. München: W. Andermann, 1953. 287 pp. Illustrated.

1242 ————. *Leitfaden für Gesangsbeflissene; eine heitere Plauderei über ernste Dinge.* In German. München: Obpacher, 1964. 51 pp. Illustrated.

1243 ────. *Mach es besser, mein Sohn; ein Tenor erzählt aus seinem Leben.* In German. Leipzig: Koehler und Amelang, 1962. 231 pp. Illustrated.

1244-T ────. *Skratta pajazzo.* Translated by Nils Edström. In Swedish. Stockholm: Medén, 1945. 332 pp. Illustrated.

Translated from the Danish original, which could not be located.

1245 Tassié, Franz. *Helge Rosvaenge.* In German. Augsburg: Schroff, 1975. 216 pp. Illustrated. Discography, pp. 213-215. Chronology, pp. 189-209. Films, p. 215.

A richly illustrated biography of the Danish tenor. It is not particularly long, yet it covers the major events of his life. The book's value lies chiefly in the supporting material. The discography lists the LP re-releases only, however the chronology is a remarkably detailed document. It includes, by year, the city and theater where Rosvaenge sang each of his operatic and operetta roles, thereby giving, indirectly, his complete repertory. The concert appearances also show the conductor. The absence of an index is a serious shortcoming for such a fine work.

See also item 1811

ROTHENBERGER, ANNELIESE, b. 1924

1246 Rothenberger, Anneliese. *Melodie meines Lebens; Selbsterlebtes, Selbserzähltes.* In German. 2nd ed. München: Lichtenberg, 1972. 191 pp. Illustrated. Discography, pp. 176-180.

1247 Lewinski, Wolf-Eberhard von. *Anneliese Rothenberger.* In German. Velber bei Hannover: Friedrich, 1968. 104 pp. Illustrated. Discography, pp. 89-98.

RÔZE, MARIE, 1846-1926

See item 1567

RUBINI, GIOVANNI BATTISTA, 1794-1854

1248 Locatelli, Agostino. *Cenni biografici sulla straordinaria carriera teatrale percorsa da Gio. Battista Rubini da Romano, cantante di camera....* In Italian. Milano: F. Colombo, 1844. 88 pp.

1249 Traini, Carlo. *Il cigno di Romano: Giovan Battista Rubini, re dei tenori.* In Italian. Bergamo: Tip. scuole professionali orfanotrofio m., 1954. 204 pp. Illustrated.

See also items 1562, 1601, 1615, 1620, 1745

RUBIO, CONSUELO, 1928-1981

1250 Rubio, Consuelo. *El canto: estética, teoría, interpretación.*
In Spanish. Madrid: Reus, 1982. 198 pp. Illustrated. Bibliography,
pp. 167-168. Repertory, pp. 197-198. Discography, p. 198.

Contains the singer's views on the various aspects of singing.
Preceded by a long preface (pp. 7-28) by Domingo Paniagua entitled
"Consuelo Rubio, profil artistico y humano." Pages 169-195 contain
a selection of Rubio's press notices in Dutch, English, French,
German, Italian and Spanish. AM

RUDENKO, BELA, b. 1933

See item 1732

RUDENKO, LARISA

1251 Grisenko, Liudmila Nikolaevna. *Larisa Rudenko.* In Ukrainian.
Kiev: Muzichna Ukraina, 1978. 54 pp. Illustrated. Repertory, pp.
49-54.

A short biography of the Ukrainian mezzo-soprano. The illustrations
show her in some of her best roles, among them: Carmen, Amneris, the
Countess.

RUFFO, TITTA, 1877-1953

1252 Ruffo, Titta. *La mia parabola; memorie.* In Italian. Milano:
Fratelli Treves Editori, 1937. 367 pp. Illustrated.

Recognized as one of the most successful autobiographies by an
opera singer, its literary quality is especially remarkable considering
that it was written by a man who never attended school--any school.
Ruffo's narrative concentrates on personal matters, the poverty of
his youth and his difficulties starting his career. As the title indicates, he was aware of the parabolic nature of his career, but in
bringing his narrative abruptly to an end in 1924 he omits the
descending trajectory of the parabola. He devotes too little space
to his operatic appearances and he gives insufficient details about
his immense successes on three continents. However, since his career
activities can be re-assembled from contemporary reviews, the book
remains a valuable document of the life and thoughts of one of the
truly great singers of the twentieth century.

1252-a ————. *La mia parabola.* With a discography by W.R. Moran.
In Italian. Opera Biographies. New York: Arno Press, 1977. 367,
xiv pp. Illustrated. Discography, pp. i-xiv.

Reprint of the 1937 edition published by Fratelli Treves Editori,
Milan (q.v.). The discography was prepared for this edition.

1252-b ————. *La mia parabola; memorie.* Riedizione del centenario
della nascita, a cura del figlio Ruffo Titta, Jr.... Omaggio di G.

Lauri-Volpi; "Parabola senza fine" di G. Gualerzi. In Italian. Roma: Staderini, 1977. xviii, 444 pp. Illustrated. Bibliography, pp. 433-434. Repertory, pp. 405-409. Index, pp. 439-444. Discography, pp. 411-431. Chronology of Performances, pp. 357-404. Notes, pp. 313-355.

This edition was prepared with loving care by the singer's son, Dr. Ruffo Titta, Jr., to celebrate the hundredth anniversary of his father's birth. If the autobiography was hailed as the paragon of musical biography, this edition deserves to be upheld as a model of scholarship, typography and book design. Titta Jr. and Gualerzi added forty pages of useful and enlightening notes. In an Epilogue the son brings his father's life story up to date from 1924, where the narrative ends, until his death. The book also has (a) a chronology of Ruffo's appearances, with casts, where available, (b) a list of his repertory and the date he first sang each role, (c) a list of the theaters where he performed with dates of his appearance, (d) a near-complete discography in collaboration with M. Tiberi, (e) a bibliography of books and magazine articles and (f) a genealogical table of the Titta family, starting with the singer's parents. 139 photographs complete this remarkable book, which is a joy to handle. It deserves to be published in English, especially since an English translation already exists in manuscript.

1253-T ———. *Parabola moei zhizni. Vospominaniia.* Translated by Aleksandr D. Bushen. In Russian. Moskva: Muzyka, 1966. 436 pp. Illustrated.

The Russian translation of *La mia parabola* (q.v.), with a long preface (32 pp.) by the translator.

1254-T ———. *Parabola moei zhizni. Vospominaniia.* Translated by Aleksandr D. Bushen. In Russian. Leningrad: Muzyka, 1968. 391 pp. Illustrated.

The Russian translation of *La mia parabola* (q.v.), with a long preface (20 pp.) by the translator.

1255 Arnosi, Eduardo, b. 1925. *Titta Ruffo, el titán de los barítonos.* In Spanish. Buenos Aires: Ayer y Hoy de la Opera, 1977. 30 pp. Illustrated.

A corrected version of the article originally published in the first issue of the Buenos Aires-based magazine *Ayer y Hoy de la Opera* (November 1977). This essay offers a good outline of Ruffo's life and the significant events of his career. Many contemporary reviews and criticisms of his artistry are quoted at length; there are also numerous references to his recordings. RT

1256 Barrenechea, Mariano Antonio, 1884-1949. *Historia estética de la música. Edición definitiva, corregida y aumentada por el autor.* In Spanish. 4th ed. Biblioteca Musical: Música y músicos a través de obras maestras, Vol. I. Buenos Aires: Editorial Claridad, 1963. Illustrated. Index, pp. 468-479.

Pages 425-467 contain an essay about Titta Ruffo. The first three editions of this book were published in 1918, 1941 and 1944 respectively. AM

1257 ————. *Titta Ruffo; notas de psicologia artistica*. In Spanish. Buenos Aires: Edición de la Revista "Música," 1911. 139 pp. Illustrated.

A thorough study by a competent critic nostalgic for the stylistic values of the past. An introductory discourse is followed by an overview of Ruffo's artistic life, the psychology of acting, a discussion of Thomas's *Hamlet* and Titta Ruffo, and the decline of the art of singing. RT

1258 *Biografía y juicio crítico de Titta Ruffo*. In Spanish. Madrid: Prudencio Pérez De Velasco, 1912. 71 pp.

Journalistic essays. One biographical essay, with some inaccuracies; two about the revolution Ruffo brought to the world of singing; and three about his interpretations of Rigoletto, Figaro and Hamlet. RT

1259 Contreras, Vicente. *Titta Ruffo y su arte; biografia y estudio en dos idiomas del eminente baritono*. In Spanish and Italian. Madrid: Imprenta Gutenberg-Castro y Compañia, 1910. 147 pp.

Chronologically the earliest book about the thirty-three-year-old Ruffo, based on and following his engagement in Madrid. The biographical chapter contains many details from his childhood and youth whose source must have been the singer himself; in fact, some of these read like passages from his autobiography written twenty-seven years later. The biographical chapter is followed by lengthy analyses of Ruffo's interpretation of three of his best-known roles: Rigoletto, Figaro and Hamlet.

1260 Farkas, Andrew, b. 1936. *Titta Ruffo, an Anthology*. With a foreword by Tito Gobbi and a discography by William R. Moran. Westport, Conn.: Greenwood Press, 1984. xiii, 289 pp. Illustrated. Bibliography, pp. 275-279. Repertory, pp. 241-244. Index, pp. 280-287. Discography, pp. 251-269. Chronology of Performances, pp. 185-240. Theaters (where Ruffo performed), pp. 245-250.

A collection of writings about Titta Ruffo drawn from international sources. Some of them were written, or translated into English, expressly for this anthology, others are reprinted for the first time. The extensive chronology, complete with casts, represents the state-of-research; the discography is believed to be complete, listing all the published and unpublished recordings Ruffo ever made since his debut. The contributions by Dr. Ruffo Titta, the singer's son, add special value to the book.

See also items 337, 1620, 1680, 1731, 1837, 1838, 1839

RUSSELL, ELLA, 1864-1935

See item 1567

RYSANEK, LEONIE, b. 1928

See items 1654, 1788

S

SACK, ERNA, 1903-1972

1261 Schäfer, Jürgen. *Erna Sack zum 75. Geburtstag und 1. Todestag.* In German. Sammlung Jürgen Schäfer. Hamburg: Jürgen Schäfer, 1973. 23 pp. Discography, pp. 13-23.

1262 ———. *Erna Sack zum 80. Geburtstag und 6. Todestag.* In German. Sammlung Jürgen Schäfer. Hamburg: Jürgen Schäfer, 1978. 28 pp. Illustrated. Discography, pp. 16-28.

See also item 1811

SADKO, KONSTANTIN

1263 Sadko, Konstantin. *Das Leben ist köstlich; ein fahrender Sänger erzählt.* In German. Tübingen: Katzman, 1951. 337 pp. Illustrated.

The autobiography of a tenor born in the Ukraine. He gave many concerts in Europe and some in America. Over half of the book is devoted to life in pre- and revolutionary Russia.

SAINT-HUBERTY, ANNE ANTOINETTE (CLAVEL), 1756-1812

1264 Goncourt, Edmond, 1822-1896. *Madame Saint-Huberty d'après sa correspondance et ses papiers de famille.* In French. Paris: Charpentier, 1885. viii, 319 pp.

1264-a ———. *Madame Saint-Huberty d'après sa correspondance et ses papiers de famille.* In French. Les actrices du XVIIIme siècle. Paris: E. Fasquelle, 1900. viii, 319 pp.

1264-b ———. *Madame Saint-Huberty d'après sa correspondance et ses papiers de famille.* In French. Les actrices du XVIIIme siècle. Westport, Conn.: Greenwood Press, 1969. viii, 319 pp.

Reprint of the 1900 edition of E. Fasquelle, Paris (q.v.).

1264-c ———. *Madame Saint-Huberty d'après sa correspondance et ses papiers de famille.* Postface de Henry Céard. Édition définitive publiée sous la direction de l'Académie Goncourt. In French. Paris: E. Flammarion, 1925? 284 pp.

See also item 1596

SALAZAR, MANUEL, 1887-1950

1265 Segura Mendez, Manuel. *Melico.* In Spanish. San José, Costa Rica: Editorial Costa Rica, 1965. 172 pp. Illustrated. Repertory, pp. 169-170.

SALÉZA, ALBERT, 1867-1916

See item 1588

SALINA, N.V.

1266 Salina, N.V. *Zhizn' i stsena. Memuary.* In Russian. Leningrad: VTO, 1941. Unverified; data obtained from secondary literature.

SÁNDOR, ERZSI, 1885-1962

1267 Balassa, Imre, b. 1886. *Sándor Erzsi.* In Hungarian. Nagy magyar elöadómüvészek, 4. Budapest: Zenemükiadó, 1968. 75 pp. Illustrated. Repertory, pp. 71-72.

A model biography despite its relative brevity. Balassa was greatly assisted in his endeavor by autobiographical sketches left behind by the artist and her devoted husband of many decades, Imre Bosnyák, and by his experiences both as a musicologist and personal acquaintance of the artist. Erzsi Sándor was the glory of Hungarian operatic life from her debut in 1905 until her retirement in 1939. The scene of most of her operatic triumphs was Budapest, strictly by choice. The partner of every major guest artist, from Ruffo and Battistini to de Luca and Stracciari, she was the only Hungarian opera singer ever to earn the Kammersängerin title of Austria.

There is a single 7" 33 rpm record accompanying this book. The four selections show a voice of great beauty and excellent schooling. Unfortunately, there is no indication when the recordings were made; the forward sound would suggest that it was late in her career. The list of her repertory gives the date of first performance for each role.

SANTLEY, CHARLES, 1834-1922

1268 Santley, Charles. *The Art of Singing and Vocal Declamation.* New York: Macmillan, 1908. xvi, 143 pp.

As the title implies, this is a book about the art of singing rather than singing technique or voice production. Santley addresses a variety of subjects, from the choice of a teacher to dramatic conception, acting, stage comportment and the use of tobacco and wine. It is an informative summary of the wisdom and experiences gained in the course of a long and distinguished career.

1269 ————. *Reminiscences of My Life.* London: I. Pitman and Sons, 1909. xiv, 319 pp. Illustrated. Index, pp. 315-319.

A Victorian autobiography by a Victorian gentleman, alternately charming, amusing and cantankerous. In addition to the expected details about his personal life and singing career, he volunteers a great deal of information about and passes judgment on a large number of subjects. His devastating opinion of the first London performance of *Mefistofele* is especially noteworthy to a posterity gifted with hindsight. His comments about composers, colleagues and singing are of value and interest.

1269-a ————. *Reminiscences of My Life*. With a discography by W.R. Moran. Opera Biographies. New York: Arno Press, 1977. xiv, ii, 319 pp. Illustrated. Index, pp. 315-319. Discography, pp. i-ii.

Reprint of the 1909 edition published by I. Pitman, London (q.v.). The discography was prepared for this edition.

1270 ————. *Student and Singer; the Reminiscences of Charles Santley*. New York: Macmillan, 1892. xvii, 358 pp. Illustrated.

A pupil of Manuel Garcia, Charles Santley made his debut in Pavia in 1858, and was a fixture of the operatic stages of Italy, France and England, with tours in the United States until 1900 when he left the operatic for the concert stage. For this first book of memoirs the author states that he has patterned his writing after that of Benvenuto Cellini "jotting down any reminiscences and reflections plainly ..." and in so doing, much of the book is not formally structured, unlike his autobiography published in 1909 (*Reminiscences of My Life*, q.v.). Santley's career had brought him into close contact with the musical world of oratorio, opera and the concert stage for some 34 years at the time this book was written, and this he describes with Victorian wit and with frankness. WRM

1271 Levien, John Joseph Mewburn, b. 1863. *Sir Charles Santley*. London: Novello, 1930? 27 pp. Illustrated. "A lecture by John Mewburn Levien."

See also items 1615, 1682

SAROBE, CELESTINO, 1892-1952

1272 Sarobe, Celestino. *Venimécum del artista lirico*. In Spanish. Barcelona: Comas, 1947. 191 pp. Illustrated.

Celestino Sarobe was the only pupil of Mattia Battistini (to whose memory this book is dedicated), and there are many quotations from the maestro throughout the text. The press extracts, arranged by city, are not all dated, but give a good deal of information about the career of this important Spanish baritone in Spain, Portugal, Italy, Switzerland, France, Hungary and Germany. In 1944 Sarobe was invited to give a master class at Salzburg, but this was cancelled due to the war. At the time of publication of this book, he was Professor of Singing and Grand Opera at the Conservatory of the Liceo in Barcelona. The book consists of a series of essays on the art of singing and characterization, an essay on "Opera in Spain," extracts from press reviews covering Sarobe's career as opera and concert singer and professor of singing from 1917 to 1944 (pp. 127-173) and finally musical extracts from a number of operas for student use. WRM

SASSE, MARIE CONSTANCE, 1838-1907

1273 Sasse, Marie Constance. *Souvenirs d'une artiste.* In French.
Paris: Librairie Molière, 1902. 233 pp. Illustrated.

This book is the autobiography of the first Elizabetta in *Don Carlo*,
the first Selika in *L'Africaine* and the first Elizabeth in the Paris
version of *Tannhäuser*. She sang in many of the world's leading opera
houses during the 1860s and 1870s. Marie Sasse writes almost as well
as she had reportedly sung and gives many fascinating insights into
the operatic life of the period. TGK

SASSONE (SUAREZ), FELIPE, b. 1884

1274 Sassone (Suarez), Felipe. *La rueda de mi fortuna (memorias).*
In Spanish. Madrid: Aguilar, 1958. 600 pp. Bibliography, pp. 597-
600.

Tenor turned writer, the author of a very large number of novels,
plays, short stories, poetry and criticism. This volume contains
his recollections of his life as singer and writer,

SCALCHI, SOFIA, 1850-1922

See item 1658

SCHAETZLER, FRITZ

1275 Schaetzler, Fritz. *Nun erst recht! Ein Schwerverwundeter geht
zur Bühne; Lebensbericht.* In German. Berlin: Deutscher Verlag,
1943. 178 pp. Illustrated.

The autobiography of a war veteran who lost one leg in combat.
He learned to control his artificial leg well enough to jump, ski
and play tennis. His singing earned him the title of Kammersänger;
his repertory included a wide variety of roles: Escamillo, Figaro,
Beckmesser, Don Alfonso, Frosch (!), Amonasro, Papageno.

SCHEBEST, AGNESE, 1813-1870

1275/A Schebest, Agnese. *Aus dem Leben einer Künstlerin.* In German.
Stuttgart: Ebner & Seubert, 1857. viii, 304 pp.

SCHEIDEMANTEL, KARL, 1859-1923

1276 Trede, Paul. *Karl Scheidemantel.* In German. Dresden-Blasewitz:
C. Reissner, 1911. 79 pp. Illustrated.

SCHELBLE, JOHANN NEPOMUK, 1789-1837

1277 Bormann, Oskar, b. 1903. "Johann Nepomuk Schelble, 1789-1837;

sein Leben, sein Wirken und seine Werke; ein Beitrag zur Musikgeschichte in Frankfurt am Main...." Dissertation, Frankfurt, 1926.
In German. 145 pp. Illustrated.

SCHICK, MARGARETE LUISE (HAMEL), 1773-1809

1278 Levezow, Konrad (Jakob Andreas Konrad), 1770-1835. *Leben und
Kunst der Frau Margarete Luise Schick, geboren Hamel, königl. preuss.
Kammersängerin und Mitgliedes des Nationaltheaters zu Berlin.* Mit dem
Bildnisse der Künstlerin nach der Büste von F. Wichmann. In German.
Berlin: Duncker und Humblot, 1809. 75 pp. Illustrated.

SCHIØTZ, AKSEL, 1906-1975

1279-T Schiøtz, Aksel. *Sangerens kunst.* Forord av Gerald Moore.
Overs. af Gerd Sciøtz. In Danish. København: Vinten, 1970. 227 pp.

1280 ————. *The Singer and His Art.* New York: Harper and Row,
1969. xvi, 214 pp. Bibliography, pp. 203-205. Index, pp. 207-214.
Discography, pp. 197-202. Appendix I: International Phonetic Association Symbols; Appendix II: Recommended Listening (LP records).

Schiøtz distills the accumulated experience of rich careers both as
performer and teacher. The main sections of the book treat the functioning of the voice; the interpretation of art song, oratorio and
opera; choice of teacher; and the various considerations of the
organization and presentation of a recital.
Gerald Moore's Preface gives the finishing touch to this highly
instructive book. The discography only lists the titles of Schiøtz's
records; the reader is referred to the discography prepared by the
Nationaldiskoteket of Copenhagen (1966), which is exhaustive and provides all recording details.

1280-a ————. *The Singer and His Art*; with a preface by Gerald
Moore. London: Hamilton, 1971. 222 pp. Discography, pp. 207-214.

1281 Schiøtz, Gerd (Haugsted), b. 1908. *Kunst og kamp.* In Danish.
København: Westermann, 1951. 232 pp. Illustrated. Discography.

This "joint autobiography" is followed by what purports to be a
full chronological discography up to 1951, i.e., 78 rpm recordings
only, including some private recordings. There are many illustrations,
personal photographs, some in costume, several cartoons, etc. Where
Aksel Schiøtz is concerned, the autobiography is immensely successful:
it limns his early life, training, concerts, operas, tours, family,
etc. There is a good amount of anecdote which certainly fills in
Schiøtz's colorful artistic life. The autobiography is topically,
rather than chronologically, arranged, so that all of Schiøtz's
English tours and performances are grouped together in a section
called "The English Adventure," subdivided into "First Trip," "Second
Trip," "Third Trip," "Glyndebourne," etc. PHS

SCHIPA, TITO, 1889-1965

1282 Schipa, Tito. *Tito Schipa si confessa*. In Italian. Roma: Pubblimusica, 1961. 107 pp. Discography, pp. 99-106.

A composite work, introduced by Giacomo Lauri-Volpi. Preface and biographical summary are by Rodolfo Celletti (pp. 6-19). Schipa recounts the events of his life with playful verve (pp. 20-98). The appendix and the discography are by Raffaele Vegeto. RT

1283 Andrea, Renzo d'. *Tito Schipa nella vita, nell'arte, nel suo tempo*. Presentazione di Lucio Caprioli. Discografia completa a cura di Daniele Rubboli. In Italian. Fasano di Puglia: Schena Editore, 1981. 246 pp. Illustrated. Discography, pp. 225-240.

SCHLUSNUS, HEINRICH, 1888-1952

1284 Naso, Eckart von, b. 1888, and Annemay Schlusnus. *Heinrich Schlusnus, Mensch und Sänger*. In German. Hamburg: W. Krüger, 1957. 335 pp. Illustrated.

1285 *Plaudereien um Heinrich Schlusnus*. In German. N.p.: Selbstverlag, n.d. 48 pp. Illustrated.

See also items 1711, 1743, 1811

SCHMIDT, JOSEPH, 1904-1942

1286 Ney-Nowotny, Karl, and Gertrud Ney-Nowotny. *Joseph Schmidt; das Leben und Streben eines Unvergesslichen*. In German. Wien: Europäischer Verlag, 1962. 190 pp. Illustrated.

1287 Rosenfelder, Carl, b. 1892. *Ein Lied geht um die Welt; ein Joseph Schmidt-Buch*, von Carl Ritter (pseud.). In German. Rothenburg ob der Tauber: J.P. Peter, 1955. 204 pp. Fictionalized biography.

SCHNORR VON CAROLSFELD, LUDWIG, 1832-1865

1288 Garrigues, Carl Henri Nicolai, b. 1869. *De første fortolkere af Richard Wagners "Tristan" og "Isolde" aegteparret Ludwig og Malvina Schnorr von Carolsfeld*. In Danish. København: I kommission hos V. Tryde, 1914. 15 pp. Illustrated.

1289 ————. *Ein ideales Sängerpaar, Ludwig Schnorr von Carolsfeld und Malvina Schnorr von Carolsfeld geborene Garrigues; zwei in einander verwobene Lebensbilder, nach eigenen und zeitgenössischen Briefen, Tagebuchblättern, Lebenserinnerungen und Berichten geschildert*. In German. Kopenhagen: Levin & Munksgaard, 1937. 492 pp. Illustrated. Bibliography, pp. 474-476.

SCHNORR VON CAROLSFELD, MALVINA (GARRIGUES), 1825-1904

See items 1288, 1289

SCHOCK, RUDOLF, b. 1915

1290 Herzfeld, Friedrich, b. 1897. *Rudolf Schock*. In German. Rembrandt-Reihe, Bd. 42. Berlin: Rembrandt, 1962. 61 pp. Illustrated.

SCHÖFFLER, PAUL, 1897-1977

1291 Christian, Hans. *Paul Schöffler. Versuch einer Würdigung*. In German. Wien: Österreichischer Bundesverlag, 1967. 40 pp. Illustrated. Discography, pp. 37-40.

SCHOLDEL, ROZÁLIA

1292 Benyovszky, Károly. *Scholdel Rozália, az elsö magyar drámai "dalnoknö."* In Hungarian. Bratislava-Pozsony: Zs. Steiner, 1927. 44 pp.

SCHORR, FRIEDRICH, 1888-1953

See item 1743

SCHOULTZ, JOHANNA CAROLINA ULRIKA VON, 1813-1883

1293 Andersson, Otto Emanuel, b. 1879. *Johanna von Schoultz i sol och skugga*. In Swedish. Åbo: Förlaget Bro, 1939. 215 pp. Illustrated. Bibliography, pp. 198-210. Index, pp. 211-215.

This is a scholarly biography of Johanna von Schoultz, with a full apparatus of notes and bibliography. There are elaborate discussions of her performances of Mozart, Bellini, Donizetti and Rossini; several reproductions of programs of concerts and a number of verses dedicated to von Schoultz. A valuable piece of work, if only as an example of the taste of the early 19th century. PHS

SCHREIER, PETER, b. 1935

1294 Schmiedel, Gottfried. *Peter Schreier*. In German. Leipzig: Deutscher Verlag für Musik, 1976. 73 pp. Illustrated. Discography, pp. 71-73.

1295 ———. *Peter Schreier: eine Bildbiographie*. In German. Berlin: Henschel, 1979. 174 pp. Illustrated. Bibliography, p. 174. Discography, pp. 167-173.

SCHRÖDER-DEVRIENT, WILHELMINE, 1804-1860

1296 (Schröder-Devrient, Wilhelmine, 1804-1860). *Pauline: Memoirs of a Singer* (Aus den Memoiren einer Saengerin). Translated from the German. Los Angeles: Holloway House Publishing Co., 1967. 312 pp.

Unlikely as it may seem, operatic biographical literature has produced one celebrated piece of hard-core pornography. Although it was published anonymously, its authorship soon came to be attributed to Wilhelmine Schröder-Devrient, in all probability for commercial reasons. The book went through several editions in the original German, also in French, Spanish and English translations (*Aus den Memoiren einer Sängerin*, Part I published around 1868, Part II in 1875; *Pauline, the Prima Donna, or Memoirs of an Opera Singer*, 1898; *Confessions of a Prima Donna*, 1924; *Memorias de una cantante alemana*, 1977; etc.). In a critical essay that precedes the main text of this edition, Philip K. Roggis presents irrefutable arguments demonstrating that Schröder-Devrient could not have written these memoirs. The "facts" in Part I do not correspond with the events in the singer's life; Part II, almost certainly written by a second author, is full of anachronisms, referring to historical events that occurred after the singer's death. The book is included in this bibliography to record in a reference work, perhaps for the first time, that this pornographic volume is neither a story of her life, nor her writing.

1297 Baudissin, Eva Fanny Bernhardine (Türk) von, b. 1869. *Wilhelmine Schröder-Devrient; der Schicksalsweg einer grossen Künstlerin, Roman*. In German. Berlin: Drei Masken Verlag, 1937. 265 pp. Illustrated.

1298 Glümer, Claire von, 1825-1906. *Erinnerungen an Wilhelmine Schröder-Devrient*. In German. Leipzig: J.A. Barth, 1862. vi, 277 pp. Illustrated.

1298-a ———. *Erinnerungen an Wilhelmine Schröder-Devrient*. In German. 3rd ed. Leipzig: P. Reclam Jun., 1904. 176 pp. Illustrated.

1299 Hagemann, Carl, 1871-1946. *Wilhelmine Schroeder-Devrient*. In German. Das Theater, Bd. VII. Berlin: Schuster & Loeffler, 1904. 85 pp. Illustrated.

1299-a ———. *Wilhelmine Schröder-Devrient*. In German. Wiesbaden: Verlag Der Greif, 1947. 79 pp. Illustrated.

1300 Richter, Hermann, b. 1887. *Das wilde Herz; Lebensroman der Wilhelmine Schröder-Devrient*. In German. Leipzig: Koehler & Amelang, 1927. 232 pp. Fictionalized biography.

1301 Wolzogen und Neuhaus, Alfred von, 1823-1883. *Wilhelmine Schröder-Devrient. Ein Beitrag zur Geschichte des musikalischen Dramas*. In German. Leipzig: F.A. Brockhaus, 1863. xii, 351 pp.

See also items 1562, 1612, 1615, 1668, 1669

SCHRÖTER, CORONA, 1751-1802

1302 Schröter, Corona, 1751-1802. *Briefe und Zeugnisse. Zum 4 Dezember 1910*. In German. Leipzig: Poeschel und Trepte, n.d. 23 pp. Only copy located in the Nationalbibliothek in Vienna.

1303 Düntzer, Heinrich, 1813-1901. *Charlotte von Stein und Corona Schröter, eine Vertheidigung.* In German. Stuttgart: J.G. Cotta, 1876. viii, 301 pp.

1304 Keil, Robert, 1826-1894. *Vor hundert Jahren. Mittheilungen über Weimar, Goethe und Corona Schröter aus den Tagen der Genie-Periode. Festgabe zur Säkularfeier von Goethe's eintritt in Weimar (7. November 1775).* In German. Leipzig: Veit und Comp., 1875. 2 vols. Illustrated. Vol. 2: *Corona Schröter. Eine Lebenskizze mit Beiträgen zur Geschichte der Genie-Periode.*

1305 Pasig, Paul Richard. *Goethe und Jlmenau. Mit einer Beigabe: Goethe und Corona Schröter.* In German. 2nd enlarged ed. Weimar: Huschke, 1902. 27 pp. Festgabe der Stadt Jlmenau zur 17. Jahres-Versammlung der Goethe-Gesellschaft.

1306 Stümcke, Heinrich, 1872-1923. *Corona Schröter.* In German. 2nd ed. Bielefeld: Velhagen und Klasing, 1926. xi, 172 pp. Illustrated.

SCHÜTZENDORF, ALFONS, 1882-1946

See item 1307

SCHÜTZENDORF, GUIDO, b. 1880

See item 1307

SCHÜTZENDORF, LEO, 1886-1931

1307 Schützendorf, Eugen. *Künstlerblut. Leo Schützendorf und seine Brüder.* In German. Berlin: N.p., 1943. 352 pp. Illustrated.

Also concerns Guido Schützendorf (b. 1880) and Alfons Schützendorf (1882-1946).

See also item 1743

SCHUMANN, ELISABETH, 1885-1952

1308 Schumann, Elisabeth. *German Song.* Translated (from manuscript) by D. Millar Craig. The World of Music. New York, 6. New York: Chanticleer Press, 1948. 72 pp. Illustrated. Index, p. 72.

Elisabeth Schumann was one of the great exponents of the Lied, and here she expresses the pleasure and joy the songs of the great masters bring her, and her pleasure in their interpretation. She feels that great songs possess some secret powers which must be absorbed to grasp their full significance. She stresses the importance of both words and music. The book is delightfully illustrated with old prints, in both black-and-white and color. WRM

1308-a ————. *German Song*. Translated (from manuscript) by D. Millar Craig. The World of Music. London, 6. London: M. Parrish, 1948. 72 pp. Illustrated. Index, p. 72.

1309 Puritz, Elizabeth. *The Teaching of Elizabeth Schumann*. London: Methuen, 1956. vii, 136 pp. Illustrated.

This work is actually a little handbook, prepared by Mme. Schumann's daughter-in-law four years after the singer's death. Elizabeth Puritz studied professionally with Schumann and knew her method and teaching habits well. From the non-technical standpoint the book makes good reading, as the effervescence of Schumann's character comes across. WRM

See also item 1702

SCHUMANN-HEINK, ERNESTINE, 1861-1936

1310 Lawton, Mary. *Schumann-Heink, the Last of the Titans*. New York: The Macmillan Company, 1928. 390 pp. Illustrated.

Written in the first person, with a bit too much emphasis on the "Achs" and "Lieber Gotts!" in an attempt to be colorful, this work has great strength in that it does get across much of the wonderful personality of the beloved singer. The atmosphere is chatty, with loving opinions of other artists and professional friends, but the dates are sketchy and there is no hint of the extremely large repertory of this admirable singer. It is good reading, but a poor reference book. The memory of Ernestine Schumann-Heink deserves better. WRM

1310-a ————. *Schumann-Heink, the Last of the Titans*. With a discography by W.R. Moran. Opera Biographies. New York: Arno Press, 1977. 390, 30 pp. Illustrated. Discography, pp. 1-30 (391-417).

Reprint of the 1928 edition by Macmillan, New York. There is a note of "Schumann-Heink on American Radio" and "Schumann-Heink on Motion Pictures" and a complete discography, none of which was part of the original edition.

1311 McPherson, James B. "Schumann-Heink." *The Record Collector* XVII, nos. 5 and 6 (June and August 1967), 99-143, 154-159. Illustrated. Repertory, pp. 115-117. Chronology of Performances, pp. 156-159.

This is a very condensed excerpt from an as-yet-unpublished complete biography of Madame Schumann-Heink (see item 1829). The article referenced here contains the main points of that excellent, thoroughly researched work. The discography, a model of its kind that accompanies the article, and an essay about her recordings, are by William R. Moran.

1312 Mayfield, John S., b. 1904. *A Conversation in 1026*. Austin, Tex., 1925. 20 pp. "One hundred ninety-nine copies printed ... each of which is numbered."

The transcript of a conversation with Madame Schumann-Heink in her hotel suite, no. 1026. The Library of Congress owns No. 198 of this edition.

See also items 1541, 1581, 1615, 1658, 1662, 1663, 1695, 1792, 1829

SCHWARZKOPF, ELISABETH, b. 1915

1313 Schwarzkopf, Elisabeth. *On and off the Record: A Memoir of Walter Legge/Elisabeth Schwarzkopf*; with an introduction by Herbert von Karajan. New York: Charles Scribner's Sons, 1982. xi, 292 pp. Illustrated. Index, pp. 289-292. Discography, pp. 243-288.

Ostensibly a biography of Walter Legge by his wife, this book is actually a compendium of articles he wrote during his long career, some including "An Autobiography," published for the first time; aside from his own life story, his writings about the Philharmonia Orchestra's founding and dissolution, Titta Ruffo, Lotte Lehmann, Rosa Ponselle, Elisabeth Schwarzkopf, Sir Thomas Beecham, Otto Klemperer, Maria Callas, Ernest Newman, Hugo Wolf and Herbert von Karajan are included. Along with that come generous doses of Legge's philosophy of music and approach to recording, and comments about many well- and not-so-well-known figures in the musical world. Two additional chapters, "Walter Legge: An Appreciation" by Dorle Soria, and "The Autocrat of the Turntable" by Edward Greenfield, round out the portrait, the whole bound together by introductions written by Schwarzkopf. Included are many informal photographs and a selected discography by Alan Sanders of the approximately 3500 records Legge produced. HCS

1313-a ————. *On and off the Record: A Memoir of Walter Legge*. With an introduction by Herbert von Karajan. London: Faber and Faber, 1982. xi, 292 pp. Illustrated. Index, pp. 289-292. Discography, pp. 243-288.

1314-T Gavoty, Bernard. *Elisabeth Schwarzkopf*. Portraits by Roger Hauert. Translated by F.E. Richardson. Great Concert Artists. Geneva: R. Kister, 195? 27 pp. Illustrated.

1315 ————. *Elisabeth Schwarzkopf*. Portraits de Roger Hauert. In French. Les grands interprètes. Genève: R. Kister, 1957. 27 pp. Illustrated.

See also items 1654, 1702, 1788

SCOTT, HENRI, 1876-1942

See item 1581

SCOTTI, ANTONIO, 1866-1936

See items 531, 1565, 1581

SCOTTO, RENATA, b. 1934

1316 Bonafini, Umberto. *Perchè sono Renata Scotto*. In Italian.
Mantova: C.I.T.E.M., 1976. 209 pp. Illustrated. Index, pp. 201-207.
Discography, pp. 197-199.

Scotto was barely 41 when this biography was published. A mediocre
journalistic effort, it consists of a loosely knit narrative interspersed with quotations by the singer, conductors, musicologists,
etc. While it is good to have the facts of her life and the development of her career available to readers, the excessive partisanship
of the author discredits his critical comments. It is impossible to
read with a straight face such statements as the caption under a
Callas-Scotto backstage snapshot "... the two greatest singers of the
last thirty years...." The discography is an insignificant, incomplete
listing of Scotto's records.

SCOVEL, EDWARD BROOKS, b. 1853

See item 1567

SEEFRIED, IRMGARD, b. 1919

1317 Fassbind, Franz. *Wolfgang Schneiderhan, Irmgard Seefried; eine
Künstler- und Lebensgemeinschaft*. In German. Bern: A. Scherz, 1960.
308 pp. Illustrated. Discography, pp. 293-308.

See also item 1813

SEMBRICH, MARCELLA, 1858-1935

1318 Armin, George. *Marcella Sembrich und Herr Professor Julius Hey.
Eine Antwort an die Streitfrage: "Was ist Koloratur?" Nebst ein
Epilog an den "Kunstgesang."* In German. Leipzig, 1898. 16 pp.

1319 Owen, Harry Goddard, b. 1905. *An Outline of the Career of
Madame Marcella Sembrich*. Bolton, N.Y.: Sembrich Memorial Association,
1940. 16 pp. Illustrated.

1320 ———. *A Recollection of Marcella Sembrich*. Bolton-on-Lake
George, N.Y.: The Marcella Sembrich Memorial, 1950. 79 pp. Illustrated.

This profusely illustrated, handsomely printed little volume,
together with the same author's article under the same title (1969,
q.v.), are among the few works written in permanent form about this
much beloved and honored Polish singer, the teacher of Dusolina
Giannini, Queena Mario, Maria Jeritza, Alma Gluck and many others.
Unfortunately, the text is badly organized and poorly written; still
it is a delightful memento because of its excellent illustrations
and quality printing. A full discography is found under the 1969
reference. WRM

1320-a ————. "A Recollection of Marcella Sembrich." *The Record Collector* XVIII, nos. 5 and 6 (May 1969), 99-138. Illustrated. Discography, pp. 110-138.

This all too brief account, together with the same author's 1950 work (q.v.) which appeared under the same title, are two of the few writings that have been published on the career of this important singer. Includes "The Recordings of Marcella Sembrich," an essay and discography by W.R. Moran. The 1950 publication does not contain the discography. WRM

See also items 1615, 1658, 1662, 1663, 1792, 1803, 1804, 1805

SHACKLOCK, CONSTANCE, b. 1913

See item 1544

SHERIDAN, ELIZABETH ANN (LINLEY), 1754-1792

1321 Black, Clementina. *The Linleys of Bath*. London: M. Secker, 1911. 339 pp. Illustrated.

SHERWIN, AMY FRANCIS, 1855-1935

1322 Fysh, Ann. *The Sherwin Family of Van Dieman's Land*. Launceston, Tasmania: Foot & Playsted, 1965. 41 pp. Illustrated. Bibliography. Title page reads: "The Early Days of the Sherwin Family of 'Sherwood', Bothwell, Tasmania, and 'Alica Place', Launceston."

Concerned with family history, there is one chapter (pp. 21-27) devoted to "The Tasmanian Nightingale." The material is taken from an article in *Parade Magazine* (September 1963). Discovered by a member of a small traveling opera company, Amy Sherwin made her debut, without benefit of any formal study, as Norina in *Don Pasquale* in Hobart, on May 1, 1878. She accompanied the company to Melbourne, where she was a sensation. She sang in New Zealand in 1878, in the United States 1879-81, and made her debut at Drury Lane in 1883 after formal study in Frankfurt and Paris. Some of the data in this account are in error. For a more accurate chronology of her career, see Mackenzie, item 1687, pp. 68-73. WRM

SHKAFER, V.P.

1323 Shkafer, V.P. *Sorok let na stsene russkoi opery. Vospominaniia 1890-1930*. In Russian. Leningrad, 1936. Unverified; data obtained from secondary literature.

SHPILLER, NATAL'IA DMITRIEVNA, b. 1909

1324 Moscow. Gosudarstvennyi akademicheskii Bol'shoi teatr. *Natal'ia Dmitrievna Shpiller*. In Russian. Moskva: Iskusstvo, 1953. Unpaged.

A brief biography followed by many illustrations. Her repertory included the major roles of Russian operas--e.g., Tatiana, Antonida (*Life for the Tzar*), Olga (*Pshkovitianka*), Countess--along with Cio-Cio-San, Marguerite, Mathilde, Micaela, etc.

SIBONI, GIUSEPPE, 1780-1839

1325 Monti, Attilio. *Giuseppe Siboni, tenore e musicista forlivese. Commemorazione letta alla Società corale "Vincenzo Bellini" di Forlì, il 2 luglio 1922.* In Italian. Forlì: Stabilimento tipografico romagnolo, 1922. 23 pp. Illustrated.

SILJA, ANJA, b. 1940

1326 Heinzelmann, Josef. *Anja Silja.* In German. Rembrandt-Reihe, Bd. 52. Berlin: Rembrandt, 1965. 58 pp. Illustrated.

SILLS, BEVERLY, b. 1929

1327 Sills, Beverly. *Bubbles: A Self-Portrait.* Indianapolis: Bobbs-Merrill, 1976. 240 pp. Illustrated. Index, pp. 233-240.

The chatty style of Sills's autobiography reflects the personality known from her many talk show appearances, interviews, and radio and television programs. The story of the artist is skillfully intertwined with the life story of the private person. The profusely illustrated book touches on all the highways, by-ways and major stops of her slow but steady rise to stardom. The book is attractively designed and beautifully printed. The first printing of the first edition contains the amusing misprint in the opening line: "When I was only three ... I sang my first aria in pubic."

1327-a ————. *Bubbles: A Self-Portrait.* New York: Warner Books, 1978. 260 pp. Illustrated. Index.

Paperback edition of the one published by Bobbs-Merrill in 1976 (q.v.).

1328 ————. *Bubbles: An Encore.* New York: Grosset & Dunlap, 1981. 280 pp. Illustrated. Index, pp. 273-280.

A listener treated to an *encore* will not be surprised to hear the same piece repeated. A reader, confronted with the subtitle "an encore," is stunned to find the unaltered text of a previously published book. It is a cheap publisher's gimmick and it is surprising that the singer agreed to it. As every "encore" differs somewhat from the first rendition, this reprinting of the 1976 edition of *Bubbles* has an Epilogue by Harvey E. Phillips that brings the Sills story up to 1981. This newly typeset section has its own fresh illustrations added. Unfortunately, with the exception of the color shots, the rest of the book is a straight photo-offset reproduction of the corrected first edition and it suffers from the inevitable loss of printing quality and clarity of detail in the excellent illustrations.

See also items 1654, 1758

SILVERI, PAOLO, b. 1913

See item 1544

SIMÁNDY, JÓZSEF, b. 1916

1329 Simándy, Jószef, and László Dalos. *Bánk bán elmondja....* In Hungarian. Budapest: Zeneműkiadó, 1983. 307 pp. Illustrated.

The autobiography of the most versatile tenor in postwar Hungary, much admired for his Italianate voice and elegant acting. The book contains the artistic wisdom of four decades spent on the operatic and concert stages in Hungary and abroad. Of particular interest to the researcher is the strict chronology of the major musical events in his career, all of them identified by exact date. Simándy allows his personal life to intrude in his narrative only if it has a bearing on his career; his undue modesty deprives the reader of getting to know him off stage.

See also item 1740

SLADEN, VICTORIA, b. 1910

1330 Sladen, Victoria. *Singing My Way.* London: Rockliff, 1951. 117 pp. Illustrated. Index, pp. 113-117.

London-born Victoria Sladen was a secretary when she won a scholarship to Trinity College of Music. There she decided on a singing career, which she pursued with study in Berlin. Her London debut was in a not-too-well received recital at Wigmore Hall, but during her stage debut when she sang opera in vaudeville she attracted the powers at Sadler's Wells. She made her debut with them as Cio-Cio-San in *Madame Butterfly.* Soon she had both Mimi and Musetta behind her, as well as Giorgetta, Lauretta, Santuzza, Pamina, Donna Anna, Octavian, Eva and Tosca (which she sang thirteen times in the 1952 season). She joined the ranks at Covent Garden in 1947. This book is the story of her career, written to prove that it can still be done in England. The book is laced with practical advice to young singers. WRM

SLEZAK, LEO, 1873-1946

1331-T Slezak, Leo. *Mani kopotie raksti.* In Latvian. N.p.: Grāmatu draugs, 1971. 239 pp.

The Latvian translations of *Meine sämtlichen Werke* (q.v.) and *Der Wortbruch* (q.v.). There is no indication of translator in the book.

1332 ———. *Mein Lebensmärchen.* In German. München: R. Piper, 1948. 206 pp.

"My life's fairy tale" is Slezak's posthumously published autobiographical work. It was written during his lonely days at Tegernsee, when the war and his growing infirmity kept him homebound and, eventually, bedridden. He finished the book only three weeks before he died. It was prepared for publication by his daughter, Margarete, who also wrote the foreword. The book is not only a retelling of his life story but, essentially, a loving tribute to his wife of over four decades. She passed away two years before death released Slezak from the unabating grief over her loss. Theirs was, reportedly, a perfect marriage; that is why Slezak entitles the chapter when she came into his life, "My life's fairy tale begins." The retelling of how he proposed to her remains a classic. Having spoken to her only once before, he stopped her on her way to a ten o'clock rehearsal with the line "Miss, you must marry me, I love you." There are many references to his career and to distinguished colleagues: Lilli and Lotte Lehmann, Burian, Caruso, Zenatello, Tauber. Slezak's special brand of humor permeates the narrative, but tears of sorrow are often mixed with tears of laughter.

1332-a ————. *Mein Lebensmärchen; Autobiographie eines Lebens-künstlers.* In German. Fischer Bücherei, no. 214. Frankfurt: Fischer Bücherei, 1958. 162 pp.

1332-b ————. *Mein Lebensmärchen.* Mit 42 Zeichnungen von Franziska Bilek. In German. Wien?: Büchergilde Gutenberg, 1960? 324 pp. Illustrated.

1332-c ————. *Mein Lebensmärchen.* Mit 42 Zeichnungen von Franziska Bilek. In German. München: Deutscher Taschenbuch Verlag, 1965. 186 pp. Illustrated.

1333 ————. *Mein lieber Bub. Briefe eines besorgten Vaters.* Herausgegeben von Walter Slezak. In German. München: Piper Verlag, 1966. 322 pp. Illustrated.

This is a selection from the hundreds of letters Slezak wrote to his actor son, Walter, in America, between 1934 and his death in 1946. One must be grateful to Walter Slezak for sharing these very touching, very personal documents of his great father with the world. In the son's own words (quoted from *his* autobiography) "this great perception, intelligence, decency, his wonderful humanity, his love of music and above all his worshipful adoration for his [wife] Elsa shimmers through every page with luminescent radiance." This statement is no exaggeration prompted by filial love. It is an accurate description of these letters written by a man who finished only eight grades, but had the inborn literary gift to put all of himself into anything he wrote. From these letters the reader can ascertain that he was--to use the appropriate German expression--a "Mensch." This volume deserves to be translated into English. It is surprising that it hasn't been done yet. (Piper Verlag published an abridged edition in 1981.)

1333-a ————. *Mein lieber Bub. Briefe eines besorgten Vaters.* Herausgegeben von Walter Slezak. Wien: Buchgemeinschaft Donauland, 1968. 330 pp.

1334 ————. *Meine sämtlichen Werke.* In German. Berlin: E. Rowohlt, 1922. 263 pp.

Following a long and distinguished international singing career that spanned thirty years (1896-1926), the celebrated Moravian tenor,

Leo Slezak, became a well-known character actor in German movies. He also had a third career: that of a successful writer. A born humorist and *raconteur*, the *göttliche Leo*, the personification of *Gemütlichkeit*, became Vienna's darling because of the instant success of his books which never, absolutely never, have been out of print. This volume contains autobiographical chapters of a musical nature and many references to his career. As the title suggests, he meant it to be his "collected works," but the enormous success that followed made him "break his word" three more times. This is probably the most enjoyable, light-hearted and entertaining book ever penned by an opera singer. All of Slezak's books went through many editions, at times with more than one publisher.

1334-a ———. *Meine sämtlichen Werke*, edited with exercises and vocabulary by Roy Temple House and Johannes Malthaner. In German. "School edition." New York: H. Holt, 1937. vi, 188, lxxiv. Illustrated.

1335 ———. *Meine sämtlichen Werke. Der Wortbruch*. In German. Stuttgart: Deutsche Verlags-Anstalt, 1927. 335 pp. Illustrated.

1336-T ———. *Összes müveim. A szószegés*. Translated by Emi Gáspár. In Hungarian. Budapest: Ruszkabányai Könyvkiadó, n.d. 319 pp.

The Hungarian translation of *Meine sämtlichen Werke* (q.v.) and *Der Wortbruch* (q.v.).

1337 ———. *Rückfall*. In German. Stuttgart: Rowohlt, 1940. 278 pp. Illustrated.

The "Relapse" is the third collection of writings by Leo Slezak. The tone and style is the same as in the first two books, yet comparing it with his previous works one senses a mild strain behind the smile and cheerfulness, as if the singer-author felt the impending collapse of his world because of world politics and old age.

1338-T ———. *Song of Motley; Being the Reminiscences of a Hungry Tenor*. London: W. Hodge, 1938. 302 pp. Illustrated.

Translations of *Meine sämtlichen Werke* (q.v.) and *Der Wortbruch* (q.v.). The translator is not identified in the book.

1338-T-a ———. *Song of Motley*. Opera Biographies. New York: Arno Press, 1977. 302 pp. Illustrated.

Translations of *Meine sämtlichen Werke* (q.v.) and *Der Wortbruch* (q.v.). Reprint of the 1938 edition published by W. Hodge, London.

1339-T ———. *Ujabb büneim*. Translated by Emi Gáspár. In Hungarian. Budapest: Ruszkabányai Könyvkiadó, 1943. 218 pp.

The Hungarian translation of *Rückfall* (q.v.).

1340 ———. *Der Wortbruch*. In German. Berlin: E. Rowohlt, 1927. 282 pp. Illustrated.

"The broken word" declares the title. Although Slezak promised his readers never to write anything beyond his one-volume "collected works" (q.v.), these are further reminiscences in much the same vein as his first book. The singer's charm and fine sense of humor radiate from every chapter. This volume contains the famous opera guide which capitalizes on the nonsensical aspects of some opera plots. The hilarity lies in Slezak's inimitable style.

1341 Klinenberger, Ludwig, b. 1873. *Leo Slezak. Ein Beitrag zur Geschichte der dramatischen Gesangkunst.* In German. Wien: Paul Knepler, 1910. 23 pp.

1342 Leitenberger, Friedrich Alfons. *Der göttliche Leo; ein Volksbuch über Leo Slezak.* In German. Wien: K. Klebert, 1948. 64 pp. Illustrated.

1343 Morgan, Paul, b. 1886. *Prominententeich; Abenteuer und Erlebnisse mit Stars, Sternchen und allerlei Gelichter; geschildert von Paul Morgan, Arm in Arm mit Leo Slezak, Fritz Grünbaum, Szöke Szakáll, Otto Wallburg und Adele Sandrock.* In German. Berlin: Amonesta-Verlag, 1934. 251 pp. Illustrated.

See also items 1344, 1345, 1346, 1811

SLEZAK, MARGARETE, 1901-1953

1344 Slezak, Margarete. *Der Apfel fällt nicht weit vom Stamm.* With 45 drawings by Franziska Bilek. In German. München: R. Piper, 1953. 233 pp. Illustrated.

"The apple does not fall far from the tree" boldly declares the title. That well may be, but this book is disappointing not only when compared with Leo Slezak's witty and charming literary efforts, but also in view of the rich material at the author's disposal which she left largely unexploited. Her stories about Papa Leo concentrate unnecessarily on his image as an amusing prankster and little else. Even though Margarete was a singer herself who sang in the operatic centers of the German speaking countries and South America (and appeared in *La Juive*, *Otello* and *Tannhäuser* partnered by her father), she barely mentions her own singing career and even less her father's. The main interest of the book lies in the details concerning the Slezak household. Curiously, Chapter 3, entitled "My Big Brother" (e.g., Walter Slezak), consists of one line, "Dieses Kapitel muss *leider* ausfallen," probably an "in" reference to the falling out of siblings. The story of her acquaintanceship with Hitler corresponds with the Führer's known penchant for being surrounded by young artists. (Leo hated Hitler. Once, at a state function he was obliged to attend, he was stuffing himself when Hitler came to his table and recounted the performances in which he heard him sing during his Vienna years. Leo cut him short: "My dear Führer, let me eat now; you can tell me all about it later.")

SLEZAK, WALTER, 1902-1983

1345 Slezak, Walter. *Wann geht der nächste Schwan?* In German. München: R. Piper & Co., 1968. 351 pp.

1346 ————. *What Time's the Next Swan? By Walter Slezak, as Told to Smith-Corona Model 88E.* Garden City, N.Y.: Doubleday, 1962. 227 pp. Illustrated.

Walter Slezak, one-time matinée idol, stage and movie actor, and quasi opera singer (he "sang" Zsupán at the Met in the 1959 production of the *Gypsy Baron*), inherited not only his famous father's features, but also his sense of humor. In his entertaining memoirs he admits to the life-long hero-worship he had for his Heldentenor father Leo, and thus devotes long passages to him. A most enjoyable book, and one wishes one could read all the passages that fell victim to editorial whims at Doubleday.

SLOBODSKAYA, ODA, 1888-1970

1347 Leonard, Maurice. *Slobodskaya: A Biography of Oda Slobodskaya.* London: Gollancz, 1979. 142 pp. Illustrated. Index, pp. 137-142. Discography, pp. 126-128.

Slobodskaya made her debut as Lisa in St. Petersburg in 1918. In 1922 she went to Paris where she created the role of Parasha in Stravinsky's *Mavra*. She made her London debut in 1931, and had a career there as a music hall and operetta singer in 1931 and 1932 under the name of Odali Careno. Her operatic appearances were at La Scala and the Colón in Buenos Aires. She was a respected teacher in London for many years. Slobodskaya was a truly amazing person, with a commanding personality on the stage and off. Unfortunately, Maurice Leonard, whose chance meeting with the singer led to a biographical collaboration and a strange friendship that lasted until her death, fails to provide a complete picture of the artist. The book is filled with generalities and very few facts and dates. The publisher states that the author had access to her personal papers; perhaps important documents relating to her career were no longer in her possession or were in a language inaccessible to her collaborator. The work ends with a group of short reminiscences by Eva Turner, Ivor Newton, Desmond Shaw-Taylor, Sylvia Fischer and Anatole Fistoulari, for which we can be grateful. The discography omits matrix numbers and gives issue rather than recording dates. WRM

SOBINOV, LEONID VITAL'EVICH, 1872-1934

1348 Sobinov, Leonid Vital'evich. *Pis'ma, stat'i, rechi, vyskazyvaniia.* Moskva: Iskusstvo, 1970. 2 vols. Illustrated.

1349 Boiarskii, IAkov O., editor. *L.V. Sobinov; zhizn i tvorchestvo. Sbornik statei.* In Russian. Moskva: Muzgiz, 1937. 267 pp. Bibliography, pp. 247-258.

1350 L'vov, Mikhail L'vovich, 1887-1957. *L.V. Sobinov.* In Russian. Mastera Bol'shogo teatra. Moskva: Muzgiz, 1951. 101 pp. Illustrated.

1351 ————. *Leonid Vital'evich Sobinov, 1872-1934.* In Russian. Moskva: Iskusstvo, 1945. 38 pp. Illustrated.

1352 Moscow. Gosudarstvennyi akademicheskii Bol'shoi teatr. *Leonid Vital'evich Sobinov*. In Russian. Moskva: Iskusstvo, 1953. Unpaged.
A short biography of the singer followed by many illustrations.

1353 Nemirovich-Danchenko, Vladimir Ivanovich, 1858-1943, editor. *Leonod Vitalievich Sobinov, 1898-1923: iubileinyi sbornik*. In Russian. Moskva: Gosizdat, 1923. 69 pp. Illustrated.

1354 Remezov, Ivan Ivanovich. *Leonod Vital'evich Sobinov; k 25-letiiu so dnia smerti*. In Russian. Muzykanty-ispolniteli. Moskva: Gos. muzykal'noe izd-vo, 1960. 137 pp. Illustrated.

1355 Sukhorukov, V.V. *Sobinov*. *Moi studencheskie vospominaniia o nem*. In Russian. Moskva: Pershinoi, 1941.

1356 Vladykina-Bachinskaia, Nina Mikhailovna. *Leonod Vital'evich Sobinov*. In Russian. Massovaia muzykal'naia biblioteka. Moskva: Gos. muzykal'noe izd-vo, 1956. 42 pp.

1357 ————. *Sobinov*. In Russian. Zhizn' zamechatel'nykh liudei; seriia biografii, vyp. 9 (257). Moskva: Molodaia gvardiia, 1958. 301 pp. Illustrated. Bibliography, pp. 299-301. Republished in 1960.

See also item 1686

SÖDERSTRÖM, ELISABETH, b. 1926

1358 Söderström, Elisabeth. *I min tonart*. In Swedish. Stockholm: Bonnier, 1978. 182 pp.

1359-T ————. *In My Own Key*. Translated by Joan Tate. London: Hamish Hamilton, 1979. 102 pp. Illustrated.
The English translation of *I min tonart* (q.v.). This little book is hardly the conventional singer's autobiography. No long chapters are devoted to childhood and growing up. Instead, it is a rather breezy account of the day-to-day life of an opera singer who views opera from backstage. There is much advice to young singers of the "how I do it" variety, all with a light touch. WRM

SOLA, WÄINÖ, b. 1883

1360 Sola, Wäinö. *Wäinö Sola kertoo*. In Finnish. Porvoo: Werner Söderström, 1951-52. 2 vols. Illustrated. Index.

SOLDENE, EMILY, 1844?-1912

1361 Soldene, Emily. *My Theatrical and Musical Recollections*. London: Downey, 1897. xviii, 315 pp. Illustrated.
Born in a suburb of London, Emily Soldene claims to have been inspired to a life of music after hearing Patti and Santley. She made

her concert debut at St. James Hall in 1864, and her first stage appearance at Drury Lane in 1865. Her early career was in London music
halls, and her specialty became the operettas of Offenbach. For some
years she had her own "English Opera Bouffe Company." She was frank
enough to admit that her success was not exactly a triumph of pure
art, as she selected her chorus for a minimum of voice and a maximum
of personal pulchritude. She toured the United States, New Zealand
and Australia. At the time of publication her memoirs were considered "naughty," although by modern standards they are tame indeed.
WRM

SONTAG, HENRIETTE, 1806-1854

1362 Gautier, Théophile, 1811-1872. *L'ambassadrice. Biographie de
la comtesse Rossi.* In French. Paris: F. Sartorius, 1850. 35 pp.

1363 Gundling, Julius, 1828-1890. *Henriette Sontag. Künstlerlebens
Anfänge in Federzeichnungen.* In German. Leipzig: F.W. Grunow, 1861.
2 vols.

1364 *Life of Henriette Sontag, Countess de Rossi.* With interesting
sketches by Scudo, Hector Berlioz, Louis Boerne, Adolphe Adam, Marie
Aycard, Julie de Margueritte, Prince Puckler-Muskau, and Theophile
Gautier. New York: Stringer and Townsend, 1852. 63 pp. Illustrated.

This is the re-publication of *A Memoir of the Countess de Rossi*
(q.v.), with some abridgements and with additional sketches by
various hands.

1365 *A Memoir of the Countess de Rossi, (Madame Sontag).* London:
Pub. by Mr. Mitchell, 1849. 111 pp.

1366 Pirchan, Emil, b. 1884. *Henriette Sontag, die Sängerin des
Biedermeier.* In German. Wien: W. Frick, 1946. 270 pp. Illustrated.
Bibliography, pp. 257-266.

1367 Rellstab, Ludwig (Heinrich Friedrich Ludwig), 1799-1860.
Henriette, oder Die schöne Sängerin. Eine Geschichte unserer Tage,
von Freimund Zuschauer (pseud.). In German. Leipzig: F.L. Herbig,
1826. 174 pp.

A satirical romance, with Henriette Sontag as the heroine.

1368 Russell, Frank. *Queen of Song; the Life of Henrietta Sontag.*
New York: Exposition Press, 1964. 282 pp. Bibliography, pp. 281-282.

1369 Stümcke, Heinrich, 1872-1923. *Henriette Sontag; ein Lebens-
und Zeitbild.* In German. Schriften der Gesellschaft für Theatergeschichte, Bd. XX. Berlin: Gesellschaft für Theatergeschichte, 1913.
xvi, 312 pp. Illustrated.

See also items 1562, 1597, 1612, 1615, 1668, 1669, 1694, 1745

SOOT, FRITZ, 1878-1965

See item 1743

SOUZAY, GÉRARD, b. 1918

See item 1813

SPANI, HINA, 1896-1969

1370 Moran, William R., and Ricardo Turro. "Hina Spani." *The Record Collector* IX, no. 4 (September 1954), 80-96, 98-99. Illustrated. Repertory. Discography, pp. 98-99.

This Argentine soprano was one of the principal singers at the Teatro Colón in Buenos Aires from 1915 to 1940. Her debut at La Scala was in 1915, and she devoted most of her operatic career and later concert appearances to the southern hemisphere. Her repertoire was large, but devoted for the most part to the works of Verdi and Puccini, and composers of the verismo school. She created a number of modern roles in Italy as well as in the Argentine. Her recordings are greatly admired by collectors. This article was written after several interviews with Mme. Spani, and her personal scrapbooks were placed at the disposal of the authors.

SPENNERT, JENNY JULIANA, b. 1879

1371 Spennert, Jenny Juliana. *Elämäni ja taiteilijanurani.* In Finnish. Helsinki: Oy Suomen Kirja, 1945. 256 pp. Illustrated.

Autobiography of the Finnish soprano who was heard in Monte Carlo as Musetta, Desdemona, Laura, Venus in Saint-Saëns's *Hélène* and other roles, with casts that included Rousselière, Chaliapin, Ruffo, Van Dyck. She was also well known as a concert artist in Scandinavia. She recorded for The Gramophone Company in Paris, in 1913. WRM

1372 ⸺⸺. *Mitt liv och min sång.* In Swedish. Helsingfors: Söderström & Co., 1946. 206 pp. Illustrated.

SPIES, HERMINE, 1857-1893

1373 (Spies, Minna). *Hermine Spies; ein Gedenkbuch für ihre Freunde, von ihrer Schwester* [Marie Spies]; mit einem Vorwort von Heinrich Bulthaupt. In German. Stuttgart: G.J. Göschen, 1894. viii, 300 pp. Illustrated.

1373-a ⸺⸺. *Hermine Spies; ein Gedenkbuch für ihre Freunde, von ihrer Schwester* [Marie Spies]; mit einem Vorwort von Heinrich Bulthaupt. 3., verb. und durch eine reihe ungedruckter Briefe von Johannes Brahms und Klaus Groth verm. Auflage. In German. Leipzig: G.J. Göschen, 1905. 316 pp. Illustrated. The "Vorwort" is signed "Minna Spiess"; the cataloging information of the New York University library shows the sister's name as: Marie Spies.

STADER, MARIA, b. 1911

1374 Stader, Maria, and Robert D. Abraham. *Nehmt meinen Dank; Erinnerungen.* München: Kindler, 1979. 460 pp. Illustrated. Bibliography, p. 426. Repertory, pp. 427-443. Index, pp. 453-458. Discography, pp. 444-452.

STAGNO, ROBERTO, 1836-1897

1375 Stagno Bellincioni, Bianca, b. 1888. *Roberto Stagno e Gemma Bellincioni intimi.* In Italian. Firenze: Casa editrice Monsalvato, 1943. 172 pp. Illustrated.

Daughter Bianca's loving memorial to her parents, Roberto Stagno and Gemma Bellincioni. This book tells the life story of these famous singers, creators of *Cavalleria rusticana.* The writing is fluid, the narrative disjointed. Written in 1942, it concludes with daughter Bianca's operatic debut in Graz, in 1909.

1376 ————. *Roberto Stagno e Gemma Bellincioni imtimi.* (Published with:) Gemma Bellincioni: *Io e il palcoscenico;* with a discography by W.R. Moran. In Italian. New York: Arno Press, 1977. 172, 137 pp. Discography, p. 140.

Reprints of the 1943 edition published by Monsalvato, Firenze (q.v.), and the 1920 edition published by R. Quinteri, Milano, item 96; William R. Moran's discography was prepared for this edition.

See also items 1733, 1757

STENBORG, CARL

See item 1088

STENHAMMAR, FREDRIKA, 1836-1880

1377 Stenhammar, Fredrika. *Brev. Utg. av Elsa Stenhammar.* In Swedish. Stockholm: Geber, 1958. 187 pp. Illustrated.

STEPHANESCU, GEORGE

1378 Stoianov, Carmen Antoaneta. *George Stephanescu.* In Rumanian. Bucureşti: Editura Muzicală, 1981. 222 pp. Illustrated.

STERLING, ANTOINETTE

1379 Sterling, Mackinlay. *Antoinette Sterling.* London: Hutchinson, 1906. 340 pp.

See also item 1658

STEVENS, RISË, b. 1913

1380 Crichton, Kyle Samuel, b. 1896. *Subway to the Met: Risë
Stevens' Story.* Garden City, N.Y.: Doubleday, 1959. 240 pp. Illustrated.

Risë Stevens's complimentary remarks notwithstanding, this biography suffers from the heavy hand of the collaborator. He seems to
have learned all he knows about opera and singing in the course of
this collaboration; whether this is the case or not, it is bad enough
if it *seems* that way. Also, he does not have a style, he has a
literary mannerism that gets in the way of an interesting life story
worth reading. It should be retold by someone else and brought up
to date to include Miss Stevens's many activities beyond 1959.

See also item 1792

STEWART, NELLIE, 1855-1931

1381 Stewart, Nellie. *My Life's Story.* Sydney: John Sands, 1923.
xx, 314 pp. Illustrated.

Known as The First Lady of the Australian Theater, Nellie Stewart
was the Yum-Yum in the first performance of *The Mikado* in Australia
in 1886. She came of a theatrical family, and first appeared on the
stage at the age of three with Charles and Ellen Kean. Her first
singing lessons were with David Miranda, father of future prima
donnas' Lalla and Beatrice. In 1879 she started on a world tour with
her family with a variety show called "Rainbow Revels." The company
played first in Calcutta and Bombay, staying three months in each
city; thence to London, where the company played at the Crystal Palace.
During their stay in London, Nellie studied voice for a time with
Alberto Randegger. Returning to Australia by way of the United
States, where the family toured a number of small towns, Nellie sang
the lead in practically every light opera from *Orphée aux Enfers* to
Patience. In 1888, during Australia's Centenary Year, she sang
Marguerite in 24 consecutive performances of Gounod's *Faust.* In
thirteen years, she sang in 35 comic operas, often for extended runs
in Sydney, Melbourne, Adelaide and Perth; then Hobart, Auckland and
Wellington, New Zealand. By the mid-1890s she began to have vocal
problems--small wonder--but she turned to acting, and made a second
career, excelling in romantic comedy. Her detailed memoirs are a
treasure-house of information on the history of the stage in Australia from the 1870s to the 1920s. WRM

STEWART, THOMAS, b. 1928

See item 1654

STIGNANI, EBE, 1904-1974

1382 Francheschi, Bruno de, and Pier Fernando Mondini. *Ebe Stignani;
una voce e il suo mondo.* In Italian. Imola: Grafiche Galeati, 1980.
231 pp. Illustrated. Repertory, pp. 178-179. Index, pp. 221-227.

Discography, pp. 180–192. Chronology, pp. 148–174. Debuts, pp. 175–177.

Born of the apparent devotion of a fan who befriended Stignani in the last three years of her life, this book is a curious mixture of a cornucopia of factual information and topical gaps. Her personal life is disposed of in a one-and-a-quarter-page chapter entitled "Birth and Studies"; then follows a season-by-season review of her career in such detail that it suggests the author's total access to the singer's scrapbooks and other memorabilia. All the important reviews of the international press are quoted in Italian and shown in photoreproduction. There are many fine illustrations, a seemingly complete chronology (with casts!) of her appearances, her repertory, a simple discography (without take or matrix numbers), and 18 pages of testimonial letters from singers, conductors and musicologists, from Barbieri to Zeani. A beautifully produced book whose reference value transcends the language barrier.

STOCKHAUSEN, JULIUS, 1826–1906

1383 Stockhausen, Julius. *Der Buchstabe G und die sieben Regeln des Herrn H. Dorn nebst einer vocal- und consonanten-Tabelle.* In German. Frankfurt am Main: Alt und Neumann, 1880. 56 pp.

1384 ————. *Gesangs-Methode.* In German. Leipzig: C.F. Peters, 1884. 155 pp.

1385 ————. *Gesangstechnik und Stimmbildung. Ausgabe für hohe Stimme.* In German. Leipzig: C.F. Peters, 1890? 115 pp.

1386 ————. *Gesangstechnik und Stimmbildung. Ausgabe für tiefe Stimme.* In German. Leipzig: C.F. Peters, 1884? viii, 117 pp.

1387 ————. *Julius Stockhausen, der Sänger des deutschen Liedes, nach Dokumenten seiner Zeit dargestellt von Julia Wirth, geb. Stockhausen.* In German. Frankfurt am Main, Historische Kommision, Frankfurter Lebensbilder, Band 10. Frankfurt: Englert und Schlosser, 1927. 537 pp. Illustrated. Bibliography, pp. 522–525. Repertory, pp. 489–498. Index, pp. 526–537.

1388-T ————. *A Method of Singing.* Translated by Sophie Löwe. Novello's Music Primers and Educational Series. London: Novello, 1884. 135 pp.

English translation of his *Gesangsmethode* (q.v.).

1389 ————. *Das Sänger-Alphabet; oder, Die Sprachelemente als Stimm-Bildungsmittel.* In German. Leipzig: B. Senff, 1901. 29 pp.

1390 Wirth, Julia (Stockhausen). *Unverlierbare Kindheit.* In German. Lebendige Welt; Erlebnisbücher und Tatsachenromane. Stuttgart: A. Spemann, 1949. 157 pp. Illustrated.

STOLTZ, ROSINE, 1815-1903

1391 Bord, Gustave, b. 1852. *Rosina Stoltz (de l'Académie de musique) (Victoire Noel) (1815-1903).* In French. Profils d'artistes. Paris: H. Daragon, 1909. 237 pp. Illustrated. Repertory, p. 236.

1392 Cantinjou, Corneille. *Les adieux de Madame Stoltz. Sa retraite de l'opéra, sa vie théatrale, ses concurrentes, son intérieur.* In French. Paris: Breteau, 1847. 72 pp. Illustrated.

1393 Pérignon, Eugénie. *Rosine Stoltz, Maxime, Mlles Lavoye.* In French. Paris, 1847. 51 pp. Illustrated. Contains a notice of Madame Stoltz only. A portrait is inserted.

STOLZ, TERESA, 1834-1902

1394 Zoppi, Umberto. *Angelo Mariani, Giuseppe Verdi e Teresa Stolz in un carteddio inedito....* In Italian. I Grandi musicisti italiani e stranieri. Milano: N.p., 1947. 402 pp. Illustrated.

STORCHIO, ROSINA, 1876-1945

See item 1731

STRACCIARI, RICCARDO, 1875-1955

See item 1731

STREICH, RITA, b. 1920

See item 1813

STREPPONI, GIUSEPPINA, 1815-1897

1395 Mùndula, Mercede. *La moglie di Verdi, Giuseppina Strepponi.* In Italian. Milano: Fratelli Treves, 1938. 317 pp. Illustrated.

1395-a ————. *La moglie di Verdi, Giuseppina Strepponi.* In Italian. Milano: Garzanti, 1941. 317 pp. Illustrated.

See also item 1620

SUCHER, ROSA (HASSELBECK), 1849-1927

1396 Sucher, Rosa Hasselbeck. *Aus meinem Leben.* In German. Breitkopf & Härtels Musikbücher. Leipzig: Breitkopf & Härtel, 1914. 95 pp. Illustrated.

See also item 1658

SUK, VIACHESLAV IVANOVICH, 1861-1933

1397 Remezov, Ivan Ivanovich. *V.I. Suk.* In Russian. Moskva: Gos. Muzykal'noe izd-vo, 1951. 61 pp. Illustrated.

SUPERVIA, CONCHITA, 1895-1936

1398 Vaudoyer, Jean Louis, b. 1883. *Dédier à l'amitié et au souvenir.* In French. Paris: Plon, 1947. 264 pp.

Contains one short chapter on Supervia. Because of the dearth of material about her it was included here.

See also item 1716

SUTHERLAND, JOAN, b. 1926

1399 Adams, Brian. *La Stupenda, a Biography of Joan Sutherland.* Melbourne: Hutchinson of Australia, 1980. 329 pp. Illustrated. Bibliography, pp. 317-318. Repertory, pp. 313-316. Index, pp. 319-329. Discography, pp. 299-312.

A detailed biography written with affection and a permissible degree of partisanship that seems to be due to admiration rather than a lack of objectivity. All the important facts relating to Sutherland's artistic and personal life are there, often in her own or husband Richard's words. The large number of excellent illustrations are in black-and-white and color. The discography is apparently complete (except for the selections re-released on 45 rpm records) up to the time of publication.

1400 Braddon, Russell. *Joan Sutherland.* New York: St. Martin's Press, 1962. 256 pp. Illustrated. Repertory, pp. 245-246. Discography, pp. 247-248.

A book-length narrative of the first half of the Sutherland story—and therein lies its value. No other full-length biography will ever again have the luxury to recount her early struggles and the seemingly endless health problems in the same detail. The book's premise is to chronicle her conquest of the four "citadels" of opera: Covent Garden, La Scala, L'Opéra (Paris) and the Metropolitan. The biography closes with her Met debut. The style is light and somewhat self-mocking, not unlike Sutherland's reported view of herself. Her gradual transformation from an overweight songster to a glamorous *prima donna assoluta* under the loving tyranny of her husband, Richard Bonynge, is well paced. Because of the date of publication, both repertory and discography are hopelessly out of date.

1401 Greenfield, Edward. *Joan Sutherland.* Recordmasters 1. London: Ian Allan, 1972. 64 pp. Illustrated. Discography, pp. 59-64. Operatic Debuts, pp. 58-59.

An ably constructed portrait of Sutherland that captures the essence of the singer, the person, the recording artist and the woman. The author's obvious affinity toward his subject does not cloud his objectivity. The repertory and discography have been rendered outdated by the passage of time.

1401-a ────. *Joan Sutherland*. New York: Drake, 1973. 64 pp. Illustrated. Operatic Debuts, pp. 58-59. Discography, pp. 59-64.

See also items 1758, 1788, 1813

SVANHOLM, SET, 1904-1964

See item 1545

SWARTHOUT, GLADYS, 1904-1969

1402 Swarthout, Gladys. *Come Soon, Tomorrow; the Story of a Young Singer*. Philadelphia: Blakiston, 1943. viii, 278 pp. Musical fiction.

SWOLFS, LAURENT, 1867-1954

1403 Swolfs, Laurent. *Souvenirs de théâtre et de coulisses*. In French. Bruxelles: H. Wellens & W. Godenne, 1950? 175 pp.

Rather than a conventional autobiography, this book by Swolf, a singer turned teacher and manager, consists of a long series of loosely knit vignettes about himself, artists and people he met or observed.

SYMINGTON, MAUDE FAY, 1878-1964

1404 Symington, Maude Fay. *Living in Awe*. Edited by Marshall Dill, Jr. San Francisco: Lawton and Alfred Kennedy, 1968. 173 pp. Illustrated.

The autobiography of the American-born soprano, Maude Fay Symington, left behind in manuscript. She studied with Aglaia Orgeni and sang for several seasons at the Royal Opera in Munich where she achieved stardom before coming to the Metropolitan. The rambling, prima donna-ish recollections are alternately fascinating and annoying despite nephew Dill's considerable skill and editorial efforts to recast the material in literary prose. The printing and book design is of the very high quality connoisseurs of fine printing have come to expect of the Kennedy firm.

SZÉKELY, MIHÁLY, 1901-1963

1405 Várnai, Péter. *Székely Mihály*. In Hungarian. Nagy magyar elöadómüvészek, 2. Budapest: Zenemükiadó, 1967. 58 pp. Illustrated.

This is the only biography of Székely, one of the few true "basso profondos" of the century. The author gives a general, somewhat sketchy overview of his career and carefully avoids any reference

to the communist regime that destroyed Székely's international career.
Upon his return home at the conclusion of the 1949–50 Met season, the
Hungarian government permanently revoked his passport. The fact that
he was to star in the role of Philip II in the opening night *Don
Carlo* of the Bing regime did not sway the authorities and he remained
captive in his own country until the end of the 1956 Revolution. Two
7" 33 rpm records inserted in the book contain eight selections from
his best roles.

See also item 1740

T

TAGLIAVINI, FERRUCCIO, b. 1913

1406 Tedeschi, Ciro. *Ferruccio Tagliavini, il signore del canto,
nuovo idolo delle folle.* In Italian. Roma: Edizioni XX secolo S.A.I.,
1942. 61 pp. Illustrated.

Not aspiring to be a full-length biography, this booklet aimed to
satisfy the public's curiosity about its new-found idol. By the time
it appeared, Tagliavini had had a successful season at La Scala, had
made his first movie (*Voglio vivere così*), was reportedly working on the
second (*La donna è mobile*), and had married soprano Pia Tassinari.
Despite its brevity, the booklet is relatively informative, giving
an outline of Tagliavini's youth, debut and early successes. The
concluding section contains excerpts from reviews. Surprisingly, this
is the only biography of the tenor to date.

See also item 1545

TAJO, ITALO, b. 1915

See item 1545

TALVELA, MARTTI, b. 1935

1407 Heikinheimo, Seppo. *Martti Talvela: jättiläisen muotokuva.*
In Finnish. Helsinki: Otava, 1978. 334 pp. Illustrated. Index.
Discography, p. 328.

See also item 14

TAKÁCS, PAULA, b. 1913

See item 1740

TAMAGNO, FRANCESCO, 1850–1905

1408 Amicis, Edmondo de, 1846–1908. *Francesco Tamagno.* In Italian.
Roma: Tip. cooperativa sociale, 1900. 16 pp. Illustrated.

1409 ———. *Francesco Tamagno. Ricordi della sua vita e annedoti interessanti*. In Italian. I nostri artisti, vol. 5. Palermo: Casa Editrice Salvatore Biondo, 1902. 23 pp. Illustrated.

A portrait that originated from meetings between the legendary tenor and the popular writer who delineates his personality with the sharp eye of a critical observer. RT

1410 Corsi, Mario, 1882-1954. *Tamagno, il più grande fenomeno canoro dell'ottocento*. In Italian. Milano: Ceschina, 1937. 214 pp. Illustrated.

A popular biography of the first interpreter of the title role of Verdi's *Otello*, which made him world famous overnight and earned him a lasting place in operatic history. Accordingly, a large portion of the book is devoted to that historical event. The quality of writing is undistinguished and factual errors diminish the book's reliability. The tenor is presented in the most favorable light without a hint of character defects, like his vanity and positively legendary stinginess. The subject deserves a more thorough, scholarly treatment. TGK

1410-a ———. *Tamagno*. With a discography by W.R. Moran. In Italian. Opera Biographies. New York: Arno Press, 1977. 214 pp. Illustrated.

Reprint of the 1937 edition published by Ceschina, Milano. The discography by William R. Moran was prepared for this edition; it consists of four unnumbered pages added at the end of the volume.

See also items 1615, 1620, 1680

TAMBERLICK, ENRICO, 1820-1889

See item 1733

TAMBURINI, ANTONIO, 1800-1876

1411 Biez, Jacques de, b. 1852. *Tamburini et la musique italienne*. In French. Paris: Tresse, 1877. iv, 128 pp. Illustrated.

Concise commemorative to Tamburini published within a year after his death, and an earnest defense of the supremacy of Italian musical art. RT

1412 Gelli-Ferraris, H. *Antonio Tamburini nel ricordo d'una nipote*. In Italian. Livorno, 1934. Unverified; information taken from the *Enciclopedia dello Spettacolo*.

See also items 1601, 1745

TASKIN, ALEXANDRE, 1853-1897

See item 1588

TAUBER, RICHARD, 1892-1948

1413 Castle, Charles, b. 1939, in collaboration with Diana Napier
Tauber. *This Was Richard Tauber.* London: W.H. Allen, 1971. 209 pp.
Illustrated. Index, pp. 202-209.

A curiously crafted biography that relies heavily on a very large
collection of unpublished letters, most of them from the personal
archives of Diana Napier Tauber, the late tenor's wife. Some of these
are most intimate: a large number of the letters were written by the
women Tauber loved, simultaneously and known to each other. The
writing is factual and detached, never penetrating or moving. Yet
the narrative that connects the epistolary material presents the life
story complete. Generously illustrated with well-chosen pictorial
material.

1414 Korb, Willi. *Richard Tauber. Biographie eines unvergessenes
Sängers.* In German. Wien: Europäischer Verlag, 1966. 171 pp.
Illustrated. Discography, pp. 149-171.

1415 Ludwigg, Heinz, editor. *Richard Tauber*; Vorwort von Leo Blech.
In German. Gesicht und Maske, Bd. 1. Berlin: O. Elsner, 1928. 95
pp. Illustrated.

1416 Schneidereit, Otto. *Richard Tauber: ein Leben, eine Stimme.*
In German. Berlin: Lied der Zeit Musikverlag, 1974. 166 pp. Illustrated.

1417 Tauber, Diana (Napier). *My Heart and I.* London: Evans Bros.,
1959. 208 pp. Illustrated.

With only slight overlap, yet filling some gaps in Diana Tauber's
first book about her husband (*Richard Tauber*, q.v.), this work is,
at times, almost an embarrassment to the reader in the intimate picture it displays of the twelve years of marriage between a world-
famous operetta, motion picture and concert artist and a less-than-
successful film actress. She is most frank about her own problems on
the stage and screen, and the extracurricular feminine attachments
which Richard maintained after their marriage. She tells unashamedly
of some of the *faux pas* which she committed from time to time because
of her lack of musical knowledge, and as if to emphasize the point she
throws in a few fresh ones, like "Puccini's original score" of
Pagliacci, as if to prove to the reader she really means it! WRM

1418 ———. *Richard Tauber.* With a foreword by Sir Charles B.
Cochran. Glasgow: Art and Educational Publishers, 1949. 237 pp.
Illustrated. Index, pp. 235-237.

The life story of Tauber written by his widow and published a year
after his death. The affection and understanding with which she
writes about her late husband is especially admirable in view of the
fact that in the last years of his life she had to share him with
another woman, a sad circumstance about which she remains discreetly—
and nobly—silent. The extensive details of Tauber's life prior to
their marriage suggest conscientious research or the contribution of
a foreign hand. There are few specifics about Tauber's early operatic

career, since Diana wasn't there and according to her own admission she was completely uneducated in matters operatic.

1418-a ————. *Richard Tauber*; with a foreword by Sir Charles B. Cochran. Da Capo Press Music Reprint Series. New York: Da Capo Press, 1980. 237 pp. Illustrated. Index, pp. 235-237.

Reprint of the 1949 edition published by Art and Educational Publishers, Glasgow (q.v.).

See also item 1743

TEBALDI, RENATA, b. 1922

1419 Casanova, Carlamaria. *Renata Tebaldi. La voce d'angelo.* In Italian. Milano: Electa, 1981. 254 pp. Illustrated. Bibliography, p. 248. Repertory, pp. 209-211. Index, pp. 249-253. Discography, pp. 246-247. Chronology of Performances, pp. 212-245.

A book obviously written with the consent of the singer. Thus one gets to know for the first time the Tebaldi who lifts the veil of reserve she has kept on her private life. A worthwhile publication. The chronology is clear and complete, the discography lists the complete operas only. RT

1420 Harris, Kenn, b. 1947. *Renata Tebaldi.* New York: Drake Publishers, 1974. xiii, 161 pp. Illustrated. Discography, pp. 155-161.

Born out of a fan's admiration, this book relies as much on published material as on personal experience and interviews. Harris's acknowledged devotion to Tebaldi interferes only minimally with his judgment of her person and not at all regarding her singing. The discussion of her roles is mostly based on her American appearances and primarily those attended by Harris. The individual analysis of her recordings is a thorough effort. The apparently complete discography excludes her three excellent 78 rpm records made for Decca.

1421 Panofsky, Walter. *Renata Tebaldi.* In German. Rembrandt Reihe, 32. Berlin: Rembrandt Verlag, 1961. 63 pp. Illustrated.

1422 Segond, André. *Renata Tebaldi.* Préface de Mario del Monaco. In French. Collection "Orphée." Lyon: J.M. Laffont, 1981. 260 pp. Illustrated. Bibliography, pp. 255-258. Discography, pp. 237-254.

1423 Seroff, Victor Ilytch, b. 1902. *Renata Tebaldi, the Woman and the Diva.* New York: Appleton-Century-Crofts, 1961. vii, 213 pp. Illustrated. Repertory, pp. 199-202. Discography, pp. 203-210.

For the first half--and possibly beyond--of her career, Victor Seroff must have been the singer's closest male friend, in the best sense of the word. Tebaldi's life story is told in the first person by the author, who seems to have been present on many important occasions in the singer's life. The events he did not witness are retold as he heard them from Tebaldi, members of her family and her teacher, Carmen Melis. The many direct quotes he takes from all of them suggest he met these individuals socially. This, the first full-length biography written with the insight and familiarity of a friend, is an excellent character-portrait of Tebaldi at the midpoint of her career. Although her professional activities are given fair treatment, it is the person, not the singer, who dominates the book.

See also item 145

TE KANAWA, KIRI, b. 1944

1424 Fingleton, David. *Kiri Te Kanawa.* Foreword by James Levine. New York: Atheneum, 1983. 192 pp. Illustrated. Index, pp. 184-192.

A detailed biography that chronicles the rise of a talented Maori girl from local (New Zealand) celebrity to international stardom. The life story has been thoroughly researched, enriched by generous quotations from reviews, articles, interviews and statements made by colleagues, friends, family and the subject herself. She emerges from these pages as a singer and a person; although an "authorized" biography, it still shows her artistic and human failings. An enjoyable narrative of one of the major contemporary operatic success stories.

1425 Harris, Norman, b. 1940. *Kiri; Music and a Maori Girl.* Text by Norman Harris in association with Kiri Te Kanawa. Wellington: A.H. and A.W. Reed, 1966. 62 pp. Illustrated. Discography, pp. 61-62.

Kiri Te Kanawa was only twenty-one years old when she left her native New Zealand to embark on an international operatic career. That she was honored by a book upon her departure speaks of the high regard in which she was held by her countrymen. Unfortunately, the book is disappointing. The style is patronizingly childish; it treats the Te Kanawa story almost as a fairy tale. Even if it was meant for young adults, which is doubtful, the reader should have been told more of her life than the succession of local and national contests young Kiri did or didn't win. The sixty-four pages of excellent photographs are arranged in an illogical sequence.

See also item 1594

TEMPLETON, JOHN, 1802-1886

1426 Husk, William Henry, 1814-1887, editor. *Templeton and Malibran. Reminiscences of These Renowned Singers, with Original Letters and Anecdotes.* Three authentic portraits by Mayall. London: W. Reeves, 1880. xii, 50 pp. Illustrated.

TEODORINI, ELENA, 1857-1926

1427 Cosma, Viorel. *Cintareaţa Elena Teodorini; schiţa monografica.* In Rumanian. Bucureşti: Editura muzicală, 1962. 210 pp. Illustrated. Bibliography, pp. 199-211.

TERNINA, MILKA, 1863-1941

See items 1658, 1663

TESI, VITTORIA, 1700-1775

1428 Croce, Benedetto, 1866-1952. *Un prelato e una cantante del
secolo decimottavo, Enea Silvio Piccolomini e Vittoria Tesi; lettere
d'amore.* In Italian. Biblioteca di cultura moderna, n. 396. Bari:
G. Laterza, 1946. 91 pp. Illustrated.

TETRAZZINI, LUISA, 1871-1940

1429 Tetrazzini, Luisa, and Enrico Caruso. *The Art of Singing.* New
York: Metropolitan Company, 1909. 71 pp. Illustrated.

   Divided into two parts, each supposedly written by the joint authors,
preceded by a short biography of both by an anonymous collaborator.
The singers offer some views about singing and the career concerns of
a performer. Considering the proficiency of both Tetrazzini and
Caruso's English in 1909, it is doubtful that any of the words are
theirs. However the facts and ideas ring true enough to suggest an
extended interview as the source, which a clever journalist turned
into a booklet.

1430 ———. *The Art of Singing*, by Luisa Tetrazzini and Enrico
Caruso. *How to Sing*, by Luisa Tetrazzini. Da Capo Press Music Reprint Series. New York: Da Capo Press, 1975. 71, 136 pp. Illustrated.

   Reprints of the 1909 edition published by Metropolitan Co., New
York, and the 1923 edition published by G.H. Doran, New York (q.v.).

1431 ———. *Caruso and Tetrazzini on the Art of Singing.* New
York: Dover Publications, 1975. 71 pp. Illustrated.

   Reprint of the 1909 edition published by Metropolitan Co., New
York, under the title *The Art of Singing* (q.v.).

1432 Tetrazzini, Luisa. *How to Sing.* New York: George H. Doran,
1923. vi, 136 pp. Illustrated.

1433 ———. *My Life of Song.* London: Cassell, 1921. 328 pp.
Illustrated. Index, pp. 323-328.

   Published in 1921, before her career went into decline, Tetrazzini
was able to recount the highlights of her life mostly in positive
terms. There is no indication who her ghost writer was or whether
the work was translated from the Italian, as one or both of the conditions must have existed. Unfortunately, her egocentric writing is too
full of prima donna-like trivia to do justice to the musical life of
the period, or even to her own distinguished career.

1433-a ———. *My Life of Song.* Philadelphia: Dorrance, 1922.
326 pp. Illustrated. Index, pp. 321-326.

This edition has been newly typeset, with different and fewer illustrations than the Cassel edition (q.v.). A curious textual change
occurs in the closing sentence of the book; the last words in the
Cassel edition are "my life of glorious song," in the Dorrance edition
"my glorious life of song."

1433-b ———. *My Life of Song*. New York: Arno Press, 1977. 328
pp. Illustrated. Index, pp. 323-328.

Reprint of the 1921 edition published by Cassell, London (q.v.).

See also items 1565, 1615, 1621, 1635, 1680, 1716

TE WIATA, INIA, 1915-1971

1434 Te Wiata, Beryl Margaret McMillan. *Most Happy Fella: A Biography of Inia Te Wiata*. Wellington: Reed, 1976. 307 pp. Index,
pp. 302-307. The copy examined had pp. 198-199, 202-203, 206-207,
210-211 blank. Are all copies defective?

The first Maori ever to receive a government scholarship to study
singing in London, Inia Te Wiata left his native New Zealand at the
relatively late age of 32. Following years of study and hardships
he became a successful concert and opera singer, but the focus of his
activities was leading roles in musicals that took him to three continents. Near the end of his life he returned to Covent Garden,
singing Pimen to Christoff's Boris Godunov. The book, written by his
second wife, is more than a tribute to his memory; it is an act of
love. The bond that united them radiates from every line. If she
wrote this memoir without editorial assistance, Beryl Te Wiata, a
former actress, deserves to be complimented on her literary skill.
Te Wiata, an accomplished wood carver, also remained faithful to
his origins. The 52-foot tall pouihi, a Maori totem pole, that
stands at the entrance of New Zealand House in London, was carved
by him. He worked on it singlehandedly for eight years, up to the
day of entering the hospital where he died of cancer after a short
but agonizingly painful period of illness. A remarkable memoir of a
remarkable man. (Te Wiata recorded for EMI.)

See also item 1594

TEYTE, MAGGIE, 1888-1976

1435 Teyte, Maggie. *Star on the Door*. London: Putnam, 1958. 192
pp. Illustrated. Discography, pp. 188-192. The discography was
compiled by David Tron.

1435-a ———. *Star on the Door*. New York: Arno Press, 1977. 192
pp. Illustrated. Discography, pp. 188-192.

Reprint of the 1958 edition published by Putnam, London (q.v.).

1436 O'Connor, Garry. *The Pursuit of Perfection; a Life of Maggie
Teyte*. New York: Atheneum, 1979. 327 pp. Illustrated. Repertory,
pp. 296-297. Index, pp. 315-327. Discography, pp. 300-314.

1436-a ————. *The Pursuit of Perfection: A Life of Maggie Teyte.*
London: Gollancz, 1979. 327 pp. Illustrated. Repertory, pp. 296-
297. Index, pp. 315-327. Discography, pp. 300-314.

See also item 1702

THALLAUG, ANITA, b. 1938

1437 Thallaug, Anita. *Veien mot nord/Anita Thallaug*; etterord av
Trygve Nordanger; med tegninger av Hammarlund. In Norwegian.
Bergen: Nordanger, 1978. 204 pp. Illustrated.

THILL, GEORGES, b. 1897

1438 Gourret, Jean, and Guy Marchal. *La technique du chant en
France depuis le XVIIe siècle; suivi d'Entretiens avec Georges Thill.*
In French. Sens: Editions I.C.C., 1973. 137 pp. Illustrated. Bib-
liography, pp. 135-136.

A treatise on singing as documented in writings about singers of
the past two centuries. It is followed by an interview with Georges
Thill. The main shortcoming of the book is the insurmountable silence
of the printed page.

1439 Mancini, Roland. *Georges Thill; biographie, discographie,
iconographie.* In French. Monstres Sacrés. Paris: SODAL, 1966.
65 pp. Illustrated. Discography, pp. 55-59.

A fairly detailed illustrated biography of one of the outstanding
French tenors of the century. A distinguished interpreter of the
French repertory, he also sang Puccini, the heavier Verdi roles and
several Wagner roles at La Scala, the Colón in Buenos Aires and at
the Metropolitan. He was also featured in the filmed version of
Charpentier's *Louise* opposite Grace Moore. The discography is a
simple, creditable effort but poorly organized. Matrix numbers are
not given, but deviations in playing speed from the standard 78 rpm
are indicated in parentheses.

1440 Segond, André, b. 1936. *Georges Thill, ou, l'âge d'or de
l'opéra.* Préface de Georges Thill. In French. Collection "Orphée."
Lyon: Éditions Jacques-Marie Laffont, 1980. 279 pp. Illustrated.
Repertory, pp. 254-260. Discography, pp. 261-278. Chronology, pp.
243-251.

The first volume in a new series dedicated to the international
history of lyric art. A biography traced by expert hands, adequately
documented. The chronology is selective. The book deserves to be
enhanced by a name index. RT

THOMAS, JESS, b. 1927

See item 1654

THOMAS, JOHN CHARLES, 1891-1960

See items 1607, 1608, 1830

THURSBY, EMMA CECILIA, 1845-1931

1441 Gipson, Richard McCandless. *The Life of Emma Thursby, 1845-1931.* New York: The New-York Historical Society, 1940. xxii, 470 pp. Illustrated. Index.

From the mid 1860s through the late 1890s, Emma Thursby was considered one of the finest concert artists to be heard. Her career took her to all parts of the world, and many critics considered her to be a close rival to both Patti and Christine Nilsson. Although impresarios from Mapleson to Strakosch and composers, including Gounod, pleaded with her to sing opera she steadfastly refused, not feeling herself to be temperamentally suited for dramatic parts. After her retirement from the concert platform she became a distinguished teacher, one of her pupils being Geraldine Farrar. It was through Thursby that Farrar was introduced to Nordica and Melba. An exceedingly well-researched work, the book is rather dryly written, but is an excellent reference work. WRM

1441-a ———. *The Life of Emma Thursby, 1845-1931.* Da Capo Press Music Reprint Series. New York: Da Capo Press, 1980. xxii, 470 pp. Illustrated. Index.

Reprint of the 1940 edition published by the New-York Historical Society, New York (q.v.).

See also item 1581

TIBBETT, LAWRENCE, 1896-1960

1442 Tibbett, Lawrence. *The Glory Road.* Brattleboro, Vt.: Privately printed by E.L. Hildreth & Co., 1933. 70 pp.

A short autobiography originally published in four consecutive installments (August-November 1933) in *The American Magazine.* The book was privately printed, presumably to be given as gifts to the singer's friends. Copies must exist; however the author knows of only one more, besides his own, in private hands, and of one in a library. Regrettably, the contents fall short of expectations. Not yet at the halfway mark of his career, thirty-eight-year-old Tibbett did not then have a story to tell. Still, the summary of his early life, his ideas and artistic concerns are of interest to those who want to learn more about the first American baritone who was born, raised and trained in this country and achieved world renown *prior* to ever having sung abroad.

1442-a ———. *The Glory Road.* With a discography by W.R. Moran. Opera Biographies. New York: Arno Press, 1977. 70, xxii pp. Illustrated. Discography, pp. i-xxii.

Reprint of the 1933 edition that was privately printed (q.v.). It con-

tains an exhaustive discography prepared by William R. Moran expressly
for this reprint edition and twenty pages of photographs, including some
movie stills, from the editor's own collection, and one unpublished
picture from Moran's private collection.

1443 Deleted

1444 Tibbett, Mrs. Lawrence. *Word Etchings*. Frontispiece, a portrait of Mr. Tibbett by Arthur Millier. New York: Flying Stag Press,
1925. 61 pp. Illustrated.

A collection of 49 short poems by the first Mrs. Tibbett (née Grace
Mackay Smith), dedicated "To Lawrence, My Husband." The Tibbetts
were married in 1919, their twin sons were born in 1920, and they
were divorced in 1931. The collection of poems, published in the
year of Tibbett's overnight fame achieved in the Met's revival of
Falstaff, is an indirect reflection of their domestic happiness. The
poems cover a wide range of subjects; husband Lawrence is the subject--
or object--of only a few. The one entitled "F. LaF." is undoubtedly
about Frank LaForge, Tibbett's voice teacher.

See also items 1607, 1608

TIETJENS, THÉRÈSE, 1831-1877

See items 1562, 1597, 1612, 1658, 1694

TINAYRE, YVES, b. 1895

See item 670

TODI, LUIZA ROSA DE AGUIAR, 1753-1833

1445 Ribeiro, Mario de Sampayo, b. 1898. *Luisa de Aguiar Todi*. In
Portuguese. Cultura artística; estudos diversos. Lisboa: Revista
Ocidente, 1943. 95 pp. Illustrated. Index, pp. 93-95.

1446 ————. *Luisa Todi; conferência realizada na rua Luisa Todi,
em Lisbon, na tarde do dia 8 de julho de 1934, primeira do ciclo de
conferencias ao ar livre, promovidas pela Câmara municipal de Lisboa.*
In Portuguese. Lisboa: S. industriais de C.M.L., 1934. 20 pp.
Illustrated.

1447 Ribeiro Guimarães, José, 1818-1877. *Biographia de Luiza de
Aguiar Todi*. In Portuguese. Lisbon: The author, 1872. 87 pp.
Illustrated.

1448 Vasconcellos, Joaquim Antonio de Fonseca e, b. 1849. *Luiza
Todi; estudo critico*. In Portuguese. Archeologia artistica, no. 1.
Porto: Imprensa portugueza, 1873. xxxi, 157 pp. Bibliography, pp.
xxv-xxxi. Edition limited to 250 copies.

1448-a ———. *Luisa Todi, estudo critico*. In Portuguese. 2nd ed.
Coimbra: Impr. da Universidade, 1929. xxi, 182 pp. Bibliography,
pp. xvii-xxi.

TOMOWA-SINTOW, ANNA, b. 1941

1449 Müller, Hans-Peter. *Anna Tomowa-Sintow*. Für Sie porträtiert
von Hans-Peter Müller. In German. Leipzig: VEB Deutscher Verlag
für Musik, 1980. 65 pp. Illustrated.

TOUREL, JENNIE, 1899-1973

See item 1654

TRAUBEL, HELEN, 1899-1972

1450 Traubel, Helen. *The Metropolitan Opera Murders*. An Inner
Sanctum Mystery. New York: Simon and Schuster, 1951. 234 pp.

Wagnerian soprano Helen Traubel loved mystery stories. Trying her
own hand at them, she wrote the amusing novelette *The Ptomaine Canary*.
It was warmly received when it was serialized in newspapers all over
the world. Encouraged by the success, Mme. Traubel wrote a full-
length mystery, whose setting, quite appropriately, is the Metropolitan Opera.

1451 ———, and Richard G. Hubler. *St. Louis Woman*. With an introduction by Vincent Sheean. New York: Duell, Sloan and Pearce, 1959.
xiv, 296 pp. Illustrated. The appendix contains a complete chronological list of her Metropolitan Opera, concert, television, radio,
stage, night club and motion picture performances, and recordings,
on pp. 275-296.

Traubel was always independent: her debut in St. Louis was in 1925,
and when she was offered a contract at the Metropolitan in 1926 she
declined in favor of further study. Her debut at the Met took place
in 1938. She stayed with the company from 1939 until March of 1953,
her roles with one exception (a single performance as the Marschallin
in *Der Rosenkavalier*) being Wagnerian heroines. Her departure from
the Metropolitan was over a dispute with manager Bing, who did not
think it dignified for one of his stars to sing in night clubs. Helen,
with typical spirit, took her leave. Her version of the Bing battle,
as well as the episode when she briefly took President Harry Truman's
singing daughter under her expansive wing, are told with humor and
poise. Traubel did not pull her punches during an active and distinguished career, and she treats her readers in the same fashion.
WRM

1451-a ———. *St. Louis Woman*. New York: Arno Press, 1977. xiv,
296 pp. Illustrated. The appendix contains a complete chronological
list of Metropolitan Opera, concert, television, radio, stage, night
club and motion picture performances, and recordings, pp. 275-296.

Reprint of the 1959 edition published by Duell, Sloan and Pearce,

New York (q.v.).

See also items 1608, 1719

TREBELLI, ZÉLIE, 1838-1892

1452 Mensiaux, Marie de. *Trebelli: A Biographical Sketch and Reminiscences of Her Life.* London: Henry Potter, 1890. 66 pp. Illustrated. Repertory, pp. 64-66.

An anecdotal biography of the French contralto Zélie Thérèse Caroline Gillebert de Beaulieu, who, not wishing to embarrass her family, took as a stage name her family name spelled backwards, minus the "G": Gillebert--Trebelli(G). According to the author's admission, in this biographical sketch "Her triumphs alone have been recorded...." An excellent musician and a great actress, her triumphs were many. Her musicianship is attested to by her stepping in for a sick tenor in Riga and singing the role of Almaviva in the *Barber of Seville* without a rehearsal. In Vienna she sang Arsace to Patti's *Semiramide*; Salvini tried to persuade her to partner him on the legitimate stage as an actress--the list goes on. An entertaining booklet of an artist deserving a full-scale biography.

See also item 1658

TREE, VIOLA, b. 1884

1453 Tree, Viola. *Castles in the Air; a Story of My Singing Days.* New York: George H. Doran, 1926. 292 pp. Illustrated.

Reminiscences of the eccentric but intelligent daughter of Herbert Beerbohm Tree, the great Shakespearean actor. This is a letter and diary-based biography of her period of vocal studies and singing. She sang in *Orpheus* opposite Bréma in London. Partial throat paralysis caused her to lose her voice before a *Salome* production in Milan.

TREIGLE, NORMAN, 1928-1975

1454 Sokol, Martin, editor. *Norman Treigle ... a Man Remembered.* New York: New York City Opera Guild, 1975? 16 unnumbered leaves. Illustrated. Repertory. Discography. Chronology.

An introduction and a short biography by Sokol and the text of Julius Rudel's speech dedicating a New York City Opera performance to the memory of Treigle. The rest of the booklet contains a generous selection of photographs, his repertory, a discography and a selective chronology.

TUCKER, RICHARD, 1914-1975

See item 1563

TULDER, LODEWIJK ALIDUS JOHANNES VAN, 1892-1969

1455 Tulder, Lodewijk Alidus Johannes van. *Van kantoorkruk tot hooge C.* In Dutch. Baarn, 1946. 152 pp. Illustrated. Information taken from the British Museum General Catalogue.

TURNER, EVA, b. 1892

See item 1544

U

UETAM

See MATEU Y NICOLAU, FRANCISCO

UNGER, CAROLINE, 1803-1877

1456 Faragó, Margit (Polgár). *Unger-Sabatier Karolina.* In Hungarian. Budapest: Danubia Könyvkiadó, 1941. 219 pp.

A superbly researched and documented biography that demands the same erudition of the reader as the author seems to have possessed: the reading knowledge of five languages. Besides the Hungarian of the main text, extensive quotations in German, Italian, French and English are incorporated throughout. Unger performed and lived in the mainstream of 19th-century musical life. She was a frequent visitor at Beethoven's, occasionally accompanied by her friend Henriette Sontag; Beethoven asked the "girls" to sing the first Viennese performance of his Ninth Symphony. Rossini also held her in very high esteem. The book also details her unhappy love affair with German poet Nikolaus Lenau, and her happy marriage with François Sabatier that lasted until her death. A superb piece of scholarship.

1457 Giordani, Pietro. *Ringraziamento de' Parmigiani a Carolina Ungher.* In Italian. Lucca, 1838. 15 pp. Information taken from the British Museum General Catalogue.

1458 *Trionfi melodrammatici di Carolina Ungher in Vienna, 1839.* In Italian. Vienna: A. Strauss?, 1839. Unpaged.

URLUS, JACQUES, 1867-1935

1459 Urlus, Jacques. *Mijn Loopbaan.* In Dutch. Amsterdam: Holkema & Warendorf, 1929. 250 pp. Illustrated.

1460 Spengler, Otto, b. 1873. *Jacques Urlus, erster Heldentenor. Heroic Tenor Metropolitan Opera House, New York-Leipzig. Ein Beitrag zur Geschichte der deutschen Oper.* In German, English. Otto Spengler's Künstler Monographien. New York, 1917? 23 pp. Illustrated.

See also item 1744

UTOR, MANUEL, 1862-1946

See items 1542, 1543

V

VÄLKKI, ANITA, b. 1926

1461 Välkki, Anita. *Taiteen vuoksi.* Muistiin merkinnyt Irmeli Sallamo. In Finnish. Helsinki: Kirjayhtymä, 1971. 115 pp. Illustrated.

VALDENGO, GIUSEPPE, b. 1914

1462 Valdengo, Giuseppe. *Ho cantato con Toscanini*; prefazione di Adriano Lualdi. In Italian. Como: P. Cairoli, 1962. 163 pp. Illustrated. Bibliography, p. 159.

Recalling the many valuable lessons received from Toscanini, Valdengo, in this lively book, full of interesting recollections, aims to pay grateful homage to the illustrious Maestro under whose guidance he had the privilege to develop and succeed. RT

VALLERIA, ALWINA (ALWINA VALLERIE SCHÖNING), 1848-1925

See item 1567

VALLIN, NINON, 1886-1961

1463 Fragny, Robert de. *Ninon Vallin, princesse du chant.* In French. Lyon: Editions et imprimeries du sud-est, 1963. 197 pp. Illustrated.

See also item 1567

VANDÅR, ELINA, 1865-1949

1464 Eibe, Inger. *Elina Vandår, en näktergal från Finland.* In Swedish. Helsingfors: Söderström, 1956. 16 pp. Illustrated.

A charming, brief essay on the career of Elina Vandår. It gives a good picture of her family and professional life, but offers too few details of performances, casts or recordings. PHS

VARNAY, ASTRID, b. 1918

1465 Wessling, Berndt Wilhelm, b. 1935. *Astrid Varnay.* In German. Bremen: Schünemann, 1965. 123 pp. Illustrated. Bibliography, pp. 121-122. Index, pp. 123-124. Discography, p. 123.

An outstanding biography that gives equal time to the person and the singer. It makes generous use of Varnay's own statements as well as comments and letters of others. The reproduction of letters, playbills, critiques and photographs are welcome; the tabulation of her Bayreuth appearances shows the extent of her annual contribution to the festival from 1951 until the publication of the book. The Wagner brothers--Wieland and Wolfgang--contributed a brief preface.

See also item 1788

VEDERNIKOV, ALEKSANDR

See item 1732

VENDRELL, EMILIO, 1893-1962

1466-T Vendrell, Emilio. *El cant: experiencies i orientacions, consells i suggeriments. Llibre per al cantant i per l'aficionat. Amb una autobiografia.* Translated by the author. In Catalan. Barcelona: E. Meseguer, 1955. 160 pp. Illustrated.

Catalan translation of his *El Canto* (q.v.).

1467 ———. *El canto, libro para el cantante y para el aficionado.* In Spanish. Manuales Meseguer, 16. Barcelona: E. Meseguer, 1955. 141 pp. Illustrated.

1468 ———. *El mestre Millet i jo: memòries.* In Catalan. Barcelona: Aymà, 1953. 251 pp. Illustrated.

Vendrell's recollections about his singing teacher. The preface is by Lluis Maria Millet (b. 1906), son of Luis Millet. AM

1469 ———. *El miracle de Sant Ponc; poema dramàtic....* In Catalan. Barcelona: Aymà, 1949. 154 pp. Illustrated.

1470 Vendrell, Emilio, b. 1924. *El meu pare, Emili Vendrell.* In Catalan. Barcelona: Toray, 1965. 190 pp. Illustrated.

VENDRELL, EMILIO, b. 1924

See item 1470

VERGNET, EDMOND, 1850-1904

See item 1588

VERLET, ALICE, 1873-1934

See item 1695

VERTINSKII, ALEKSANDR

1471 Vertinskii, Aleksandr. *Chetvert' veka bez rodiny.* In Russian.
Information taken from the Polish edition of Vertinskii's book which
contains a chapter on Chaliapin (pp. 112-122). A complete bibliographic entry could not be located for this book.

1472 ————. *Podróze z piesnia; wspomnienia.* Translated by Stanislaw
Ludkiewicz. In Polish. Warszawa: Czytelnik, 1967. 158 pp.

Russian translation of *Chetvert' veka bez rodiny* (q.v.). Contains
a chapter on Chaliapin (pp. 112-122).

1473 Kalmykov, Nikolai Nikolaievich. *Pevets Aleksandr Vertinskii--
artist, poet i kompozitor.* In Russian. Leningrad, 1963. 9 typescript pp. Information taken from the British Museum General Catalogue.
Author's name is spelled: "Kalmuikov."

VESTRIS, LUCIA ELIZABETH, 1787-1856

1474 Capon, Gaston. *Les Vestris; le "diou" de la danse et sa famille
1730-1808; d'après des rapports de police et des documents inédits....*
In French. Paris: Société du Mercure de France, 1908. 307 pp.

1475 *Memoirs of the Life of Madame Vestris, of the Theatres Royal
Drury Lane and Covent Garden.* London: Privately printed, 1830.
72 pp.

1476 *Memoirs of the Life, Public and Private Adventures of Madame
Vestris ... with Interesting and Amusing Anecdotes of Celebrated
Characters in the Fashionable World....* London: Printed for the book-
sellers, 1839. 61 pp. Illustrated.

1477 Pearce, Charles E. *Madame Vestris and Her Times.* London: S.
Paul, 1923. 314 pp. Illustrated.

1478 Williams, Clifford John. *Madame Vestris--a Theatrical Biography.* London: Sidgwick and Jackson, 1973. xiv, 240 pp. Illustrated.
Bibliography, pp. 232-233. Index.

VEZZANI, CÉSAR, 1888-1951

1479 Païta, François. *César Vezzani, 1888-1951.* In French. Bastia:
Chez l'auteur, 1971. 10 pp. Illustrated.

VIARDOT-GARCIA, PAULINE, 1821-1910

1480 Fitzlyon, April. *The Price of Genius; a Life of Pauline Viardot.*
London: Calder, 1964. 520 pp. Illustrated. Bibliography, pp. 495-
505. Index, pp. 506-520.

This thoroughly researched and very readable account of Pauline
Viardot-Garcia would have been even more valuable if more attention

had been paid to the singer's career and less to her relationship with Turgenev. For example, no mention is made of the fact that she sang the first Lady Macbeth in the British Isles, or that she created *Halka* in its four-act version in Warsaw on January 1, 1858. Nor is the book entirely accurate. To cite just one factual error: on page 227 it is incorrectly stated that *Les Huguenots* had not been heard in London before 1848; the opera had been previously given there in 1842 and 1845. While slips like these diminish its value as a reference work, it is still one of the finest books available on any singer of the period, and easily outdistances all other volumes published thus far on Viardot. TGK

1480-a ————. *The Price of Genius; a Life of Pauline Viardot.*
New York: Appleton-Century, 1965. 520 pp. Illustrated. Bibliography, pp. 495-505. Index, pp. 506-520.

1481 Grevs, Ivan Mikhailovich, 1860-1941. *Istoriia odnoi liubvi: I.S. Turgenev i Polina Viardo.* In Russian. Moskva, 1927.

1481-a ————. *Istoriia odnoi liubvi: I.S. Turgenev i Polina Viardo.* In Russian. 2nd enlarged ed. Moskva: Sovremennye problemy, 1928. 369 pp.

1482 Hoyer, Galina (Diuriagina) von, b. 1898. *Die Liebe eines Lebens: Iwan Turgenjew und Pauline Viardot*, von Alja Rachmanowa (pseud.). Aus dem russischen Manuskript ins Deutsche übersetzt [von] Arnulf von Hoyer. In German. Frauenfeld: Huber, 1952. 399 pp. Bibliography, pp. 393-399.

1483 Lipsius, Ida Maria, 1837-1927. "Pauline Viardot-Garcia." Von La Mara (pseud.). *Sammlung musikalische Vorträge*, 4. Reihe, nr. 43 (1882), 259-278. Leipzig, 1879-98, 20 pp. In German. Double pagination.

1484 Rozanov, A. *Polina Viardo-Garsia; monografiia.* In Russian. Leningrad: N.p., 1982. 239 pp.

1485 Sand, George, pseud. of Mme. Dudevant, 1804-1876. *Lettres inédites de George Sand et de Pauline Viardot (1839-1849).* Recueillies, annotés et précédées d'une introd. par Thérèse Marix-Spire. In French. Paris: Nouvelles Éditions latines, 1959. 316 pp. Illustrated. Bibliography, pp. 289-300.

1486 Schoen-René, Anna Eugénie. *America's Musical Inheritance; Memories and Reminiscences.* New York: G.P. Putnam's Sons, 1941. xi, 244 pp. Illustrated.

As the title implies, these are the musical reminiscences of a singer turned teacher, the pupil of Pauline Viardot-Garcia and teacher of Risë Stevens. In addition to her recollections of Viardot-Garcia she devotes sub-chapters to Melba, Lehmann, Sembrich, Caruso and Schumann-Heink.

1487 Thomsen, Ferde. *Ivan Turgenjew og Pauline Viardot Garcia. Et Tidsbillede.* In Danish. København: Vilhelm Prior, 1915. 226 pp. Illustrated.

A fascinating "dual-biography" of Turgenev and Viardot, incorporating
a large number of musical anecdotes and incidents, e.g., Viardot's
first performance in Meyerbeer's *Prophet* (April 16, 1849); correspondence with Princess Wittgenstein concerning Liszt; and the premiere of
Gounod's *Sappho*. The largest part of the volume, however, concerns
Turgenev and his relationship to Viardot, with a very large number of
letters relating to Dostoevsky, Tolstoy and other Russian authors.
There is a lovely cameo of Viardot as Norma. PHS

1488   Turgenev, Ivan Sergeevich, 1818-1883. *Lettres à Madame Viardot*;
publiées et annotées par E. Halpérine-Kaminsky. In French. Paris:
Charpentier, 1907. 263 pp.

1489 ――――. *Pis'ma I.S. Turgeneva k g-zh Polin Viardo i ego
frantsuzskim druz'iam: Gustavu Floberu (i dr.), sobrannyia i
izdannyia'g.* In Russian. Moskva: D.P. Efimova, 1900. 10, xiii,
361 pp. At head of title: "Lettres inédites d'Ivan Tourguénew."

1490 ――――. *Pis'ma I.S. Turgeneva k Paulin Viardo.* In Russian.
Moskva: Univ. tip., 1900. iv, 252 pp.

See also items 903, 1588, 1601, 1612, 1615, 1643, 1681, 1682, 1689,
1745

VICKERS, JON, b. 1926

See items 1563, 1654

VILLANI, LUISA, 1884-1961

1491   Bott, Michael F. *Luisa Villani--Forgotten Diva.* Hamilton,
Bermuda: Published by the author, 1981. 21 pp. Illustrated. Bibliography, p. 15. Repertory, p. 16. Discography, p. 14. Numbered
edition, limited to 100 copies.

A brief, but well-researched account of the highlights of the life
of the San Francisco-born, Milan-trained soprano who created the role
of Fiora in Montemezzi's *L'Amore de Tre Re* at La Scala, on April 10,
1913. Hers was not a spectacular career, but she was often entrusted
with leading roles in the company of artists of international reputation (e.g., Slezak, Zenatello, Pertile) and performed with leading
conductors of her time. Reviews are quoted from performances in
Europe, as well as with such organizations as The Boston Grand Opera
Company. Twenty-one known roles are cited, ranging from Nedda and
Santuzza to Leonora (in *Il Trovatore*), Desdemona, Elsa and Eva.
Details of her brief recorded legacy are listed. WRM

VIÑAS, FRANCISCO, 1863-1933

1492   Viñas, Francisco. *El arte del canto; datos históricos, consejos y normas para educar la voz.* In Spanish. Barcelona: Salvat,
1932. iv, 384 pp. Illustrated.

1492-a ———. *El arte de canto; datos históricos, consejos y ejercicios-musicales para la educación de la voz.* Con un prologo de Victoria de los Angeles. In Spanish. 2nd ed. Barcelona: Casa del Libro, 1963. iv, 388 pp. Illustrated.

Except for the slight change in the wording of the title and the addition of de los Angeles's preface, this is identical with the 1932 edition by Salvat, Barcelona (q.v.).

1493 ———. *Parsifal: leyendas del santo Graal y de Parsifal.* In Spanish. Barcelona: Emporium, 1934. 110 pp. Illustrated.

1494 Bilbao, José. *Teatro real; recuerdos de las cinco temporadas del empresario Arana.* In Spanish. Madrid: Norma, 1936. 163 pp. Illustrated. Chronology of Performances, pp. 49-134. Edition limited to 300 copies.

1495 Gregori, Luigi de, 1874-1947. *Francesc Viñas, el gran tenor catala, fundador de la Lliga de Defensa de l'Arbre Fruiter.* In Catalan. Barcelona: Emporium, 1935. 269 pp. Illustrated. Repertory, p. 228. Chronology, pp. 223-227.

1496-T ———. *Francisco Viñas, el gran tenor español, fundador de la "Liga Defensa del Arbol Frutal."* Translated by the publishers. In Spanish. Barcelona: Emporium, 1936. 318 pp. Illustrated. Repertory, p. 289. Chronology of Performances, pp. 277-287.

VINCENT, JO, b. 1898

1497 Vincent, Jo. *Zingend door het leven; memoires.* Mit inleidigen van Rudolf Mengelberg (et al.). In Dutch. Amsterdam: Elsevier, 1955. 127 pp. Illustrated.

This peculiar but interesting volume of Jo Vincent's memoirs begins with four introductions, one of them by Rudolf Mengelberg, cousin of conductor Willem who was the first to recognize Vincent's talent. Her memoirs trace her childhood, her training by Cornelie van Zanten, her career through her farewell on December 25, 1953, and her personal life. A successful oratorio and concert singer, she had only one operatic role, the Countess in the *Marriage of Figaro*. The volume deals too little with music and too much with personalia, but Vincent comes across as a charming person. PHS

VISCARDI, MARIA, 1887-1966

1498 Falzetti, Giulia, and Tommaso Falzetti. *Maria Viscardi: una vita per il canto.* In Italian. Roma: A. Signorelli, 1966. 307 pp. Illustrated.

Uncritical reproduction of a huge collection of newspaper clippings relating to the career of the soprano. There is a listing of singers and conductors mentioned in the book but without page references. Has very few notes. RT

VÖLKER, FRANZ, 1899-1965

1499 Schäfer, Jürgen. *Franz Völker.* In German. Sammlung Jürgen Schäfer. Hamburg: Jürgen Schäfer, 1978. 22 pp. Discography, pp. 7-22.

See also item 1811

VOGL, HEINRICH, 1845-1900

1500 Pfordten, Hermann von der. *Heinrich Vogl. Zur Erinnerungen und zum Vermächtnissen.* In German. München: C. Haushalter, 1900. 27 pp.

1501 Wünnenberg, Rolf. *Das Sängerehepaar Heinrich und Therese Vogl. Ein Beitrag zur Operngeschichte des 19. Jahrhunderts.* In German. Tutzing: Hans Schneider, 1982. 164 pp. Illustrated. Bibliography, pp. 159-161. Index, pp. 162-164.

VOGL, JOHANN MICHAEL, 1768-1840

1502 Liess, Andreas, b. 1903. *Johann Michael Vogl, Hofoperist und Schubertsänger.* In German. Graz: Hermann Böhlaus Nachf., 1954. 224 pp. Illustrated. Bibliography, pp. 201-202. Repertory, pp. 195-200. Index, pp. 220-224. The piano-vocal score of "Süsse heilige Natur" from *Die Erbschaft* (Kotzebue) is appended at the end.

A detailed, well-researched, scholarly biography of Schubert's first major vocal interpreter.

VOGL, THERESE, 1845-1921

See items 1501, 1658

VULPESCU, MIHAIL

1503 Obreja, C. *Mihail Vulpescu.* In Rumanian. Bucureşti: Editura Muzicală, 1967. 179 pp. Illustrated.

W

WAGNER, JOHANNA JACHMANN, 1826-1894

1504 Jachmann, Hans. *Wagner and His First Elisabeth.* Translated by Maria A. Trechman. London: Novello, 1944. vii, 63 pp. Illustrated.

1505 Kapp, Julius, b. 1883, and Hans Jachmann. *Richard Wagner und seine erste "Elisabeth", Johanna Jachmann-Wagner; ein neuer Beitrag zur Wagnerforschung. Mit unveröffentlichten Briefen von Richard Wagner*

und anderen nebst 16 Bildbeilagen und 9 Faksimiledrucken. In German.
Berlin: Dom-Verlag, 1927. 237 pp. Illustrated.

WAKEFIELD, AUGUSTA MARY, 1853-1910

1506 Newmarch, Rosa Harriet (Jeaffreson), 1857-1940. *Mary Wakefield,
a Memoir.* Kendal: Atkinson and Pollitt, 1912. 142 pp. Illustrated.

WALKER, FRANCIS

1507 Walker, Francis. *Letters of a Baritone.* New York: C. Scribner's
Sons, 1895. xii, 298 pp. Illustrated.

A collection of letters written by the author to his sister during
his years of study in Italy. In tone, style and depth of observation
these letters project the observations of a person with limited
literary gifts who never penetrated the mainstream of European musical
life.

WALLACE, IAN, b. 1919

1508 Wallace, Ian. *Promise Me You'll Sing Mud!: The Autobiography
of Ian Wallace.* London: J. Calder, 1975. 240 pp. Illustrated.
Index, pp. 235-240.

The story of the Scottish opera singer, actor, popular entertainer
and TV show host. Wallace has the rare ability to find the humor
in many of the unusual situations of his eventful life. His innate
wit and gift of a raconteur is well captured in his easy-flowing
prose that guarantees the reader's sustained interest.

WALSKA, GANNA

1509 Walska, Ganna. *Always Room at the Top.* New York: R.R. Smith,
1943. 504 pp. Illustrated.

The very diligent researcher might possibly find that the number
of those performances by Polish soprano Ganna Walska which actually
took place almost equals those which were cancelled, frequently at
the last moment. Critics seemed unanimous that her vocal resources
were limited, but at one thing she excelled: she had an extraordinary
talent for collecting very wealthy husbands, among them society Doctor
Joseph Fraenkel; Alexander Cochran, multimillionaire sportsman and
carpet king; and Harold F. McCormick of International Harvester. Her
memoirs are a grand miscellany of philosophical wanderings from the
Ouija Board (which guided her early career) through the teachings of
Yoga, materialization (Abraham Lincoln once sat in her lap and
"assured me that my singing teacher was a perfect choice"), meta-
physics, telepathy, the doctrine of reincarnation ("even if it per-
plexed me for a while when I was unable to grasp which of my departed
husbands would be my husband in heaven") to stories of universal per-
secution by the press as well as the ex-wives of her various husbands.
At one point she "took complete possession" of the Théâtre des Champs-

Élysées where she sponsored concerts and opera for the benefit of Paris music lovers. Throughout the 500 pages of pap runs a thin trail of social and operatic history which only the brave will be willing to attempt to extract. WRM

WALTER, AUGUST, 1821-1896

1510 Niggli, Arnold, 1843-1927. *Biographieen schweizerischer Tonkünstler. Das Künstlerpaar August und Anna Walter-Strauss; ein biographisch-kritischer Essay.* In German. Zürich: Gebrüder Hug, 1893. 56 pp. Illustrated.

WALTER, GUSTAV, 1834-1910

1511 Nunnenmacher-Röllfeld, Maria. *Der Schubertsänger Gustav Walter. Ein Künstlerleben.* In German. Berlin: Ernst Menda, 1930. 142 pp. Illustrated.

WALTER-STRAUSS, ANNA SUSANNA, b. 1846

See item 1510

WARD, GENEVIÈVE, 1838-1922

1512 Ward, Geneviève, and Richard Whiteing. *Both Sides of the Curtain.* London: Cassell, 1918. 291 pp. Illustrated.

1513 Ward, Geneviève. *Geneviève Ward Souvenir Supplement. Polite Society.* London: The Forget-me-not Company, 1917. 4 pp. Illustrated.

Contains a message and reminiscences of Miss Ward. Laid in a pale green folder, printed on blue paper, with a portrait of Geneviève Ward.

1514 Wikoff, Henry, 1813-1884. *Memoir of Ginevra Guerrabella....* New York: T.J. Crowan, 1863. 63 pp. Guerrabella is Geneviève Ward's *nom de théâtre*, an Italian form of her Russian name.

WARFIELD, SANDRA, b. 1929

See item 890

WEGENER, PAUL

1515 Hindermann-Wegener, Aenny. *Lied eines Lebens; Wegstrecken mit Paul Wegener.* In German. Minden in Westf.: J.C.C. Bruns, 1950. 229 pp. Illustrated.

WELITSCH, LJUBA, b. 1913

1516 Bonchev, Marin TS. *Slaveiat s ime Liubov: Liuba Velichkova.*
In Bulgarian. Sofiia: Muzika, 1979. 121 pp. Illustrated. Bibliography.

See also items 1544, 1654

WERMINSKA, WANDA, b. 1900

1517 Werminska, Wanda. *Na obu polkulach.* Spisal i opracowal Alek-
sander Jerzy Rowinski. In Polish. Warszawa: Czytelnik, 1978. 176
pp. Illustrated. Repertory, pp. 173-174.

Autobiography of the Polish soprano. She had a successful international career concentrated mostly in the central European countries.
She was engaged at the Colón in Buenos Aires on Gigli's recommenda-
tion; she also appeared in *Faust* in Budapest (1934) opposite
Chaliapin at the basso's explicit invitation and coached by him.
This was the memorable performance when a cat mysteriously appeared
during the "Jewel song" and had to be coaxed off-stage with a bowl
of milk. Her repertory included the major Verdi, Wagner and Puccini
roles.

WERRENRATH, REINALD, 1883-1953

See items 1565, 1581

WETTERGREN, GERTRUD PÅLSON, b. 1897

1518 Wettergren, Gertrud Pålson. *Mitt ödes stjärna.* In Swedish.
Stockholm: Rabén & Sjögren, 1964. 293 pp.

WHITEHILL, CLARENCE, 1871-1932

1519 Williams, Frank. "Clarence Whitehill." *The Record Collector*
XXII, nos. 10 and 11 (April 1975), 221-263. Illustrated. Discography,
pp. 247-263.

Clarence Whitehill was born in Marengo, Iowa, and spent a long and
useful career in grand opera in Germany, England and America. He
appeared 381 times with the Metropolitan, in 26 roles, from 1909 to
1932. There appears to be no other biographical work on this singer.
The details of his career in Europe as well as in America have been
well researched. The discography is by W.R. Moran. WRM

WIATA, INIO TE

See Te Wiata, Inio

WILLIAMS, EVAN, 1867-1918

1520 Lewis, Gareth H. "Evan Williams." *The Record Collector* XXIV, nos. 11 and 12 (December 1978), 242-277. Illustrated. Discography, pp. 258-277.

The popular concert and oratorio singer, born in Ohio of Welsh parents, Evan Williams, seems to have been neglected by biographers. This well-researched article presents some details on the singer's vocal difficulties and how he overcame them, in clear and well-written prose. It is followed by a discography and an essay on the recordings by W.R. Moran. WRM

See also item 1581

WILSON, STEUART, 1889-1966

1521 Stewart, Margaret. *English Singer: The Life of Steuart Wilson.* London: Duckworth, 1970. 320 pp. Illustrated. Bibliography, pp. 313-314.

Biography of the English tenor Steuart Wilson by his widow. An interesting book with a broad coverage of topics. It has passages relating to John Christie, Glyndbourne, and other musical matters of British interest.

WINDGASSEN, WOLFGANG, 1914-1974

1522 Honolka, Kurt. *Wolfgang Windgassen.* In German. Stuttgart: Deutscher-Opern-Verlag, n.d. 62 pp. Illustrated.

1523 Wessling, Berndt Wilhelm, b. 1935. *Wolfgang Windgassen.* In German. Bremen: Schünemann, 1967. 126 pp. Illustrated.

WITHERSPOON, HERBERT, 1873-1935

1524 Witherspoon, Herbert. *Singing; a Treatise for Teachers and Students.* New York: G. Schirmer, 1925. 126 pp. Illustrated. Index, pp. 125-126.

A treatise on singing, its technique and the functioning and care of the singing equipment. Space is also devoted to proper living, physical and mental hygiene, and common sense. Witherspoon writes-- and all singers should read--that: "Vanity, conceit, pomposity, will do you even more harm than lack of poise and self-confidence. Just because you are an artist you are no different from all the rest of mankind."

1524-a ————. *Singing; a Treatise for Teachers and Students.* Da Capo Press Music Reprint Series. New York: Da Capo, 1980. 126 pp. Illustrated. Index, pp. 125-126.

Reprint of the 1925 edition published by G. Schirmer, New York.

1525 ———. *Thirty-six Lessons in Singing for Teacher and Student.* Chicago: Miessner Institute of Music, 1930. 51 pp. Illustrated.

See also item 1565

WITTRISCH, MARCEL, 1901-1955

See item 1811

WOOD, JOSEPH, 1801-1890

1526 *Memoir of Mr. and Mrs. Wood, Containing an Authentic Account of the Principal Events in the Lives of These Celebrated Vocalists....* Boston: J. Fisher, 1840. 36 pp. Illustrated.

Also includes memoirs of Mary Ann Paton Wood (1802-1864).

1526-a *Memoir of Mr. and Mrs. Wood, Containing an Authentic Account of the Principal Events in the Lives of These Celebrated Vocalists: Including the Marriage of Miss Paton to Lord William Lennox; and the Causes Which Led to Their Divorce: Her Subsequent Marriage to Joseph Wood, and a Full Statement of the Popular Disturbance at the Park Theatre, New York.* Philadelphia: Turner and Fisher, 1840. 36 pp. Illustrated.

WRONSKI, THADDEUS, b. 1915

1527 Wronski, Thaddeus. *The Singer and His Art; Including Articles on Anatomy and Vocal Hygiene by John F. Levbarg, M.D.* New York: D. Appleton, 1921. xx, 265 pp. Illustrated. Index, pp. 263-266.

Written by a singer turned voice teacher, this book is dedicated to Giulio Gatti-Casazza and bears the signatorial endorsement of many prominent Met artists. The book is divided into three parts: the voice, acting and mimicry, and makeup. The text is elementary; Wronski's photographs of himself enacting various emotions are unintentionally hilarious, showing acting, operatic or legitimate, at its worst.

WÜLLNER, LUDWIG, 1858-1938

1528 Ludwig, Franz, b. 1889. *Ludwig Wüllner, sein Leben und seine Kunst. Mit vierzehn Beiträgen zeitgenössischer Persönlichkeiten.* In German. Leipzig: E. Weibezahl, 1931. xxxii, 252 pp. Illustrated.

1529 Rapsilber, Maximilian, 1862-1934, editor. *Ludwig Wüllner, ein musikalisches Charakterbild dargestellt in deutschen und ausländischen Zeitungsstimmen aus den Jahren 1896 bis 1907.* In German. Berlin: G. Braunbeck und Gutenberg-Druckerei, 1907. 82 pp.

See also item 1615

Z

ZABELA, NADEZHDA IVANOVNA, 1868-1913

1530 IAnkovskii, Moisei Osipovich, b. 1898. *N.I. Zabela-Vrubel'*. In Russian. Moskva: Gos. muzykal'noe izd-vo, 1953. 141 pp. Illustrated. Bibliography, pp. 137-142.

ZAMORA, ELENA

1531 Zamora, Elena. *Am slujit cintecul; amintiri dupa 50 ani de teatru*. In Rumanian. Bucureşti: Editura Muzicală, 1964. 136 pp. Illustrated.

ZANDT, MARIE VAN, 1858-1919

See item 1588

ZANELLI, RENATO, 1892-1935

1532 Saavedra R., Oscar, and William R. Moran. "Renato Zanelli, Baritone and Tenor." *The Record Collector* VII, no. 9 (September 1952), 194-207. Illustrated. Discography, pp. 204-207.

   Renato Zanelli was born in Valparaiso, Chile, and made his operatic debut in Santiago in 1916. From 1919 to 1923 he sang at the Metropolitan, where his baritone competitors were Amato, de Luca and Scotti. After a year of further study in Italy, he emerged as a tenor, and eventually became famous as one of the great interpreters of Otello. His brother, Carlos Zanelli Morales, had an excellent career in opera as Carlo Morelli. This article appears to be the only "authorized" biographical record of Zanelli's career, having been written with the assistance and approval of the singer's widow. Zanelli recorded as a baritone for Victor and as a tenor for HMV.

ZENATELLO, GIOVANNI, 1876-1949

1533 Zenatello Consolaro, Nina. *Giovanni Zenatello, tenore; ideatore degli spettacoli lirici dell'Arena di Verona (1913)*. In Italian. Verona: Novastampa di Verona, 1976. 157 pp. Illustrated.

   A respectable effort by the tenor's daughter to commemorate her father with a biography. Unfortunately, familiarity with the operatic world must have come to her entirely through her father, as she does not dare to venture beyond the facts and events affecting Zenatello's life. Even these are insufficiently covered, with many obvious holes in the fabric of her narrative. The most curious omission is the sparse mention of Maria Gay, Zenatello's wife and--presumably--Nina's mother. Her person and career are merely referred to four or five times throughout the book. A woman who sang for years with and without her husband, under the name Maria Gay-Zenatello, should have

deserved more extensive treatment in father Giovanni's biography, regardless of what the causes for this exclusion may have been. If
nothing else, the fact that she lost her two sons within two weeks in
1913 is a tragedy noteworthy enough to deserve mention. A detailed
biography of both is in order. For such a work the present book can
serve as good source material.

ZENI, PIETRO, 1870-1932

1534 *Commemorazione ufficiale del 50. anniversario della morte del
tenore Pietro Zeni (1932-1982).* In Italian. Bolletino No. 4--
27 Giugno 1982. Acquanegra sul Chiese, Modena: Biblioteca Pubblica
Popolare Communale "Gianni Bosio," 1982. 7 pp. Illustrated.

ZERNY, FRIEDA, 1864-1917

1535 Wolf, Hugo, 1860-1903. *Briefe an Frieda Zerny.* Hrsg. von Ernst
Hilmar und Walter Obermaier. In German. Wien: Musikwissenschaftlicher
Verlag, 1978. 83 pp. Illustrated. Index, pp. 81-83.

A collection of Hugo Wolf's love letters to the foremost contemporary
interpreter of his songs, mezzo-soprano Frieda Zerny (née Zimmer).
In addition to intimate subjects, these letters contain discussions
of musical matters and other concerns of the composer. After her
marriage to music director Karl Hallwachs in 1901, Zerny gave up her
stage career but remained active as a recitalist. Considering her
remarkable poetic gifts it is particularly regrettable that none of
her letters to Wolf survived.

ZIEGLER, ANN, b. 1910

1536 Ziegler, Anne, and Webster Booth. *Duet.* London: S. Paul, 1951.
223 pp. Illustrated.

The joint authors of this joint autobiography tell their respective
life stories, intertwined by marriage, in alternate chapters. Although
they were active mostly in musicals and film, they often sang and
recorded operatic excerpts as concert artists. Booth, who was a
member of the D'Oyly Carte Company for more than four years in his
youth, frequently sang in oratorio, and appeared as the Italian Singer
in *Der Rosenkavalier* under Kleiber during the International Season at
Covent Garden in 1938. The fast moving life stories are interesting,
the chapters by Booth have marginally more depth.

Part II
Multi-Subject Monographs

1537 Aldrich, Richard, 1863-1937. *Concert Life in New York, 1902-1923*. New York: G.P. Putnam's Sons, 1941. xvii, 795 pp. Illustrated. Index, pp. 741-786.

This volume contains a selection from Aldrich's articles and reviews published in the *New York Times* during the years indicated in the title. They give an accurate idea of the range and quality of musical life in New York City. Aldrich's style is occasionally archaic and somewhat clumsy, but his observations are dependable, reasoned and objective, and his judgments well supported by recordings of the period. The selections presented here review and analyze the concert and operatic performances of instrumentalists as well as vocalists.

The index of this work indexes *all* the reviews published by Aldrich in the *New York Times*, including those not contained in this volume. It serves, therefore, as an index to his writings for the *New York Times* over the years and a locator for every piece.

1537-a ————. *Concert Life in New York, 1902-1923*. Edited by Harold Johnson. Freeport, N.Y.: Books for Libraries Press, 1971. xvii, 795 pp. Illustrated.

Reprint of the 1941 edition published by G.P. Putnam's Sons, New York (q.v.).

1538 Aleksandrovich, A. *Zapiski pevtsa*. In Russian. N'iu Iork: Izdatel'stvo Chekhova, 1955. 409 pp.

A collection of singers' biographies.

1539 Alfonso, José. *Del Madrid del cuplé (Recuerdos pintorescos)*. In Spanish. Colección Veinteduros, 2. Madrid: Cunillera, 1972. 252 pp.

A picturesque description of intellectual life in Madrid during the first three decades of the century. Consisting of a merry collection of anecdotes about people of all walks of life, the author mentions over fifty opera and zarzuela singers. Many of them are treated at length, depending on the story the author has to tell about them. AM

1539/A Allegri, Renzo. *Il prezzo del succeso. Trenta cantanti lirici raccontano la loro storia*. In Italian. Milano: Rusconi, 1983. 320 pp. Illustrated.

1540 Arditi, Luigi, 1822-1903. *My Reminiscences*. Ed. and compiled with introduction and notes by the Baroness von Zedlitz. New York: Dodd, Mead, 1896. xxii, 314 pp. Illustrated.

Conductor and composer (of vocal waltzes such as "Il bacio," "Se saren rose" and "L'incantatrice" sung by every soprano from Patti to Sutherland), Luigi Arditi was an important ingredient in things operatic and musical in general on both sides of the Atlantic for many years. In an appendix to this book are many of Arditi's "firsts": a list of 26 "Operas first produced in England under my Direction" includes *I Vespri Siciliani*, *Forza del Destino*, *Ballo in Maschera*, *Faust*, *Hamlet*, *Mignon* and *Cavalleria*. The list of "Composers I have personally known" begins with Rossini, Donizetti, Verdi, Wagner and

Meyerbeer, and ends with Humperdinck. The list of "Singers who have appeared under my Direction" occupies nine double-columned pages and includes such names as Grisi, Lilli Lehmann, Sontag, Alboni, Tamagno, Patti, Maurel, Capoul, Campanini, Tietjens, Melba, a veritable who's who of the period. From 1878 to 1883 Arditi was principal conductor for the notorious Col. James H. Malpeson in his famous operatic tours of the United States. He was conductor at Her Majesty's Theatre in London, as well as at Covent Garden, and with the Carl Rosa Opera Company. His stories about the people he knew are endless. An absolutely fascinating and very important book. WRM

1540-a ————. *My Reminiscences*. Ed. and compiled with introduction and notes by the Baroness von Zedlitz. 2nd ed. London: Skaffington, 1896. xxv, 352 pp. Illustrated.

1541 Armstrong, William, b. 1856. *The Romantic World of Music*. New York: E.P. Dutton and Company, 1922. ix, 239 pp. Illustrated.

These are the author's recollections of singers of his time, with the inclusion of one pianist, Paderewski. The singers are: Amato, Bori, Caruso, D'Alvarez, Easton, Galli-Curci, Garden, Gates, Gordon, Hempel, Jeritza, McCormack, Melba, Nordica, Patti, Ponselle and Schumann-Heink. Armstrong's literate portraits of these operatic celebrities gain by his personal acquaintance or friendship with most of them. He enriches his writing with the many incidents he witnessed. An entertaining, lightweight work.

1542 Artís, Andrés Avelino. *Aquella entremaliada Barcelona*, (por) Sempronio (Andrés-Avelino Artís). In Spanish. Biblioteca Selecta, vol. 500, Història XLV. Barcelona: Selecta, 1978. 205 pp. Illustrated.

Includes some information about Manuel Utor.

1543 ————. *Sonata a la Rambla*, por Sempronio (Andrés-Avelino Artís). In Spanish. Barcelona: Barna, 1961. 273 pp. Illustrated.

The author, a well-known Spanish journalist recollects in this pleasant book a large number of anecdotes linked with the Rambla, a famous avenue in Barcelona leading from the center of the city to the harbor. The four parts of chapter 1 are devoted to Barrientos, Lázaro, Palet and Utor. AM

1543/A Barilli, Bruno, 1880-1952. *Il paese del melodramma*. Prefazione di Emilio Cecchi. In Italian. Lanciano: G. Carabba, 1930. 218 pp.

Short sketches by an outstanding journalist, music critic and composer of two operas, containing his personal impressions about a number of opera singers. Most of the writings gathered here first appeared in *Il Tempo* and *Tevere*. Barilli's graceful, almost poetic command of Italian makes this volume a delight to read. AM

1544 Barker, Frank Granville. *Stars of the Opera*. With a foreword by Geoffrey Handley-Taylor. London: Published for British Poetry-Drama Guild by Lotus Press, 1949. 51 pp. Illustrated.

On Dal Monte, Gigli, Gobbi, Infantino, Melchior, Shacklock, Silveri, Turner and Welitsch.

1545 ————. *Voices of the Opera*. London: A. Unwin, 1951. 61 pp.

An insignificant book with brief, superficial biographical sketches of nine singers (Christoff, Coates, Flagstad, Guerrini, Hammond, Midgley, Svanholm, Tagliavini and Tajo) and conductor Victor de Sabata.

1546 Battaglia, Fernando. *L'arte del canto in Romagna. I cantanti lirici romagnoli dell'Ottocento e del Novecento*. In Italian. Bologna: Bongiovanni, 1979. 263 pp. Illustrated. Bibliography, pp. 246-247. Index, pp. 249-256.

The author's objective was to bring order and clarity to the large amount of confusing and often fictitious information about singers regarded as Romagnese by birth, origin or adoption. They are divided into three groups, arranged alphabetically. The first contains 27 singers for whom extensive, interesting, and occasionally unpublished documentation exists; the second lists 40 lesser singers whose career summary could be reconstructed from secondary sources only; the last six singers are still active, thus the author did not want to pass judgment on them. There is a chronology and bibliography for the first group only. Two short appendices list the singing teachers and theaters of Romagna. RT

1547 Bazzetta de Vemenia, Nino, b. 1881. *Le cantanti italiane dell'-ottocento: ricordi, aneddoti, intimità, amori*. In Italian. Novara: G. Volante, 1945. 298 pp. Illustrated.

Colorful gallery of more than 110 portraits and miniatures of individuals, families and groups. The author dips his brush into history as well as cosmopolitan sophistication. RT

1548 Bennati, Nando. *Musicisti ferraresi. Note biografiche*. In Italian. Ferrara: G. Zuffi, 1901. 56 pp.

1549 Bennett, Joseph, 1831-1911. *Forty Years of Music, 1865-1905*. London: Methuen, 1908. xvi, 415 pp. Illustrated. Index, pp. 411-415.

Reminiscences of the English music critic who had seen, heard and met seemingly every major musical figure living, performing or staying in London. While it contains little biographical material of singers, the cumulation of the numerous vignettes lend value to this book.

1550 Bernsdorf, Eduard, 1825-1901, editor. *Neues Universal-Lexikon der Tonkunst. Für Künstler, Kunstfreunde und alle Gebildeten....* In German. Dresden: Robert Schaefer, 1856-65. 4 vols. (vol. 3 and suppl.).

1551 Berutto, Guglielmo. *I cantanti piemontesi. Dagli albori del melodramma ai nostri giorni*. In Italian. Torino: Italgrafica, 1972. 285 pp. Illustrated. Bibliography, pp. 275-283.

Dictionary of more than 320 singers of Piemontese birth, blood or adoption. Uniform data, collected through many years of patient research. RT

1552-T Bing, Rudolf, b. 1902. *5000 Abende in der Oper. Mit 32 Bildseiten und einer Chronik der Bing-Jahre 1950-1972 an der Metropolitan Opera, New York.* Translated by Evelyn Linke. In German. München: Kindler, 1973. 333 pp. Illustrated. At head of title: *Die Sir Rudolf Bing Memoiren.*

This, the German edition of Bing's book, differs from the original only in the supporting material that has been added. There is a year-by-year fact sheet of the Bing-years at the Met listing new productions, new artists and a summary of the year entitled "highlights"; there is also a name index that had been badly missed in the original edition.

1553 ———. *5000 Nights at the Opera.* Garden City, N.Y.: Doubleday, 1972. 360 pp. Illustrated.

The long-awaited memoirs of the colorful General Manager of 22 years of New York's Metropolitan Opera House. Bing palpably contains his caustic wit throughout and the book fails only through the reader's intuition as to what Bing chose—or was forced—to leave out. What *is* there is a fascinating document of a career spent at the center of international operatic life.

1553-a ———. *5,000 Nights at the Opera.* London: Hamilton, 1972. 285 pp. Illustrated. Index.

1553-b ———. *5000 Nights at the Opera; the Memoirs of Sir Rudolf Bing.* New York: Popular Library, 1972. 360 pp. Illustrated.

1554-T ———. *5000 sere all'Opera.* Roma?: Vallecchi, 197?

1555 ———. *A Knight at the Opera.* New York: Putnam, 1981. 287 pp. Repertory, pp. 265-268. Index, pp. 281-287. New Productions, pp. 269-278. List of Conductors, Singers, Dancers, Choreographers, Actors, pp. 241-261.

A poor sequel to Bing's first book, it neither amplifies nor completes the original life story. There is a fascinating exchange of letters with Callas quoted in full about projects that did not materialize, and a terribly sad chapter about the prolonged illness of Mrs. Bing. Beyond that, Sir Rudolf makes an effort to say only good things about his former associates and Met artists, a posture that renders his value judgments almost meaningless.

1556 Blaukopf, Kurt. *Grosse Oper, grosse Sänger.* In German. Bücher der Weltmusik, Bd. 7. Teufen/St. Gallen: A. Niggli und W. Verkauf, 1955. 170 pp. Illustrated. Bibliography, p. 170. Discography, pp. 154-169. 2nd enlarged edition published by the same publisher in 1959.

Competent discussion of diverse musical subjects, ranging from tradition to stage directors, composers to vocal art. This is followed by a section of capsulized biographies of 28 singers from Caruso to Windgassen. Most subjects—excepting Caruso—are given only one page or less space. The inconsequential discography lists a few dozen works available on LPs at the time of publication, presumably chosen by the author to illustrate some of his points.

1557 Blum, Daniel C. *A Pictorial Treasury of Opera in America*. New York: Greenberg, 1954. 315 pp. Illustrated.

1558 Bonaventura, Arnaldo, 1862-1952. *Musicisti livornesi*. In Italian. Livorno: S. Belforte, 1930. 91 pp.

Contains in a continuous narrative the very brief outline of activities and accomplishments of musicians of Livornese origin from the eighteenth to the twentieth century. The term "musician" is interpreted broadly to include anyone whose professional endeavors were in the field of music, from composers (Mascagni) to vocalists, among the latter Celeste Coltellini, Nicola Tacchinardi, Enrico delle Sedie, and Mario Ancona (pp. 66-67).

1559 ————. *Ricordi e ritratti (fra quelli che ho conosciuto)*. In Italian. Quaderni dell'Accademia chigiana, 24. Siena: Ticci, 1950. 77 pp. Edition limited to 300 numbered copies.

1560 Bossan, George S. de. *Nederlandsche zangeressen*. In Dutch. Caecilia-reeks, no. 7. Amsterdam: Bigot & Van Rossum, 1941. 128 pp. Illustrated. Bibliography, p. 128. Index, pp. 126-128.

Biographies of Dutch women singers, two or three pages in length, in chronological order. They begin in the mid-nineteenth century and end with the events in the late 1930s. Discusses the characteristics of their voices, their performances, most famous roles, etc. There are pictures of the singers, none in costume. HCS

1561 Bracale, Adolfo. *Mis memorias*. In Spanish. Caracas: Elite, 1931. 217 pp. Illustrated.

An unsophisticated yet fascinating narrative of his successes and adventures as an impresario. Of particular value and interest is his story of Caruso's Cuban engagement which netted the tenor $90,000 for ten performances. Bracale concluded this volume of his memoirs with the promise of a second volume, which could not be traced. We assume that he never wrote it. The English translation of this book has circulated in manuscript (see item 1840).

1561-a ————. *Mis memorias*; prólogo de José Ramírez. In Spanish. 2nd ed. Bogotá: Editorial ABC, 1931. 193 pp. Illustrated.

1562 Brémont, Anna (Dunphy) de. *The World of Music.... The Great Singers....* London: W.W. Gibbings, 1892. 227 pp.

Subjects are Braham, Billington, Catalani, Garcia, Giuglini, Grisi, Hayes, Lablache, Lind, Malibran, Mario, Parepa-Rosa, Pasta, Rubini, Ronconi, Schröder-Devrient, Sontag and Tietjens.

1563 Breslin, Herbert H., editor. *The Tenors*. New York: Macmillan, 1974. xv, 203 pp. Illustrated. Index, pp. 197-203.

Public relations manager Herbert Breslin, generally credited with Pavarotti's media ubiquity, is the editor of this collection of "portraits" of the five leading tenors of the early seventies:

Corelli, Domingo, Pavarotti, Tucker and Vickers. Each chapter has a different author and thus the writing varies from workmanlike journalism to literary portraiture. The best piece of writing is Breslin's own preface.

1564 Brook, Donald. *Singers of Today*. London: Rockliff, 1949. 226 pp. Illustrated. 2nd revised edition by same publisher in 1958.

This is a collection of brief sketches of forty singers, 36 of them from the British Commonwealth (the exceptions are Flagstad, Gigli, Silveri and Schumann) and therein lies the particular value of the book. Most of these artists are not known outside the British Isles, and even for many of those who are, this is the only source of biographical material. The chapters are based on interviews, although the singers' statements are rephrased, "reported" by the author.

1564-a ————. *Singers of Today*. Freeport, N.Y.: Books for Libraries Press, 1971.

Reprint of the 1949 edition of Rockliff, London (q.v.).

1565 Brower, Harriette Moore, b. 1869. *Vocal Mastery; Talks with Master Singers and Teachers, Comprising Interviews with Caruso, Farrar, Maurel, Lehmann, and Others*. New York: Frederick A. Stokes, 1920. 292 pp. Illustrated.

Those interviewed are Barrientos, Bispham, Braslau, Caruso, Case, D'Alvarez, De Luca, Easton, Farrar, Galli-Curci, Hempel, Homer, Johnson, Kingston, Lilli Lehmann, Martinelli, Maurel, Muzio, Raisa, Scotti, Tetrazzini, Werrenrath and Witherspoon.

1566 Buffen, Frederick Forster. *Musical Celebrities*. London: Chapman Hall, 1889.

The unnumbered first series of Buffen's musical biographies, it gives a short, 4-8 page biographical summary of 18 musicians, among them three singers, Henschel, Adelina Patti and Reeves. The artists are of the first rank, thus the tone of the writing is justifiably laudatory. The information given is not exclusive to this publication; the portraits are uniformly excellent for the period.

1567 ————. *Musical Celebrities*. *Second Series*. London: Chapman & Hall, 1893. 120 pp. Illustrated.

Short, 3- to 6-page biographical sketches of several pianists and 19 singers, all but three of them women. They are Albani, Brema, Calvé, De Lussan, Eames, Hauk, Melba, Moody, Nevada, Nordica, Ponti, Giulia Ravogli, Sofia Ravogli, Edouard Reszke, Jean de Reszke, Rôze, Russell, Scovel and Valleria. The writing is superficial and the contents an unsatisfactory mixture of biography and adulation, stressing the glitter and glamour of a career. There is a magnificent portrait of each artist made by the best photographers of the period.

1568 Callejo Ferrer, Fernando. *Música y músicos portorriqueños*. In Spanish. San Juan, Puerto Rico: Cantero Fernandez, 1915. 313 pp. Illustrated.

A history of Puerto Rican music and musicians from 1660 until 1914. An entire chapter is devoted to Spanish tenor Antonio Paoli, who was born on the island. The rest of the book includes a large number of vocalists not well known internationally; it is possibly the only source of information on them. AM

1569 Camner, James, editor. *The Great Opera Stars in Historic Photographs: 343 Portraits from the 1850's to the 1940's.* New York: Dover Publications, 1978. 199 pp. Index, pp. 197-199.

Without doubt the best collection of photographs of opera singers in its breadth of coverage. The 343 portraits show singers of a whole century, from the 1850s to the 1940s. The quality of reproductions is excellent.

1569/A Caputo, Pietro. *Cotogni, Lauri-Volpi, e ...: breve storia della scuola vocale romana.* Prefazione di Laura Padellaro. In Italian. Bologna: Bongiovanni, 1980. 151 pp. Illustrated. Index, pp. 143-147.

Contains short biographies of about forty singers, including Antonio Cotogni and Giacomo Lauri-Volpi.

1570 Carpentier, Alejo, 1904-1980. *Ese músico que llevo dentro.* Selección de Zoila Gómez. In Spanish. La Habana: Editorial Letras Cubanas, 1980. 3 vols.

An excellent collection of the writings of the celebrated Cuban novelist and journalist, several times nominated for the Nobel Prize in literature. Over fifty of these short masterpieces focus on opera singers, among them Amato, Caruso, Chaliapin, Gigli, Kapitan Zaporojetz, Lázaro, Ruffo, Stracciari and others. AM

1571 Celletti, Rodolfo, editor. *Le grandi voci; dizionario critico-biografico dei cantanti con discografia operistica.* Consulenti per le discografie: Raffaele Vegeto (e) John B. Richards. Redattore Luisa Pavolini. In Italian. Collana Scenario, 1. Roma: Istituto per la collaborazione culturale, 1964. xiv, 1044 columns. Illustrated.

The bulk of this "critical-biographical dictionary of singers" has been taken from the monumental 15-volume set (plus supplements) of the *Enciclopedia dello Spettacolo*, often augmented, supplemented or rewritten by the editor. A discography listing most of a singer's operatic (only) recordings is appended to each biography. The undertaking was ambitious, the execution typographically beautiful, the overall results flawed. The objection centers on the excessive number of factual errors. It ranges from such obvious ones as Antonio Magini-Coletti's being born three years *after* his stage debut, through Christoff's 1949-50 recordings identified as "acoustics," to the absurdity of Jadlowker's having recorded the "Ansprache des Landgrafen" from *Tannhäuser*. Celletti's informative biographies vary in length according to the historical importance of the singer. Bearing the above caveat in mind, this is an important and useful work. There is a 127-column listing of complete operas on 78s and LPs. The photographic material is uniformly excellent, the reproduction good.

1572 Chapin, Schuyler. *Musical Chairs: A Life in the Arts.* New York: Putnam, 1977. 448 pp. Illustrated. Index, pp. 437-448.

After a professional life spent in the music world and among musicians, through a succession of unfortunate events (among them the death of Goeran Gentele), Chapin found himself in 1972 at the helm of the Metropolitan Opera House, the successor of Rudolf Bing. According to Chapin's presentation, he fell victim to an internal power struggle and when he realized he was expendable he resigned, three years, almost to the day, after being named general manager.

1573 Charnacé, Guy de, 1825-1909. *Les étoiles du chant.* Livraison 1-3. In French. Paris: Plon, 1869. 3 parts in 1 vol. Illustrated.

The subjects: Krauss, Christine Nilsson and Adelina Patti.

1574 Chorley, Henry Fothergill, 1808-1872. *Thirty Years' Musical Recollections.* London: Hurst and Blackett, 1862. 2 vols.

Chorley was one of the most important music critics and writers on matters operatic in London in the period covered by this work. His strength was in his writing on Italian opera; however, he misjudged the importance of the works of Wagner and for this he has been highly criticized. The book describes each musical season in London, beginning with the year 1830 and ending with 1860. This was the period when many works of Bellini, Rossini, Donizetti and Verdi were heard for the first time in London, and with casts which boggle the modern mind. Authoritative descriptions of these performances and these artists are of the greatest historical importance. Chorley's style makes for easy reading; he has wit and frankness in his opinions, which make delightful history. WRM

1574-a ———. *Thirty Years' Musical Recollections.* Edited with an introduction by Ernest Newman. New York: A.A. Knopf, 1926. xxv, 411 pp. Illustrated. Index, pp. 403-411.

1575 *Cincuenta entrevistas con gente importante del mundo de la música.* In Spanish. Colección Monografías Monsalvat, no. 4. Barcelona: Ediciones de Nuevo Arte Thor, 1980. 236 pp. Illustrated.

Contains fifty interviews made by some twenty journalists and published in the opera magazine *Monsalvat* during the first five years (1974-1978) of its existence. AM

1576 Clayton, Ellen Creathorne, 1834-1900. *Queens of Song: Being Memoirs of Some of the Most Celebrated Female Vocalists Who Have Appeared on the Lyric Stage, from the Earliest Days of Opera to the Present Time. To Which Is Added a Chronological List of All the Operas That Have Been Performed in Europe.* London: Smith, Elder, 1863. 2 vols. Illustrated.

Biographies of 42 singers who achieved international renown, mostly in the first half of the nineteenth century, among them Arnould, Billington, Catalani, Pasta, Sontag, Grisi, Novello, Viardot, Lind, Alboni, Hayes, Piccolomini and Tietjens. Three chapters are devoted to two singers each; the balance of the artists are given complete chapters. The biographies are quite detailed, with dates, places and roles performed. Many biographies contain quotations from their subjects, suggesting that the author knew many of these singers personally. The chronological list of operas is arranged by composer, beginning with Lulli (1673) and ending with Mellon (1859). Verdi is listed through *Forza del Destino* (1862); the last entry appears to be Balfe's *The Armorer of Nantes* (London, February 12, 1863). Wagner's name appears in a separate list headed "Alphabetical List of Dramatic Composers not pre-eminent as operatic writers." WRM

1576-a ————. *Queens of Song: Being Memoirs of Some of the Most Celebrated Female Vocalists Who Have Performed on the Lyric Stage from the Earliest Days of Opera to the Present Time. To Which Is Added a Chronological List of All the Operas That Have Been Performed in Europe.* New York: Harper, 1864. xiv, 543 pp. Illustrated. Bibliography, pp. xiii-xiv.

The American edition in one volume of the two-volume London edition of Smith, Elder and Company (q.v.).

1576-b ————. *Queens of Song; Being Memoirs of Some of the Most Celebrated Female Vocalists Who Have Performed on the Lyric Stage from the Earliest Days of Opera to the Present Time....* Freeport, N.Y.: Books for Libraries Press, 1972. xiv, 543 pp. Illustrated. Bibliography, pp. xiii-xiv.

Reprint of the 1865 edition by Harper and Brothers, New York.

1577 Cohen, F. *L'Opéra*. In French. Paris, 1876. Edition limited to 500 copies.

As per the dealer's catalog that was the source of this citation, one page is devoted to each artist; half of them singers, the other half dancers; with a poem addressed to them by the author.

1578 Conrad, Max Alfred Wilhelm, b. 1872. *Im Schatten der Primadonnen; Erinnerungen eines Theaterkapellmeisters.* In German. Atlantis-Musikbücherei. Zürich: Atlantis Verlag, 1956. 208 pp. Illustrated.

1579 Cook, Ida. *We Followed Our Stars*. New York: Morrow, 1950. 246 pp. Illustrated.

A wonderfully constructed autobiographical narrative of the author's life that led her, and her sister Louise, into the intimate circle of opera stars, among them Pinza, Rethberg, Ponselle and Galli-Curci. At midpoint the narrative shifts the focus of attention away from opera, to the illegal rescue work the two ladies undertook in Hitler's Germany, first by accident, later by design. Following their "stars" to Germany and Austria, with the active help of their operatic friends, Viorica Ursuleac and her husband, Clemens Krauss, they helped dozens of the persecuted people of Europe to escape to England. An eminently readable book by a skilled writer, author of over eighty books for young women, under the pen name of Mary Burchell. She is also the "ghost" of Tito Gobbi's autobiography, *My Life* (item 583).

1579-a ————. *We Followed Our Stars*. London: H. Hamilton, 1950. 246 pp. Illustrated.

1579-b ————. *We Followed Our Stars*. London: Mills & Boon, 1956. 246 pp. Illustrated.

1580 ————. *We Followed Our Stars*. Toronto: Harlequin—Mills and Boon, 1976. 287 pp. Illustrated.

Not a mere republication of the 1950 edition, but rather an updated version of the original life story. As Ida Cook writes, "it seems to me unnecessarily arbitrary to break the narrative abruptly ... in 1947." The new chapter adds the appropriate finishing touch to the book.

1581 Cooke, James Francis, b. 1875. *Great Singers on the Art of Singing: Educational Conferences with Foremost Artists; a Series of Personal Study Talks with the Most Renowned Opera, Concert and Oratorio Singers of the Time, Especially Planned for Voice Students*. Philadelphia: Theo. Presser, 1921. 304 pp. Illustrated.

After an introduction ("Vocal Gold Mines and How They are Developed") and a chapter on the "Technique of Operatic Production," the balance of this book is made up of a series of interviews, each written in the first person, with the following singers: Alda, Amato, Bispham, Butt, Campanari, Caruso, Claussen, Dalmorès, Dippel, Eames, Easton, Farrar, Gadski, Galli-Curci, Garden, Gluck, de Gogorza, Hempel, Melba, De Pasquali, Schumann-Heink, Scott, Scotti, Thursby, Werrenrath and Williams. Each interview is prefaced by a brief biographical sketch and covers a wide range of subjects: Eames tells of studying with Gounod; Bispham talks of the main elements of interpretation; Schumann-Heink discusses "Keeping the Voice in Prime Condition," etc. These interviews originally appeared in the monthly magazine, *The Etude*, over a period of several years. WRM

1582 Corte, Andrea della, b. 1883. *L'interpretazione musicale e gli interpreti*. In Italian. Torino: Unione tipografico-editrice torinese, 1951. xvi, 574 pp. Illustrated.

1583 Crowest, Frederick James, 1850-1927. *Advice to Singers, by a Singer*. New, enlarged ed. London: Frederick Warne, 1880. The book went through at least ten editions and revisions.

1584 ————. *A Book of Musical Anecdote, from Every Available Source*. London: R. Bentley, 1878. 2 vols.

A collection of anecdotes about musicians. A revised edition appeared in 1902 under the title *Musicians' Wit, Humour, & Anecdote* (q.v.).

1585 ————. *Musician's Wit, Humour & Anecdote*. Illustrated by J.P. Donne. London: The Walter Scott Publishing Co., 1902. 423 pp. Illustrated.

A real miscellany of stories about musicians, arranged in no particular order—an expansion of a former collection published under the title *A Book of Musical Anecdote* (q.v.). Fortunately, an index is supplied, in which one notes such names as Albani (2 entries), Alboni (3), Mrs. Billington (5), Blauvelt (1), Butt (6), Calvé (3), Eames (1) and so on through Lind (10), Malibran (19), Patti (9), etc. Some of the stories are familiar; some are not. How many of them have merit? Who knows? WRM

1586 Culshaw, John, 1924-1980. *Putting the Record Straight; the Autobiography of John Culshaw*. New York: Viking Press, 1981. 362 pp. Index, pp. 355-362.

Culshaw's autobiography, left incomplete by his premature death, contains numerous vignettes and extensive discussions devoted to many singers with whom he worked during his remarkable career as record producer for English Decca. There are many passages relating to Price, Björling, Tebaldi, McCracken, Corelli and others. Culshaw's easy style and sense of proportion make his book a delight to read.

1586-a ————. *Putting the Record Straight; the Autobiography of John Culshaw*. London: Secker & Warburg, 1981. 362 pp. Index.

1587 ————. *Ring Resounding*. New York: Viking, 1967. 276 pp. Illustrated. Index, pp. 271-276. Discography, pp. 268-270.

Culshaw's famous saga of the Solti *Ring* for English Decca (London Records) contains many important statements about the work and personalities of the soloists who participated in the project. In addition to the central theme, the first complete recording of Wagner's *Der Ring des Nibelungen*, Culshaw's observations about Flagstad, Windgassen, Nilsson and many others are documents of lasting interest. It bears recording that the tenor referred to as "our Siegfried," who dropped out of the project before it began, was Ernst Kozub; the ill-tempered egocentric Viennese conductor (pp. 25-26) was Joseph Krips.

1587-a ————. *Ring Resounding*. London: Secker & Warburg, 1967. 284 pp. Illustrated. Index.

1587-b ————. *Ring Resounding*. New York: Time-Life Records Special Edition, 1972. 278 pp. Illustrated. Index, pp. 275-278. Discography, pp. 271-272.

Considerably more than a re-publication of the 1967 first edition, this superbly designed and executed book has a new author's note and acknowledgment, a publisher's biography of Culshaw and an outstanding collection of illustrations gathered, or especially made, for this edition. It was published in a presentation box with G.B. Shaw's *The Perfect Wagnerite* and Robert W. Gutman's *Richard Wagner*.

1588 Curzon, Henri de, 1861-1942. *Croquis d'artistes*. In French. Paris: Librairie Fischbacher, 1898. xiv, 252 pp. Repertory. Chronology of Performances.

Excellent biographical sketches of 16 prominent singers (Caron, Carvalho, Faure, Fugère, Galli-Marié, Isaac, Krauss, Lassalle, Maurel, Christine Nilsson, Renaud, Saléza, Taskin, Vergnet, Viardot-Garcia and van Zandt) of the late nineteenth and early twentieth centuries, each with a chronological list of roles assumed to date of publication. Gives an interesting appraisal of a number of these artists near the ends, at the midpoints, or at the beginnings of their careers. Handsome photographic reproductions. WRM

1589 Davidson, Gladys. *Opera Biographies*. London: W. Laurie, 1955. 352 pp. Illustrated. Bibliography, pp. 345-346.

Index, pp. 347-352.

In covering the lives of 119 singers in sketches which usually
average 2 or 3 pages, each author has tended to include a smattering
of the great names of the distant past, such as Grisi, Lind and
Mario, and a large number of the great from the more recent past:
Albani, Caruso, Chaliapin, Destinn, Edvina, Farrar, Galli-Curci,
Jeritza, McCormack, Melba, Nordica, etc. British singers of the 20s
and 30s receive still more attention, and we find names like
Austral, Coates, Lawrence, Radford, Teyte and Turner. Still more space
is given to singers popular at the time of publication, and while we
find Björling, Grandi, Schumann, Schwarzkopf and other well-known
names, they are intermixed with many lesser artists who never ful-
filled the promise expected of them. Although the selection of
artists covered in the book is lopsided towards today's singers, this
is still a remarkable collection. It contains many hard-to-find facts
about some singers of perhaps lesser importance in the history of
opera, which are hard to locate elsewhere. WRM

1589-a ———. *A Treasury of Opera Biography.* New York: Citadel
Press, 1955. 352 pp. Illustrated.

The American edition of the 1955 edition of *Opera Biographies,*
W. Laurie, London (q.v.).

1590 De Bekker, Leander Jan, 1872-1931. *Black's Dictionary of
Music and Musicians, Covering the Entire Period of Musical History
from the Earliest Times to 1924.* London: A. and C. Black, 1924.
757 pp. First published under the title: *Stokes' Encyclopedia of Music
and Musicians.*

1591 ———, and Winthrop Parkhurst. *The Encyclopedia of Music and
Musicians.* New York: Crown, 1937. viii, 662 pp. Illustrated.

A universal musical dictionary, it went through many editions.
After the death of De Bekker, Winthrop Parkhurst prepared the subsequent editions. Crown reissued this edition in 1939.

1592 Donnay, Maurice. *Nos vedettes.* In French. Paris: Joe Bridge,
1924? 308 pp. Index, pp. 303-308.

1593 Downes, Olin, 1886-1955. *Olin Downes on Music; a Selection
from His Writings During the Half-Century 1906 to 1955.* Edited by
Irene Downes, with a preface by Howard Taubman. New York: Simon and
Schuster, 1957. 473 pp. Illustrated.

A chronological arrangement of over 170 of Olin Downes's reviews published in the Boston *Post* and *The New York Times*, selected by his
wife, Irene Downes. They cover the whole spectrum of classical and
contemporary music; the reviews of operatic and vocal interest include
Calvé's recital with her tenor husband (!) Galileo Gaspari, Mary
Garden's Tosca, Tibbett's Emperor Jones, Jeritza's Carmen, Chaliapin's
obituary and several others. The quality of writing is uneven.

1594 Downes, Peter. *Top of the Bill: Entertainers Through the Years.*
Wellington, N.Z.: A.H. and A.W. Reed, 1979. 98 pp. Illustrated.

A history of stage entertainment in New Zealand, with chapters on various stage celebrities, popular and classical, including Buckman, D'Oisly, Natzke, Te Kanawa and Te Wiata. Profusely illustrated. WRM

1595 Dupêchez, Charles. *Les divas*. In French. Collection nostalgie-- L'univers des voix. Paris: Ramsay, 1980. 189 pp. Illustrated. Discography, pp. 187-189.

1596 Edwards, Henry Sutherland, 1828-1906. *Idols of the French Stage*. London: Remington and Co., 1889. 2 vols.

A cleverly written book in the style of literate gossip: amusing, rapid narrative, superficial and revealing at the same time. The singers are Arnould, Dugazon, Favart and Saint-Huberty. The book also has chapters on French actresses, from the wife of Molière to Sarah Bernhardt.

1597 ———. *The Prima Donna, Her History and Surroundings from the Seventeenth to the Nineteenth Century*. London: Remington and Co., 1888. 2 vols. Index, Vol. 2, pp. 293-302.

A distinctly nineteenth-century discussion, both in style and attitudes, of mostly nineteenth-century prima donnas. The originality lies in the organization of the material and in the style; otherwise these artists' portraits are the intelligent synthesis of written records, published commentary and the public opinion at the author's disposal, occasionally assisted by personal experience. They are Albani, Arnould, Bosio, Cuzzoni Sandoni, Fenton, Gabrielli, Grisi, Hasse, Lind, Lucca, Malibran, Mara, Mingotti, Christine Nilsson, Pasta, Adelina Patti, Robinson, Sontag and Tietjens.

1598 Eisenberg, Ludwig Julius, b. 1858. *Ludwig Eisenberg's grosses biographisches Lexikon der deutschen Bühne im XIX. Jahrhundert. Mit einem Titelbild*. In German. Leipzig: Paul List, 1903. 1180 pp. Illustrated. Bibliography, pp. 1174-1176.

1599 Engel, Louis. *From Mozart to Mario. Reminiscences of Half a Century*. London: R. Bentley, 1886. 2 vols.

These musical reminiscences deal mostly with composers. However, volume 2 contains three chapters of opera-biographical interest: Patti, pp. 245-289; Nilsson, pp. 290-331; Mario, pp. 332-371.

1600 Ertel, Paul, 1865-1933. *Künstler-Biographieen*. In German. Berlin: Hermann Wolff, 1898-? 10 vols.

1601 Escudier, Marie Pierre Yves, and Léon Escudier. *Études biographiques sur les chanteurs contemporains, précédées d'une Esquisse sur l'art du chant, par mm. Escudier frères*. In French. Paris: J. Tessier, 1840. 268 pp.

Following a brief introductory chapter on the art of singing, the book contains a collection of short, entertaining biographies of the most prominent singers of the Parisian operatic scene at the time it was published. Of great value are the biographies of singers not represented elsewhere, specifically the career of Eugénie (Mayer) Garcia, pupil of Garcia, Sr., and later the wife of Manuel Garcia,

Jr. The list also includes Cinti-Damoreau, Dorus-Gras, Duprez, Grisi, Lablache, Fanny, Rubini, Tamburini and Viardot-Garcia.

1602 ————. *Vie et aventures des cantatrices célèbres; précedées des Musiciens de l'empire et suivies de la Vie anecdotique de Paganini.* In French. Paris: E. Dentu, 1856. 380 pp.

1603 Esser, Grace Denton, b. 1890. *Madame Impresario; a Personal Chronicle of an Epoch.* Foreword by Merle Armitage. Yucca Valley, Calif.: Manzanita Press, 1974. 230 pp. Illustrated.

One of the founders of The Music Academy of the West in Santa Barbara, California, Grace Denton had a long career as an impresario. Trained as a musician, the author served an apprenticeship as a music teacher and later was on the staff of *The Musical Courier* in New York. She became involved in concert management in Toledo, where she got to know such artists as Galli-Curci, Mary Garden, Schumann-Heink, McCormack, Tibbett, Homer, Paderewski, Kreisler, Gabrilowitsch and Stokowski. Later she was connected with the Chicago Opera and various musical associations in the Midwest and on the West Coast. The text of the book is rather brief; the illustrations are spectacular. The author has shared with the reader literally hundreds of autographed photos of famous artists from her personal collection. WRM

1604 Ewen, David, b. 1907, comp. *Living Musicians.* New York: H.W. Wilson, 1940. 390 pp. Illustrated.

Ewen devotes a quarter to one page to each of the 500 musicians of American or international fame who were alive--as opposed to active-- at the time this book was published. All the major and several lesser known singers of the epoch are included, and while anyone can spot an omission, for many artists this is the sole source of biographical in- formation. The contents of the popular biographical sketches suggest that Ewen interviewed or consulted his subjects. There is a portrait for most biographees.

1605 ————. *Living Musicians. Supplement.* New York: H.W. Wilson, 1957. 178 pp. Illustrated.

Ewen continues in this volume the work he began with the main volume in 1940 (q.v.); the approximately 150 biographies follow the same plan in layout, style, length. As was the case with the first volume, the supplement also stresses American artists and artists active in America. One inexplicable omission is Mario Lanza, particularly in view of the fact that both George London and Frances Yeend, the other members of the Bel Canto Trio, are listed and so credited. At the time of publication Lanza was at the height of his fame, so the ex- clusion is all the more puzzling.

1606 Ewen, David. *Men and Women Who Make Music.* New York: Thomas Y. Crowell, 1939. xiv, 274 pp. Illustrated.

The singers are Flagstad, Lotte Lehmann, Melchior and Pinza.

1607 ————. *Men and Women Who Make Music.* New York: The Readers Press, 1945. xii, 244 pp. Illustrated.

Included are Anderson, Flagstad, Lotte Lehmann, Melchior, Moore, Pinza, Pons, Thomas and Tibbett.

1608 ————. *Men and Women Who Make Music*. New York: Merlin Press, 1949. x, 233 pp. Illustrated.

This is a reworking of Ewen's earlier works under the same title. There have been some additions and deletions in the coverage. These are short, popular biographies of singers (in addition to pianists, violinists, cellists), easy to read and moderately informative. The singers: Anderson, Flagstad, Lawrence, Lotte Lehmann, Melchior, Peerce, Pinza, Pons, Thomas, Tibbett and Traubel.

1609 ————. *Musicians Since 1900: Performers in Concert and Opera*. New York: H.W. Wilson Co., 1978. 974 pp. Illustrated.

This work was designed to replace the author's *Living Musicians* (1940, q.v.) and *Living Musicians: First Supplement* (1957, q.v.), both long out of print. The volume "provides detailed biographical, critical, and personal information about 432 of the most distinguished performing musicians in concert and opera since 1900," regardless of whether the artist is alive or dead. The individual articles are written in the same popular style as the ones in the *Living Musicians* volumes, but they are considerably longer, ranging from one to five pages. The printing and layout are identical. Most biographies are illustrated with a portrait, and the majority carry bibliographic citations of magazine or newspaper articles of recent vintage. A useful, popular reference work.

1610 Farga, Franz, b. 1873. *Die goldene Kehle, Meistergesang aus drei Jahrhunderten*. In German. Wien: A. Franz Göth, 1948. 315 pp. Illustrated. Index, pp. 305-315.

In an overview of singing and singers the book covers the timespan between the seventeenth and early twentieth centuries. Farga moves from the castrati to Faustina Bordoni and her circle, to Lully and his singers, to La Mara, Billington, Catalani, the two Leonoras (Milder and Schröder) and—a hundred pages later—ends up with Caruso and "a glance at today," including Jeritza and Slezak. Farga writes in a fluid and readable manner. His early chapter on the history of singing and the "golden throat" of the title, while cursory, is interesting. His materials concerning three centuries of "masters" are quite valuable. An excellent book. PHS

1611 Fenston, Joseph. *Never Say Die; an Impresario's Scrapbook*. London: A. Moring, 1958. 205 pp. Illustrated.

The autobiography of a "colorful" impresario from England, who seems to have dabbled in everything which seemed profitable. He dealt in jewelry and pearls in China, W.D. Griffith's films in England and France, and eventually became an impresario for singers and instrumentalists. The book is poorly written, yet interesting. It has more name-dropping than substance. Its most important segment is an extensive passage about Piccaver whom Fenston re-introduced in his own country amidst general acclaim. A brief but especially noteworthy vignette (p. 109) is of a "grand old lady" singing "Vissi d'arte" in a Buenos Aires cabaret, who turns out to be Ada Giachetti, Caruso's common-law wife and mother of his two sons.

1612 Ferris, George Titus, b. 1840. *Great Singers*. Appleton's New Handy-Volume Series, vols. 48, 66. New York: D. Appleton, 1880-81.

2 vols. The two volumes constitute the First Series (from Bordoni to Sontag), published in 1879, and the Second Series (Malibran to Tietjens), published in 1880. The two-volume set went through more than ten editions in the span of 25 years.

The author notes at the beginning of this work: "In compiling and arranging the material which enters into the following sketches of distinguished singers, it is only honest to disclaim any originality except such as may be involved in a picturesque presentation of facts. The compilor has drawn freely from a great variety of sources.... [T]he opinions and descriptions of writers and critics contemporary with the subjects have been used at length...." The "sketches" are fairly comprehensive, usually running to 30 or more pages for each singer. The singers are Alboni, Arnould, Billington, Catalani, Cruvelli, Gabrielli, Hasse, Grisi, Lind, Malibran, Pasta, Persiani, Schröder-Devrient, Sontag, Tietjens and Viardot. An important reference work. WRM

1612-a ————. *Great Singers*. Freeport, N.Y.: Books for Libraries Press, 1972. 2 vols. For a detailed list of subjects see the 1880-81 edition of this title.

Reprint of the 1880-81 edition of D. Appleton and Company, New York (q.v.).

1613 Ffrench, Florence, compiler. *Music and Musicians in Chicago; the City's Leading Artists, Organizations and Art Buildings, Progress and Development....* Chicago: F. Ffrench, 1899. 238 pp. Originally appeared as "the special Chicago edition of the *Musical Courier* two seasons ago." Illustrated.

A brief history of music in Chicago, with notations on musical organizations and theaters (to page 53), is followed by an alphabetical section made up of biographical essays (usually accompanied by photographs of the subjects) on local musicians. The work provides information on many obscure (on the international scene) artists, some of whom are known today from recordings which they left (e.g., Genevra Johnstone Bishop, Charles W. Clark), as well as information on the early careers of other artists who later became well known (e.g., George Hamlin, Bernice de Pasquali). There are over 150 biographical sketches. WRM

1614 Finck, Henry Theophilus, 1854-1926. *My Adventures in the Golden Age of Music*. New York: Funk & Wagnalls, 1926. xvi, 462 pp. Illustrated.

A mediocre autobiography, with musical emphasis, poorly written. There are brief sub-chapters on Caruso, Calvé, Eames, Nordica, Sembrich, Farrar, Homer, Fremstad, Schumann-Heink, Lehmann, Materna, Brandt, Niemann, Fischer, Alvary, de Gogorza, Renaud, Garden, Raisa, the de Reszke brothers, Jeritza, Bori, Galli-Curci, Easton and other musicians.

1614-a ————. *My Adventures in the Golden Age of Music*. Da Capo Press music reprint series. New York: Da Capo Press, 1971. xvi, 462 pp. Illustrated.

Reprint of the 1926 Funk and Wagnall, New York, edition (q.v.).

1615 ————. *Success in Music and How It Is Won; with a Chapter on Tempo Rubato by Ignace Jan Paderewski.* New York: Charles Scribner's Sons, 1924. 471 pp.

Subjects are Brandt, Calvé, Campanini, Catalani, Eames, Farrar, Garden, Lilli Lehmann, Lind, Lucca, Malibran, Mara, Mario, Maurel, Melba, Christine Nilsson, Nordica, Pasta, Adelina Patti, Renaud, Reszke, Rubini, Santley, Schröder-Devrient, Schumann-Heink, Sembrich, Sontag, Tamagno, Tetrazzini, Viardot-Garcia and Wüllner.

1616 Firner, Walter, editor. *Wir von der Oper, ein kritisches Theaterbildbuch, mit Beiträgen von Gitta Alpar, Fritz Busch, Willy Domgraf-Fassbaender....* Einleitung: Oscar Bie. Mit 40 Porträtstudien in Kupfertiefdruck nach Originalaufnahmen von Walter Firner. In German. München: F. Bruckmann, 1932. 126 pp. Illustrated.

1617 Flor, Kai, b. 1886. *Store tonenkunstnere jeg mødte.* In Danish. København: Berlingske forlag, 1954. 117 pp. Illustrated.

This is a volume of nine essays, each a reminiscence of a notable conductor or singer: Busch, Gigli, Furtwängler, Stokowski, Tango, Chaliapin, Høeberg, Forsell and Battistini. This small volume is of tremendous interest and should be made more accessible through translation. It is full of otherwise unavailable photographs from Flor's personal collection. The anecdotes concerning performances and contacts with musical personalities are interesting and entertaining. PHS

1618 Gaisberg, Frederick William. *The Music Goes Round.* New York: Macmillan, 1942. 273 pp. Illustrated.

1618-a ————. *The Music Goes Round.* New York: Arno Press, 1977. 273 pp. Illustrated. Index, pp. 269-273.

Reprint of the 1942 edition published by Macmillan, New York (q.v.).

1618-b ————. *Music on Record.* Foreword by Compton Mackenzie. London: R. Hale, 1946. 269 pp. Illustrated. First published under the title *The Music Goes Round* (q.v.).

1619 Ganz, Wilhelm, 1833-1914. *Memories of a Musician; Reminiscences of Seventy Years of Musical Life.* London: J. Murray, 1913. xv, 357 pp. Illustrated.

The recollections of a pianist-violinist-composer's life spent with music and among musicians. There are numerous references to singers: Lind, Cruvelli, Lablache, Alboni, Tietjens, Trebelli, Mario, Grisi, Reeves, Patti, Carvalho, Scalchi, Albani, Hauk, Nordica, de Lussan, de Reszke, Melba, Tetrazzini, Calvé, Destinn, Butt, Teyte, Ackté, with a whole chapter devoted to Patti--a veritable who's who of nineteenth-century opera.

1620 Gara, Eugenio, b. 1888. *Cantarono alla Scala.* In Italian. Milano: Teatro alla Scala/Electa, 1975. 180 pp. Illustrated.

A collection of excellent biographical sketches (on Bellincioni, Bonci, Borgatti, Caruso, Gayarre, Kaschmann, Lablache, Malibran,

Mirate, Pasta, Adelina Patti, Pertile, Rubini, Ruffo, Strepponi and Tamagno) previously published in the Milanese Review *Scala*. AM

1621 Gattey, Charles Neilson. *Queens of Song*. London: Barrie and Jenkins, 1979. 248 pp. Illustrated. Bibliography, pp. 235-238. Index, pp. 239-248.

An exceptionally well-researched book about five divas--Lind, Malibran, Melba, Adelina Patti and Tetrazzini--written with a delightful light touch that sustains reader interest throughout. Although each of the five main chapters is devoted to one singer, their stories as well as the introductory chapter offer valuable information about several other "queens of song." The extensive bibliography appended at the end suggests that the author has conducted comparative research to verify his facts.

1622 Gatti-Casazza, Giulio, 1869-1940. *Memories of the Opera*. New York: C. Scribner, 1941. xii, 326 pp. Illustrated. Index, pp. 319-326.

The anecdotal reminiscences of the General Manager of La Scala and later of the Metropolitan. Written--or dictated--by a tired old man whose style reflects his countenance well known from photographs and contemporary accounts. What could have been a major documentary of "the" golden age of opera is just a minor contribution by the man who not only witnessed it but helped it happen.

1622-a ———. *Memories of the Opera*. New York: Vienna House, 1973. xxvi, 326 pp. Illustrated. Index, pp. 319-326.

Reprint of the 1941 edition published by Scribner, New York (q.v.); with a new introduction.

1622-b ———. *Memories of the Opera*. Opera Library. London: John Calder, 1977. xxix, 326 pp. Illustrated. Index, pp. 319-326.

Reprint of the 1941 edition published by Scribner, New York (q.v.); with a new preface.

1623 Gelatt, Roland, b. 1920. *Music Makers, Some Outstanding Musical Performers of Our Day*. New York: Knopf, 1953. 286 pp. Illustrated.

Contains biographical sketches of 21 musicians: conductors, violinists, pianists, etc. Only three singers among them, ten pages devoted to each: Bernac, Flagstad and Lotte Lehmann.

1624 Gentile, Enzo, b. 1955. *Guida critica ai cantautori italiani*. In Italian. Guida 11. Milano: Gammalibri, 1979. 144 pp.

1625 Giovine, Alfredo. *Musicisti e cantanti lirici baresi*. In Italian. Biblioteca dell'archivio delle tradizioni popolari baresi. Bari: N.p., 1968. 63 pp. Illustrated.

1626 Glennon, James. *Australian Music and Musicians*. Adelaide: Rigby, 1968. 291 pp. Illustrated. Index, pp. 285-291.

Concise, one-or-two-page, biographies of 31 singers, 12 pianists, organists, instrumentalists, conductors, composers, conservatorium directors. The biographies are of well-known and lesser known Australian artists; the brief biographical section entitled "Profiles" (pp. 217-240) also has considerable value to the researcher. It is rather amazing how often Melba is mentioned as lending a hand to her musical countrymen and women. WRM

1627 Gourret, Jean, and Jean Giraudeau. *Encyclopédie des fabuleuses cantatrices de l'Opéra de Paris*. Préface de François Lesure. In French. Paris: Mengès, 1981. 317 pp. Illustrated. Bibliography, pp. 315-316. Index, pp. 307-314.

Fairly long biographies of 18 "fabulous" singers, followed by biographical notes on some 1,300 others. As these are obviously less "fabulous," some biographies are no longer than two lines. AM

1628 Grau, Robert, 1858-1916. *Forty Years Observation of Music and the Drama; Profusely Illustrated from Photographs and Prints*. New York: Broadway Publishing Co., 1909. iv, 370 pp. Illustrated.

The author was the brother of Maurice Grau (1849-1907). Maurice had brought Anton Rubinstein and Henri Wieniawski to the United States in 1872; in 1873 he formed the Kellogg Opera Company, and introduced Salvini, Ristori, Offenbach, and Bernhardt to the American public. As Manager of the Metropolitan Opera from its opening in 1883, he introduced such singers as Nilsson, Sembrich, Nordica, Melba, Eames, Plançon, Schumann-Heink and the two de Reszkes. Brother Robert, the author of this book, was associated with Maurice in one way or another during most of this period. He managed Patti's 1904 "farewell" tour of the United States, and describes a visit to Craig-y-Nos, Patti's castle in Wales, to arrange the details of this tour, and tells how he persuaded Mme. Patti to include in her programs a song called "The Last Farewell," written by Grau's friend, Charles K. Harris (composer of "After the Ball"). At least it can be said in Patti's defense that she was most reluctant about the whole affair!

This is probably one of the most poorly written reminiscences of this sort ever published! If there is any scheme of organization, it is difficult to find. The author wanders on about this and that, discussing Billie Burke in one paragraph and Marcella Sembrich in the next. There is no index, and it is next to impossible to find anything ... but the careful searcher will find bits and pieces of biographical detail about many singers who seldom figure in any literature. Along with Tetrazzini, Melba and others one can find material on Bessie Abott, Blanche Arral, Ellen Beach Yaw, Edith Helena, Alan Hinckley and scores of others whose voices are still known to record collectors, but about whose careers relatively little is known. There is also much about actors and actresses, as well as vaudeville stars. WRM

1629 Grew, Sydney, b. 1879. *Favourite Musical Performers*. Edinburgh: T.N. Foulis, 1923. 266 pp. Illustrated.

Musicians of all kinds are the subjects of this book: violinists, organists, conductors and four singers (Buckman, Coates, Mullings and Radford). The author claims personal acquaintanceship with them; some were his fellow voice students. The brief chapters are poorly organized, chatty and somewhat shallow, yet useful if taken in conjunction with other, more scholarly material.

1630 ————. *Makers of Music, the Story of Singers and Instrumentalists.* London: G.T. Foulis, 1924. 365 pp. Illustrated. Index, pp. 363-365.

A survey of performers through the ages, divided into three parts: violinists, pianists, singers. The section on singers discusses the most outstanding exponents of vocal art in the seventeenth, eighteenth and nineteenth centuries, from Siface (Giovanni Francesco Grossi) to Clara Novello. The selection of singers seems arbitrary, the style uninspired and the discussion a mere synthesis of the state of scholarship without particular insight or originality.

1631 Grial, Hugo de. *Músicos mexicanos.* In Spanish. Colección moderna, no. 44. Mexico: Diana, 1965. 283 pp.

Short biographies of some 150 Mexican musicians, among them 11 opera singers: Anitúa, Caraza, Castro-Escobar, Castro-Padilla, De Castro, Llera, Mojica, Negrete, Peralta, Romero and Romero-Malpica. AM

1632 Gunsbourg, Raoul, 1859-1955. *Cent ans de souvenirs ... ou presque.* In French. Monaco: Editions du Rocher, 1959. 228 pp.

The reminiscences of the colorful impresario-general manager of the Monte Carlo Opera during its golden epoch. This posthumous volume contains an autobiography and a long series of anecdotes which may be entertaining, but alas, so full of fiction that it discredits the entire volume. If Gunsbourg hadn't tried to "improve" on a good story about his singers, the book would be a valuable contribution to the literature. And if he had written it twenty years sooner....

1633-T ————. *Zwischen Petersburg und Monte Carlo.* In German. München: Langen-Müller, 1959. 232 pp.

The German translation of *Cent ans de souvenirs ... ou presque* (q.v.).

1634 Haas, Walter, b. 1921. *Nachtigall in Samt und Seide. Das Leben der grossen Primadonnen.* In German. Hamburg: v. Schroder, 1969. 402 pp. Illustrated.

Biographical sketches of all the "big" names. You name her, she is here. The writing is mediocre, the overview of each career is adequate.

1635 Hadden, James Cuthbert, 1861-1914. *Modern Musicians; a Book for Players, Singers and Listeners.* Boston: Phillips, 1913. 266 pp. Illustrated.

This is a companion volume to the same author's *Master Musicians*, which deals with composers only. He accomplishes his objective as stated in his preface, of writing musical biography "in a popular style ... for popular reading." The four- to eight-page biographies reflect the prevailing contemporary view of these artists. The book is divided into four sections: composers, pianists, singers, violinists and cellists. The singers are Butt, Calvé, Caruso, Kirkby-Lunn, Melba and Tetrazzini.

1635-a ————. *Modern Musicians; a Book for Players, Singers and*

Listeners. London: T.N. Foulis, 1913. 266 pp. Illustrated.

For subjects see the entry for the 1913 Phillips, Boston edition.

1635-b ————. *Modern Musicians; a Book for Players, Singers and Listeners*. London: P. Davies, 1928. 266 pp.

For subjects see the entry for the 1913 Phillips, Boston edition.

1636 Hartog, Jacques, 1837-1917. *Beroemde zengeressen*. In Dutch. Amsterdam: J.M. Meulenhoff, 1916. 315 pp. Illustrated.

Brief biographies of 23 female vocalists are contained in this volume. Their dates of birth (given for all but Barbi) range from 1749 to 1872. While the chapters dealing with the most prominent singers contain little or no material that could not be obtained from other, superior sources, the volume is important in one respect: it is possibly the only source of biographical information about six of the seven Dutch singers. A curious omission is Sembrich's name from the table of contents. PHS

1637 Hedberg, Frans Teodor, 1828-1908. *Svenska operasångere; karakteristiker och porträtter*. In Swedish. Stockholm: C.E. Fritze's K. Hofbokhandel, 1885. 319 pp. Illustrated.

1638 Hemel, Victor van. *De zangkunst; geschiedenis, over het lied en zijn componisten, beroemde zangers en zangeressen, methodes e.a....* In Dutch. Antwerpen: Cupido-Uitgave, 194? 53 pp. Illustrated. Bibliography, pp. 52-53.

This book begins with a history of music in general, from its beginnings to ca. 1600, a period when most music was sung. It traces the development of the Lied and song forms from the twelfth century to the present; it includes one-paragraph biographies of many great singers from the eighteenth century to the present, arranged nation-by-nation; it discusses the various vocal ranges and types (e.g., coloratura and dramatic) and illustrates their ranges with music on the staff. There is a one-and-a-half page discussion of technique. A later edition was published in 1958 (q.v.). HCS

1638-a ————. *De zangkunst; geschiedenis, over het lied en zijn komponisten, beroemde zangers en zangeressen, metodes, e.a.* In Dutch. 2nd enlarged ed. Antwerpen: Cupido-Uitg., 1958. 111 pp. Illustrated. Bibliography. Index, pp. 105-106. Discography, pp. 91-95.

An updated, expanded version of the edition from the 1940s. In addition to the musical and anatomical illustrations in the first edition, this edition contains portraits of composers and fairly uninteresting pictures of some instruments. There are several bibliographies: methods, pp. 80-85; textbooks on singing, pp. 96-98; short vocal works, pp. 86-90. The general bibliography for the book is on pp. 107-110. HCS

1639 Henderson, William James, 1855-1937. *The Art of Singing*. Introduction by Oscar Thompson. New York: The Dial Press, 1938. xviii, 509 pp.

This volume constitutes a reprinting of the author's 1906 book,

"The Art of the Singer" (q.v.) to which has been added a selection from Henderson's later works, made up of articles published during a lifetime of reviewing in *The New York Sun*, *Munsey's Magazine* and the *Laryngoscope*. The original articles date from 1896 to 1927, the first describing the nineteenth century's great singers, and the last devoted to "Flagstad and other great Isoldes." In between are articles on Calvé, Tetrazzini, Galli-Curci, Patti, Farrar, Caruso, Maurel, Jean de Reszke, Lilli Lehmann, Ponselle, Melba, Scotti, Renaud, Sembrich, Schumann-Heink and others. This selection from the pen of one of the most astute and knowledgeable of critics was selected by Oscar Thompson and Irving Kolodin to form a memorial volume for Mr. Henderson. WRM

1639-a ————. *The Art of Singing*. Introduction by Oscar Thompson. Freeport, N.Y.: Books for Libraries Press, 1968. xviii, 509 pp.

Reprint of the 1938 edition published by the Dial Press, New York (q.v.).

1640 ————. *The Art of the Singer: Practical Hints About Vocal Techniques and Style*. New York: C. Scribner's Sons, 1906. viii, 270 pp.

In the author's preface, he expresses the hope that the teacher, the student and the lover of singing will find set forth clearly and comprehensively what he had been able to learn in twenty-five years of careful study and original research pertaining to the singer's art. Today's reader can but agree that he succeeded in a most admirable manner. Mr. Henderson continued to produce "remarkably discussional articles" until his death in 1936. "Considered in detail or in their entirety, no more thoughtful and influential articles on music have appeared in the American press," said Oscar Thompson in a Henderson memorial volume entitled *The Art of Singing* (q.v.), which not only reprinted the 1906 work but presented a selection from the author's later articles. WRM

1641 Heriot, Angus, b. 1927. *The Castrati in Opera*. London: Secker & Warburg, 1956. 243 pp. Illustrated. Bibliography, pp. 229-232.

An intelligent, scholarly discussion of the role castrati played in the history and development of vocal music. The exhaustive bibliography is indicative of the author's familiarity with the subject which is reflected in his writing. Chapter 5 (pp. 84-199), as its title indicates, contains the "Careers of Some Well-Known Castrati." This is perhaps the most important source book on the subject.

1641-a ————. *The Castrati in Opera*. Da Capo Press Reprint Series. New York: Da Capo Press, 1974. 243 pp. Illustrated. Bibliography, pp. 229-232. Also issued in 1975 as a Da Capo paperback.

Reprint of the 1956 edition of Secker & Warburg, London (q.v.).

1642-T ————. *I castrati nel teatro d'opera*. Translated by Testi Piceni and Maria Grazia. In Italian. Milano: Rizzoli, 1962. 261 pp. Bibliography. Discography.

The Italian translation of the English-language original (q.v.).

1643 Héritte de la Tour, Louis. *Mémoires de Louise Héritte-Viardot. Une famille de grands musiciens; notes et souvenirs anecdotique sur Garcia, Pauline Viardot, la Malibran, Louise Héritte-Viardot et leur entourage.* In French. Paris: Stock, 1923. xi, 266 pp. Illustrated.

1644 Herzfeld, Friedrich, b. 1897. *Magie der Stimme; die Welt des Singens, der Oper und der grossen Sänger.* In German. Berlin: Ullstein, 1961. 263 pp. Illustrated. Bibliography, pp. 259-260. Index, pp. 261-263.

This is a thorough, though occasionally overly pedantic history of the use of the human voice in song. Divided into two major parts, singing and singers, it begins with an exposition of anatomy and physiology (including an excursus on the birth cry); moves on to a discussion of the voice in belief and in myth, in saga and legend; to the use of the voice in the early church; to polyphony and song; to the opera in the seventeenth century. The second half of the book, on singers, discusses most major singers from the sixteenth to the twentieth century. The chapters group singers first by period, then from the nineteenth century on by nationality. For the historian this is an indispensable volume; yet it is difficult to imagine anyone reading it for pleasure, despite its wealth of detail. An excellent collection of unusual photographs adds interest to the book. PHS

1645 Heylbut, Rose, b. 1899, and Aimé Gerber. *Backstage at the Opera.* New York: Thomas Y. Crowell, 1937. ix, 325 pp. Illustrated.

The Foreword states, "Aimé Gerber, paymaster of the Metropolitan opera association is responsible for the facts of the opera's life from 1898 to 1931, Rose Heylbut is responsible for the arrangement and writing." The contents are interesting, the writing excellent. There are long chapters devoted to the managerial and artistic personalities, the one about Caruso is perhaps the best portrait of the singer outside a full-length biography. Part III, entitled "The Factory," gives the reader a glimpse at the behind-the-scenes efforts it takes to prepare a performance.

1645-a ———. *Backstage at the Metropolitan Opera.* New York: Arno Press, 1977. ix, 325 pp. Illustrated.

Reprint of the 1937 edition published by T.Y. Crowell, New York, under the title *Backstage at the Opera* (q.v.).

1646 Honolka, Kurt. *Die grossen Primadonnen, von der Bordoni bis zur Callas.* In German. Stuttgart: Cotta, 1960. 286 pp. Illustrated.

1647 *How to Become a Successful Singer.* By Madame Clara Butt, Madame Melba, Signor Caruso, Mr. Ben Davies. London: George Newnes, 1912. 64 pp. Located as a title entry in the British Museum General Catalogue. No other library copy traced.

1648 Hurok, Solomon, 1888-1974, and Ruth Goode. *Impresario, a Memoir.* New York: Random House, 1946. 291 pp. Illustrated.

Hurok's first book is not an autobiography, although it contains material relating to his own life, but rather contains recollections of the great artists he managed over the years. There are long chapters about Chaliapin, Marian Anderson and, of course, Hurok's great personal interest: ballet and its stars. The writing is light and entertaining, the contents informative and exceptionally interesting. The book badly needs an index.

1648-a ———. *Impresario; a Memoir*. London: Macdonald, 1947. 272 pp. Illustrated.

1649 Deleted

1650 Hurst, Peter G. *The Golden Age Recorded; a Collector's Survey*. Henfield, Sussex: The author, 1946. 175 pp. Illustrated. Discography, pp. 133-175.

It is perhaps difficult in this day and age to realize that the author of this book took himself perfectly seriously, and moreover had an immense following, especially in England, who believed, as he most assuredly did, that he had invented record collecting. As it was his personal creation, he felt that he alone could "set the rules," and woe be unto the upstart who dared question his authoritatively stated "facts." Fortunately, the Hurst cult with its attendant puffery has nearly died out. Care should be exercised in using this work for reference purposes in serious work. Read as an example of a--fortunately--passing fad, one can enjoy the book as one may Monty Python. WRM

1651 ———. *The Golden Age Recorded*. Lingfield, Surrey: Oakwood Press, 1963. 187 pp. Discography, pp. 147-187.

In this completely revised and almost wholly re-written edition of his original book under the same title (1946, q.v.), Hurst seems to have mellowed a bit from his previous position of the record collector's dictator of sixteen years before. His inclusion of operatic cartoons from *Punch* suggests that in the mellowing process he has decided to convey that he does not take himself quite so seriously. Unlike Bunthorne in Gilbert and Sullivan's *Patience*, he does not go so far as to admit that he is an aesthetic sham, but there is just a hint of Bunthorne's tactics (see his song "Am I alone and unobserved?"). The warning issued in the annotation of his earlier book still applies: there is much wheat in these pages, but many of the statements so boldly made as fact prove, on close inspection, to be indeed chaff. WRM

1652 *Ispoved tenora*. In Russian. Moskva: V. Rikhter, 1896. 2 vols. in 1.

1653 Jacobs, Esther. *Love and Law. A Story of Joy and Woe in a Singer's Life*. New York: G.W. Dillingham, 1895. vi, 243 pp.

1654 Jacobson, Robert. *Reverberations; Interviews with the World's Leading Musicians*. New York: W. Morrow, 1974. 308 pp.

These interviews were conducted in the late sixties and early seventies by music critic and editor of *Opera News*, Robert Jacobson. About half of the interviews, 17 to be exact, are devoted to opera singers from Arroyo to Welitsch; the remaining 18 deal with composers, conductors, pianists, etc. The singers are Arroyo, Baker, Domingo, Farrell, Kirsten, Lear, Milnes, Birgit Nilsson, Price, Rysanek, Schwarz--·

kopf, Sills, Stewart, Thomas, Tourel, Vickers and Welitsch. Interviews with living and active musicians become obsolete upon publication. At the same time, as researchers are aware, they are invaluable pieces of mosaic that eventually make up the total picture of an artist's career. Jacobson adds currency to the interviews with an introductory paragraph that precedes each piece. They are well-written literary snapshots of the subjects who are allowed to do most of the "talking." Jacobson must be a pleasant and skilled interviewer.

1655 Jeri, Alfredo. *Bellegole; trecent'anni al teatro d'opera*. In Italian. Milano: A. Corticelli, 1947. 204 pp. Illustrated. Index, pp. 201-204.

A somewhat rambling discourse of singers and singing, embedded in a succession of stories, histories, anecdotes, views and appraisals. The clumsy style gets in the way of the message. A curious feature is a four-page quasi index without page references.

1656 Kingston, Claude, 1888-1978. *It Don't Seem a Day Too Much*. Adelaide: Rigby, 1971. 208 pp. Illustrated.

These are the memoirs of an Australian impresario. He devotes long passages to Melba, Chaliapin and Tibbett, among others, and his stories relating to these singers are not to be found elsewhere in the literature.

1656-a ———. *It Don't Seem a Day Too Much*. London: Hale, 1972. 208 pp. Illustrated.

1657 Klein, Hermann, 1856-1934. *The Golden Age of Opera*. London: G. Routledge, 1933. xxvi, 275 pp. Illustrated.

In his introduction, the author states: "That the richest and most productive period in the history of opera coincided in date and length with what is known as the Victorian Era is a fact that must be generally conceded. Hence the title of the present book, which, unlike my *Thirty Years of Musical Life in London* (q.v.), deals exclusively with opera and cognate subjects, and provides the first consecutive account of the 'Golden Age' of this much-admired form of lyric art. Nor is the title a merely fanciful one. Opera has flourished more or less for about 250 years; but during no period other than the Victorian-Edwardian did there ever occur such an amazing concentration of great works and great performances in the domain of the lyric drama...." In the present work, Klein covers the same territory as in his *Thirty Years*, but, in addition, brings the story well into the twentieth century, including the arrival of Caruso, the advent of Emmy Destinn, the affairs of Oscar Hammerstein and Sir Thomas Beecham, and discusses the effect of, and his appraisal of, the gramophone, with a few words on such singers as Alda, Amato, Annseau, Dux, Farrar and Chaliapin and their recordings. The importance the words of one who heard them all gives those of us who know only some of the last, and many of these only through recordings, cannot be overemphasized. WRM

1657-a ———. *The Golden Age of Opera*. New York: E.P. Dutton, 1933. xxvi, 275 pp. Illustrated.

American edition, "Printed in Great Britain."

1658 ———. *Great Women-Singers of My Time.* With a foreword by
Ernest Newman. New York: E.P. Dutton, 1931. vi, 244 pp. Illustrated.

Critic and teacher of singing in the Garcia tradition, Klein heard
most of the singers about whom he writes at their London debuts and
farewells; he also knew most of them personally throughout their professional careers. He was in a unique position to observe and compare
voices and musicianship. From his descriptions of the voices of those
singers the present generation knows from early recordings (i.e.,
Patti, Albani, Sembrich, Melba, Calvé, Schumann-Heink, Brandt and
Lehmann) we, who have no other way of knowing the qualities and failings of the others, can be better appraised of the reasons for their
fame. He tells about Albani, Alboni, Brandt, Calvé, Di Murska,
Klafsky, Lilli Lehmann, Lucca, Malten, Materna, Melba, Christine
Nilsson, Nordica, Patey, Adelina Patti, Ravogli, Reicher-Kindermann,
Scalchi, Schumann-Heink, Sembrich, Sterling, Sucher, Ternina, Tietjens,
Trebelli and Vogl. WRM

1658-a ———. *Great Women-Singers of My Time.* With a foreword by
Ernest Newman. Freeport, N.Y.: Books for Libraries, 1968. vi, 244
pp. Illustrated.

Reprint of the 1931 edition by E.P. Dutton, New York (q.v.).

1659 ———. *Musical Notes; Annual Critical Record of Important
Musical Events.* London: Carson & Comerford, 1887-1890. 4 vols. in 3.
3rd and 4th issue called 3rd and 4th year, and published by Novello,
Ewer.

1660 ———. *Musicians and Mummers.* London: Cassell and Company,
1925. xi, 340 pp.

In his preface to this book, the author states: "On the busy highways of Music and the Drama it is inevitable that the active critic
... should come into contact with what are commonly called 'celebrities'. During my journalistic career of over half a century I must
have personally encountered scores of them. Nevertheless I do not
limit the characters of this book to celebrities only.... I intro-
duce, together with these people, some of the forgotten labourers who
stood in the background...." The work covers some of the same ground,
with some important filling in, as his *Thirty Years of Musical Life
in London, 1870-1900* (q.v.), but carries the story onward for an
additional twenty-five years. In this work, the author surveys a
broader field, with more emphasis on dramatic, in addition to musical,
events. Klein was a pupil of Manuel Garcia, distinguished teacher of
singing in both London and New York, as well as a critic. His comments
on the great singers of his time are worthy of attention. WRM

1661 ———. *Thirty Years of Musical Life in London, 1870-1900.*
London: W. Heinemann, 1903. xvii, 481 pp. Illustrated.

Published simultaneously by the Century Co., in New York.

1662 Kobbé, Gustav, 1857-1918. *Opera Singers; a Pictorial Souvenir,
with Biographies of Some of the Most Famous Singers of the Day.* New
York: R.H. Russell, 1901. (87) pp. Illustrated.

Brief, generalized, flattering chapters about seven prominent
singers of the Metropolitan Opera at the turn of the century. They

include Calvé, Melba, Nordica, Edouard de Reszke, Jean de Reszke, Sembrich and Schumann-Heink. Each article is generously illustrated with excellent photographs. At the end of the volume there is an extensive photographic section containing pictures of many prominent singers of the period: Saléza, de Lussan, Gadski, Bréval, Plançon, Ternina, Scotti and others. The chapter entitled "Opera-Singers Off Duty" is illustrated with "snapshots" of famous singers clowning alongside a railroad car during an early transcontinental tour.

1663 ————. *Opera Singers; a Pictorial Souvenir, with Biographies of Some of the Most Famous Singers of the Day.* Boston: Oliver Ditson Company, 1906. 95 pp. Illustrated.

This edition is identical with the first, 1901, edition (q.v.) except that it has been expanded to include a chapter on Enrico Caruso (1873-1921) and Milka Ternina (1863-1941). Since neither edition was paginated, the addition of new material could be conveniently made.

1664 Kohut, Adolph, 1848-1917. *Die Gesangköniginnen in den letzten drei Jahrhunderten.* Berlin: H. Kuhz, 1905-06. 2 vols. in 1. Illustrated.

Four- to ten-page biographical summaries of the lives and activities of 46 singers. As the title indicates, these were the queens of song of the last three centuries. For many singers this volume well may be the only source of biographical information. It deserves to be translated into English for wider international accessibility.

1665 Kopecký, Emanuel, and Vilém Pospíšil. *Slavní pěvci Národního divadla.* In Czech. Edice umělcu Národního divadla, svazek 4. Praha: Panton, 1968. 223 pp. Illustrated.

Biographies of 32 Czech opera singers, with summaries in German.

1666 Krause, Ernst, b. 1911. *Opernsänger. 44 Porträts aus der Welt des Musiktheaters.* In German. Berlin: Henschelverlag, 1965. 145 pp. Illustrated.

Biographical sketches of opera singers, mostly "unknown" in the West, and, with some exceptions, mostly East Germans.

1667 ————, and Marion Schöne. *Opernsänger: 60 Porträts.* In German. Berlin: Henschelverlag, 1979. 183 pp. Illustrated.

An East Berlin publication, it contains the artistic portrait in prose and photographs of 60 singers active in East Germany, regardless of national origin. Only few are known in the West, the obvious examples who fall in this category are Adam, Dvorakova, Schreier, Tomowa-Sintow and Wenkoff. One to three pages are devoted to each singer, the articles are guardedly laudatory: they accentuate the positive and avoid mentioning anything unfavorable. There are no biographical data given or any discussion of the private lives of the artists. A selective repertory of each singer is given on pp. 175-183.

1668 Kühner, Hans. *Genien des Gesanges aus dem Zeitalter der Klassik und Romantik.* In German. Basel: Trias-Verlag, 1951. 309 pp. Illustrated.

Long, detailed chapters on Mara, Sontag, Malibran and Schröder-Devrient.

1669 ───────. *Grosse Sängerinnen der Klassik und Romantik; ihre Kunst, ihre Grosse, ihre Tragik.* In German. Stuttgart: Victoria Verlag, M. Koerner, 1954. 325 pp. Illustrated. Bibliography, pp. 318-320.

The main difference between this volume and the author's *Genien des Gesanges aus dem Zeitalter der Klassik und Romantik* (q.v.) is one added chapter, on Jenny Lind.

1670 Kuhe, Wilhelm, 1823-1912. *My Musical Recollections.* London: R. Bentley, 1896. xxviii, 394 pp. Illustrated. Index, pp. 387-394.

The recollections of a concert pianist-composer. He dwells on his own activities only to provide continuity to his anecdotes and reminiscences about the major musical personalities of the nineteenth century. Kuhe seems to have had a great affinity towards vocal music and opera in particular. He devotes nearly half of his book to his operatic experiences as a spectator, accompanist and personal friend of many singers. The critical comments of a trained musician about his colleagues are particularly noteworthy to a generation which never heard those singers, thus his lengthy observations about Mario, Lablache, Lind, Christine Nilsson, Patti and others are of great importance.

1671 Kun, Imre. *30 év müvészek között; egy hangversenyrendezö naplója.* In Hungarian. 2nd revised and enlarged ed. Budapest: Zenemükiadó, 1965. 236 pp. Illustrated.

As the title implies, Imre Kun spent thirty years (1920-1950) among artists as an impresario. The operatic interest of the book is limited. Although Kun and his agency handled the majority of domestic and foreign artists, the bulk of his clients were instrumentalists and conductors. However, in addition to brief mention of such singers as Tibbett, Giannini, Lehmann, Tauber, Schumann, Crooks, Björling and Völker, there are important eyewitness accounts of greater length of a Chaliapin recital, his Mephisto and Don Quixote, and a report of Galli-Curci's spectacular fiasco in *La Traviata.* The first edition of this book, published in 1960, could not be located for a complete bibliographic citation.

1672 Kurucz, Ladislao, b. 1923. *Vademecum Musical Argentino.* In Spanish. Buenos Aires: VAMUCA, 1983. 142 pp. Illustrated.

1673-T Kutsch, Karl J., and Leo Riemens. *A Concise Biographical Dictionary of Singers; from the Beginning of Recorded Sound to the Present.* Translated from German, expanded and annotated by Harry Earl Jones. Philadelphia: Chilton Books, 1969. xxiv, 487 pp.

1674 ───────. *Unvergängliche Stimmen; kleines Sängerlexikon.* Sammlung Dalp, Bd. 92. In German. Bern: Francke, 1962. 429 pp.

1674-a ───────. *Unvergängliche Stimmen. Kleines Sängerlexikon.* In German. 2nd revised and enlarged ed. Sammlung Dalp, Bd. 92. Bern: Francke, 1966. 555 pp.

1675 ───────. *Unvergängliche Stimmen; Sängerlexikon. Ergänzungsband.* In German. Bern: Francke, 1979. 263 pp.

This volume contains additional biographies to the main volume, and

a substantial section (pp. 211-263) of addenda and corrigenda to the
main volume.

1676 ————. *Unvergängliche Stimmen; Sängerlexikon.* In German.
2nd newly revised and enlarged ed. Bern: Francke, 1982. 782 pp.

The most complete collection of detailed biographies of all the
important operatic singers of the world, provided they meet one
criterion: they made recordings. The biographies have been thoroughly
researched and, apparently, the errors that crept into the first
edition and its supplement have been corrected. The entries vary in
length according to the activities, rather than the relative merits,
of a given artist. The typography and design are excellent; in every
respect a major reference work for the specialist, one of the best of
its kind.

1677 Lahee, Henry Charles, b. 1856. *Famous Singers of To-day and
Yesterday.* Boston: L.C. Page, 1898. ix, 337 pp. Illustrated.
Index, pp. 333-337. Chronological Table of Famous Singers, pp. 325-
332.

As Lahee states in his preface, his book is "as complete a record
as possible of the 'Famous Singers' from the establishment of Italian
Opera down to the present day." Considering the time span this
modest sized volume covers (the pages are small), the author accomplishes his stated objective and the reader obtains basic information
about the outstanding vocalists of three centuries. An important
appendix of the book is the chronological table of singers, giving
birth and death dates, years of debut and retirement. Useful as it
may be, the researcher should not rely on this information without
confirmation from other sources.

1677-a ————. *Famous Singers of To-day and Yesterday.* New revised
ed. Boston: L.C. Page, 1936. ix, 421 pp. Illustrated. Chronological Table of Famous Singers, pp. 407-414.

1678 ————. *The Grand Opera Singers of To-day; an Account of the
Leading Operatic Stars Who Have Sung During Recent Years, Together
with a Sketch of the Chief Operatic Enterprises.* Boston: L.C. Page,
1912. x, 461 pp. Illustrated. Index, pp. 453-461.

In a preface, the author states: "In writing 'The Grand Opera
Singers of To-day' the object has been to give some account of the
leading singers who have been heard in America during the present
century. Those whose careers have been touched upon in 'Famous
Singers of To-day and Yesterday' and in 'Grand Opera in America' are
not mentioned, except perhaps casually, in this book." This work is
a perfect joy to collectors of recordings of the early twentieth
century, as in it will be found a great deal of factual information
about well-known as well as lesser known singers who recorded. The
book is organized by discussions about performances and artists from
(1) The Metropolitan Opera House under Maurice Grau; (2) The Metropolitan Opera House under Heinrich Conreid; (3) The Manhattan Opera
House under Oscar Hammerstein; (4) The Metropolitan Opera House under
Gatti-Casazza and Dippel; (5) The Boston Opera under Henry Russell
and (6) The Chicago-Philadelphia Company under Andreas Dippel. WRM

1678-a ————. *The Grand Opera Singers of To-day; an Account of the Leading Operatic Stars Who Have Sung During Recent Years, Together with a Sketch of the Chief Operatic Enterprises.* New revised ed. The Music Lovers' Series. Boston: The Page Company, 1922. x, 543 pp.

1679-T Lancelotti, Arturo, b. 1877. *Voces de oro; semblanzas anec-dóticas.* Translated by José M. Borrás. In Spanish. Barcelona: Ediciones Ave, 1943. 223 pp.

Spanish translation of *Le voci d'oro* (q.v.).

1680 ————. *Le voci d'oro.* In Italian. 2nd ed. Roma: Fratelli Palombi, 1942. 361 pp. Illustrated. Bibliography, pp. 363-364.

For biographees see entry for 3rd edition.

1680-a ————. *Le voci d'oro.* In Italian. 3rd revised enlarged edition. Roma: Fratelli Palombi, 1953. 407 pp. Illustrated. Bibliography, pp. 405-407.

The author's preface states that these biographical sketches, more anecdotal than critical, are enough to indicate the enthusiasm and excitement which prevailed in the times of great singers, and of the fortunes which they were able to accumulate. The singers are Battistini, Bellincioni, Caruso, Cavalieri, Cotogni, Mario, De Lucia, Gayarre, Gigli, Kaschmann, Lablache, Malibran, Marconi, Masini, Pampanini, Adelina Patti, Ruffo, Chaliapin, Tamagno and Tetrazzini. Entertaining reading, but nothing of great depth. WRM

1681 Levien, John Joseph Mewburn, 1863-1953. *The Garcia Family.* London: Novello and Company, 1932. 29 pp. Illustrated. Advertising Matter, pp. 28-29.

On Manuel del Popolo Vicente Garcia, Manuel Garcia, Malibran and Viardot-Garcia.

1682 ————. *Six Sovereigns of Song,* lectures delivered by John Mewburn Levien. London: Novello and Co., n.d. 84 pp.

They are, in chronological order of birth: Braham, Manuel del Popolo Vicente Garcia, Manuel Garcia, Malibran, Viardot-Garcia and Santley.

1683 Linfield, John Henry. *Singers of Bygone Days; a Retrospect of the Fifty Years--1894 to 1944, and Some of the Sleeping Memories It Awakens of Those Who Sang and Charmed in These Far-off Yesterdays.* 2nd ed. N.p., 1952 or 3. 17 pp. First edition could not be located.

1684 Lipsius, Ida Maria, b. 1837. *Die Frauen im Tonleben der Gegen-wart.* By La Mara (pseud.). In German. Musikalische Studienköpfe, Bd. 5. Leipzig: Breitkopf & Härtel, 1882. xi, 393 pp. There is no indication whether this is the first or second edition.

1684-a ————. *Die Frauen im Tonleben der Gegenwart.* By La Mara (pseud.). In German. 3rd revised ed. Musikalische Studienköpfe, Bd. 5. Leipzig: Breitkopf & Härtel, 1902. xi, 379 pp. Illustrated.

1685 Lumley, Benjamin, 1812-1875. *Reminiscences of the Opera.* London: Hurst and Blackett, 1864. xx, 448 pp. Illustrated.

First as solicitor and later as manager, Lumley was intimately connected with Her Majesty's Theater, the London home of Italian opera, from 1836 to 1858. This brought him into close contact with such singers as Malibran, Grisi, Mario, Rubini, Pasta, Sontag, Piccolomini, Lablache, Alboni, Tietjens; he knew and worked with them all. He was responsible for presenting Jenny Lind in opera in England, and has much to say about the Swedish Nightingale. Here we have the manager's view, with all the legal and political frustrations of running an opera company. The work is a companion piece to Henry F. Chorley's *Thirty Years' Musical Recollections* (see item 1574), which covers many of these same events from the viewpoint of a critic. WRM

1686 L'vov, Mikhail L'vovich, 1887-1957. *Russkie pevtsy*. In Russian. Moskva: Muzyka, 1965. 263 pp. Illustrated.

On Lemeshev, Maksakova, Mikhailov, Nezhdanova, Petrov, Pirogov, Reizen and Sobinov.

1687 Mackenzie, Barbara (Kruger), 1903-1975, and Findlay Mackenzie. *Singers of Australia: From Melba to Sutherland*. Melbourne: Lansdowne Press, 1967. xvii, 309 pp. Illustrated. Bibliography, pp. 298-302. Index, pp. 303-309.

Beginning with a chapter on the history of opera in Australia, this well-conceived book goes on to discuss musical traditions and pioneer activities before introducing an extensive biographical section which begins with an accurate biographical sketch of Melba (pp. 32-67). This is followed by biographical accounts of Melba's contemporaries, with much original research on the careers of Amy Sherwin, Marie Narelle, Ada Crossley, Horace Stevens, Peter Dawson, Malcolm McEachern, Frances Alda, Rosina Buckman, Elsa Stralia and others. A chapter featuring singers of the period between the two wars brings us John Brownlee, Gertrude Johnson, Margherita Grandi, Florence Austral and many more. The final section gives biographical details about postwar singers, beginning with Joan Hammond and ending with Joan Sutherland. While there are a few omissions and a few errors, this is an excellent reference work, with much hard-to-come-by information. Profusely illustrated, with a foreword by Harold Rosenthal. WRM

1687-a ————. *Singers of Australia: From Melba to Sutherland*. London: Newnes, 1968. xvii, 309 pp. Illustrated. Bibliography, pp. 298-302. Index, pp. 303-309.

1688 Mahalin, Paul, 1838-1899. *Les Jolies actrices de Paris*. Série 1-5. In French. Paris: Pache & Deffaux, 1868-89. 5 vols. Illustrated.

In each of the five volumes (or "série"), published and sold separately, Mahalin writes about 50-80 performers of the Parisian stage of his time. Each lady is identified by her theatrical affiliation; those of operatic interest are the ones of the Opéra, Opéra-Comique and Théâtre des Italiens. Mahalin's treatment and style is low, gossipy, prejudiced journalism marked by excessive vindictiveness or loyalties. Because of this shortcoming none of his statements can be taken at face value without corroborating evidence from an independent source. The main value of his work is that he provides some information, unreliable as it may be at times, about singers not represented anywhere else in the literature.

1689 Malvern, Gladys. *The Great Garcias*. Decorations by Alan Moyler.
New York: Longmans, Green, 1958. 210 pp. Illustrated.

They are Manuel del Popolo Vicente Garcia, Manuel Garcia, Malibran
and Viardot-Garcia.

1690 Mapleson, James Henry, 1830-1901. *The Mapleson Memoirs 1848-
1888*. New York: Belford, Clarke, 1888. 2 vols. Illustrated.

1690-a ————. *The Mapleson Memoirs, 1848-1888*. 2nd ed. London:
Remington, 1888. 2 vols. Illustrated.

1690-b ————. *The Mapleson Memoirs; the Career of an Operatic Impresario, 1858-1888*. Edited and annotated by Harold Rosenthal.
London: Putnam, 1966. 346 pp. Illustrated.

1690-c ————. *The Mapleson Memoirs; the Career of an Operatic Impresario, 1858-1888*. Edited and annotated by Harold Rosenthal. New
York: Appleton-Century, 1966. 346 pp. Illustrated.

1691 Maretzek, Max, 1821-1897. *Crotchets and Quavers; or, Revelations of an Opera Manager in America*. New York: S. French, 1855.
viii, 346 pp.

1691-a ————. *Revelations of an Opera Manager in 19th Century
America. Crotchets and Quavers & Sharps and Flats*. With a new introduction by Charles Haywood. New York: Dover Publications, 1968.
xxxv, 346, 94 pp. Illustrated.

"This Dover edition is an unabridged and slightly corrected republication of *Crotchets and Quavers* (q.v.) originally published in 1855,
and *Sharps and Flats* (q.v.) originally published in 1890."

1692 ————. *"Sharps and Flats;" A Sequel to "Crotchets and Quavers."*
New York: American Musician Publishing Co., 1890. 87 pp. Illustrated.

1693 Mariz, Vasco, b. 1921. *Dicionário bio-bibliográfico musical
(brasileiro e internacional)*. Prefácio de Renato Almeida. In Portuguese. Rio de Janeiro: Livraria Kosmos, 1948. 250 pp.

A biographical dictionary of musicians. The coverage is international, but only the most prominent musicians--composers, singers,
instrumentalists, etc.--are represented. The coverage is historical,
without an apparent emphasis on contemporary (living) musicians.

1694 Marks, Edward Bennett, 1865-1945. *They All Had Glamour, from
the Swedish Nightingale to the Naked Lady*. New York: Julian Messner,
1944. xvii, 448 pp. Illustrated. Index, pp. 445-448. Old-Time
Colloquialisms, pp. 431-438.

A collection of show business stories about celebrities of the 19th
century, ranging from clowns to courtesans. The book is divided into
three parts, part two consisting of fifteen chapters, each devoted to
a famous prima donna--Alboni, Bishop, Grisi, Hauk, Kellogg, Lind,
Lucca, Malibran, Christine Nilsson, Parepa-Rosa, Adelina Patti,
Carlotta Patti, Piccolomini, Sontag and Tietjens. The approach is
anecdotal rather than scholarly, stressing the strange or, at the

very least, the unusual aspects of these lives. While the basic
facts are corroborated by more detailed biographies, the anecdotes
perhaps ought to be taken "cum grano salis."

1694-a ————. *They All Had Glamour, from the Swedish Nightingale
to the Naked Lady.* Westport, Conn.: Greenwood Press, 1972. xvii,
448 pp. Illustrated.

Reprint of the 1944 edition by J. Messner, New York (q.v.).

1695 Martens, Frederick Herman, 1874-1932. *The Art of the Prima
Donna and Concert Singer.* New York: D. Appleton and Company, 1923.
xiv, 292 pp. Illustrated.

In the author's introduction he states: "Here the greatest singers
of our age have placed at the student's disposal the results of their
actual technical and artistic experience. In a direct, informal
manner [they] tell what they did to achieve their abiding success
on the operatic and concert stage...." Interesting reading for the
record collector! (One wonders how Ursula Greville got into this
distinguished company. In her chapter she states: "although I made
my debut in Covent Garden as the Queen of the Night...," yet Harold
Rosenthal, in a 1967 letter to this annotator, says that he can find
no trace of her in the Covent Garden archives....) The singers are
Bori, Braslau, Calvé, Case, Easton, Farrar, Galli-Curci, Garrison,
Greville, Hempel, Homer, Ivogün, Jeritza, Miura, Onegin, Ponselle,
Raisa, Rethberg, Schumann-Heink and Verlet. WRM

1695-a ————. *The Art of the Prima Donna and Concert Singer.*
Opera Biographies. New York: Arno Press, 1977. xiv, 292 pp. Illustrated.

Reprint of the 1923 edition published by D. Appleton, New York
(q.v.). For names of biographees see the entry for that edition.

1696 Martin, Jules, b. 1860. *Nos artistes. Annuaire des théâtres
et concerts suivis d'une notice sur les droits d'auteurs, la censure,
les associations artistiques, les principaux théâtres, etc.* In
French. Paris: Société d'éditions littéraires et artistiques, 1895,
1901. 2 vols. Illustrated.

Pocket size books, measuring 3" x 5", containing excellent short--
6-15 lines--biographical summaries and photos of all the important
artists on the Parisian stages, legitimate and lyric, at the turn of
the century. An exceptionally important publication, as it is the
sole source of biographical information, including birth dates, debut
dates and repertory, of many lesser known artists.

1696-a ————. *Nos artistes. Portraits et biographies....* Préface
par M. Aurélien Scholl. In French. Paris: L'Annuaire Universel,
1895. 448 pp. Illustrated.

1696-b ————. *Nos artistes: annuaire des théâtres et concerts,
1901-1902. Portraits et biographies, suivis d'une notice sur les
droits d'auteur, la censure, les associations artistiques, les principaux théâtres, etc.* Préface par Alfred Capus. Gravure de M. Louis
Geisler. In French. Paris: Paul Ollendorff, 1901. 392 pp. Illustrated.

1697 Matz, Mary Jane. *Opera Stars in the Sun; Intimate Glimpses of Metropolitan Personalities*. With a foreword by Milton Cross. Illustrated by Susan Perl. New York: Farrar, Straus & Cudahy, 1955. xiv, 349 pp. Illustrated.

Thumbnail sketches of 96 Metropolitan Opera artists, mostly singers. The few (less than a dozen) non-singers are conductors, stage directors, etc. These mini-portraits run one to two pages each, ending in a brief list of biographical data (place of birth, early training, debut role and place, and early experience), followed by a list of the artist's Metropolitan roles, with dates of first performance. Because of this feature, and the fact that this is the only source for some lesser artists, the book holds an important place in the literature.

1697-a ————. *Opera Stars in the Sun; Intimate Glimpses of Metropolitan Personalities*. Westport, Conn.: Greenwood Press, 1973. xiv, 349 pp. Illustrated.

Reprint of the 1955 edition published by Farrar, Straus & Cudahy (q.v.).

1698 Miller, Basil William, b. 1897. *Ten Singers Who Became Famous*. Grand Rapids, Mich.: Zondervan Pub. House, 1954. 87 pp. Illustrated.

1699 Monaldi, Gino, 1847-1932. *Cantanti celebri del secolo XIX*. In Italian. Biblioteca della Nuova antologia, 12. Roma: Nuova antologia, 192? 310 pp. Illustrated.

Faithful to his title, Monaldi gives an overview of the vocal scene of the entire nineteenth century. He discusses most of the prominent singers from Grassini to Caruso. His writing is erudite and his statements well researched and competent. A two-page index of great interest to researchers gives, in lire, the earnings of several prominent nineteenth-century singers. No other edition of this book could be located. References to Bonci and Carsuo suggest that the book was written--and perhaps first published--around 1916-1917.

1699-a ————. *Cantanti celebri (1829-1929)*. In Italian. Roma: Edizioni Tiber, 1929. 316 pp. Illustrated.

This is a partially revised edition of the same author's *Cantanti celebri del secolo XIX* (q.v.). This edition drops the first chapter of the former work, and adds two chapters at the end, in which are discussed the successors of Caruso (Martinelli, Gigli), as well as Muzio, Borgioli, Pertile, De Muro, Lauri-Volpi, Franci, Dal Monte, Schipa, De Luca, Ruffo, Galeffi, De Angelis, Merli, Scacciati, Rethberg, Raisa, Della Rizza, etc. In between, the chapters cover much the same ground as the former edition, but in a somewhat shorter form. This is a well-written and very interesting book for a general review of singers of the period covered. The researcher will fault the lack of specific dates and an index. WRM

1700 ————. *Cantani evirati celebri del teatro italiano*. In Italian. Roma: Ausonia, 1920. 127 pp. Illustrated. Cover-title: Cantani evirati celebri, secoli XVII-XVIII.

The story of the art and lives of the numerous castrati who delighted audiences in the eighteenth and nineteenth centuries. The narrative is concise without strict chronological order. RT

1701 ————. *I miei ricordi musicali*. In Italian. L'Italia musicale moderna. Roma: Ausonia, 1921. 151 pp.

1702 Moore, Gerald, b. 1899. *Am I Too Loud? Memoirs of an Accompanist*. London: H. Hamilton, 1962. 304 pp. Illustrated. Index, pp. 295-304.

Gerald Moore, the "unashamed accompanist," has elevated his métier to such artistic excellence that it now ranks with that of the soloist. He accompanied many of the great singers of his time during his long career. He devotes entire chapters to the most outstanding artists of his generation whom he accompanied in live concerts and on records. They are de los Angeles, Chaliapin, Coates, Ferrier, Fischer-Dieskau, Gerhardt, McCormack, Schumann, Schwarzkopf and Teyte. Moore is a great story-teller, his book is a joy to read.

1702-a ————. *Am I Too Loud? Memoirs of an Accompanist*. Harmondsworth: Penguin, 1966. 286 pp. Illustrated. Index.

For subjects see the entry for the 1962 H. Hamilton edition.

1703 Moran, William R. "The Legacy of Gianni Bettini." *The Record Collector* XVI, nos. 7 & 8 (September 1965), 148-185. Illustrated. Bibliography. Discography, pp. 169-179.

This article was an attempt to gather together in one place all the bits and pieces of information on this famed entrepreneur who had his own recording "laboratory" in New York in the 1890s and early 1900s. There he managed to make cylinder recordings of such artists as Suzanne Adams, Mario Ancona, Sigrid Arnoldson, Blanche Arral, Sarah Bernhardt, Emma Calvé, Lina Cavalieri, Italo Campanini, Jean de Reszke, Lillie Langtry, Jean Laselle, Mark Twain, Nellie Melba, Lillian Nordica, Antonio Scotti, Ernest Van Dyck, Anton Van Rooy and many others. A chronological list of printed references to Bettini is given, with a summary of each, 42 in all. Known Bettini catalogs and other material are detailed; a complete listing of known Bettini artists is given (121), together with a description of some 66 known Bettini recordings. Material on Bettini phonographs (recorders, reproducers, etc.) is also presented. The result of a tremendous amount of research, and to date the definitive summary of known information about the products of this pioneer in the history of recorded sound.

1704 Moreau, Mário, b. 1926. *Cantores de ópera portugueses*. In Portuguese. Amadora: Livraria Bertrand, 1981. 879 pp. Illustrated. Volume 1 only; volume 2 is in preparation.

The author, a physician by profession, is a passionate and dedicated scholar of music, lyric art in particular. It is evidenced by this work, an outstanding example of rigorously methodical and thorough-going research that could almost be termed "archaeological." It is a gallery of chronologically arranged monographs about Portuguese singers. Each contains the singer's biography and chronology supported by profuse annotations; illustrations, for the most part previously unpublished; and sources of data. The first volume, covering about half of the eighteenth and nineteenth centuries, discusses 56 singers. RT

1705 Moresby, Isabelle. *Australia Makes Music*. London: Longmans, Green, 1948. 197 pp. Illustrated. Bibliography.

Biographical sketches of Australian artists, mostly singers (pp. 26-123), Australian composers (pp. 124-143) and Australian conductors (pp. 144-156). Also chapters on Australian violin makers, broadcasting in Australia, etc. Apart from the sketches of the lives of such well-known Australians as Ada Crossley, Florence Austral, Nellie Melba, John Brownlee, Marjorie Lawrence, there are brief biographies of a number of lesser known singers such as Browning Mummery, Dorothy Helmrich, Horace Stevens and Evelyn Scotney. While the book has largely been replaced by the generally more complete *Singers of Australia* (1967) by Barbara and Findlay Mackenzie (see item 1687), one notes that there are sketches of Essie Ackland, John Dudley and Alan Eddy, who were not included in the Mackenzie work. WRM

1706 Moscheles, Charlotte (Embden), d. 1889. *Aus Moscheles' Leben. Nach Briefen und Tagebüchern herausgegeben von seiner Frau.* In German. Leipzig: Duncker & Humbolt, 1872-73. 2 vols. A complete catalog of the compositions by I. Moscheles is in Vol. 2, pp. 347-355.

1707-T ————. *Life of Moscheles, with selections from his diaries and correspondence, by his wife.* Translated by A.D. Coleridge. London: Hurst and Blackett, 1873. 2 vols. Illustrated. "A complete catalogue of compositions by I. Moscheles" is in Vol. 2, pp. 302-311.

Ignaz Moscheles (1794-1870) was a pianist, teacher and composer. He prepared the piano score of *Fidelio* under the composer's supervision; he was a close friend of Mendelssohn, and was active in musical affairs in Vienna, London and Leipzig. There are many personal observations about Jenny Lind, Lablache, Clara Novello, Malibran, Mario, Pauline Viardot-Garcia and others. The author kept a detailed diary and supplemented this with extensive letters to his wife; these have been skillfully combined to give a well-documented and dated, as well as observant, record of musicians and musical affairs of the period covered (1814-1870). WRM

1707-T-a ————. *Recent Music and Musicians as Described in the Diaries and Correspondence of Ignatz Moscheles, edited by his wife.* New York: H. Holt, 1873. xviii, 434 pp. Illustrated. "A complete catalogue of compositions by I. Moscheles": pp. 421-428.

English translation of *Aus Moscheles' Leben* (q.v.) and previously published in London by Hurst and Blackett, in 1873, under the title *Life of Moscheles* (q.v.), in 2 volumes. The American edition went through many subsequent editions.

1708 Moscow. Gosudarstvennyi akademicheskii Bol'shoi teatr. *Biograficheskie ocherki artistov Bol'shogo teatra.* In Russian. Moskva, 1953. 11 nos. in 1 vol. Illustrated.

Contains biographies on Baturin, Derzhinskaia, Golovkina, Ivanov,

Lisitsian, Maksakova, Pirogov and Rejzen.

1709 Moses, Montrose Jonas, b. 1878. *The Life of Heinrich Conried.*
New York: Thomas Y. Crowell, 1916. xv, 367 pp. Illustrated.

1709-a ————. *The Life of Heinrich Conried.* New York: Arno Press,
1977. xv, 367 pp. Illustrated.

Reprint of the 1916 edition published by Crowell, New York (q.v.).

1710 Mount-Edgcumbe, [Richard Edgcumbe], 2nd earl of, 1764-1839.
*Musical Reminiscences of an Old Amateur Chiefly Respecting the Italian
Opera in England for Fifty Years, from 1773 to 1823.* The second
edition, continued to the present time. 2nd ed. London: W. Clarke,
1827. xii, 183 pp.

For an annotation, see the entry for the 4th edition.

1710-a ————. *Musical Reminiscences, Chiefly Respecting the Italian
Opera in England, from the Year 1773 to the Present Time.* The 3rd
edition. 3rd ed. London: G. Clarke, 1828. xvi, 192 pp.

1710-b ————. *Musical Reminiscences, Containing an Account of the
Italian Opera in England from 1773.* The 4th ed., continued to the
present time, and including the festival in Westminster Abbey. 4th ed.
London: J. Andrews, 1834. xvi, 294 pp.

Musical reminiscences characteristic of the period, of which the
best example is the one written by H. Fothergill Chorley (see item
1574). This edition, like the earlier ones, comments on the artistry
of Pacchierotti, Mara, Billington, Grassini, Braham, Catalani, Col-
bran, Pasta, Sontag, Malibran, Grisi and several others. The absence
of an index is a drawback; it would have greatly improved the usefulness of the volume. The subtitle varies from edition to edition.

1711 Müller, Martin, and Wolfgang Mertz, editors. *Diener der Musik.
Unvergessene Solisten und Dirigenten unserer Zeit im Spiegel der
Freunde.* In German. Tübingen: Wunderlich, 1965. 274 pp. Illus-
trated.

Short biographical recollections of outstanding musicians; only
three singers among many conductors and instrumentalists. The three
articles are of Kathleen Ferrier by Bruno Walter (pp. 60-67), Karl
Erb by Gerd Scheider (pp. 197-211) and Heinrich Schlusnus by Eckart
von Naso (pp. 227-239).

1712 Müller-Marein, Josef, b. 1907, and Hannes Reinhardt, editors.
*Das musikalische Selbstportrait von Komponisten, Dirigenten, Instru-
mentalisten, Sängerinnen und Sängern unserer Zeit.* In German. Hamburg: Nannen-Verlag, 1963. 508 pp. Illustrated. Index, pp. 499-508.
Discography, pp. 461-497.

This is a fascinating book. It arose from brief taped interviews
with 50 internationally famous musicians of various nationalities
and talents. The 24 singers include, among others, Erna Berger, Max
Lorenz, Margarete Klose, Lawrence Winters, Tiana Lemnitz, Lauritz
Melchior. What has resulted is a set of extremely interesting autobiographical narratives. The illustrations, grouped together (pp.

429-460), are good but unexciting. There is a selective discography
containing a representative sampling of long playing records for most
artists, performers and composers. PHS

1713 *Musicisti e artisti forlivesi. Note storiche e biografiche.*
In Italian. Forlì: Tip. A. Raffaelli, 1957. 22 pp. Published for
the Associazione "Amici del Teatro" Forlì.

Contains short--3 to 25 lines--biographies of 69 musicians and
artists who were born, or professionally active, in Forlì. The best
known singer of those included is Angelo Masini.

1714 Natan, Alex, b. 1906. *Primadonna; Lob der Stimmen.* In German.
Basel: Basilius Presse, 1962. 141 pp. Illustrated. Discography,
pp. 117-135.

Short, one-page, popular biographies of fifty sopranos, from Patti
to Nilsson. There is neither discernible criteria for inclusion nor
a logical sequence, which is not chronological nor alphabetical. The
biographies are superficial and derivative. The book's most valuable
feature is the excellent and unusual pictorial material, including a
photo of the short, overweight, aging Tetrazzini beaming on the arm
of her newly acquired young husband; the picture speaks volumes! The
discography of each biographee covers LP records only. The releases
are broken down by country of origin and numbers are given for
monophonic and stereo recordings; however, there is no label identification beyond the record number prefix. This leaves the majority
of records unidentified. Also, no casts or co-performers are shown.
A volume entitled *Primo uomo* (q.v.) devoted to male singers was
published by the same author a year later.

1715 ————. *Primo uomo; grosse Sänger der Oper.* In German. Basel:
Basilius Presse, 1963. 152 pp. Illustrated. Discography, pp. 121-
147.

A companion volume to the same author's *Prima Donna* (q.v.), it contains brief, popularly written biographies of fifty male opera
singers from Battistini to Vickers. As in the case of the earlier
work, the page-long biographies are written for the casual reader
rather than the scholar. The arrangement lacks a logical plan; it
is neither chronological nor alphabetical. The discography covers
LP records only, broken down by country of origin. Record numbers
are given for both mono- and stereophonic records, but record labels
aren't identified (except in the prefix of American releases). A
further shortcoming is the omission of co-performers: soloists, conductor or accompanist. This volume has an added feature: *Kurz-
Biographier*, which contains 6- to 15-line biographical summaries
for each artist.

1716 Newton, Ivor, b. 1892. *At the Piano--Ivor Newton: The World
of an Accompanist.* London: H. Hamilton, 1966. ix, 309 pp. Illustrated. Index, pp. 303-309.

One of a handful of outstanding pianists who elevated the role of
accompanist to a position co-equal with that of the soloist, Newton
collaborated with many outstanding vocalists. He devotes an entire
chapter to seven of them in this gentle, pleasant, informative volume

of reminiscences, written with a penchant for the typically British understatement. The seven are Chaliapin, Flagstad, Melba, Moore, Rosing, Supervia and Tetrazzini.

1717 Novák, Ladislav, 1872-1946. *Stará garda Národniho divadla; cinohra, opera, balet.* In Czech. 3rd ed. Praha: J.R. Vilímek, 1944. 455 pp. Illustrated. Index, pp. 449-453.

Contains the biographies of 28 Czech singers. The first edition of this book appeared in 1937.

1718 Núñez y Dominguez, Roberto. *Descorriendo el telón; cuarenta años de teatro en México.* Prólogo de Tomás Borras. In Spanish. Madrid: Gráficas Editorial Rollán, 1956. 617 pp.

A collection of the reviews of the Mexican drama critic originally printed in the newspaper *Excelsior* and the weekly magazine *Revista de Revistas*, both published in Mexico City. His introductory essay summarizes the theatrical and operatic events of Mexico City from 1910 to 1950 (pp. 13-31). The rest of the book is an anecdotal, unorganized recollection of the events of each theatrical and operatic establishment. Many singers are mentioned: the author devotes one or more articles to Caruso, Besanzoni, Constantino, Ruffo, Fleta and Peralta. The writing is lightweight, the style that of a newspaper reporter. AM

1719 O'Connell, Charles, b. 1900. *The Other Side of the Record.* New York: A.A. Knopf, 1947. xi, 332, xi pp. Index, pp. i-xi.

Charles O'Connell wrote these cathartic recollections upon his resignation after two decades of service from the powerful post of musical director of RCA. (If he is the man Arthur Rubinstein refers to in his memoirs as Charles O'Connor, his resignation was not voluntary.) His caustic wit and deft style make this book enjoyable reading; his familiarity with his subjects--singers, conductors and instrumentalists--affords the reader a glimpse of the great and super-great at an uncomfortably close range. If familiarity breeds contempt, O'Connell must have been quite familiar with some of his subjects. The singers are Flagstad, Melchior, Moore, Pons and Traubel.

1719-a ———. *The Other Side of the Record.* Westport, Conn.: Greenwood Press, 1970. xi, 332, xi pp. Index, pp. i-xi.

1720 O'Donnell, Josephine. *Among the Covent Garden Stars.* Foreword by Sir Thomas Beecham, bart. London: Stanley Paul & Co., 1936. 295 pp. Illustrated. Index, pp. 289-295.

A loosely knit collection of stories and anecdotes witnessed, heard and overheard by the secretary of Covent Garden for eleven years between World Wars I and II. The writing is affected and only mildly amusing; however, the large number of stars mentioned in these pages makes this book entertaining reading for opera lovers.

1721 Orovio, Helio, b. 1938. *Diccionario de la música cubana: biográfico y técnico.* In Spanish. La Habana: Editorial Letras Cubanas, 1981. 442 pp. Illustrated.

The book contains some 800 short biographies about Cuban musicians, along with historical data about Cuban music, musical styles, instruments, orchestras and ensembles. The biographies include a large number of Cuban opera and zarzuela singers. AM

1722 Padoan, Paolo. *Profili di cantanti lirici veneti.* In Italian. Bologna: Bongiovanni, 1977. 209 pp. Illustrated.

Excellent profiles of 29 opera singers in chronological order by their date of birth. The preface is by Giacomo Lauri-Volpi; a discography of 26 singers by D. Rubboli. RT

1723 Pahissa, Jaime, 1880-1969. *Sendas y cumbres de la música española.* In Spanish. Colección El Mirador. Buenos Aires: Hachette, 1955. 189 pp. Illustrated.

1724-T Pahlen, Kurt, b. 1907. *Grandes cantantes de nuestro tiempo.* In Spanish. Buenos Aires: Editores, 1973. 334 pp. Illustrated.

Spanish translation of his *Grosse Sänger unserer Zeit* (q.v.).

1725-T ———. *Great Singers from the Seventeenth Century to the Present Day.* Translated by Oliver Coburn. London: W.H. Allen, 1973. 266 pp. Illustrated.

The English translation of his *Grosse Sänger unserer Zeit* (q.v.).

1725-T-a ———. *Great Singers, from the Seventeenth Century to the Present Day.* Translated by Oliver Coburn. New York: Stein and Day, 1974. 266 pp. Illustrated. Index, pp. 260-266.

The English translation of his *Grosse Sänger unserer Zeit* (q.v.). A stylish overview of singing and singers, whose value is greatly impaired by many factual inaccuracies that a competent editor with the appropriate subject knowledge could have spotted upon first reading. (The details, dates, opera titles, number and sequence of performances and events in Caruso's last season at the Met are mostly incorrect.) Bearing this defect in mind, the book makes pleasant reading.

1726 ———. *Grosse Sänger unserer Zeit.* In German. Gütersloh, Wien: Bertelsmann Sachbuchverlag, 1971. 287 pp. Illustrated.

1727 Papp, Viktor. *Arcképek az Operaházból.* In Hungarian. Budapest: Stadium, 1924.

The title in English means "Portraits from the Opera House." Presumably contains biographical materials of the soloists of the Hungarian Royal Opera House, current as of 1924. The bibliographic information was taken from the Széchenyi Library, Budapest, where the only library copy is located. The book was not available for examination at the time of the editor's visit.

1728 Parets i Serra, Juan. *La ópera en Mallorca (siglo XIX).* In Spanish. Panorama Balear, Serie XI, No. 108. Palma de Mallorca: Luis Ripoli, 1982. 16 pp. Illustrated. Bibliography, p. 16.

A very brief history of opera on the island of Mallorca, followed by a section of major singers born there (pp. 5-14). The only exception included is Dionisia Fité de Goula (1847-1873) who was born in Barcelona. AM

1729 Payne, Albert, 1842-1921. *Berühmte Sängerinnen der Vergangenheit und Gegenwart. Eine sammlung von 91 Biographien und 90 Porträts.* Hrsg. von A. Ehrlich (pseud.). In German. Leipzig: A.H. Payne, 1896. ix, 228 pp. Illustrated.

1730 Peltz, Mary Ellis (Opdycke), b. 1896. *Spotlights on the Stars; Intimate Sketches of Metropolitan Opera Personalities.* New York: Metropolitan Opera Guild, 1943. 114 pp. Illustrated.

One-page biographies and full-page illustrations of 43 major Met stars (of 1943), along with several dozen shorter entries of 8-15 lines for lesser artists, conductors and other individuals affiliated with the Metropolitan.

1731 Pérez Lugín, Alejandro, 1870-1926. *De Titta Ruffo a la Fons pasando por Machaquito. Notas de un reporter.* Prologo de Domingo Blanco. Dibujos de Tovar. In Spanish. Madrid: Establecimiento Tipográfico, 1912. 227 pp. Illustrated.

Brief, unbiased interviews conducted locally by a Madrid-based reporter with a large variety of stage personalities. The volume opens with twelve pages devoted to Titta Ruffo. The volume also contains interviews with Giuseppe Anselmi (9 pp.), Cecilia Gagliardi (7 pp.), Maria Gay (7 pp.), Rosina Storchio (6 pp.) and Riccardo Stracciari (8 pp.). RT

1732 *Pevtsy Bol'shogo teatra SSSR; odinnatsat' portretov.* In Russian. Moskva: Muzyka, 1978. 178 pp. Illustrated.

Eleven short chapters by diverse authors, each devoted to one currently active major soloist of the Bol'shoi theater, all of them recipients of the Lenin prize. They are Arkhipova, Atlantov, Eizen, Guliaev, Mazurok, Milashkina, Nesterenko, Obraztsova, Ognitsev, Rudenko and Vedernikov. The individual chapters consist of 12-16 pages, half of them devoted to a short essay about the artist, the balance filled with excellent photographs reproduced at the level of Western standards of printing. The last two pages give a very brief trilingual (English, French, German) summary of the book. A beautiful volume, deserves to be translated.

1733 Piccini, Giulio, 1849-1915. *Attori, cantanti, acrobati; memorie umoristiche di Jarro* (pseud.). In Italian. Firenze: Tipografia di M. Cappelli, 1887. 193 pp. Illustrated.

The singers are Bellincioni, Nevada, Stagno and Tamberlick.

1733-a ————. *Attori, cantanti, concertisti, acrobati; ritratti, macchiette, aneddoti*; memorie umoristiche di Jarro (pseud.). In Italian. Firenze: R. Bemporad & Figlio, 1897. 317 pp.

1734 Pleasants, Henry. *The Great Singers; from the Dawn of Opera to Our Own Time.* New York: Simon and Schuster, 1966. 382 pp. Illustrated.

1734-a ————. *The Great Singers; from the Dawn of Opera to Our Own Time*. London: Gollancz, 1967. 382 pp. Illustrated.

1735 Pössiger, Günter. *Die grossen Sänger und Dirigenten; Kurzbiographien der bedeutendsten Sänger und der führenden Dirigenten unserer Zeit*.... In German. München: Wilhelm Heyne Verlag, 1968. 220 pp. Illustrated. Bibliography, pp. 219-220.

Short biographies of 101 opera singers and 56 conductors of "our time."

1736 Poliakova, Liudmila Viktorovna. *Molodezh opernoi stseny Bol'shogo teatra*. In Russian. Moskva: Gos. muzykal'noe izd-vo, 1952. 110 pp. Illustrated.

1737 *Portrete şi autoportrete. Cîntăreţi Români*. In Rumanian. Bucureşti: Editura Muzicală, 1974. 429 pp. Illustrated.

1738 Pougin, Arthur, 1834-1921. *Figures d'Opéra-Comique: Madame Dugazon, Elleviou, les Gavaudan*. In French. Paris: Tresse, 1875. 234 pp. Illustrated.

1739 Pujol, Rámon. *Mundo lirico; semblanzas biograficas de primerisimas figuras de la opera*. In Spanish. Barcelona: Ediciones Rondas, 1965. 206 pp. Illustrated.

A collection of writings about 35 twentieth-century singers, ranging --chronologically speaking--from Hipólito Lázaro to Joan Sutherland. It seems that Pujol has personally known, or at least met, all of his subjects. The majority of the numerous illustrations are unusual shots of these artists, many of them taken in the course of their Madrid engagements.

1740 Rajk, András. *Hogy volt?! Hogy volt?!* In Hungarian. Budapest: Szépirodalmi Könyvkiadó, 1979. 272 pp. Illustrated on dust jacket.

A collection of short biographies of twenty-one prominent Hungarian artists, among them eight opera singers (Joviczky, Orosz, Osváth, Palánkay, Palló, Simándy, Székely and Takács). Except for Palló and Székely, there is no biographical material available about the rest of these important soloists apart from brief entries in musical dictionaries. The chapters are sketchy overviews of the career of each singer, enlivened by quotations from interviews conducted by the author. A recurring theme is the singers' displeasure with the current (1970s) management of the Hungarian Opera House. In the absence of comparable works this is an important biographical anthology.

1741 Rasponi, Lanfranco. *The Last Prima Donnas*. New York: Knopf (Distributed by Random House), 1982. 633 pp. Illustrated. Index, pp. 607-633.

1742 Reissig, Elisabeth, b. 1883. *Erlebte Opernkunst: Bilder und Gestalten der Berliner Staatsoper*. In German. Berlin: Oesterheld, 1927. 98 pp. Illustrated.

On Bohnen, Kemp, Mann and Reinhardt.

1743 ————. *Erlebte Opernkunst: Bilder und Gestalten der Berliner Staatsoper*, zweite Folge. Mit sechzehn Tafeln. In German. Berlin: Oesterheld, 1928. 132 pp. Illustrated.

Contains a general discourse about singing and the work of ten singers of the Berlin Opera House. They are Arndt-Ober, De Garmo, Henke, Leider, Pattiera, Schlusnus, Schorr, Schützendorf, Soot and Tauber. The treatment is superficial; there is an excellent photograph of each artist.

1744 Riemens, Leo. *Uren der zangkunst*. In Dutch. Amsterdam: Voor de Bezige Bij uitg., 1954. 178 pp.

The heart of this book is a series of 25 brief essays on singers and opera. These are preceded by an introduction and followed by a near-polemic on "The Gramophone and the Singer's Art." Singers included are Brouwenstijn, Caruso, Ferrier, Hayes, Melba and Urlus. In addition to entire chapters devoted to individual singers, the essays concern Mascagni, Boito's *Mefistofele*, Italian opera, Black singers, opera and radio, Bel Canto, etc. For the most part they are well written and interesting. The slight piece, "An Opera Encounter with Sherlock Holmes," is an excellent example of pure "fun." PHS

1745 Rogers, Francis, 1870-1951. *Some Famous Singers of the 19th Century*. New York: H.W. Gray Company, 1914. 128 pp. Illustrated.

A thin little book containing excellent, concise essays about fifteen singers who represent the cream of the operatic crop of the nineteenth century. They are Catalani, Duprez, Manuel Garcia, Manuel del Popolo Vicente Garcia, Grisi, Lablache, Lind, Malibran, Mario, Nourrit, Pasta, Rubini, Sontag, Tamburini and Viardot-Garcia. The writing is economical and direct; if the reader wants only a casual acquaintance with the singers discussed these essays contain the essentials. In spite of the absence of a bibliography or footnotes the writer seems to have been thoroughly familiar with the source materials relating to his subjects; the occasional errors are probably due to the "state-of-research" rather than negligence.

1745-a ————. *Some Famous Singers of the 19th Century*. New York: Arno Press, 1977. 128 pp. Illustrated.

Reprint of the 1914 edition by H.W. Gray, New York (q.v.). It has a list of the subjects.

1746 Rosenthal, Harold D., b. 1918, and John Warrack. *Concise Oxford Dictionary of Opera*. London: Oxford University Press, 1964. xiv, 446 pp. Bibliography, pp. ix-xii.

1746-a ————. *Concise Oxford Dictionary of Opera*. 1st edition reprinted with corrections. London: Oxford University Press, 1972. xv, 446 pp. Bibliography, pp. ix-xii.

1746-b ————. *The Concise Oxford Dictionary of Opera*. 2nd ed. London: Oxford University Press, 1979. 561 pp. Bibliography.

The best contemporary English-language dictionary of matters operatic. The entries vary from a few lines to a full column on a double-column page. There is a generous listing of important opera singers through

the ages, also entries under composers, conductors, producers, designers, opera managers, theaters, plots, operatic characters, even first
lines of the most popular musical excerpts. Considering the wealth
of information crammed into this compact volume one can have but a
single complaint: it ought to have been double in size to accommodate
twice as many entries. As is the case with all reference works of
this nature, the birth dates of some of the singers conflict with the
dates given in other sources.

1747-T ——————. *Dictionnaire de l'opéra*; revu et complété par Jacques
Bourgeois et Eric Deschamps; préf de Jacques Bourgeois. Translated
by Azziz Izzet. In French. Paris: Fayard, 1974. 420 pp.

French translation of the *Concise Oxford Dictionary of Opera* (q.v.).

1748 Rosenthal, Harold D. *Great Singers of Today*. London: Calder
and Boyars, 1966. 212 pp. Illustrated.

One hundred singers of the postwar era are represented by a 1- to
2-page biography and a generous selection of excellent photographs.
Some of the singers are merely prominent rather than great, thus there
are many artists listed who are not represented in other biographical
anthologies. As Rosenthal himself states in his postscript, "Everyone, including the author, can think of another hundred names that
deserve to have been included...." The style is straightforward and
simple, as readers of *Opera* (London) have come to expect of its long-
time editor.

1748-a ——————. *Great Singers of Today*. New York: Arno Press, 1977.
212 pp. Illustrated.

Reprint of the 1966 edition published by Calder & Boyars, London
(q.v.).

1749 ——————. *My Mad World of Opera*. London: Weidenfeld and Nicolson,
1982. 234 pp. Illustrated. Index, pp. 221-234.

The *double entendre* of the title refers to the author's world of
Opera with capital "O," the London-based magazine whose editor Rosenthal has been for over three decades. Although this is his life story,
it is so richly populated by opera singers that its inclusion in
this bibliography seems justified.

1750 ——————. *Sopranos of Today; Studies of Twenty-Five Opera Singers*.
London: J. Calder, 1956. 102 pp. Illustrated.

Concise, two-page biographies of twenty-five sopranos of the author's
choice, admittedly chosen subjectively for his liking of their voice
and singing and, in some instances, for the additional circumstance
of friendship. With the exception of four singers (Cross, Flagstad,
Pons and Welitsch), the biographies of the others are incorporated in
the author's *Great Singers of Today* (q.v.), with only minor textual
changes and additions. With many excellent photographs.

1751 Rubboli, Daniele, b. 1944. *Cronache di voci modenesi*. In Italian.
Milano: Nuove edizioni, 1981. 107 pp. Index, pp. 105-106. Discography, pp. 99-101.

Each of the seven loosely organized, eclectic chapters that make up

this book covers about a century and a half, beginning with 1800. As
in a constellation, there are "stars" and voices of all sizes in every
chapter. The more or less informative entries provide data about 103
Modenese singers. KT

1752 ————. *Le voci raccontate: (Ferrara, 1200-1977)*. In Italian.
Bologna: Bongiovanni, 1976. 202 pp. Illustrated. Discography, pp.
187-202.

1753 Russell, Henry, 1871-1937. *The Passing Show*. London: T. Butterworth, 1926. 295 pp. Illustrated.

1753-a ————. *The Passing Show*. Boston: Little, Brown, 1926. 295
pp. Illustrated.

1754 Sagardia, Angel. *Músicos vascos*. In Spanish. Colección
Auñamendi, 93-95. San Sebastián: Auñamendi, 1972. 3 vols.

A biographical dictionary of 269 Basque musicians and musical
organizations, among them a large number of singers for whom this
work seems to be the sole source. AM

1755 Saleski, Gdal, b. 1888. *Famous Musicians of a Wandering Race;
Biographical Sketches of Outstanding Figures of Jewish Origin in the
Musical World*. New York: Bloch Publishing Co., 1927. 464 pp. Illus-
trated.

1755-a ————. *Famous Musicians of Jewish Origin*. New York: Bloch
Publishing Co., 1949. 716 pp. Illustrated. First edition published
in 1927 under title: *Famous Musicians of a Wandering Race* (q.v.).

1756 Sánchez Torres, Enrique. *Nueve músicos clásicos y seis artistas
españoles: característica*. Biblioteca popular del filarmónico. Barcelona: Tipografia Universal, 1891. 96 pp.

The singers are Cepeda, Gayarre, Labán and Mateu ("Uetam").

1757 ————. *Stagno, Gayarre, Massini; las tres grandes escuelas del
canto moderno. Conferencia concierto dada en el Ateneo de Madrid la
noche del 25 de febrero de 1910*. In Spanish. Madrid: M.G. Hernández,
1911. 77 pp.

1758 Sargeant, Winthrop, b. 1903. *Divas*. New York: Coward, McCann
and Geoghegan, 1973. 192 pp. Illustrated.

This is a collection of six independent articles, five of which were
previously published in *The New Yorker* in slightly altered form. The
tone, weight and style conform to what one expects of a *New Yorker*
piece: polished journalism at its best, informative, not too deep,
easily accessible to all would-be intellectuals, yet full of important
and revealing information about the subject in every well-crafted
paragraph. The articles are on Farrell, Horne, Birgit Nilsson, Price,
Sills and Sutherland.

1759 Schürmann, Joseph Johan, b. 1857. *Derrière le rideau; secrets
et indiscrétions de coulisses, 2me série*. In French. Paris: M. Bauche,
1912? 188 pp.

1760 ————. *Impresario Schürmann; une tournée en Amérique.* In French. Paris: F. Juven, 1896? 248 pp.

1761 ————. *Secrets de coulisses.* In French. Paris: M. Bauche, 1911. 220 pp.

1762 Scott, Michael. *The Record of Singing to 1914.* London: Duckworth, 1977. 243 pp. Illustrated. Bibliography, pp. 235-236. Index, pp. 237-243.

In a beautifully produced book Scott offers an "illustrated survey of the art of singing as it survives on gramophone recordings." This volume, the first of a projected three-volume set (planned to conclude in 1951, at the end of the 78rpm era), covers the infancy of the gramophone until 1914. It was specifically designed to accompany the 12-record set of EMI with the same main title (EMI RLS 724). The introduction gives a historical overview of singing through the ages; the main body contains a critical appraisal of each major vocalist who left recordings to posterity, in addition to a mention of those singers before them whose legacy influenced the styles and singing methods of their artistic heirs.

As is the case with encyclopedic works of this sort, it is not entirely free of errors. But the flaws are minor if measured against the overall importance of the work which is, in many instances, the sole source of biographical information for several singers. The continuous narrative moves from subject to subject with graceful ease, the concise biographical sentences or paragraphs are followed by an evaluation of the singer's recorded artistry. The book has 209 magnificent illustrations, some of them quite rare.

1762-a ————. *The Record of Singing to 1914.* New York: Scribner's Sons, 1977. xii, 243 pp. Illustrated. Bibliography, pp. 235-236. Index, pp. 237-243.

The unchanged American edition of the one published by Duckworth in London (q.v.).

1763 ————. *The Record of Singing; Volume Two, 1914-1925.* London: Duckworth, 1979. viii, 262 pp. Illustrated. Bibliography, pp. 253-254. Index, pp. 257-262.

Scott's second volume, bearing the same main title as the first, covers the period 1914-1925. As in the case of volume I, this too was designed to accompany the 13-record album of EMI (EMI RLS 743) with the same main title, covering the stated period as preserved on 78 rpm records. Arrangement, layout, approach, style and illustrations conform to and dovetail with the first of this (projected) three-volume work. However, in this volume more than in the first, the author's personal likes and dislikes color and cloud his judgments and become obtrusive and irritating. Also, there are, again, some factual errors, although none of them significant enough to discredit the work. With this caveat the reader can beneficially use this important reference book.

1763-a ————. *The Record of Singing.* New York: Holmes and Meier Publishers, 1979. x, 262 pp. Illustrated. Bibliography, pp. 253-254. Index, pp. 257-262.

The subtitle of the British edition of this book (London, Duckworth, q.v.) is "volume two, 1914-1925." The American publisher omitted this for obvious commercial reasons, intentionally withholding from the prospective buyer the fact that even though this is a bibliographically self-contained work, it has a preceding part, covering an earlier period, which, incidentally, was the publication of another publisher.

1764 Seidl, Anton, 1850-1898, editor. *The Music of the Modern World Illustrated in the Lives and Works of the Greatest Modern Musicians and in Reproductions of Famous Paintings, etc.* New York: D. Appleton, 1895-97. 2 vols. in 4. Illustrated.

Originally issued in 25 parts. Volume 1, consisting of two physical volumes, contains the texts; volume 2, also in two physical volumes, contains music. There are several pompous articles by Melba, Maurel, Marchesi, Lilli Lehmann, and about Tamagno; and a handful of absolutely magnificent photographs of Tamagno, Maurel, Melba, Sanderson (as Thaïs), Marchesi mother and daughter, Niemann, Lehmann and others.

1765 Sguerzi, Angelo. *Le stirpi canore*. In Italian. Bologna: Bongiovanni, 1978. 221 pp. Index, pp. 205-215.

Consists of three parts. The first two are discussions on the art of singing (pp. 9-72); the third, entitled "Cameos and Portraits" (pp. 73-203), is of short notices on 157 Italian and foreign singers, in alphabetical order. The author maintains that all the singers were appraised on the basis of first-hand experience, in some cases supported by recordings. The only exceptions are Rethberg and Pinza, who are judged exclusively through their numerous records. RT

1766 Sheean, Vincent, b. 1899. *Oscar Hammerstein I; the Life and Exploits of an Impresario*. With a preface by Oscar Hammerstein II. New York: Simon and Schuster, 1956. 363 pp. Illustrated.

A delightfully written, well-researched, detailed biography of the colorful German immigrant and cigar manufacturer-turned-impresario whose success presented the only competition to the Metropolitan that venerable institution ever had domestically in its first century.

1767 Simpson, Harold. *Singers to Remember*. Lingfield, Eng.: Oakwood Press, 1972? 223 pp.

Contains 1- to 2-page biographical notices of 71 singers and less than one page for 29 more, 100 in all, most of them famous and all of them active in the first half of the twentieth century. The author, apparently not a professional writer, did a creditable job assembling the basic facts about his subjects. He presents the material at his disposal concisely and objectively. Since the majority of singers are not represented elsewhere in similar works, this is a useful addition to the ever-expanding reference literature. A list of suggested recordings, mostly LP transfers of 78s, is appended to the longer entries.

1768 Steane, John B. *The Grand Tradition; Seventy Years of Singing on Record*. London: Gerald Duckworth & Co., 1974. xii, 628 pp. Illustrated. Bibliography, pp. 611-612. Index, pp. 620-628. Composer Index, pp. 613-619.

This book is the result of what must have been countless hours of attentive and highly critical listening to several thousand vocal recordings. Every major and many secondary singers are represented, their singing accorded a fair appraisal exclusively on the basis of their records, and their position in the history of singing identified. Steane's lucid presentation and reasoned value judgments command attention even on those occasions when the reader disagrees with his conclusions. The feature that deserves the utmost admiration is the quality of writing. The ability to write about a single aspect--singing--of several hundred artists without becoming repetitive or boring is a gift uncommon among writers of any field. An indispensable reference work.

1768-a ————. *The Grand Tradition; Seventy Years of Singing on Record*. New York: C. Scribner's Sons, 1974. xii, 628 pp. Illustrated. Bibliography, pp. 611-612. Index, pp. 620-628. Composer Index, pp. 613-628.

The United States edition of the same work published by Duckworth in London (q.v.).

1769-T Steiner, Christian, and Robert Jacobson. *Grandes de la opera*. Translated by Luís Romano-Haces and Juan José Olives. In Spanish. Barcelona: Editorial Blume, 1982. 112 pp. Illustrated.

Spanish translation of *Opera People* (q.v.).

1770 Steiner, Christian. *Opera People*. Photographs, Christian Steiner; text, Robert M. Jacobson; introduction, Michael Scott. New York: Vendome Press; distr. by Viking, 1982. 112 pp. Illustrated.

Despite a knowledgeable introduction by Michael Scott and excellent short essays by Robert Jacobson, the dominant element of this book is Christian Steiner's glorious photographs. Steiner explains his work in extensive notes relating to each subject at the end of the volume. He is a contemporary master of portrait photography whose work ranks, in modern terms, with the work of such famous predecessors as Mishkin, Aimé Dupont and Cecil Beaton.

1770-a ————. *Opera People*. Photographs, Christian Steiner; text, Robert M. Jacobson; introduction, Michael Scott. London: Weidenfeld and Nicolson, 1982. 112 pp. Illustrated.

1771 Steinitzer, Max, 1864-1936. *Meister des Gesangs*. In German. Berlin: Schuster & Loeffler, 1920. 230 pp. Bibliography, pp. 219-222. Index, pp. 223-230.

Rather than devoting entire chapters to an individual singer, this work discusses singing at large and the artistry of major vocalists from Lind to Caruso. The critical observations that vary from a single sentence to two pages are valid and defendable, even though the author has his obvious favorites. Considering his competence and apparent listener's experience, one wishes he had elaborated at greater length about the performances he had seen and the singers heard.

1772 Strang, Lewis Clinton, 1869-1935. *Famous Prima Donnas*. Boston: L.C. Page, 1900. xiv, 270 pp. Illustrated. Index, pp. 261-270.

Intended to review the careers of current (1900) musical comedy stars, these excellent biographical sketches prove a source for information on a number of artists who later became famous in grand opera, motion pictures, etc. Among the 22 singers who each receive a separate chapter are listed Alice Nielsen, Lillian Russell, Jessie Bartlett Davis, Edna Wallace Hopper, Edna May, Christie MacDonald, Marie Dressler, Marie Tempest and Della Fox. WRM

1773 ————. *Famous Stars of Light Opera*. Boston: L.C. Page, 1900. 293 pp. Illustrated.

1774 ————. *Prima Donnas and Soubrettes of Light Opera and Musical Comedy in America*. Boston: L.C. Page, 1900. xiv, 270 pp. Illustrated.

1775 Strantz, Ferdinand von, b. 1821. *Persönliche Erinnerungen an berühmte Sängerinnen des XIX. Jahrhunderts*. In German. Berlin: H. Lazarus, 1906. 44 pp.

1776 *Světovi pevci 20. stoleti*; výber z textu provázejicich porady Divadla hudby z nahrávek svetových pevcu usporádala Bedriska Adamicková. In Czech. Edice Divadla hudby, sv. 4. Praha: Státni hudebni vydavatelstvi, 1966. 93 pp. Illustrated. Discography, pp. 89-93.

1777 Szabolcsi, Bence, 1899, and Aladár Tóth, eds. *Zenei lexikon; a zenetörténet és zenetudomány enciklopédiája*. In Hungarian. Budapest: Gyözö Andor, 1930-31. 2 vols. Illustrated. Supplemented edition published in 1935.

1778 Taubman, Hyman Howard, b. 1907. *Opera--Front and Back*. New York: C. Scribner's Sons, 1938. x, 388 pp. Illustrated.

1779 Tegani, Ulderico, b. 1877. *Cantanti di una volta*. In Italian. Milano: Valsecchi, 1945. 332 pp. Illustrated.

Forty articles about 43 singers, all of whom were born in the nineteenth century. The articles, written in an easy-going, journalistic style, are alternately informative and superficial, often both. They are a combination of the author's opinions based on first-hand experiences, hearsay and information culled from a variety of no longer identifiable sources. All in all, good supportive material to secondary literature.

1780 Thalberg, Gustave Jonathan, 1854-1917. *Artist-profiler och impresario-historier; pikanta inblickar i artistlifvet*. In Swedish. Stockholm: Skoglund, 1915. 287 pp. Illustrated.

1781 ————. *Bland "stjärnor"; en svensk impresarios erinringar från artistlif, resor och äfventyr i främmande länder*. In Swedish. Stockholm: Nordiska Bokhandeln, 1906. viii, 351 pp. Illustrated.

1782 Thompson, Oscar, b. 1887. *The American Singer; a Hundred Years of Success in Opera*. New York: Dial Press, 1937. 426 pp. Illustrated. Index, pp. 415-426.

An indispensable reference book; full chapters are devoted to certain prominent singers, with others grouped under voice classification.

It is a popular sport, in some circles, to dredge up names of American singers not found in Thompson's book, thus criticizing the work as "incomplete." So is every encyclopedia! It is a source of constant amazement to find the names one does in this book, if no more than passing mention. An amazing compilation, written in a readable style, the work has stood the test of time with relatively few errors being found in frequent usage during the years. Appendices include tables of early New York appearances of American singers; first appearances of American singers at the Academy of Music; a listing in alphabetical order giving names, roles and dates of debuts of American singers at the Metropolitan; and a similar list for the Chicago Opera Company (1910-1916). WRM

1783 Thurner, Auguste, b. 1833. *Les reines du chant.* In French. Paris: A. Hennuyer, 1883. 335 pp. Illustrated.

The life and artistry of 61 "queens of song" are discussed in this informative, enjoyable book. Some singers are accorded a full chapter, others only extensive passages. Although the book lacks documentation, the writing reflects the author's familiarity with previously published material and, in the instances of his contemporaries, first-hand knowledge of his subjects.

1784 Tikholov, Petko. *Kum vurkhovete na izkustvo: 105 nashi i chuzhdi operni deitsi razkazvat....* In Bulgarian. Sofiia: Muzika, 1979. 516 pp. Illustrated.

A collection of interview-type articles of varying length about 105 singers, dancers, conductors, directors, choreographers currently (as of the date of publication) active in Bulgarian musical life.

1785 Todd, Mrs. R.H. *Looking Back; Some Early Recollections.* Sydney: Snelling Printing Works, 1938. 50 pp. Illustrated.

1786 Tosi, Pietro Francesco, ca. 1650-ca. 1732. *Opinioni de' cantori antichi e moderni, o siano Osservazioni sopra il canto figurato....* In Italian. Bologna, 1723. 118 pp.

1787 Tóth, Aladár, 1898-1968. *Tóth Aladár válogatott zenekritikái, 1934-1939.* Az elöszót irta Lukács György. In Hungarian. Budapest: Zeneműkiadó, 1968. 638 pp. Illustrated. Index, pp. 627-631.

In the words of Walter Legge, "Aladár Tóth was one of the wisest and most cultivated of men and certainly the gentlest I have known. He was, so Hungarians tell me, one of their best writers." Tóth was indeed a noted musicologist and music critic before he became the director of the Hungarian Opera House for a decade immediately following World War II. The present collection is a selection from his reviews published in the six years before the outbreak of the war. They represent a summary of musical life in Budapest for that period. The operatic interest of the volume is in his long essays about important revivals, and reviews of the multiple guest appearances of such celebrities as Chaliapin, Gigli, Stracciari, Pertile, Müller, Cigna and Rimini. In addition there are many articles about the operatic and concert work of native singers. Although Tóth is prone to indulge in superlatives and some of his convoluted sentences are an obstacle course of adjectives, his reviews are always interesting,

informative, competent and unbiased. György Lukác's pitiful effort
to put music criticism on Marxist-Leninist footing is more ludicrous
than annoying.

1788 Tubeuf, André, b. 1930. *Le chant retrouvé; sept divas, renaissance de l'opéra.* In French. Paris: Fayard, 1979. 271 pp. Illustrated. Discography, pp. 255-270.

The author devotes a long chapter to each of his seven subjects,
who, in his opinion, have given us a renaissance of beautiful singing,
reviving the best in bel canto tradition. Tubeuf recounts each diva's
life, her early struggles and eventual success, with love, devotion
and psychological insight. The divas are Caballé, Crespin, Jurinac,
Rysanek, Schwarzkopf, Sutherland and Varnay. AM

1789 Tuggle, Robert. *The Golden Age of Opera.* With the photographs of
Herman Mishkin. Foreword by Anthony A. Bliss. New York: Holt, Rinehart and Winston, 1983. 246 pp. Illustrated. Bibliography, pp.
223-234. Index, pp. 235-246.

This book succeeds in every respect. Director of Archives for the
Metropolitan Opera, Robert Tuggle had direct access to one of the
richest treasure troves of operatic documentation. In his extensive
research he left no resources untapped: human, printed or photographic.
His comments on New York's resident operatic greats of 1906-1932 are
informative, stylish and engagingly informal, well supported by a
large number of often lengthy quotations from contemporary reviews.
The majority of the large number of illustrations are Mishkin's
photographs, most of them reproduced from original glass negatives.
The book is a superb example of modern book design and printing.

1790 Turner, Patricia. *Afro-American Singers: An Index and Preliminary Discography of Long-Playing Recordings of Opera, Choral
Music, and Song.* Minneapolis: Turner, 1976. xvi, 240 pp. Bibliography, pp. 220-228. Index, pp. 239-240.

A selective long-playing discography of 72 Afro-American singers
and eight choral groups affiliated with Black institutions. The
arrangement is alphabetical by artist, a brief list of recordings
follow, giving composer, title and record number only, and occasionally excerpts from published critiques. An important feature of the
book is a listing of sources of biographical articles appended to each
singer's entry.

1791 Uda, Michele. *Arte e artisti.* In Italian. Napoli, 1900. 2
vols.

1792 Ulrich, Homer, b. 1906. *Famous Women Singers.* Famous Biographies for Young People. New York: Dodd, Mead, 1953. 127 pp.
Illustrated.

Simple, 6- to 8-page biographies of world famous prima donnas,
written for young adults. The singers are Anderson, Calvé, Farrar,
Flagstad, Galli-Curci, Garden, Kirsten, Lind, Melba, Nordica, Adelina
Patti, Pons, Schumann-Heink, Sembrich and Stevens.

1793 *Ungarischer Künstler Almanach; das Kunstleben Ungarns in Wort und Bild*. Musik Chefredakteur: Béla Diósy. Redaktionskomitee: Julius Fodor et al. Verantwortlicher Redakteur: Julius Vásárhelyi. In German. Budapest: Königlich Ungarische Universitätsdr., 1929. 400 pp. Illustrated. Index, pp. 375-382.

An exhaustive overview of Hungarian musical life at the time of publication. Positively all aspects of music and musical personalities are covered: educational and performing institutions, choral groups, composers, instrumental and vocal soloists, musicologists and music historians, pedagogues, etc. There is a photograph for each prominent musical personality. The mystery of the publication is the language: why in German, why isn't there a traceable Hungarian edition?

1794 Ungern-Sternberg, Alexander, Freiherr von, 1806-1868. *Berühmte deutsche Frauen des achtzehnten Jahrhunderts*. In German. Leipzig: F.A. Brockhaus, 1848. 2 vols.

1795 Van Vechten, Carl, 1880-1964. *Interpreters and Interpretations*. New York: A.A. Knopf, 1917. 368 pp.

The only book of predominantly opera-biographical interest by the well-known essayist and patron of the arts and artists. The book contains long, 18- to 40-page, essays of five opera singers (Chaliapin, Farrar, Fremstad, Garden and Mazarin), plus *diseuse* Yvette Guilbert and dancer Waslaw Nijinsky. Van Vechten's erudition and highly developed critical faculties are in evidence throughout. He can claim credit for being one of the few to recognize and publicly acknowledge Chaliapin's interpretative genius in face of the universal condemnation he reaped from the New York critics during his first Met season in 1907-08 that was partially responsible for his 13-year absence that followed. Van Vechten's writing has a freshness and immediacy that could serve as a model to other musical essayists.

1796 ————. *Interpreters*. New revised ed. New York: A.A. Knopf, 1920. 201 pp. Illustrated.

This is the revised version of the first half of *Interpreters and Interpretations*, 1917 (q.v.).

1796-a ————. *Interpreters*. Opera Biographies. New York: Arno Press, 1977. 201 pp. Illustrated.

The reprint of the 1920 edition published by Knopf, New York (q.v.), which is a revised version of the first half of *Interpreters and Interpretations*, 1917 (q.v.). For biographees see the entry for the 1920 edition.

1797 Várnai, Péter. *Operalexikon*. In Hungarian. Budapest: Zenemükiadó, 1975. 533 pp.

1798-T Vehanen, Kosti, b. 1887. *Efter applåderna*. Translated by Ole Torvalds. In Swedish. Göteborg: Aktiebolaget Bokförmedlingen, 1946. 227 pp. Illustrated.

Swedish translation of Vehanen's autobiography written in Finnish (q.v.)

1799 ————. *Muistojen mosaiikkia*. Kuvittanut Roy. In Finnish. Helsinki: Söderström, 1944. 260 pp.

1800 ————. *Rapsodia elämastä.* Kuvittanut Ole Kandelin. In Finnish. Porvoo: W. Söderström, 1944. 249 pp.

The autobiography of the celebrated Finnish accompanist, best known to American audiences through his long association with Marian Anderson (1935-1941). His recollections contain chapters on Titta Ruffo, Mercedes Capsir, Mme. Charles Cahier, Marian Anderson, Jacques Urlus, Richard Crooks, Irma Tervani, Aino Ackté and others. WRM

1801 Vizentini, Albert, 1841-1906. *Derrière la toile (foyers, coulisses et comédiens). Petites physiologies des théatres parisiens.* In French. Paris: A. Faure, 1868. vi, 292 pp.

The author devotes a chapter to each of the major theatrical establishments and their leading personalities of Second Empire Paris. Theaters of operatic interest covered are the Théatre Impérial de l'Opéra and the Opéra Comique, the Théatre Italien, and the Théatre Impérial Lyrique. Brief mention of contemporary French singers and frequent visitors lends some importance to this generally superficial book.

1802 Volkov, IUrii Aleksandrovich. *Pesni, opera, pevtsy Italii.* In Russian. Moskva: Iskusstvo, 1967. 218 pp. Illustrated.

Contains a discussion of the artistry and singing of every major Italian singer, with particular emphasis on those who appeared at the Bol'shoi: del Monaco, Scotto, Simionato. The illustrations are good; there is a magnificent shot of Nilsson, Freni and Cossotto in Moscow wearing identical mink stoles.

1803 Wagnalls, Mabel, b. 1871. *Opera and Its Stars; a Description of Music and Stories of the Enduring Operas, and a Series of Interviews with the World's Famous Sopranos.* New York: Funk & Wagnalls, 1924. xiv, 410 pp. Illustrated.

Amplified from previous editions of her *Stars of the Opera* (q.v.) and written in the worst style of girlie magazines, this volume contains the author's interviews with famous prima donnas: Calvé, Eames, Farrar, Galli-Curci, Garden, Hempel, Jeritza, Lilli Lehmann, Melba, Nordica and Sembrich. Interspersed throughout the volume are opera guide-type chapters of works associated with each artist. The book's value--if there is any--lies in the passages where the sopranos are allowed to speak for themselves. The writing often borders on the ludicrous. "In the prehistoric ooze of time it may have been that Mary Garden, in her 'tadpole' days, disported herself in ways unheard of" is a truly memorable sentence. The opera guide chapters are an inexhaustible source of unintentional hilarity. *The Magic Flute*, whose "libretto is all top-heavy with names ... could well be given *sans* Papageno and his mate," is Wagnalls's conclusion. Let readers draw theirs.

1804 ————. *Stars of the Opera; a Description of Twelve Operas and a Series of Personal Sketches, with Interviews, of Marcella Sembrich, Emma Eames, Emma Calvé, Lillian Nordica, Lilli Lehmann and Nellie Melba.* New York: Funk & Wagnalls, 1899. 368 pp. Illustrated.

1805 ———. *Stars of the Opera: A Description of Operas and a Series of Personal Interviews with Marcella Sembrich, Emma Eames, Emma Calvé, Lillian Nordica, Lilli Lehmann, Geraldine Farrar, and Nellie Melba.* Revised and enlarged ed. New York: Funk and Wagnalls, 1907. 402 pp. Illustrated.

1806 Wagner, Alan. *Prima Donnas and Other Wild Beasts.* Larchmont, N.Y.: Argonaut Books, 1961. 250 pp. Cast of Characters, pp. 237-250.

An entertaining little book, collecting and retelling some new and many old operatic anecdotes. The writing is appropriately light-hearted and occasionally tongue-in-cheek. While familiarity with the subjects—both human and musical—greatly enhances the appreciation of the humor of some stories, the special merit of the book is that it can be enjoyed by the casual operagoer as well. A biographical dictionary entitled "Cast of Characters" is appended at the end of the book for easy identification of the protagonists of the stories.

1806-a ———. *Prima Donnas and Other Wild Beasts.* New York: Collier Books, 1961. 187 pp. Cast of Characters, pp. 171-187.

1807 Wagner, Charles Ludwig. *Seeing Stars.* New York: G.P. Putnam's, 1940. ix, 403 pp. Illustrated. Index, pp. 391-403.

The "stars" in the title of this book are the stage variety, mostly musical and predominantly operatic. In this autobiography Wagner, a successful American impresario, sums up his experiences (until 1940). His enterprise brought him in close contact with celebrities like Alda, Tibbett, Kipnis, Fremstad and Moore. He devotes an entire chapter each to McCormack, Galli-Curci and Mary Garden. An interesting book about the "marketing" of performers and the money they earned for themselves and their agents.

1807-a ———. *Seeing Stars.* New York: Arno Press, 1977. ix, 403 pp. Illustrated.

Reprint of the 1940 edition published by Putnam, New York (q.v.).

1808 Waldstein, Max, b. 1836. *Heitere Bilder aus der Opernwelt.* In German. Chemnitz: B. Richter's Verlag, 1900. 186 pp. Illustrated.

1809 Warriner, John, b. 1858, editor. *National Portrait Gallery of British Musicians.* With an introduction by Joseph Bennett. London: Sampson Low, Marston and Co., 1896. 75 pp. Illustrated with 521 portraits on xxxv plates.

Brief biographical sketches of "British" musicians with "current" addresses. Patti-Nicolini's address is given as "Craig-y-Nos, Swansea"; Melba's as "Savoy Hotel, W.C." Important for information on many lesser known singers. To be included one apparently had to be a "resident" of England, as included are such singers as the American, Esther Palliser. The editor notes: "For natural and sufficient reasons it has not been always possible to obtain particulars as to the date of birth, etc., of all those whose names appear...." The introduction is by Joseph Bennett; the book has 35 photographic plates, each with 15 photographs. WRM

1810 Watkins, Mary Fitch. *Behind the Scenes at the Opera; Intimate Revelations of Backstage Musical Life and Work.* New York: Frederick A. Stokes, 1925. vii, 328 pp.

As a young girl, Mary Watkins became enamored of the voice and personality of Olive Fremstad; Fremstad took an interest in her, and made her her secretary and "buffer." Watkins's life with Fremstad has been delightfully told in the book *The Rainbow Bridge* (published under the name Mary Fitch Watkins Cushing), which is the only full-length biography of that singer (see item 493). During her seven years with Fremstad, the author came in contact with many singers "backstage at the Metropolitan," and this early work tells many interesting stories and anecdotes of those contacts. Miss Watkins later authored a number of articles of the "as told to" variety for such magazines as the *Saturday Evening Post*, notably about Geraldine Farrar. She was also the author of *First Aid to the Opera-Goer*. For many years she was on the staff of the *New York Herald Tribune*. WRM

1811 Weinschenk, Harry Erwin, editor. *Künstler plaudern.* In German. Berlin: Wilhelm Limpert, 1941. 336 pp. Illustrated.

These "chats with artists" are brief, well-written interviews, with many quotations by the subjects. While they are rather lightweight, they are nonetheless interesting and informative. The term "artist" here means musicians only, from conductors and composers to instrumentalists and theater intendants, and includes 23 singers. The generous illustrations contain some highly unusual photographs. The artists are Baklanov, Bockelmann, Bohnen, Bollmann, Chaliapin, Dal Monte, Giannini, Gigli, Graveure, Ivogün, Leider, Leisner, Lorenz, Müller, Onegin, Prohaska, Rode, Rosvaenge, Sack, Slezak, Schlusnus, Völker and Wittrisch.

1812 Weissmann, Adolf, b. 1873. *Die Primadonna.* In German. Berlin: Paul Cassirer, 1920. 223 pp. Illustrated.

A brilliantly written, highly entertaining, very informative volume written by a "fan." Weissmann is an unabashed follower of that singular type of virtuoso we know as the Prima Donna. He does not restrict his discussion to the female voice only; in separate chapters he considers Farinelli, Catalani and Pasta, the Garcias, and goes on to groupings such as "The Demigoddesses," "The Tenor," "The Operetta Diva," and "The Wagner Diva." The volume is profusely illustrated, but not with photographs: there are engravings, drawings and watercolors. More than a hundred performers over a period of 150 years are mentioned in this highly recommended book. PHS

1813 Westering, Paul Christiaan van, b. 1911. *De mens achter musicus; gesprekken met Yehudi Menuhin, Robert Casadesus, Maria Callas, Daniel Wayenberg, Pierre Boulez, Joan Sutherland en anderen.* In Dutch. Toorts-contacten. Haarlem: De Toorts, 1964. 209 pp. Illustrated.

This little volume is composed of eighteen interviews with musical personalities, only five of them singers: Callas, Streich, Sutherland, Souzay and Seefried. None of the interviewees really "open up" and the results are rarely engaging. There is one interesting recollection of Callas by Menuhin (p. 55). PHS

1814 Whelbourn, Hubert, b. 1901. *Celebrated Musicians, Past and Present.* London: T.W. Laurie, 1930. xi, 227 pp. Illustrated. Subsequent editions published under the title: *Standard Book of Celebrated Musicians, Past and Present* (q.v.).

1815-T ————. *Diccionario de músicos célebres del pasado y del presente; con un apéndice, agregado por los editores de la present edición argentina....* In Spanish. Buenos Aires: Ediciones Anaconda, 1942. 349 pp.

   Spanish translation of *Standard Book of Celebrated Musicians, Past and Present* (q.v.).

1816 ————. *Standard Book of Celebrated Musicians, Past and Present.* Rev., enlarged ed. Garden City: Garden City Publishing Company, 1937. xiii, 305 pp. Illustrated.

1816-a ————. *Standard Book of Celebrated Musicians, Past and Present.* Rev., enlarged ed. London: F. Werner Laurie, 1937. 315 pp.

1817 *Who's Who in Opera: An International Biographical Directory of Singers, Conductors, Directors, Designers, and Administrators, also Including Profiles of 101 Opera Companies.* Maria F. Rich, editor. New York: Arno Press, 1976. xxi, 684 pp.

   One of the most ambitious undertakings of its kind within memory, this work aimed at nothing less than the biographical listing of all the leading and active operatic soloists, conductors, stage directors and designers, and administrators of every major opera house in the world. The 2,350 entries include 497 sopranos, 197 mezzo-sopranos and contraltos, 351 tenors, 508 baritones and basses, 287 conductors, 188 stage directors, 187 designers and 135 administrators. The uniform biographical entries contain date of birth, marital status, citizenship, education, debut, awards, related professional activities, company affiliations, recordings, film, television, world premiers, agents and address. The bulk of each entry is taken up by the listing of the singer's repertory, in some cases (i.e., Hans Hopf) absolutely staggering in size and variety.
   The great value of this work beyond its scope of coverage is its authority. The data were gathered directly from the subjects or primary sources and checked for authenticity, giving this reference work greater reliability than most others of its kind. Because of its importance and universal coverage of the current operatic scene, it should be updated at least once every decade.

1818 Zavadskaia, Nina Petrovna. *Pevets i pesnia: metodicheskoe posobie.* In Russian. Samodeiatel'nyi teatr, 8. Moskva: Iskusstvo, 1979. 85 pp. Illustrated.

Part III
Manuscripts—Monographs
Manuscripts—Translations

ARRAL

1819 Arral, Blanche, 1865-1945. "Bravura Passage." Translated by
Ira Glackens. Unpublished manuscript. 368 typescript pp. Transcribed,
translated (from the French) and heavily edited by Ira Glackens, who
was largely responsible for instigating the project. With a discography by William R. Moran.

This is a fascinating manuscript which should be read more as a
historical novel than a true biography. The singer, who was born in
Belgium, studied with Marchesi and made her debut at the Opéra
Comique in 1880. Massenet wrote a "walk-on" part for her, which she
created in the first performance of *Manon* in 1884. She led a roving
life, with many adventures in the Middle and Far East, Russia and
Australia, eventually settling in New York. Her book is full of
these adventures, told with a flare for the bizarre and not always
with the strictest attention to the facts; it is immensely entertaining but difficult to verify with places and dates. Taken in the
proper spirit, it is an excellent work. Mary Ellis Peltz once wrote
this annotator that she considered it fully on a par with *Anna and
the King of Siam*. The manuscript could be further edited to make a
very worthwhile publication. Mme. Arral left some excellent recordings.
WRM

CALLAS

1820 Laque, Rosemarie S. "Maria Callas: The Controversial Career of
a Prima Donna." Master's thesis, Catholic University of America,
Washington, D.C., 1979, iii, 50 leaves. Bibliography, pp. 48-50.

CARUSO

1821 Mouchon, Jean-Pierre, b. 1937. "Enrico Caruso, l'homme et
l'artiste." Doctoral dissertation, the Sorbonne, Paris, 1978. In
French. 1605 typescript pp. Illustrated. Bibliography, pp. 976-1049.
Index, pp. 1076-1605. Discography, pp. 796-974. Chronology, pp. 1050-
1075.

This unpublished dissertation, submitted to the Sorbonne (Paris) on
November 28, 1978, is probably the most complete, thorough and well-
documented study of this legendary singer. His life, vocal technique,
linguistic abilities and the special characteristics of his artistry
are analyzed in great detail. A discography of his published and
unpublished records with commentary, an extensive annotated bibliography, a chronology of his career and a large number of illustrations
lend added value to this important manuscript. It deserves to be
published. RT

FLAGSTAD

1822 Sanner, Howard C., b. 1954. "Kirsten Flagstad Discography."
Master's thesis, University of Maryland, 1981. vi, 244 pp. Bibliography, pp. 207-215. Artist Index, pp. 216-225. Composer/Title Index,
pp. 226-244.

Manuscripts

Compiled and submitted as a Master's thesis, and cataloged by the Library of Congress, this is the definitive discography of Kirsten Flagstad's recordings. It is a model discography in coverage, organization, layout and scholarship, listing all known published and unpublished recordings whose existence could be ascertained at the time of compilation.

LABIA

1823 Labia, Maria, 1880-1953. "Memorie e confessioni." Con prefazione di Arnaldo Fraccaroli. In Italian. 85 typescript pp. Manuscript dated: 24 luglio 1947. Done at Val di Sogno sul Garda.

McCORMACK

1824 McCormack, John, 1884-1945. "Memoirs." Unpublished manuscript. 1936-? 175 handwritten pp.

These memoirs consist of 175 pages written in pencil by McCormack, narrating the principal incidents of his career, along with his views of life as a concert artist. There are 14 additional pages of inserts to the original draft for the benefit of a future editor or collaborator, and 14 pages of quotations from reviews between 1906 and 1928. There are also 21 typed pages of copy at the beginning of the memoirs. McCormack dedicates his story "To the ideal wife of a singer--I married her." Portions of the memoirs were incorporated in Lily McCormack's *I Hear You Calling Me* (see item 887), including the epitaph that concludes his manuscript: "I live again the days and evenings of my long career. I dream at night of operas and concerts in which I have had my share of success. Now, like the old Irish minstrels, I have hung up my harp because my songs are all sung."

MARCHESI

1825 Marchesi, Blanche, 1863-1940. "La foi (Droit d'enfant); drame en trois actes." In French. Paris, 1914. 91 pp. Typescript, copy held by the New York Public Library.

MELBA

1826 Rothermel, Henry McK., comp. "Annotated List of Ninety-eight Records by Dame Nellie Melba." Reading, Pa., 1931. Typescript. Information taken from the British Museum General Catalogue.

MORTON

1827 Morton, Rachel, 1888-1982. "The Steep Climb Up" (Original title: Three Times an Outcast). With a foreword by Sir John Barbirolli. Unpublished manuscript. 105 typescript pp. With a discography by William R. Moran. A portion of this manuscript appeared in very slightly altered form as an appendix (pp. 317-321) under the title

"Jean de Reszke as a Teacher" in Clara Leiser's *Jean de Reszke and the Great Days of Opera* (see item 1181).

Rachel Morton was born in Webster, Massachusetts, and died in Carmel, California. She began her studies in Boston, later working in Berlin with Frau Niklas-Kempner. She recounts, in her autobiography, hearing Lilli Lehmann in her farewell recital, hearing Battistini and others of the period. She auditioned for the Metropolitan Opera, and was told to gain stage experience in Europe, where she returned in 1922. She auditioned for Jean de Reszke in 1922, and studied with the famous tenor until his death in 1925; later she sang with the British National Opera Company, and appeared with Sir Henry Wood in his famous Promenade Concerts. In the United States she was sponsored by Walter Damrosch, and made many concert tours. She taught singing in New York and in Carmel, California; from 1947 to 1967 she was Music Critic for the *Long Beach Telegram*. She made test recordings for Victor in 1917 and 1920, and electrical recordings for HMV in 1925/26. The account of her life is of minor interest, and will probably never be published. WRM

PATTI

1828 Tribble, Edwin. "The Prima Donna as Goddess: A Life of Adelina Patti." Manuscript. 1972, Revised 1976. Typescript. Bibliography. Discography.

The author worked for close to ten years on the first version of his text; the completely re-written second version was completed in 1976. Both versions were rejected by a number of publishers. This work, in its original form, was an immense labor of love: the author obviously spent years digging up material on his subject, and made the mistake of attempting to get it all within the covers of his book. The result is a really tremendous accumulation of facts. His bibliography is one of the most complete on the singer. But this was obviously (as it proved on submission to several publishers) "not commercial." The revised version cut out much detail, but was still unfortunately a rather dry recitation of facts; as such, it was still not acceptable for commercial publication. I made available to the author (via the Library of Congress) photocopies of "The Woodford Collection" (scrapbooks and letter-copy books of correspondence from the Craig-y-Nos period, originally collected by Patti's goddaughter and secretary, Mabel Woodford), which form a unique source base. These unpublished manuscripts are the only works on Patti to date that have made use of these important materials, and as such are an important collation of material about Adelina Patti. WRM

SCHUMANN-HEINK

1829 McPherson, James B. "'Madame'; the Life and Times of Ernestine Schumann-Heink." Toronto. 528 typescript pp. Illustrated. Bibliography. Repertory. Index. Discography. Chronology of Performances.

An excellent, full-length biography which shows the results of several years of extensive research, this work manages to capture the essence of the spirit and tremendous personality of Madade Schumann-

Heink that made her one of the most beloved artists ever to be adored
by the American public. There is also a great deal of insight into
her daily life, the fears, anxieties and tribulations that "Mother"
Schumann-Heink managed to hide from the public, much of it gleaned
from family files and discussions with her descendants. The repertory
list, which contains some real surprises, was taken from Mme. Schumann-
Heink's own notebooks. This is a work which simply *must* be published.
WRM

THOMAS

1830 Armitage, Merle. "J.C.T.: A Biography of John Charles Thomas."
Manuscript. 1961? 291 typescript pp.

   This unpublished manuscript was written after Thomas's death
(Dec. 13, 1960), but according to the author's introduction, it was
informally commissioned by the singer in the Spring of 1951. Armitage
first met the singer in 1916, and was long his close friend and
manager. There are many lengthy quotes, taken from notes during discussions between author and singer, and much of the material could
only have been obtained from personal sources. Included is a chapter
(pp. 223-266) entitled "J.C.T. by His Friends" that quotes many letters
containing stories and anecdotes from fellow singers (such as John
McCormack, Mario Chamlee, Frank Chapman, James Melton), businessmen
and other friends who have added a personal touch. The book is written
with admiration and love and provides an excellent, if uncritical,
portrait of a most interesting personality. It deserves to be published. The manuscript also includes an outline for a motion picture
scenario by Armitage, Charles Strickland and Len Ross. This was
written "in the 1950s" and was apparently seriously considered for production by M.G.M. WRM

MANUSCRIPT TRANSLATIONS (INTO ENGLISH)

BATTISTINI

1831 Palmegiani, Francesco. "Mattia Battistini, il re dei baritoni."

See item 90

BORGATTI

1832 Borgatti, Giuseppe. "La mia vita d'artista, ricordi e aneddoti."

See item 121

DE MURO

1833 De Muro, Bernardo. "Quand'ero Folco."

See item 358

LAURI-VOLPI

1834 Lauri-Volpi, Giacomo. "Voci parallele."

See item 737-a

LITVINNE

1835 Litvinne, Félia. "Ma vie et mon art; souvenirs."

See item 867

RUBINI

1836 Traini, Carlo. "Il cigno di Romano: Giovan Battista Rubini, re dei tenori."

See item 1249

RUFFO

1837 Ruffo, Titta. "La mia parabola."

See item 1252

1838 Arnosi, Eduardo. "Titta Ruffo, el titán de los barítonos."

See item 1255

Manuscripts

1839 ————. "Biografía y juicio crítico de Titta Ruffo."

See item 1258

BRACALE (impresario)

1840 Bracale, Adolfo. "Mis memorias."

See item 1561

ABOUT THE EDITOR

Andrew Farkas is Director of Libraries and Professor of Library Science
at the University of North Florida. He was previously Assistant Man-
ager of Walter J. Johnson, Inc., and Chief Bibliographer and Assistant
Head of the Acquisitions Department at the University of California
Library at Davis. He is the editor and contributor of *Titta Ruffo,
an Anthology*, principal co-editor of the annual publication, *Librarian's
Calendar and Pocket Reference*. A 42-volume reprint series entitled
Opera Biographies was published under his advisory editorship in 1977.
He has published articles, reviews and photography in *Opera* (London),
Opera News, *The Opera Quarterly*, *The Record Collector*, *Advances in
Collection Development and Resources Management*, *Library Journal*,
The Library Scene, *Florida Libraries*, *Previews* and *The Negro Educational
Review*. He is currently collaborating with Enrico Caruso, Jr., on
a volume of reminiscences dealing with Enrico Caruso, Ada Giachetti
and the Caruso family.